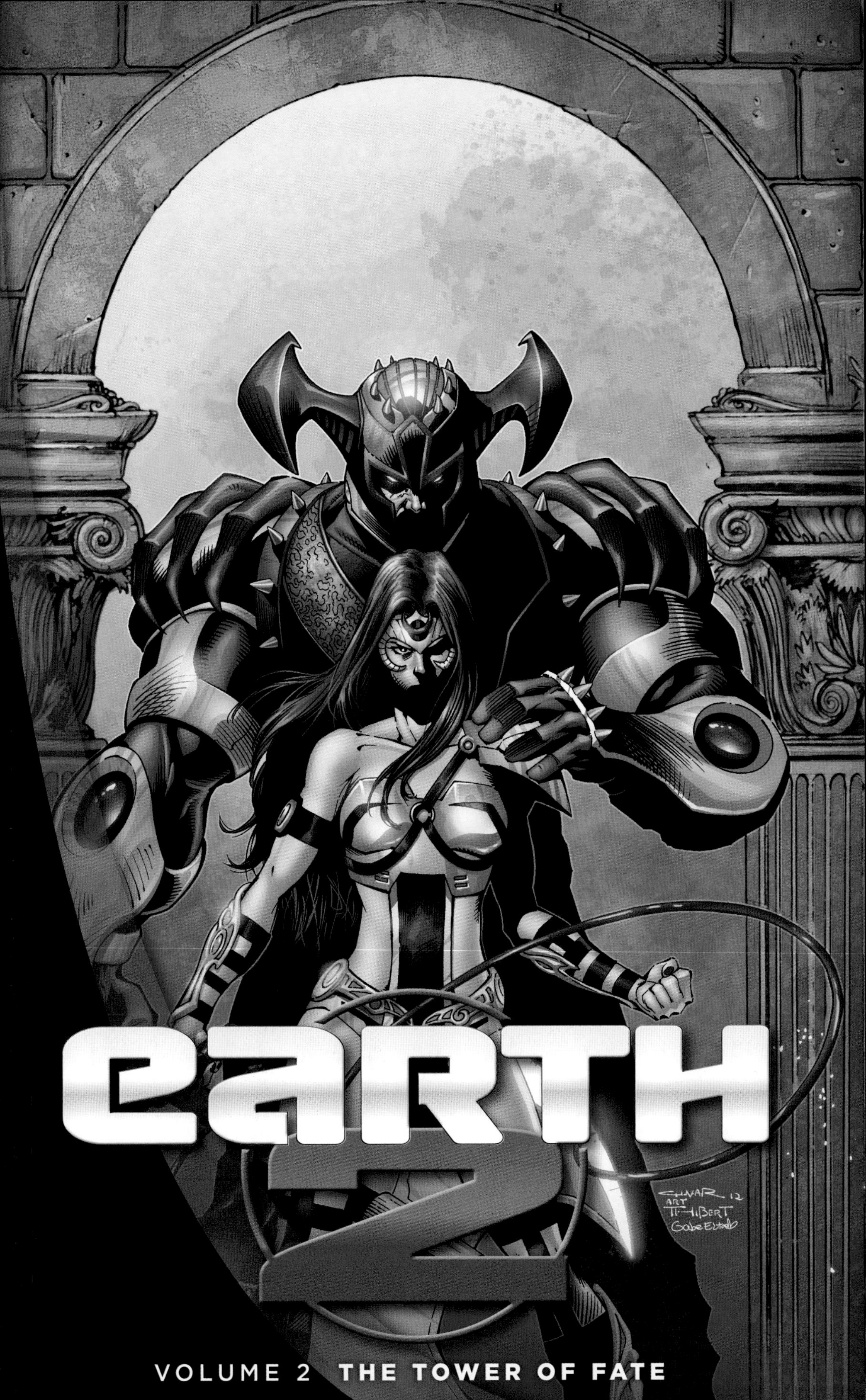
EARTH
2

VOLUME 2 **THE TOWER OF FATE**

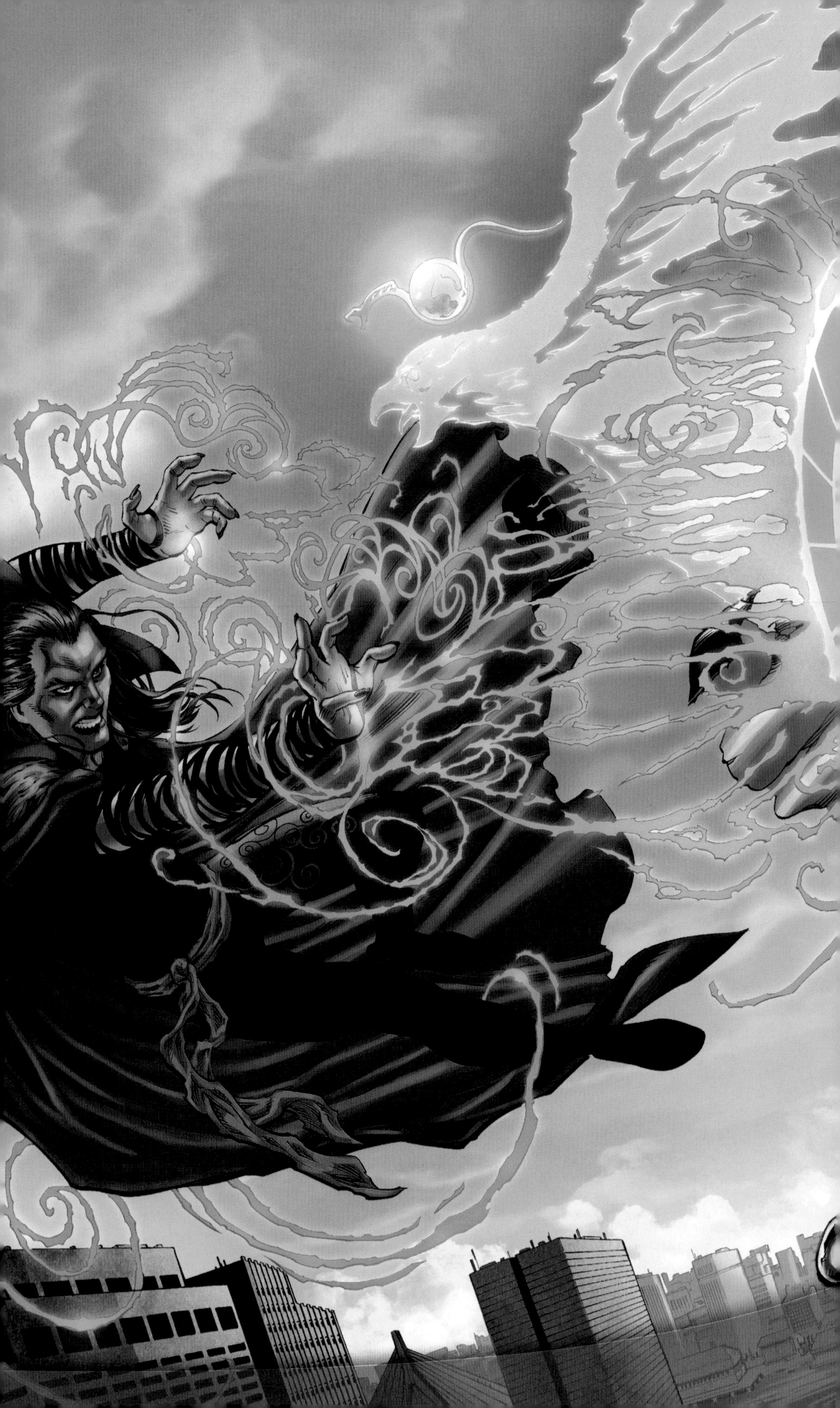

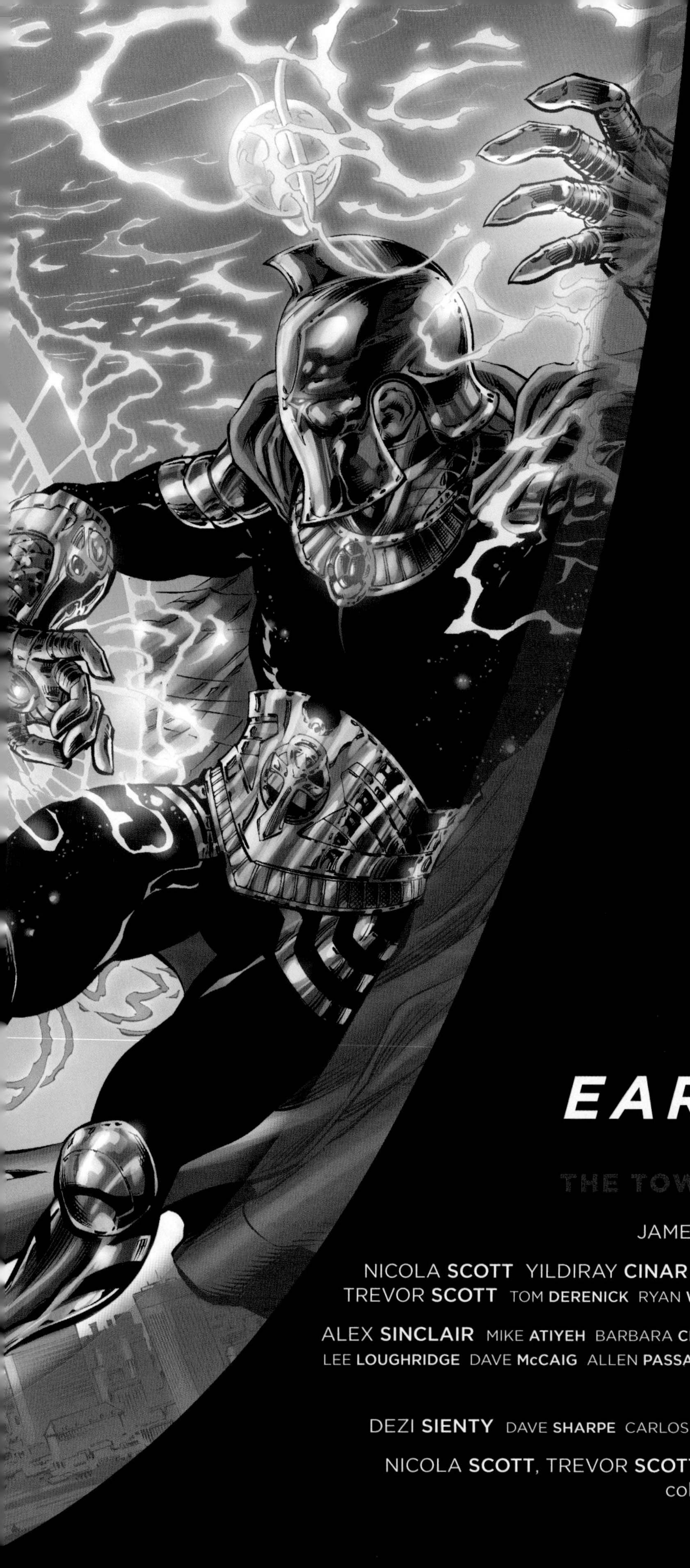

EARTH 2

VOLUME 2

THE TOWER OF FATE

JAMES **ROBINSON** writer

NICOLA **SCOTT** YILDIRAY **CINAR** TOMÁS **GIORELLO**
TREVOR **SCOTT** TOM **DERENICK** RYAN **WINN** RUY **JOSÉ** artists

ALEX **SINCLAIR** MIKE **ATIYEH** BARBARA **CIARDO** NATHAN **EYRING**
LEE **LOUGHRIDGE** DAVE **McCAIG** ALLEN **PASSALAQUA** PETE **PANTAZIS**
colorists

DEZI **SIENTY** DAVE **SHARPE** CARLOS M. **MANGUAL** letterers

NICOLA **SCOTT**, TREVOR **SCOTT** & ALEX **SINCLAIR**
collection cover artists

MIKE COTTON PAT McCALLUM JOEY CAVALIERI Editors – Original Series
WIL MOSS Associate Editor – Original Series ANTHONY MARQUES SEAN MACKIEWICZ KATE STEWART Assistant Editors – Original Series
ROBIN WILDMAN Editor ROBBIN BROSTERMAN Design Director – Books
ROBBIE BIEDERMAN Publication Design

BOB HARRAS Senior VP – Editor-in-Chief, DC Comics

DIANE NELSON President DAN DIDIO and JIM LEE Co-Publishers
GEOFF JOHNS Chief Creative Officer
JOHN ROOD Executive VP – Sales, Marketing and Business Development
AMY GENKINS Senior VP – Business and Legal Affairs NAIRI GARDINER Senior VP – Finance
JEFF BOISON VP – Publishing Planning MARK CHIARELLO VP – Art Direction and Design
JOHN CUNNINGHAM VP – Marketing TERRI CUNNINGHAM VP – Editorial Administration
ALISON GILL Senior VP – Manufacturing and Operations HANK KANALZ Senior VP – Vertigo and Integrated Publishing
JAY KOGAN VP – Business and Legal Affairs, Publishing JACK MAHAN VP – Business Affairs, Talent
NICK NAPOLITANO VP – Manufacturing Administration SUE POHJA VP – Book Sales
COURTNEY SIMMONS Senior VP – Publicity BOB WAYNE Senior VP – Sales

EARTH 2 VOLUME 2: THE TOWER OF FATE
Published by DC Comics. Copyright © 2013 DC Comics. All Rights Reserved.

Originally published in single magazine form in EARTH 2 #0, 7-12; DC UNIVERSE PRESENTS #0 Copyright © 2012, 2013 DC Comics.
All Rights Reserved. All characters, their distinctive likenesses and related elements featured in this publication
are trademarks of DC Comics. The stories, characters and incidents featured in this publication are entirely fictional.
DC Comics does not read or accept unsolicited ideas, stories or artwork.

DC Comics, 1700 Broadway, New York, NY 10019
A Warner Bros. Entertainment Company.
Printed by RR Donnelley, Salem, VA, USA. 8/30/13. First Printing.

ISBN HC: 978-1-4012-4311-1
ISBN SC: 978-1-4012-4614-3

Library of Congress Cataloging-in-Publication Data

Robinson, James Dale, author.
Earth 2. Volume 2, The tower of fate / James Robinson, Nicola Scott.
pages cm
"Originally published in single magazine form as Earth 2, 0, 7-12; DC Universe Presents 0."
ISBN 978-1-4012-4311-1
1. Graphic novels. I. Scott, Nicola, illustrator. II. Title. III. Title: Tower of fate.
PN6727.R58E24 2013
741.5'973—dc23
                                2013020539

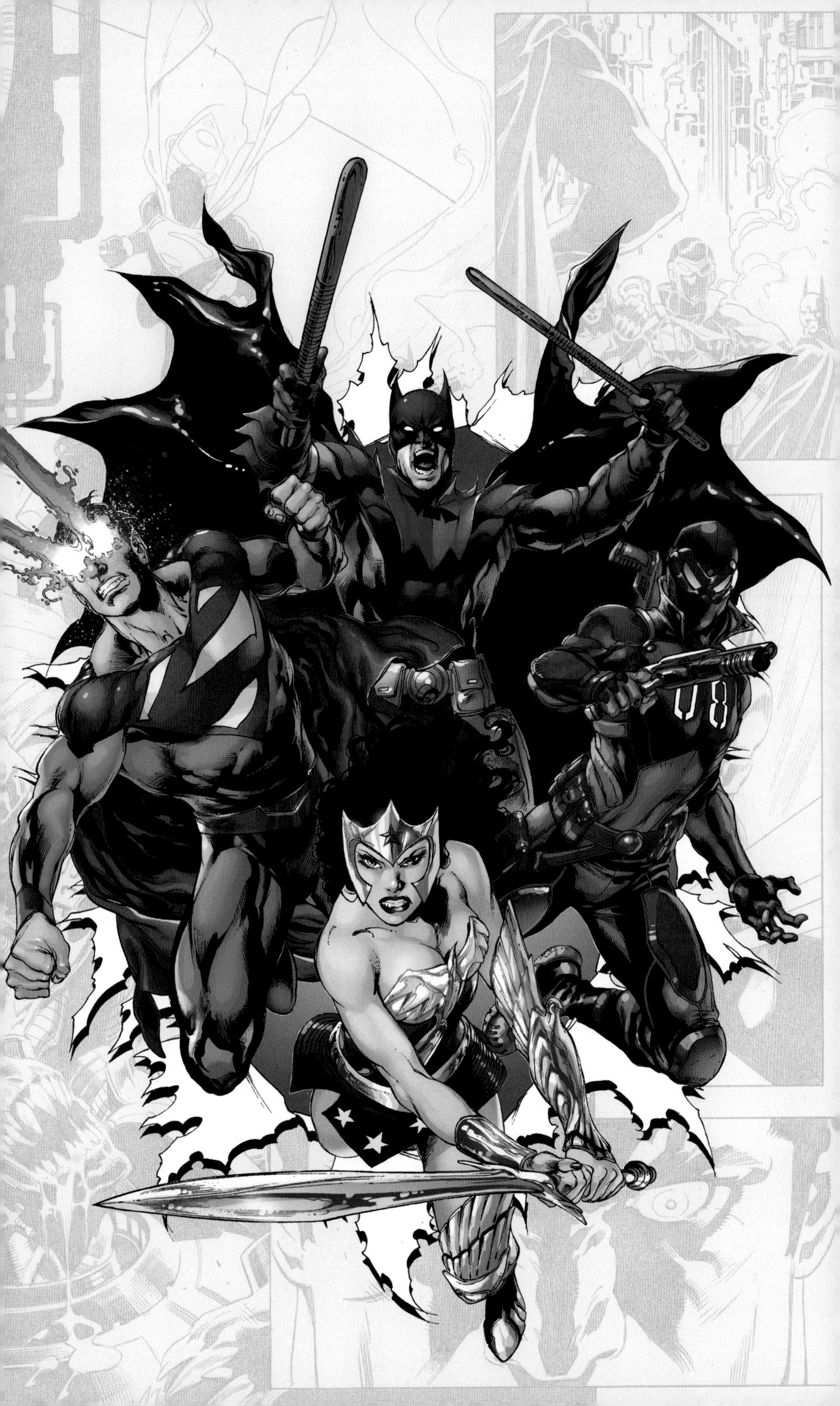

JAMES ROBINSON writer TOMAS GIORELLO artist (main story) TOM DERENICK artist (Mister Terrific) cover by IVAN REIS, JOE PRADO & ROD

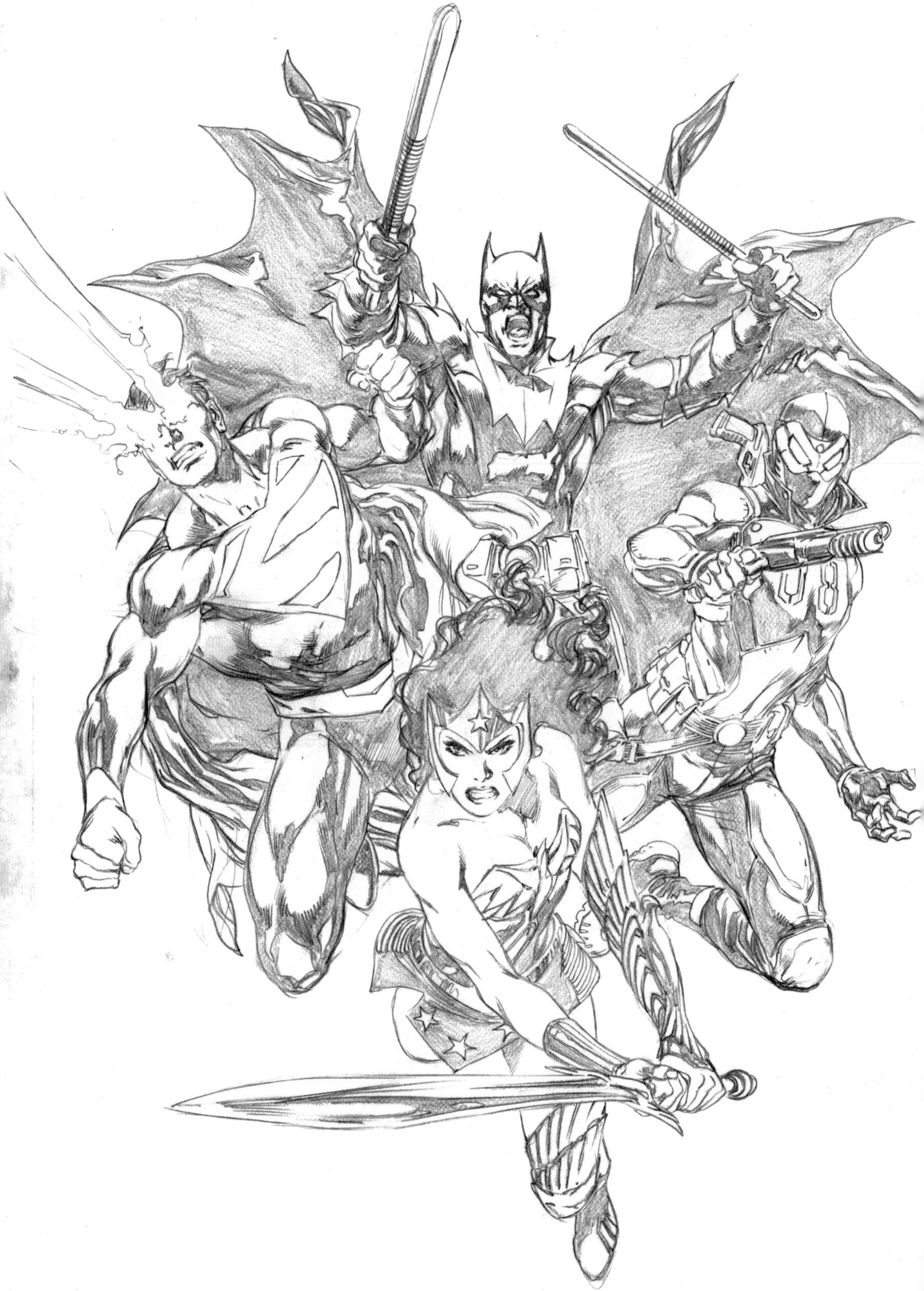

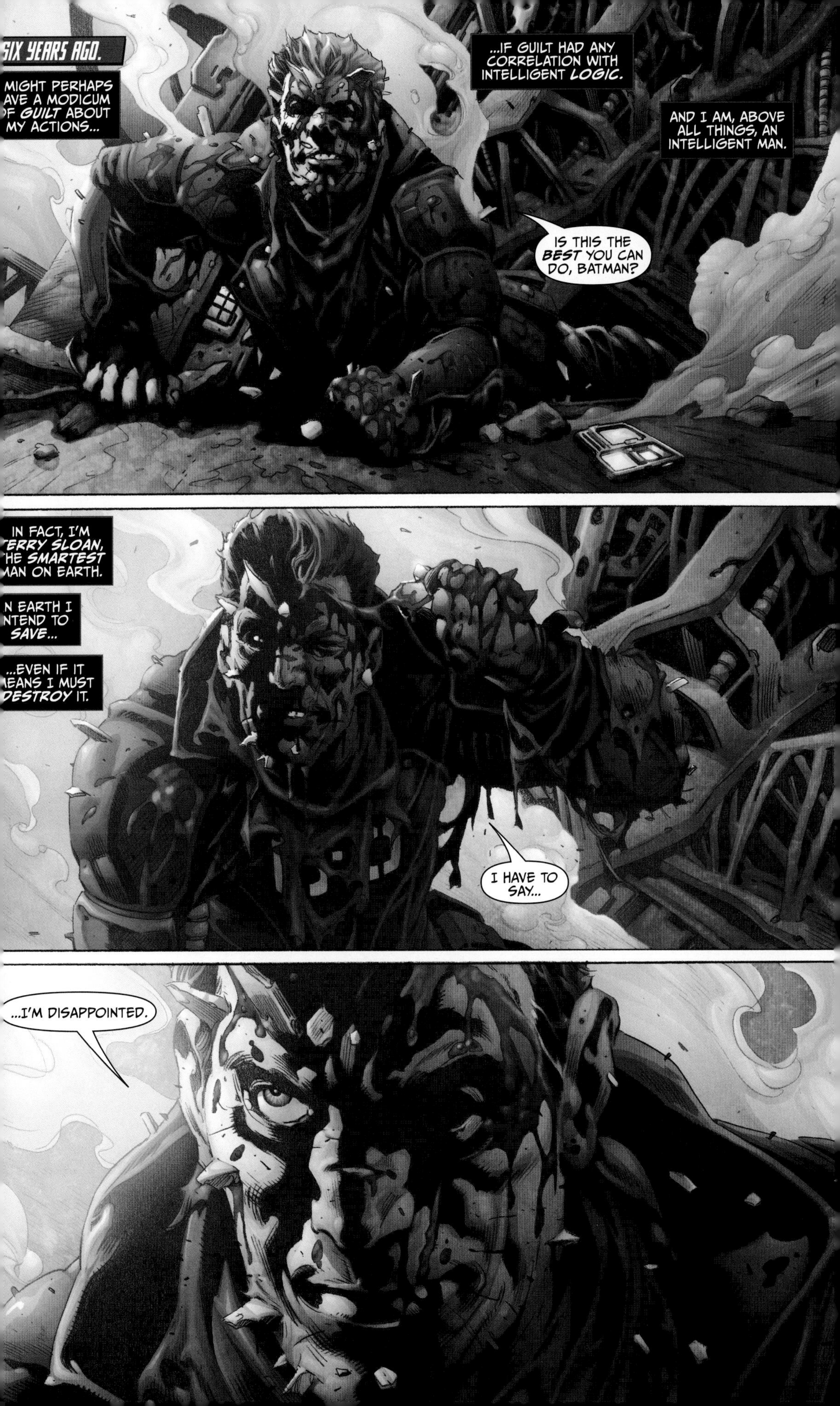
SIX YEARS AGO.
MIGHT PERHAPS AVE A MODICUM F *GUILT* ABOUT MY ACTIONS...
...IF GUILT HAD ANY CORRELATION WITH INTELLIGENT *LOGIC.*
AND I AM, ABOVE ALL THINGS, AN INTELLIGENT MAN.
IS THIS THE *BEST* YOU CAN DO, BATMAN?
IN FACT, I'M ERRY SLOAN, HE *SMARTEST* AN ON EARTH.
N EARTH I NTEND TO *SAVE*...
...EVEN IF IT EANS I MUST *DESTROY* IT.
I HAVE TO SAY...
...I'M DISAPPOINTED.

SEVENTEEN MINUTES PREVIOUS.
IT'S BEEN THREE YEARS ALMOST TO THE DAY, SINCE THE ARMIES OF APOKOLIPS BURST THROUGH THEIR PORTALS, SEEMINGLY WITH ONE GOAL.
CONQUEST.
AND SINCE THEN, MY PARTNERS IN RESISTANCE (IN THIS INSTANCE WONDER WOMAN, SUPERMAN...

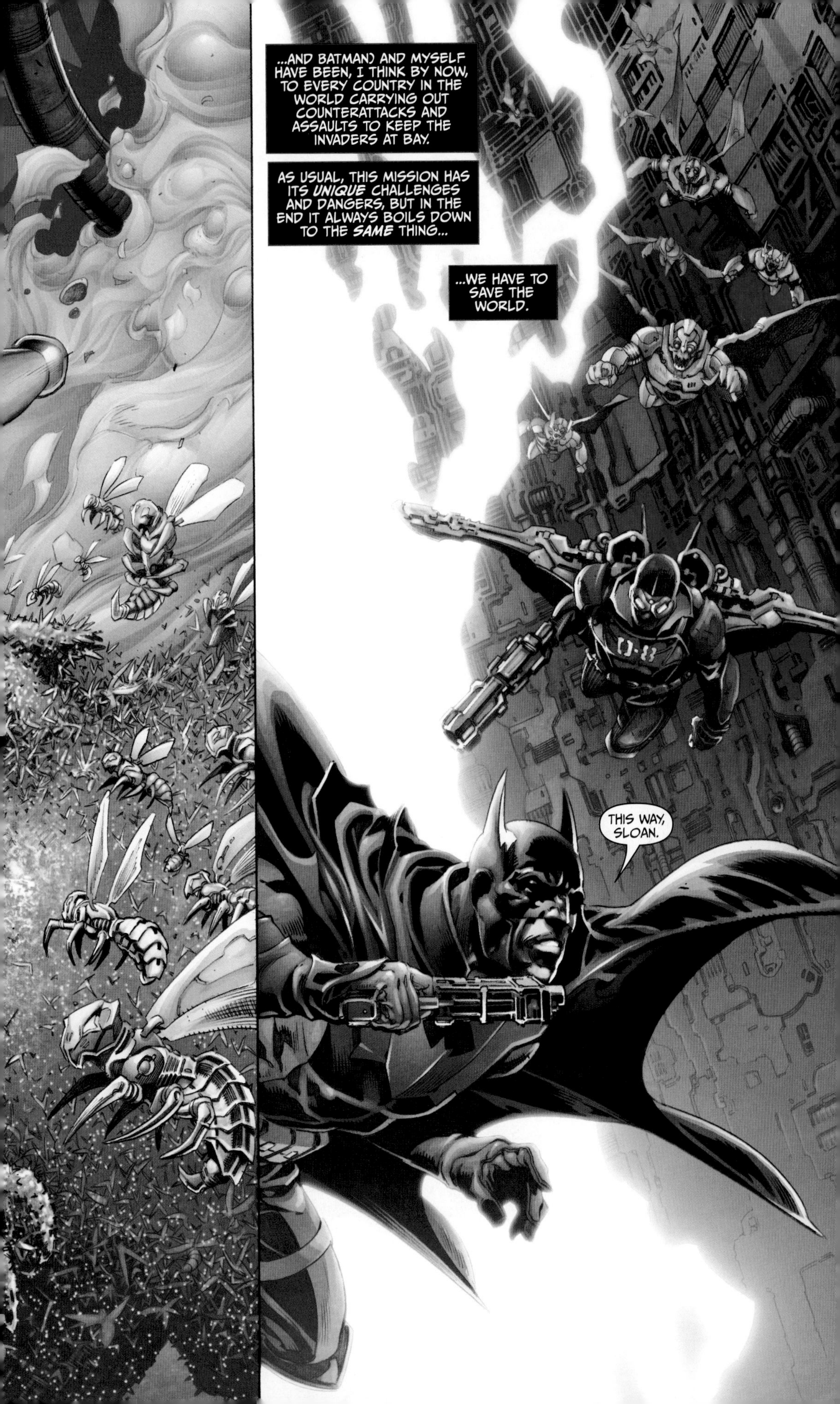
...AND BATMAN) AND MYSELF HAVE BEEN, I THINK BY NOW, TO EVERY COUNTRY IN THE WORLD CARRYING OUT COUNTERATTACKS AND ASSAULTS TO KEEP THE INVADERS AT BAY.
AS USUAL, THIS MISSION HAS ITS UNIQUE CHALLENGES AND DANGERS, BUT IN THE END IT ALWAYS BOILS DOWN TO THE SAME THING...
...WE HAVE TO SAVE THE WORLD.
0-8
THIS WAY, SLOAN.

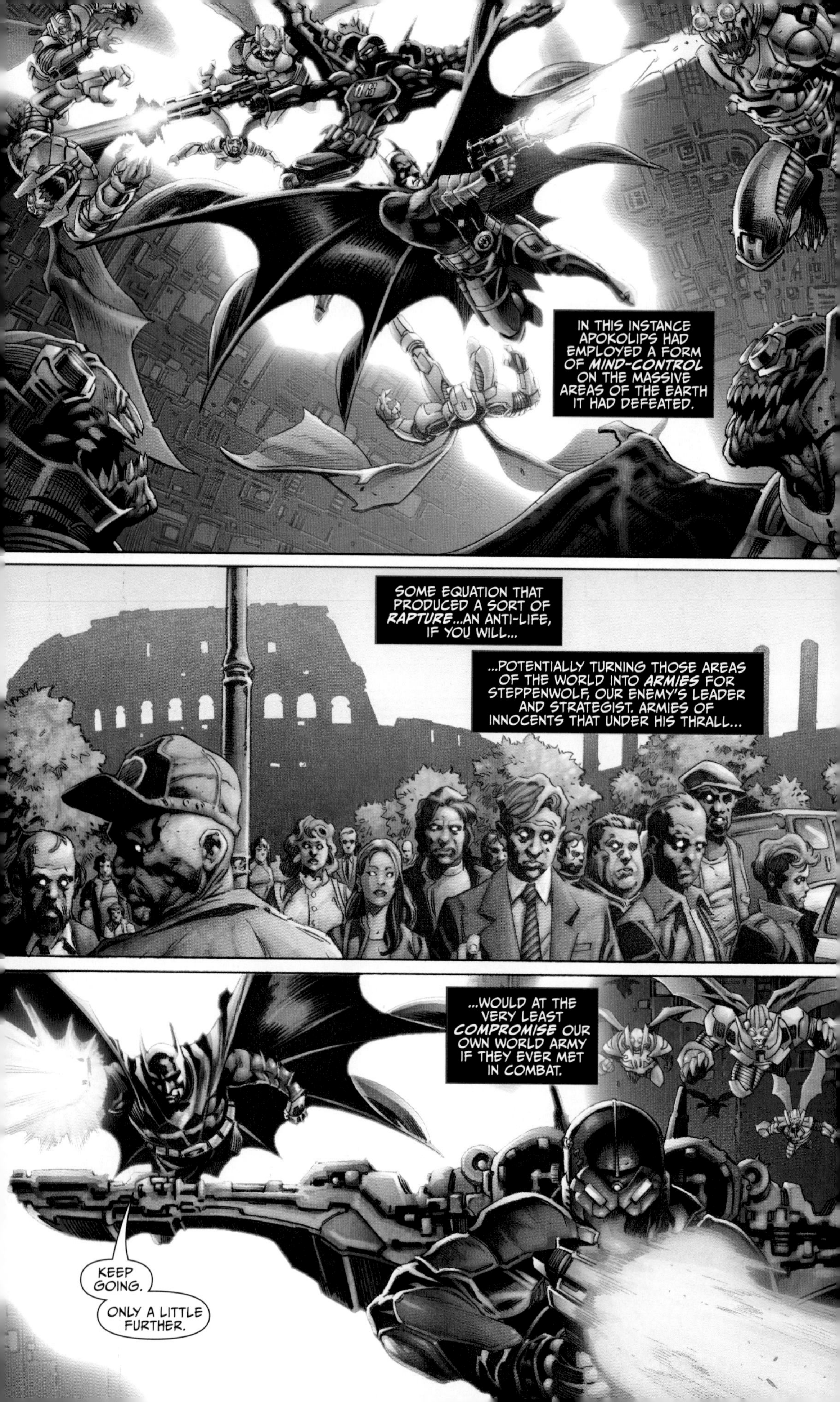
IN THIS INSTANCE APOKOLIPS HAD EMPLOYED A FORM OF MIND-CONTROL ON THE MASSIVE AREAS OF THE EARTH IT HAD DEFEATED.
SOME EQUATION THAT PRODUCED A SORT OF RAPTURE...AN ANTI-LIFE, IF YOU WILL...
...POTENTIALLY TURNING THOSE AREAS OF THE WORLD INTO ARMIES FOR STEPPENWOLF, OUR ENEMY'S LEADER AND STRATEGIST. ARMIES OF INNOCENTS THAT UNDER HIS THRALL...
...WOULD AT THE VERY LEAST COMPROMISE OUR OWN WORLD ARMY IF THEY EVER MET IN COMBAT.
KEEP GOING.
ONLY A LITTLE FURTHER.

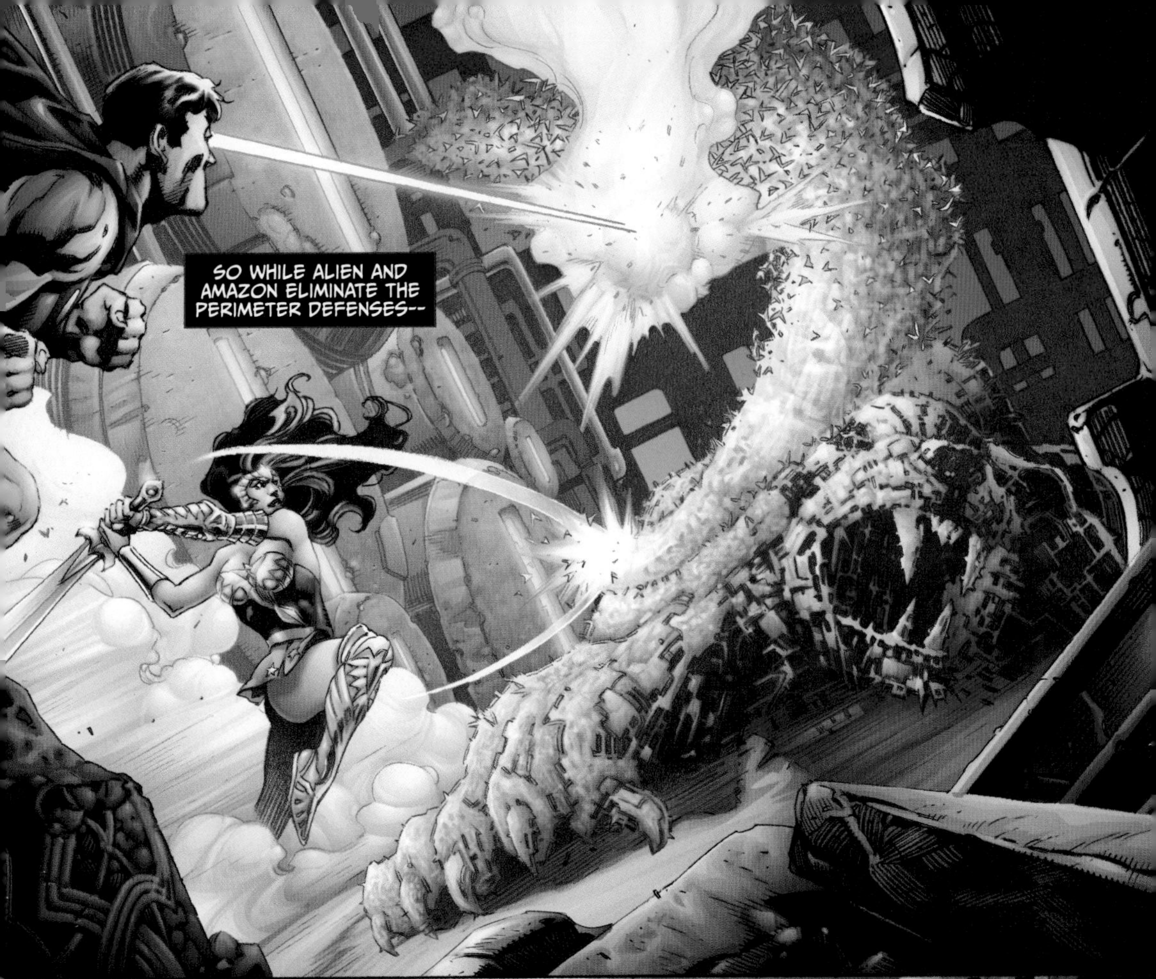
SO WHILE ALIEN AND AMAZON ELIMINATE THE PERIMETER DEFENSES--

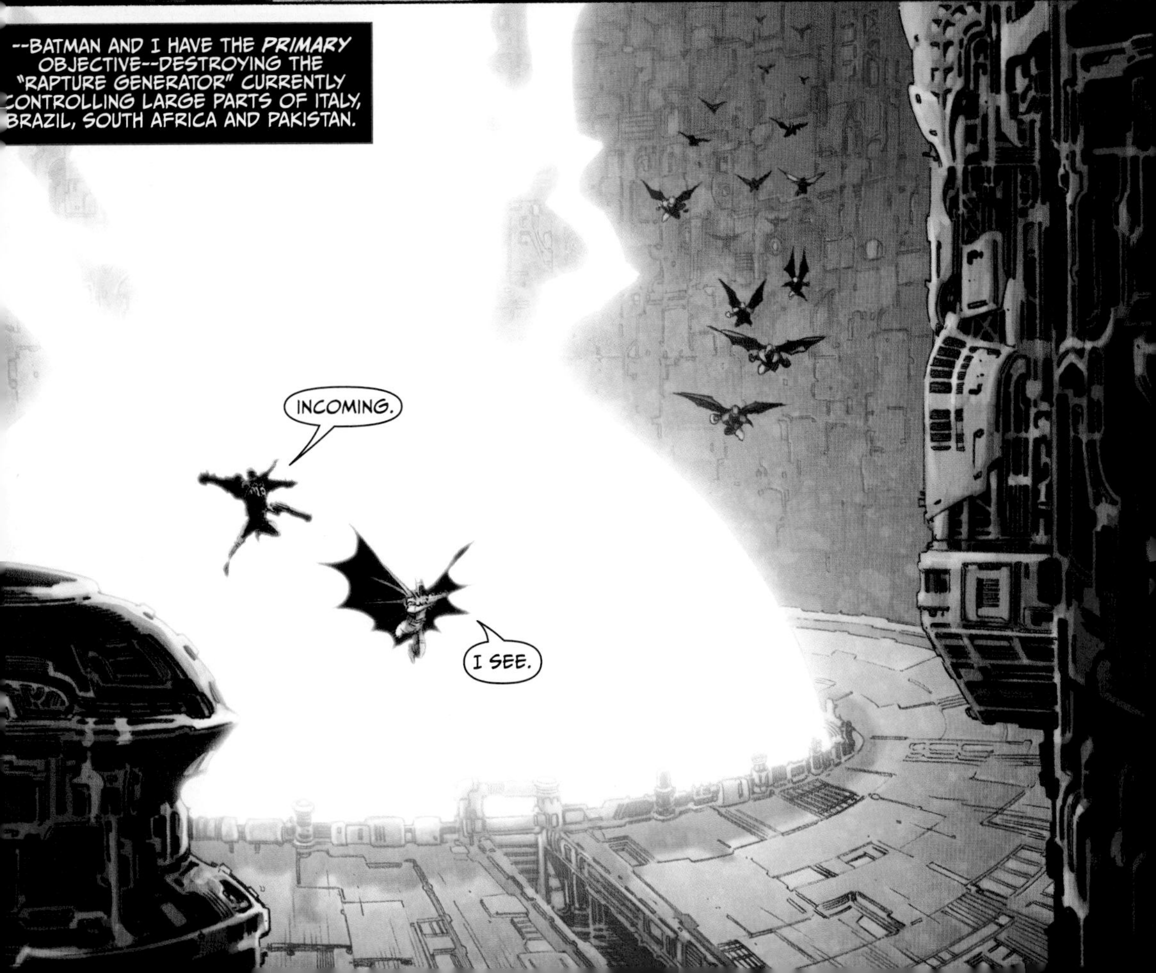
--BATMAN AND I HAVE THE *PRIMARY* OBJECTIVE--DESTROYING THE "RAPTURE GENERATOR" CURRENTLY CONTROLLING LARGE PARTS OF ITALY, BRAZIL, SOUTH AFRICA AND PAKISTAN.
INCOMING.
I SEE.

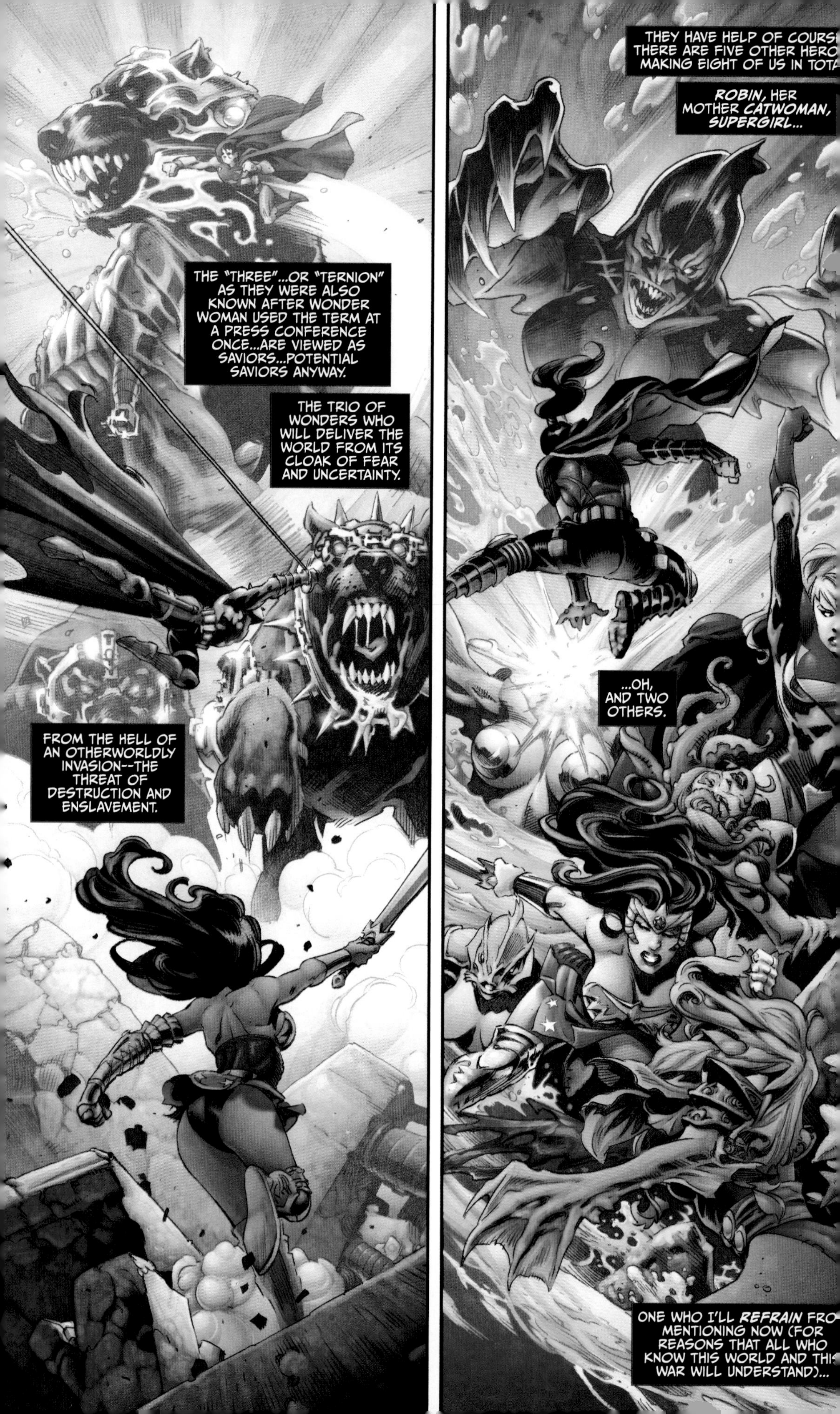
THE "THREE"...OR "TERNION" AS THEY WERE ALSO KNOWN AFTER WONDER WOMAN USED THE TERM AT A PRESS CONFERENCE ONCE...ARE VIEWED AS SAVIORS...POTENTIAL SAVIORS ANYWAY.
THE TRIO OF WONDERS WHO WILL DELIVER THE WORLD FROM ITS CLOAK OF FEAR AND UNCERTAINTY.
FROM THE HELL OF AN OTHERWORLDLY INVASION--THE THREAT OF DESTRUCTION AND ENSLAVEMENT.
THEY HAVE HELP OF COURS THERE ARE FIVE OTHER HERO MAKING EIGHT OF US IN TOTA
ROBIN, HER MOTHER *CATWOMAN*, *SUPERGIRL*...
...OH, AND TWO OTHERS.
ONE WHO I'LL *REFRAIN* FRO MENTIONING NOW (FOR REASONS THAT ALL WHO KNOW THIS WORLD AND THI WAR WILL UNDERSTAND)...

...AND ME.

"MR. 8"--THE EIGHTH AND FINAL WONDER.

TERRY SLOAN, FREELANCE GOVERNMENT LIAISON AND A PART OF SO MANY OF THE PLANS AND STRATE-GIES THAT HAVE AT LEAST KEPT THIS CONFLICT TO A STALEMATE, IF NOT OUTRIGHT VICTORY.

I CONFESS, IT WAS THE "STALE-MATE" PART OF ALL OUR EXPLOITS THAT HAD BOTHERED ME OF LATE.

OUR FRUSTRATING INABILITY TO TURN THE TIDE.

BUT THEN I DISCOVERED THE SOLUTION FOR THIS...THE ANSWER. IRONICALLY NOT ON THIS WORLD OR EVEN APOKOLIPS...

...BUT IN ANOTHER DIMENSION ENTIRELY.

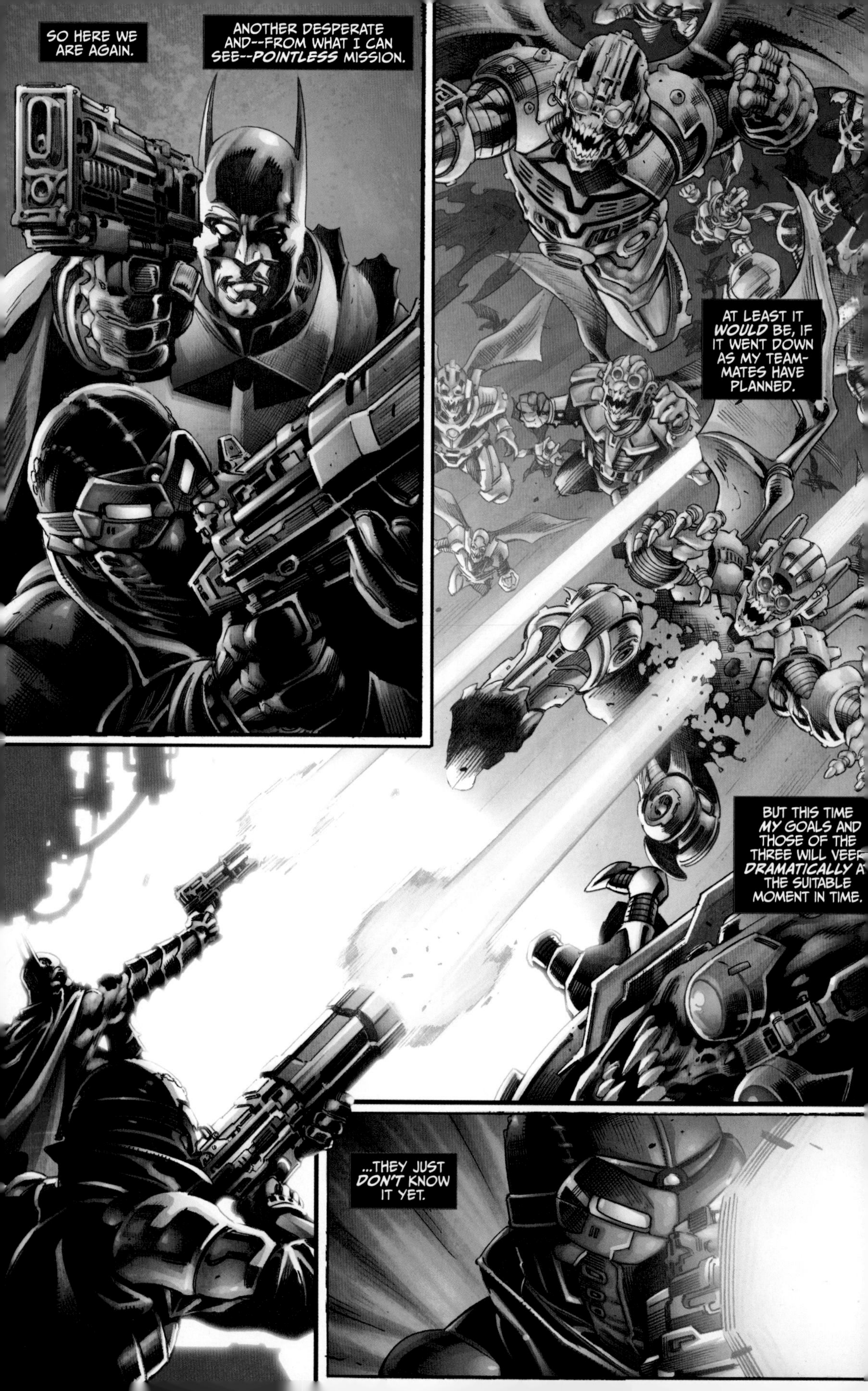
SO HERE WE ARE AGAIN.
ANOTHER DESPERATE AND--FROM WHAT I CAN SEE--*POINTLESS* MISSION.
AT LEAST IT *WOULD* BE, IF IT WENT DOWN AS MY TEAM-MATES HAVE PLANNED.
BUT THIS TIME *MY* GOALS AND THOSE OF THE THREE WILL VEER *DRAMATICALLY* A THE SUITABLE MOMENT IN TIME.
...THEY JUST *DON'T* KNOW IT YET.

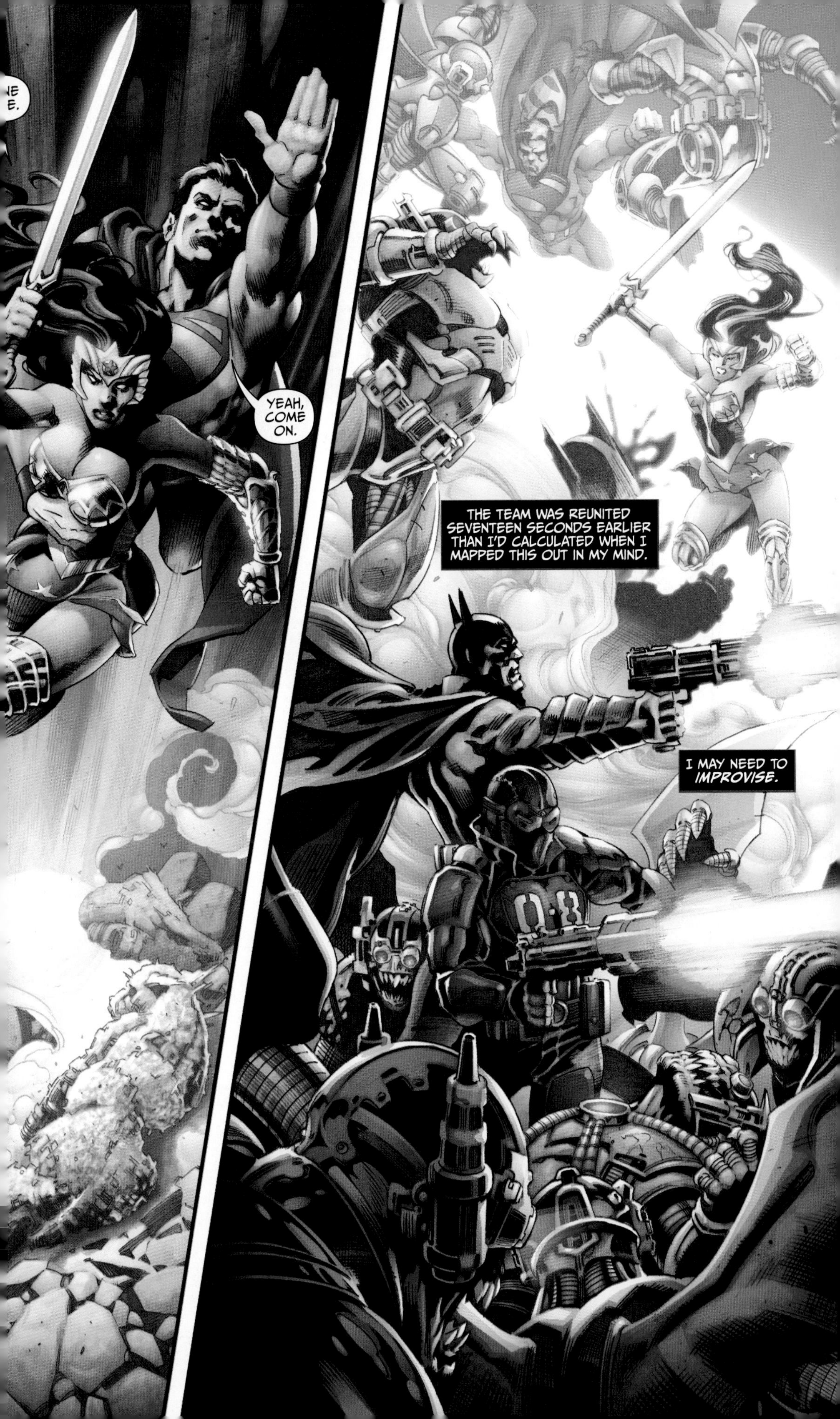
NE
E.
YEAH, COME ON.
THE TEAM WAS REUNITED SEVENTEEN SECONDS EARLIER THAN I'D CALCULATED WHEN I MAPPED THIS OUT IN MY MIND.
I MAY NEED TO *IMPROVISE.*

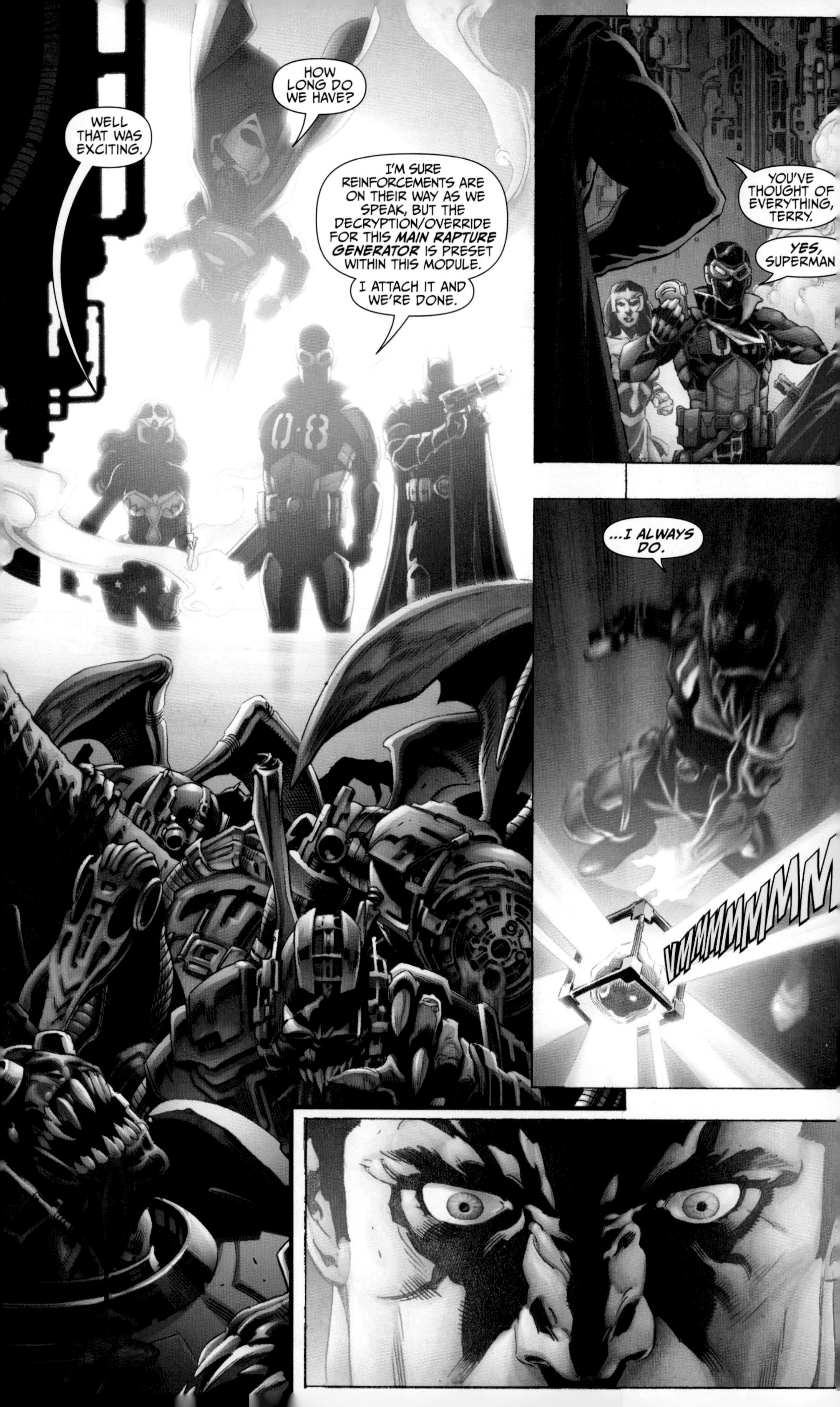

WELL THAT WAS EXCITING.
HOW LONG DO WE HAVE?
I'M SURE REINFORCEMENTS ARE ON THEIR WAY AS WE SPEAK, BUT THE DECRYPTION/OVERRIDE FOR THIS ***MAIN RAPTURE GENERATOR*** IS PRESET WITHIN THIS MODULE.
I ATTACH IT AND WE'RE DONE.
YOU'VE THOUGHT OF EVERYTHING, TERRY.
YES, SUPERMAN
...***I ALWAYS DO.***
VMMMMMMMMM

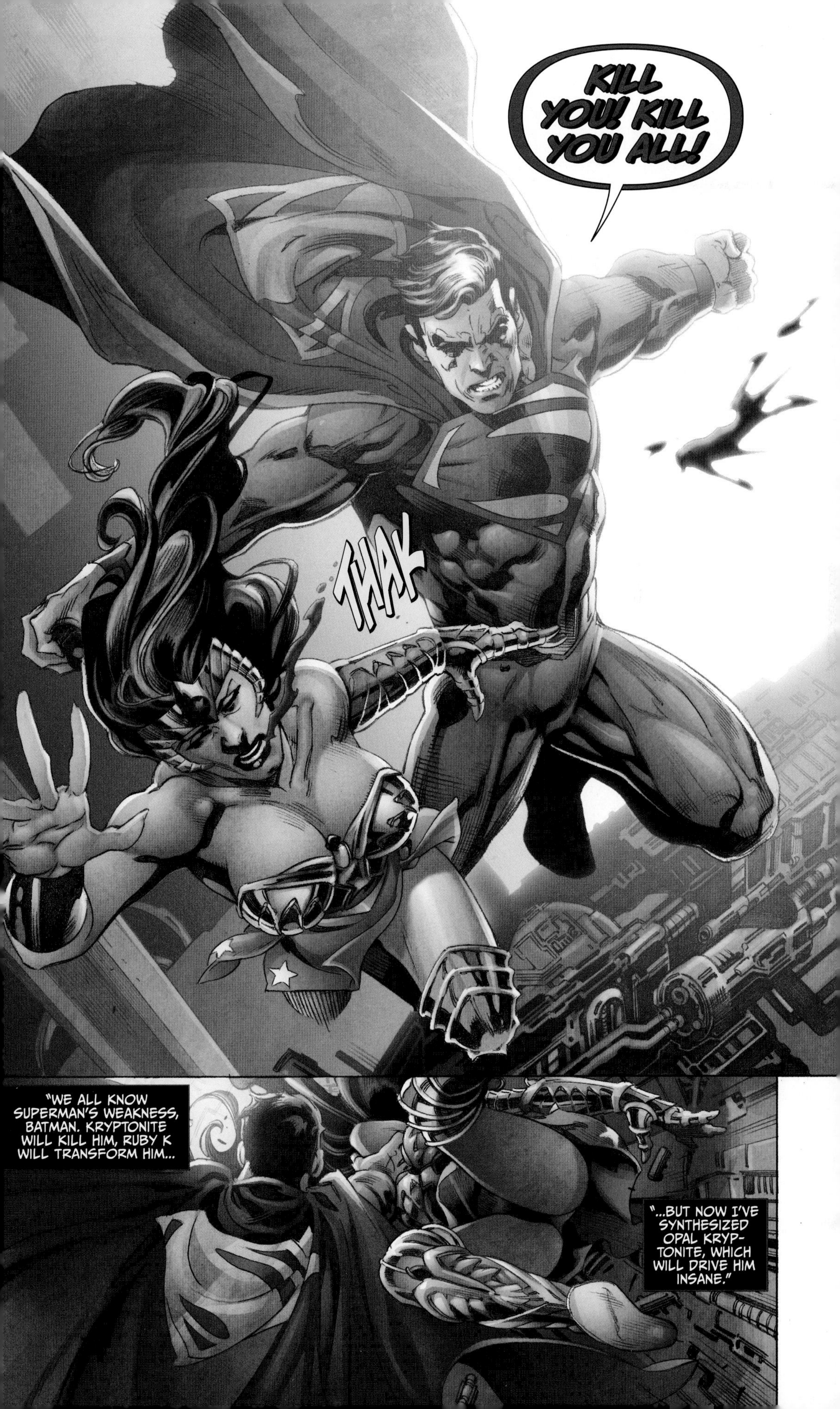
KILL YOU! KILL YOU ALL!
THAK
"WE ALL KNOW SUPERMAN'S WEAKNESS, BATMAN. KRYPTONITE WILL KILL HIM, RUBY K WILL TRANSFORM HIM...
"...BUT NOW I'VE SYNTHESIZED OPAL KRYP-TONITE, WHICH WILL DRIVE HIM INSANE."

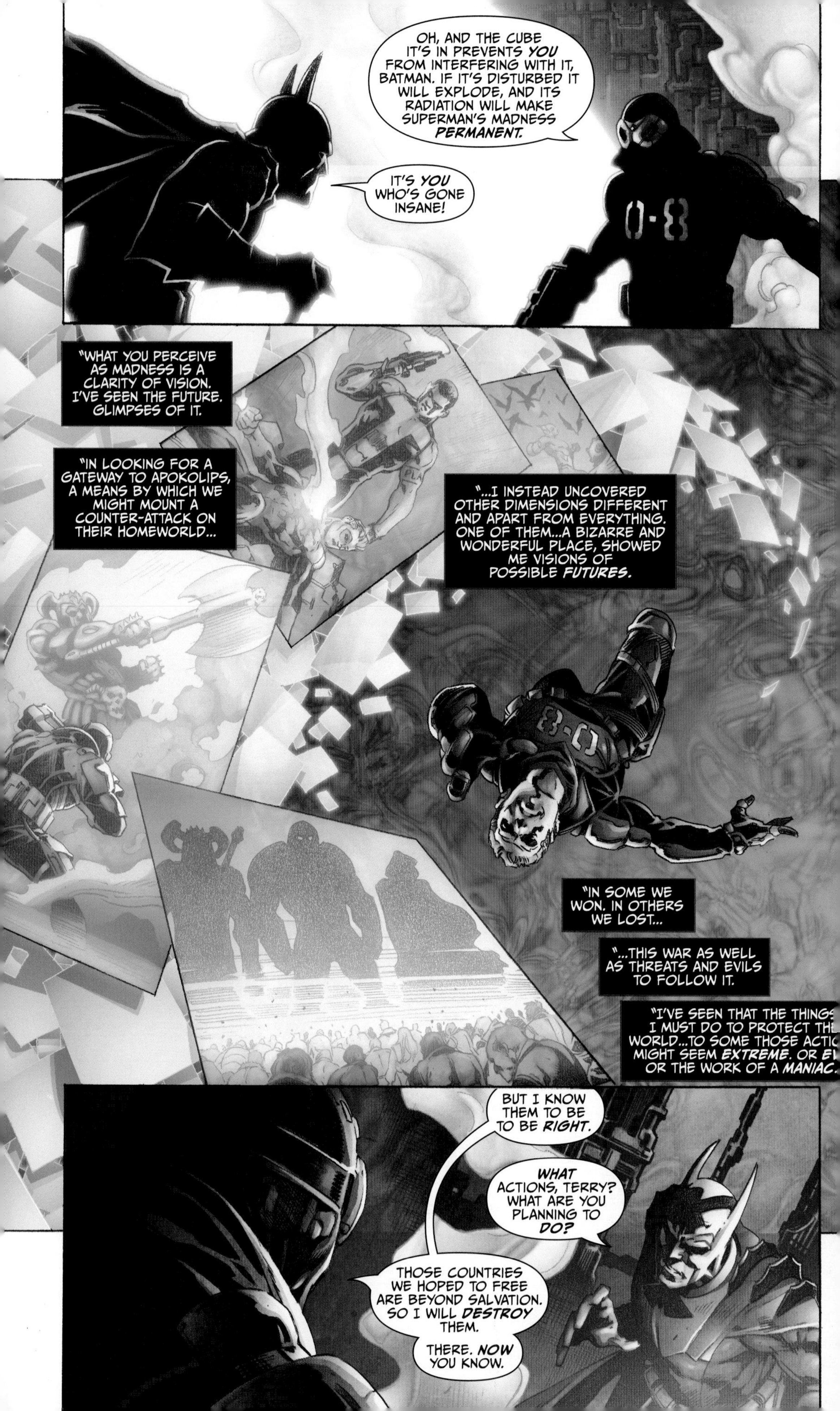

OH, AND THE CUBE IT'S IN PREVENTS *YOU* FROM INTERFERING WITH IT, BATMAN. IF IT'S DISTURBED IT WILL EXPLODE, AND ITS RADIATION WILL MAKE SUPERMAN'S MADNESS ***PERMANENT.***
IT'S *YOU* WHO'S GONE INSANE!
O-8
"WHAT YOU PERCEIVE AS MADNESS IS A CLARITY OF VISION. I'VE SEEN THE FUTURE. GLIMPSES OF IT.
"IN LOOKING FOR A GATEWAY TO APOKOLIPS, A MEANS BY WHICH WE MIGHT MOUNT A COUNTER-ATTACK ON THEIR HOMEWORLD...
"...I INSTEAD UNCOVERED OTHER DIMENSIONS DIFFERENT AND APART FROM EVERYTHING. ONE OF THEM...A BIZARRE AND WONDERFUL PLACE, SHOWED ME VISIONS OF POSSIBLE ***FUTURES.***
"IN SOME WE WON. IN OTHERS WE LOST...
"...THIS WAR AS WELL AS THREATS AND EVILS TO FOLLOW IT.
"I'VE SEEN THAT THE THINGS I MUST DO TO PROTECT THE WORLD...TO SOME THOSE ACTI MIGHT SEEM ***EXTREME.*** OR EV OR THE WORK OF A ***MANIAC.***
BUT I KNOW THEM TO BE TO BE ***RIGHT.***
WHAT ACTIONS, TERRY? WHAT ARE YOU PLANNING TO ***DO?***
THOSE COUNTRIES WE HOPED TO FREE ARE BEYOND SALVATION. SO I WILL ***DESTROY*** THEM.
THERE. ***NOW*** YOU KNOW.

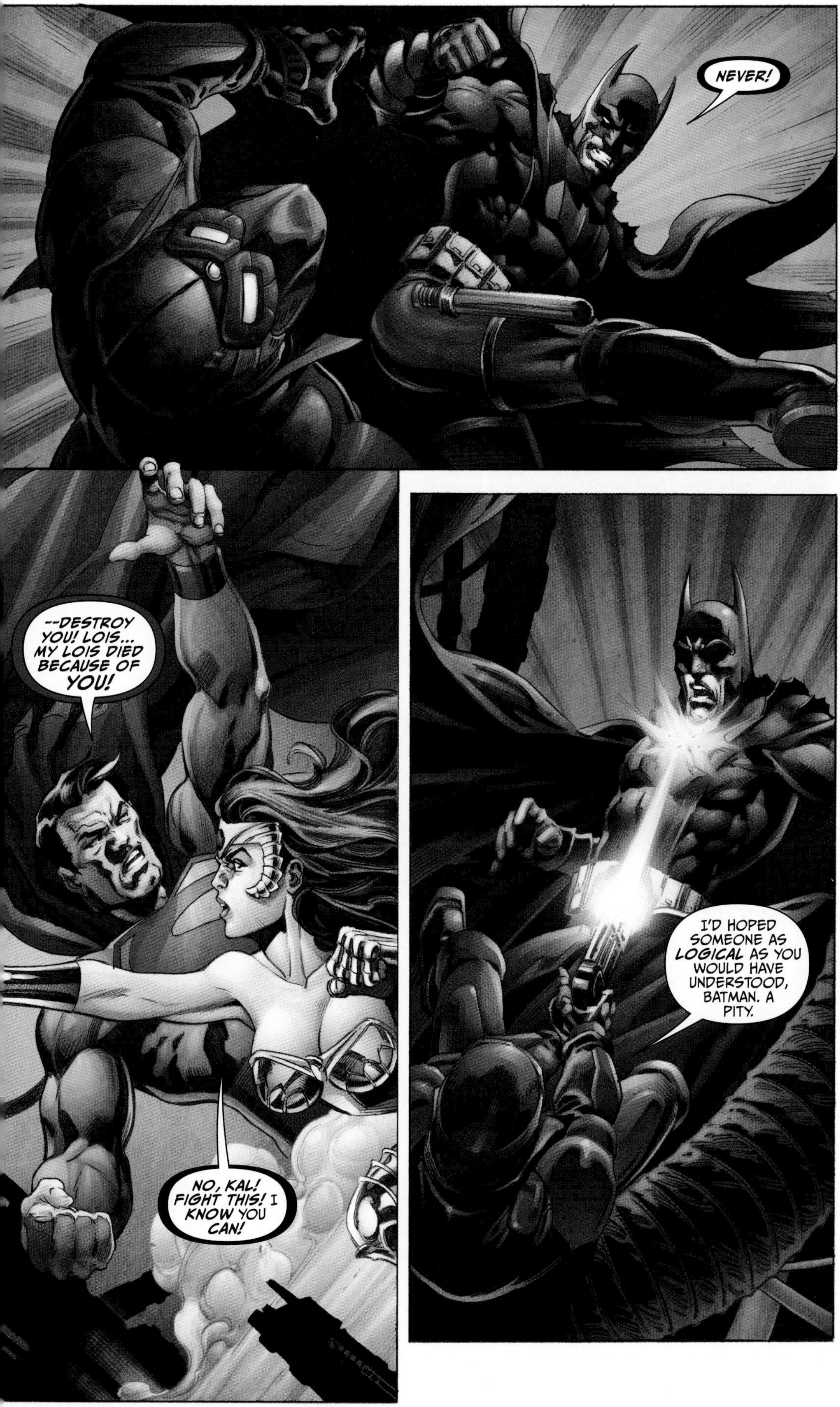
NEVER!
--DESTROY YOU! LOIS... MY LOIS DIED BECAUSE OF YOU!
NO, KAL! FIGHT THIS! I KNOW YOU CAN!
I'D HOPED SOMEONE AS LOGICAL AS YOU WOULD HAVE UNDERSTOOD, BATMAN. A PITY.

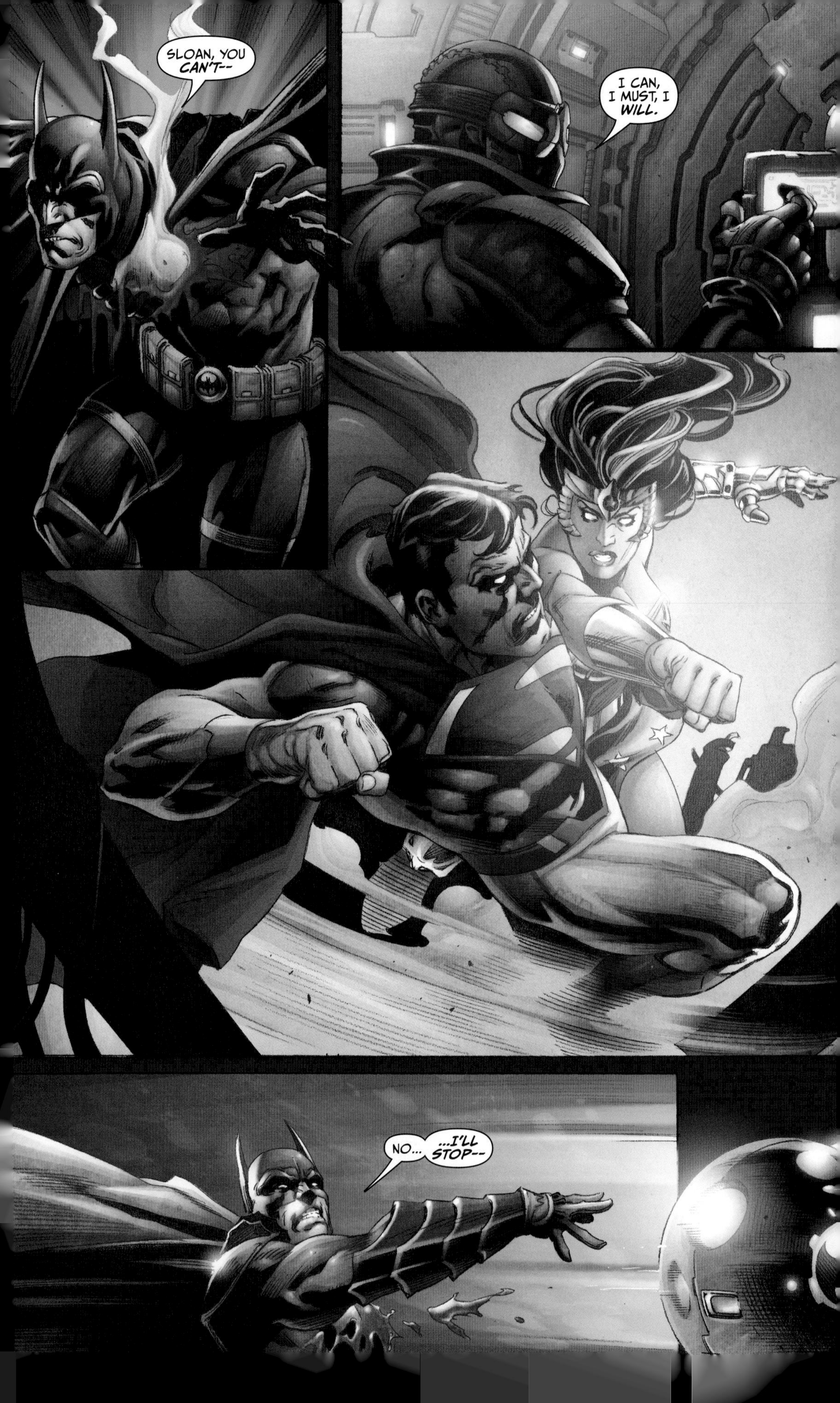
SLOAN, YOU CAN'T--
I CAN, I MUST, I WILL.
NO...
...I'LL STOP--

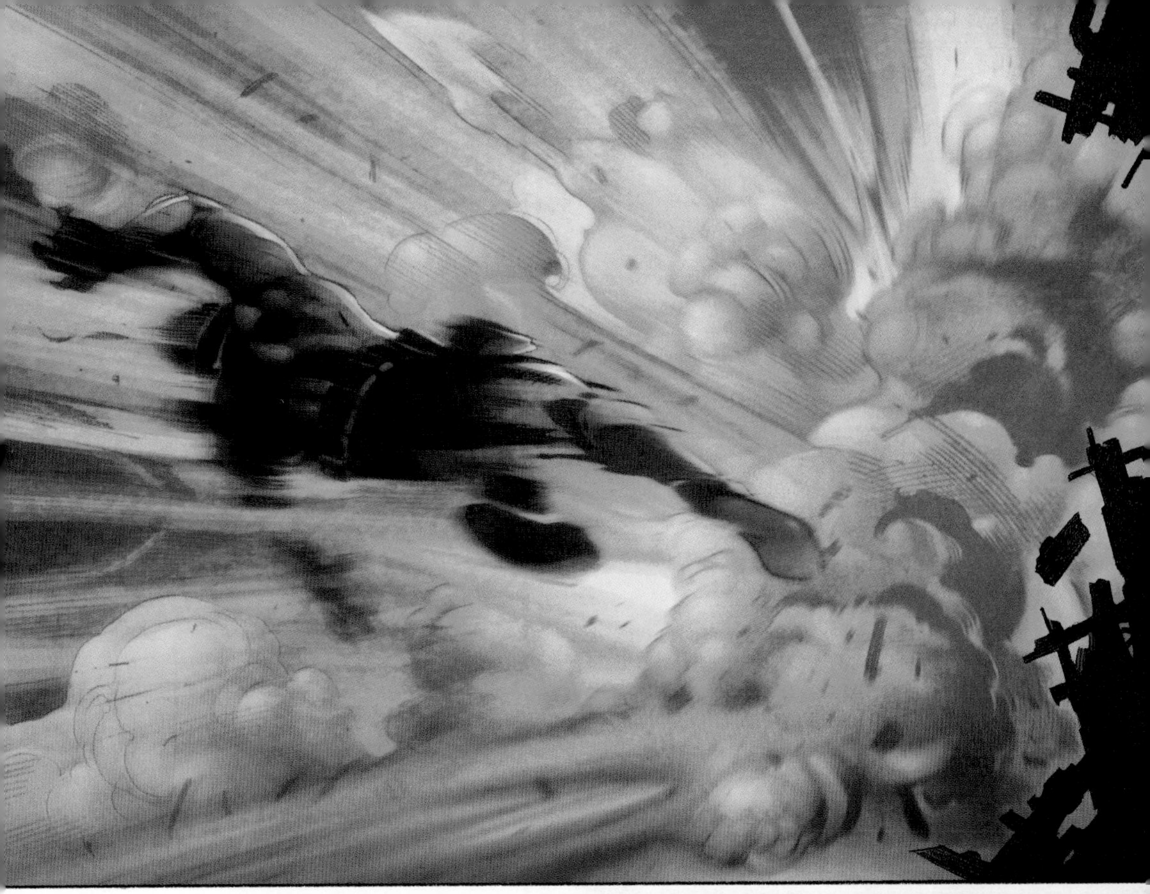

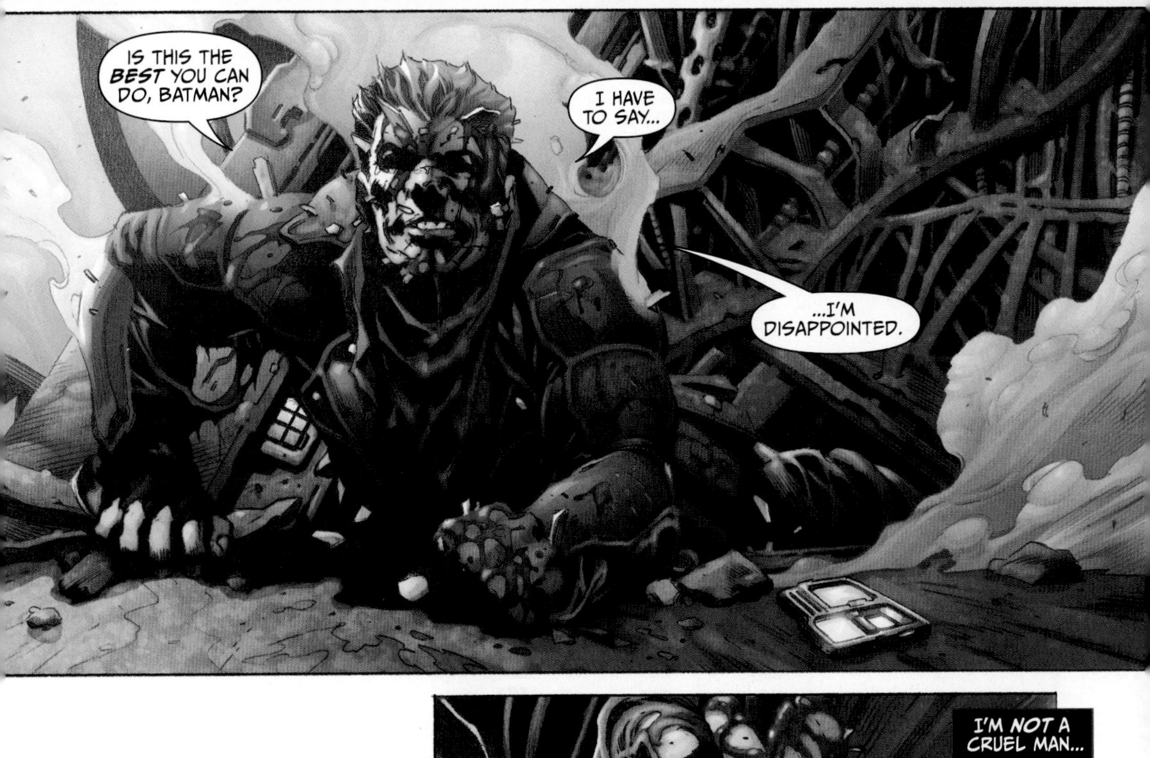
IS THIS THE BEST YOU CAN DO, BATMAN?
I HAVE TO SAY...
...I'M DISAPPOINTED.

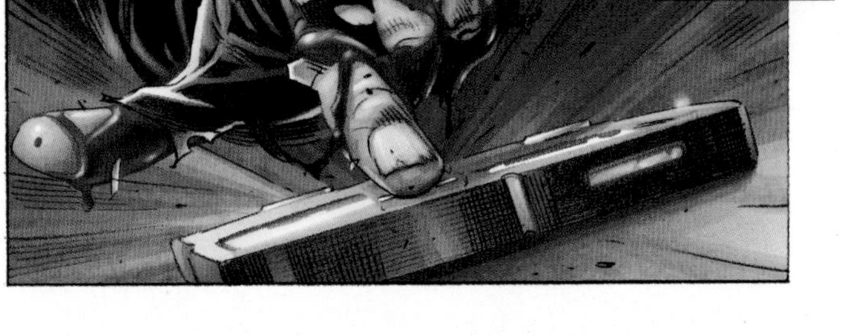
I'M NOT A CRUEL MAN...

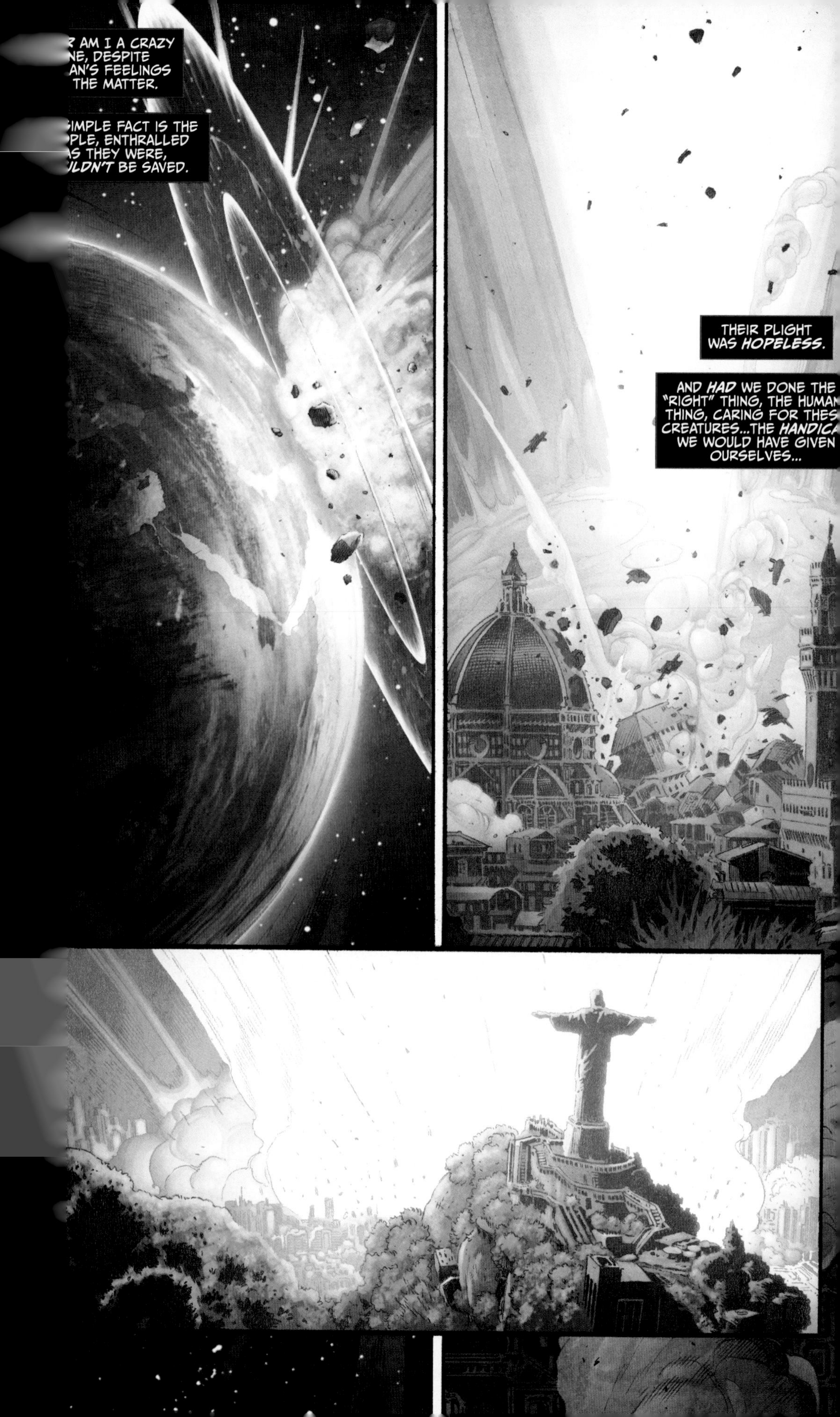
R AM I A CRAZY NE, DESPITE AN'S FEELINGS THE MATTER.
SIMPLE FACT IS THE PLE, ENTHRALLED AS THEY WERE, ULDN'T BE SAVED.
THEIR PLIGHT WAS *HOPELESS.*
AND *HAD* WE DONE THE "RIGHT" THING, THE HUMAN THING, CARING FOR THES CREATURES...THE *HANDICA* WE WOULD HAVE GIVEN OURSELVES...

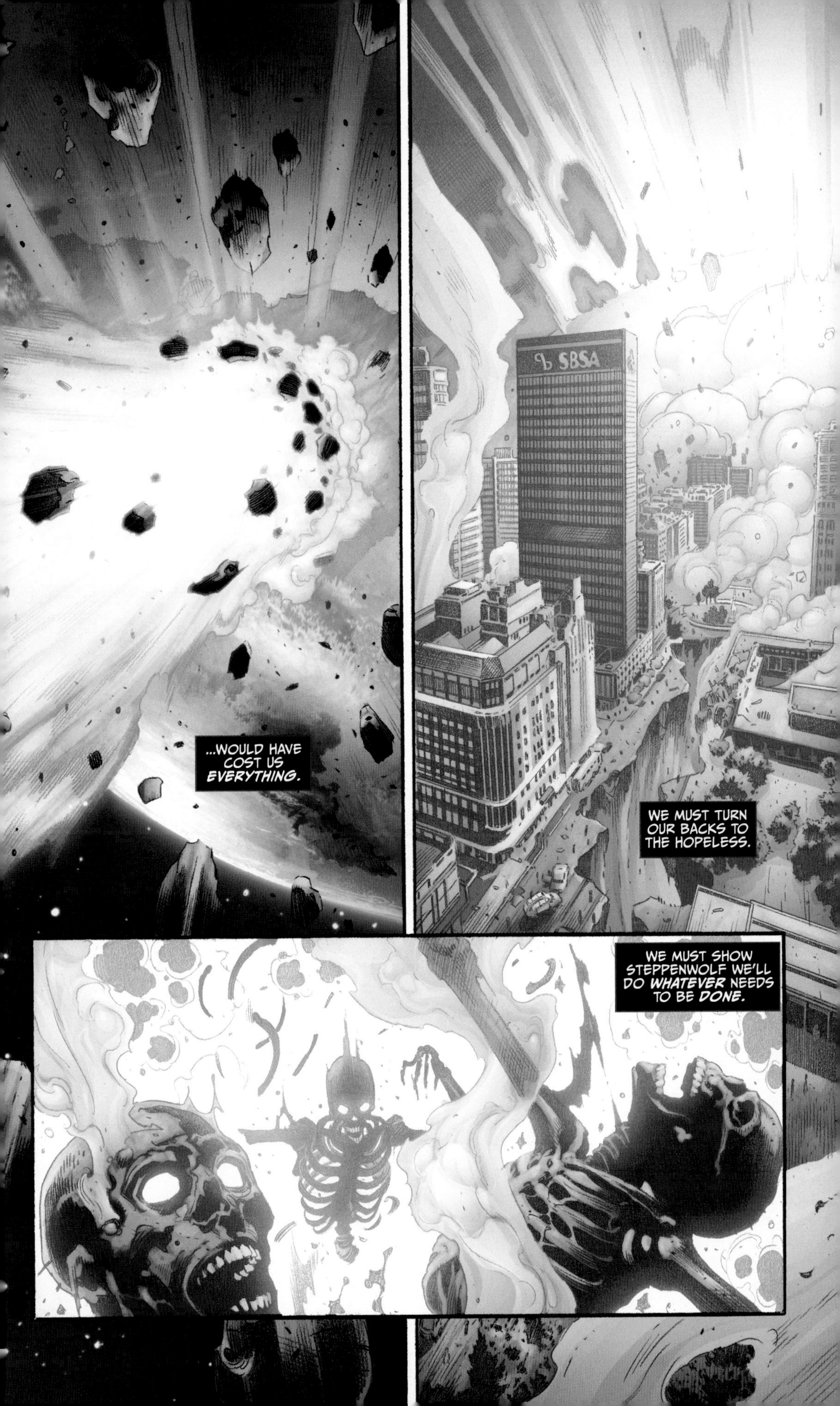
...WOULD HAVE COST US EVERYTHING.
SBSA
WE MUST TURN OUR BACKS TO THE HOPELESS.
WE MUST SHOW STEPPENWOLF WE'LL DO WHATEVER NEEDS TO BE DONE.

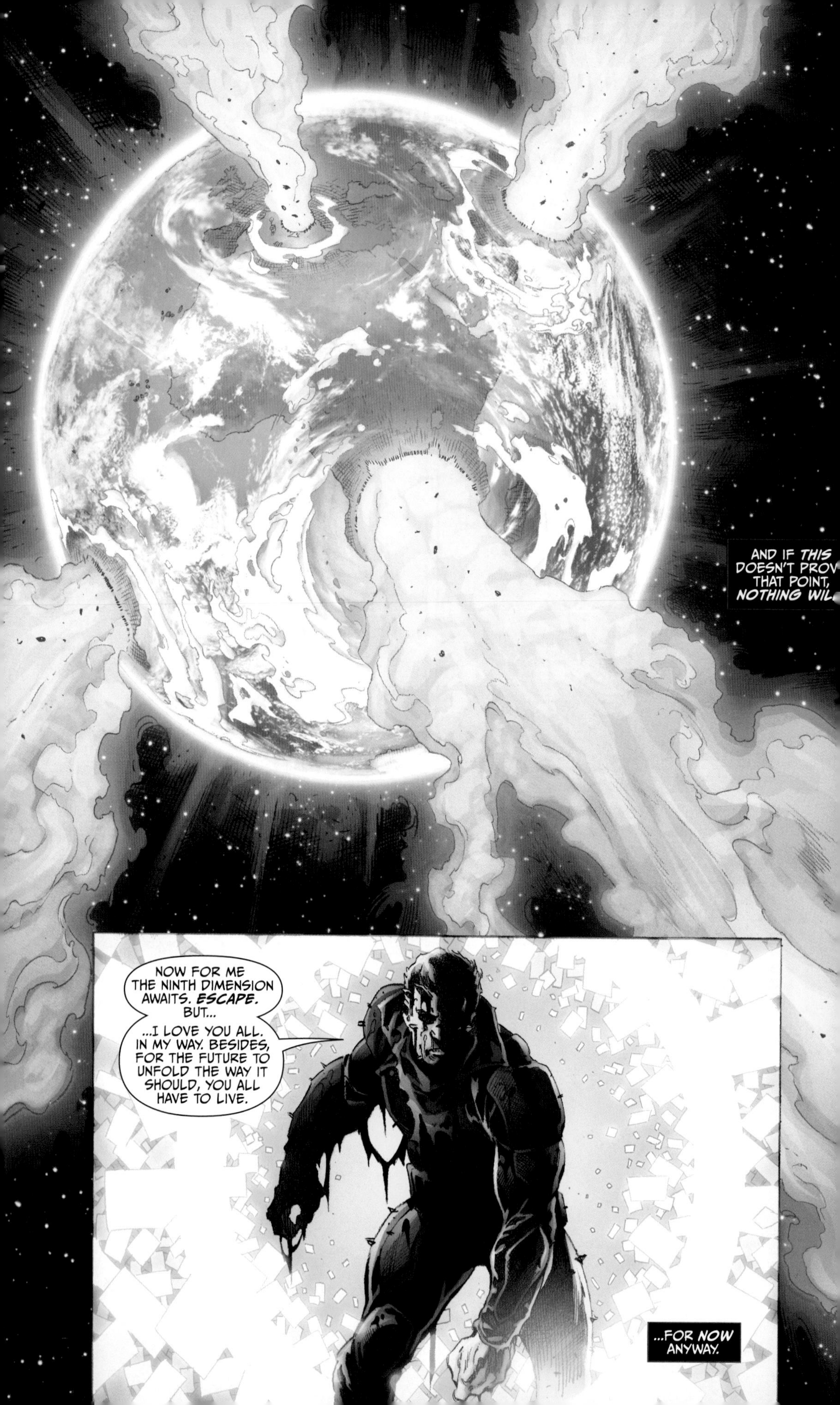
AND IF THIS DOESN'T PROV THAT POINT, NOTHING WIL
NOW FOR ME THE NINTH DIMENSION AWAITS. ESCAPE. BUT...
...I LOVE YOU ALL. IN MY WAY. BESIDES, FOR THE FUTURE TO UNFOLD THE WAY IT SHOULD, YOU ALL HAVE TO LIVE.
...FOR NOW ANYWAY.

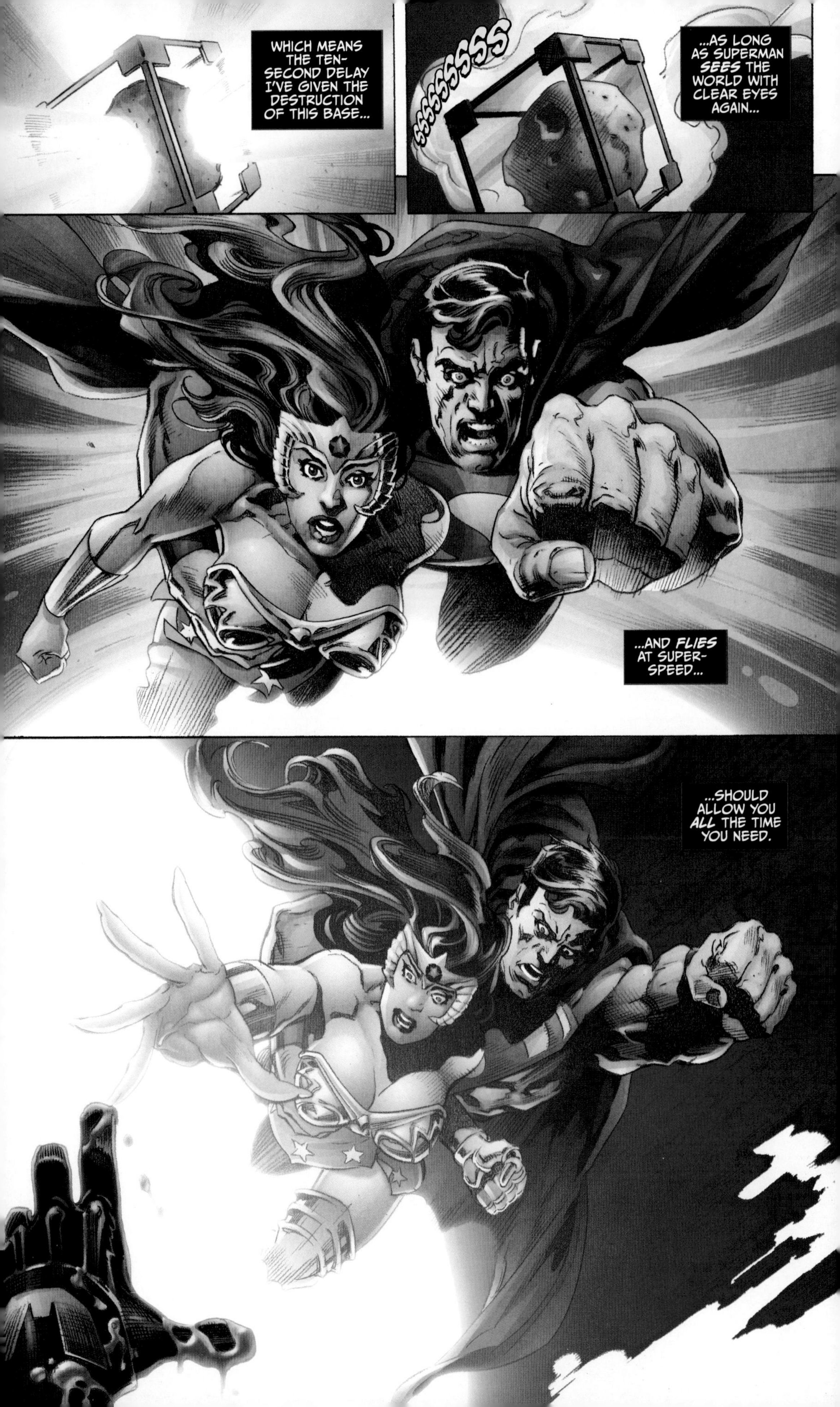
WHICH MEANS THE TEN-SECOND DELAY I'VE GIVEN THE DESTRUCTION OF THIS BASE...
SSSSSSSSSS
...AS LONG AS SUPERMAN SEES THE WORLD WITH CLEAR EYES AGAIN...
...AND FLIES AT SUPER-SPEED...
...SHOULD ALLOW YOU ALL THE TIME YOU NEED.

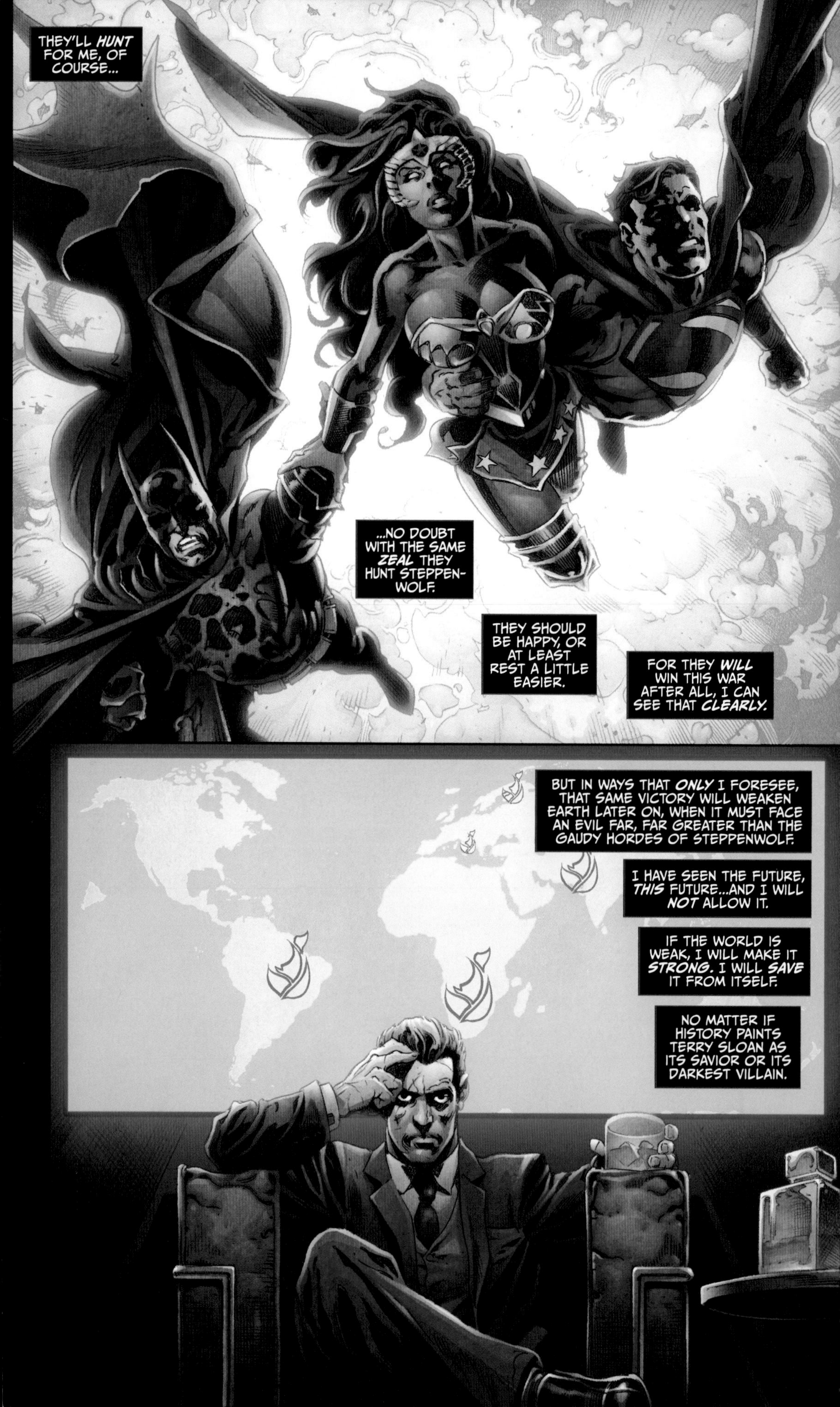
THEY'LL HUNT FOR ME, OF COURSE...
...NO DOUBT WITH THE SAME ZEAL THEY HUNT STEPPEN-WOLF.
THEY SHOULD BE HAPPY, OR AT LEAST REST A LITTLE EASIER.
FOR THEY WILL WIN THIS WAR AFTER ALL, I CAN SEE THAT CLEARLY.
BUT IN WAYS THAT ONLY I FORESEE, THAT SAME VICTORY WILL WEAKEN EARTH LATER ON, WHEN IT MUST FACE AN EVIL FAR, FAR GREATER THAN THE GAUDY HORDES OF STEPPENWOLF.
I HAVE SEEN THE FUTURE, THIS FUTURE...AND I WILL NOT ALLOW IT.
IF THE WORLD IS WEAK, I WILL MAKE IT STRONG. I WILL SAVE IT FROM ITSELF.
NO MATTER IF HISTORY PAINTS TERRY SLOAN AS ITS SAVIOR OR ITS DARKEST VILLAIN.

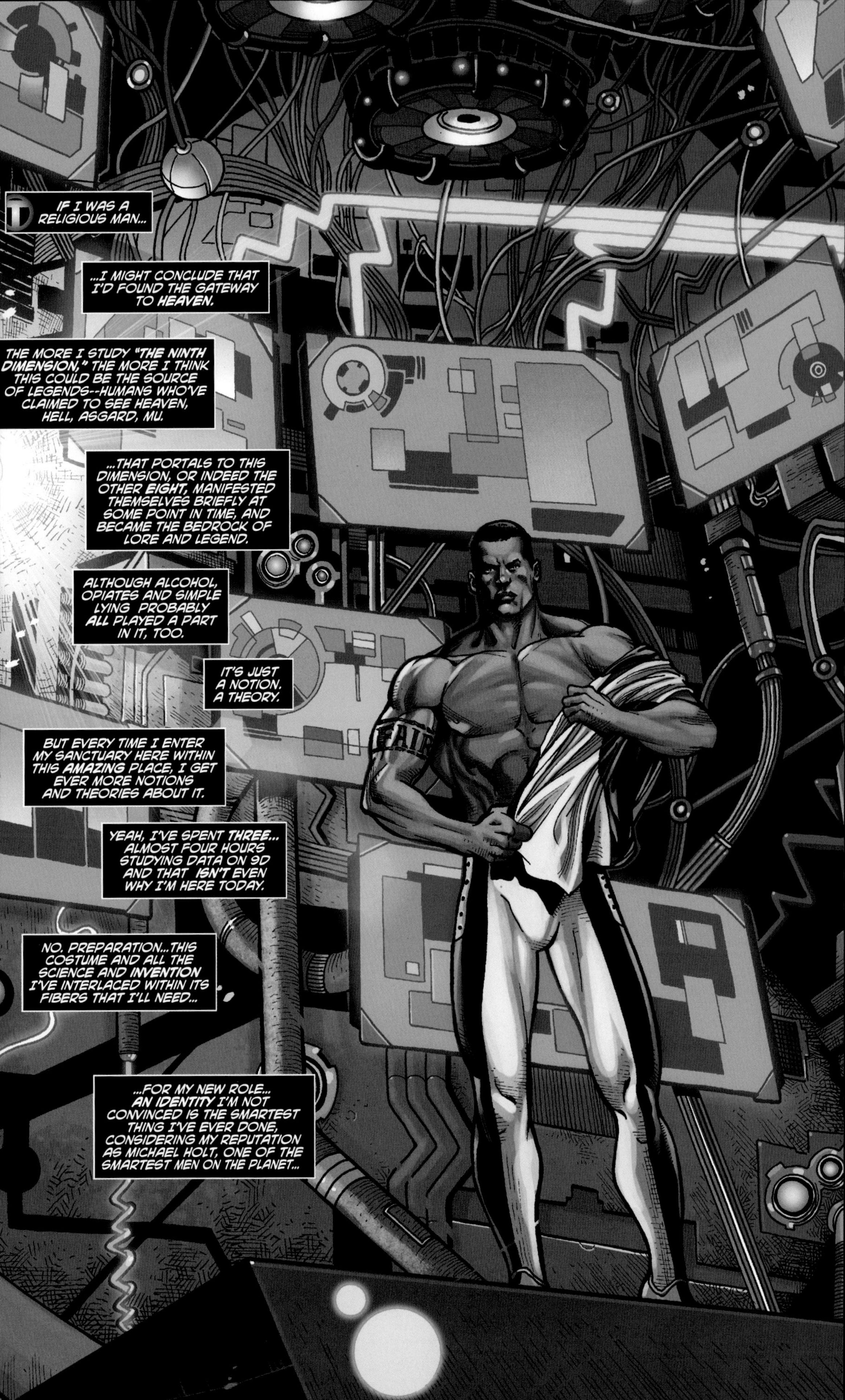
IF I WAS A RELIGIOUS MAN...
...I MIGHT CONCLUDE THAT I'D FOUND THE GATEWAY TO HEAVEN.
THE MORE I STUDY "THE NINTH DIMENSION," THE MORE I THINK THIS COULD BE THE SOURCE OF LEGENDS--HUMANS WHO'VE CLAIMED TO SEE HEAVEN, HELL, ASGARD, MU.
...THAT PORTALS TO THIS DIMENSION, OR INDEED THE OTHER EIGHT, MANIFESTED THEMSELVES BRIEFLY AT SOME POINT IN TIME, AND BECAME THE BEDROCK OF LORE AND LEGEND.
ALTHOUGH ALCOHOL, OPIATES AND SIMPLE LYING PROBABLY ALL PLAYED A PART IN IT, TOO.
IT'S JUST A NOTION. A THEORY.
BUT EVERY TIME I ENTER MY SANCTUARY HERE WITHIN THIS AMAZING PLACE, I GET EVER MORE NOTIONS AND THEORIES ABOUT IT.
YEAH, I'VE SPENT THREE... ALMOST FOUR HOURS STUDYING DATA ON 9D AND THAT ISN'T EVEN WHY I'M HERE TODAY.
NO. PREPARATION...THIS COSTUME AND ALL THE SCIENCE AND INVENTION I'VE INTERLACED WITHIN ITS FIBERS THAT I'LL NEED...
...FOR MY NEW ROLE... AN IDENTITY I'M NOT CONVINCED IS THE SMARTEST THING I'VE EVER DONE, CONSIDERING MY REPUTATION AS MICHAEL HOLT, ONE OF THE SMARTEST MEN ON THE PLANET...

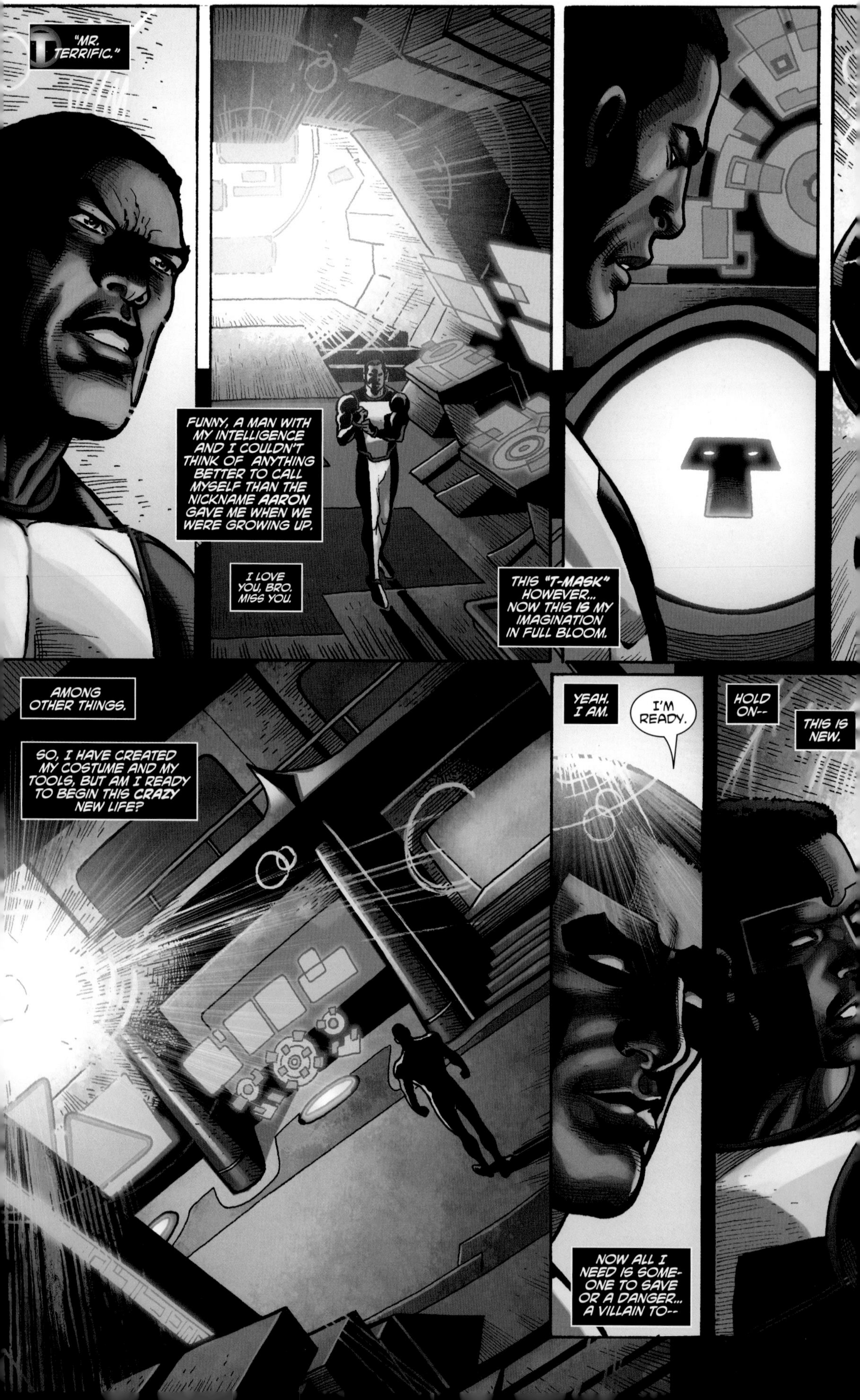
"MR. TERRIFIC."
FUNNY, A MAN WITH MY INTELLIGENCE AND I COULDN'T THINK OF ANYTHING BETTER TO CALL MYSELF THAN THE NICKNAME AARON GAVE ME WHEN WE WERE GROWING UP.
I LOVE YOU, BRO. MISS YOU.
THIS "T-MASK" HOWEVER... NOW THIS IS MY IMAGINATION IN FULL BLOOM.
AMONG OTHER THINGS.
SO, I HAVE CREATED MY COSTUME AND MY TOOLS, BUT AM I READY TO BEGIN THIS CRAZY NEW LIFE?
YEAH. I AM.
I'M READY.
NOW ALL I NEED IS SOME-ONE TO SAVE OR A DANGER... A VILLAIN TO--
HOLD ON--
THIS IS NEW.

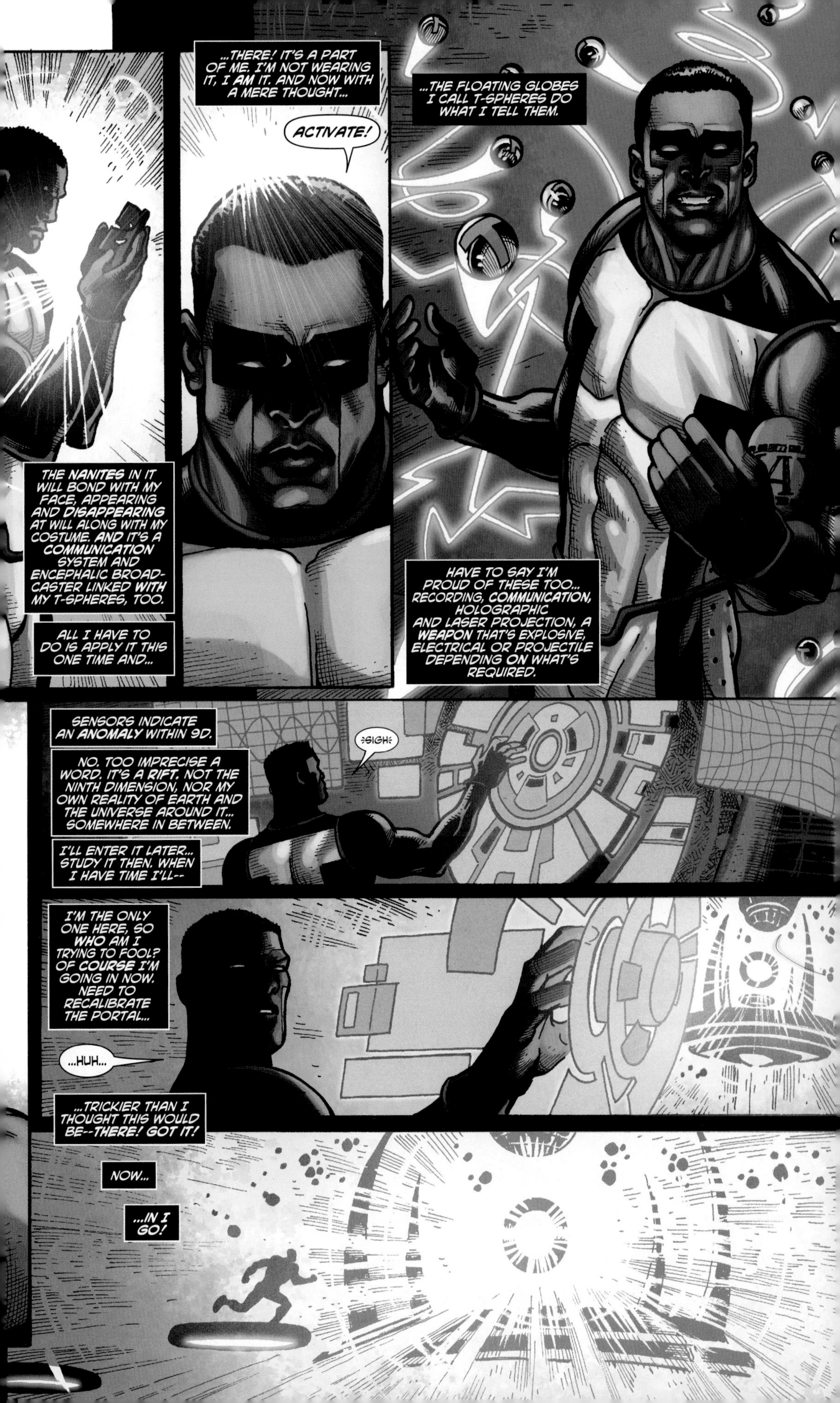

THE NANITES IN IT WILL BOND WITH MY FACE, APPEARING AND DISAPPEARING AT WILL ALONG WITH MY COSTUME. AND IT'S A COMMUNICATION SYSTEM AND ENCEPHALIC BROAD-CASTER LINKED WITH MY T-SPHERES, TOO.
ALL I HAVE TO DO IS APPLY IT THIS ONE TIME AND...
...THERE! IT'S A PART OF ME. I'M NOT WEARING IT, I AM IT. AND NOW WITH A MERE THOUGHT...
ACTIVATE!
...THE FLOATING GLOBES I CALL T-SPHERES DO WHAT I TELL THEM.
HAVE TO SAY I'M PROUD OF THESE TOO... RECORDING, COMMUNICATION, HOLOGRAPHIC AND LASER PROJECTION, A WEAPON THAT'S EXPLOSIVE, ELECTRICAL OR PROJECTILE DEPENDING ON WHAT'S REQUIRED.
SENSORS INDICATE AN ANOMALY WITHIN 9D.
NO. TOO IMPRECISE A WORD. IT'S A RIFT. NOT THE NINTH DIMENSION, NOR MY OWN REALITY OF EARTH AND THE UNIVERSE AROUND IT... SOMEWHERE IN BETWEEN.
SIGH
I'LL ENTER IT LATER... STUDY IT THEN. WHEN I HAVE TIME I'LL--
I'M THE ONLY ONE HERE, SO WHO AM I TRYING TO FOOL? OF COURSE I'M GOING IN NOW. NEED TO RECALIBRATE THE PORTAL...
...HUH...
...TRICKIER THAN I THOUGHT THIS WOULD BE--THERE! GOT IT!
NOW...
...IN I GO!

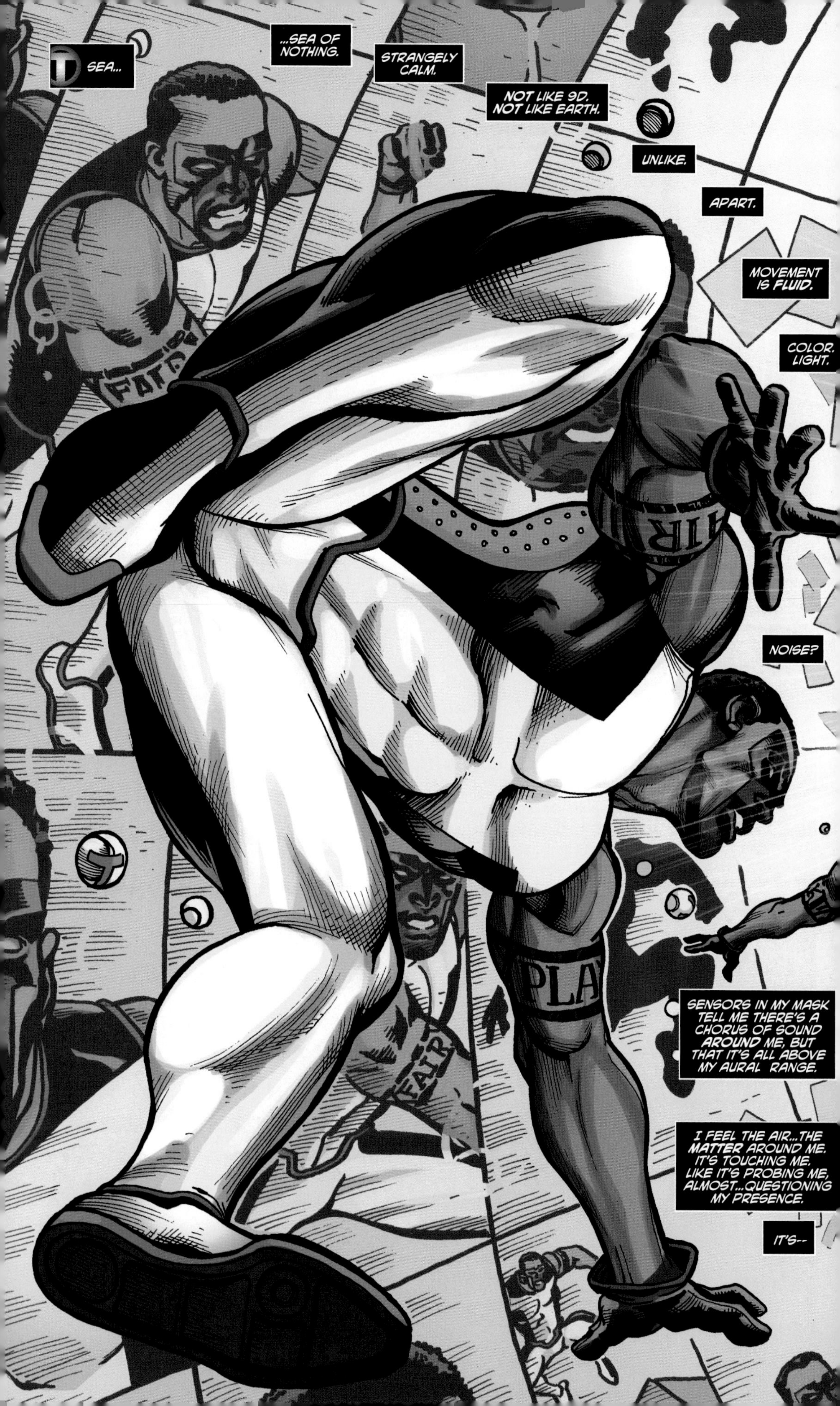
SEA...
...SEA OF NOTHING.
STRANGELY CALM.
NOT LIKE 9D. NOT LIKE EARTH.
UNLIKE.
APART.
MOVEMENT IS FLUID.
COLOR. LIGHT.
NOISE?
SENSORS IN MY MASK TELL ME THERE'S A CHORUS OF SOUND AROUND ME, BUT THAT IT'S ALL ABOVE MY AURAL RANGE.
I FEEL THE AIR...THE MATTER AROUND ME. IT'S TOUCHING ME. LIKE IT'S PROBING ME, ALMOST...QUESTIONING MY PRESENCE.
IT'S--

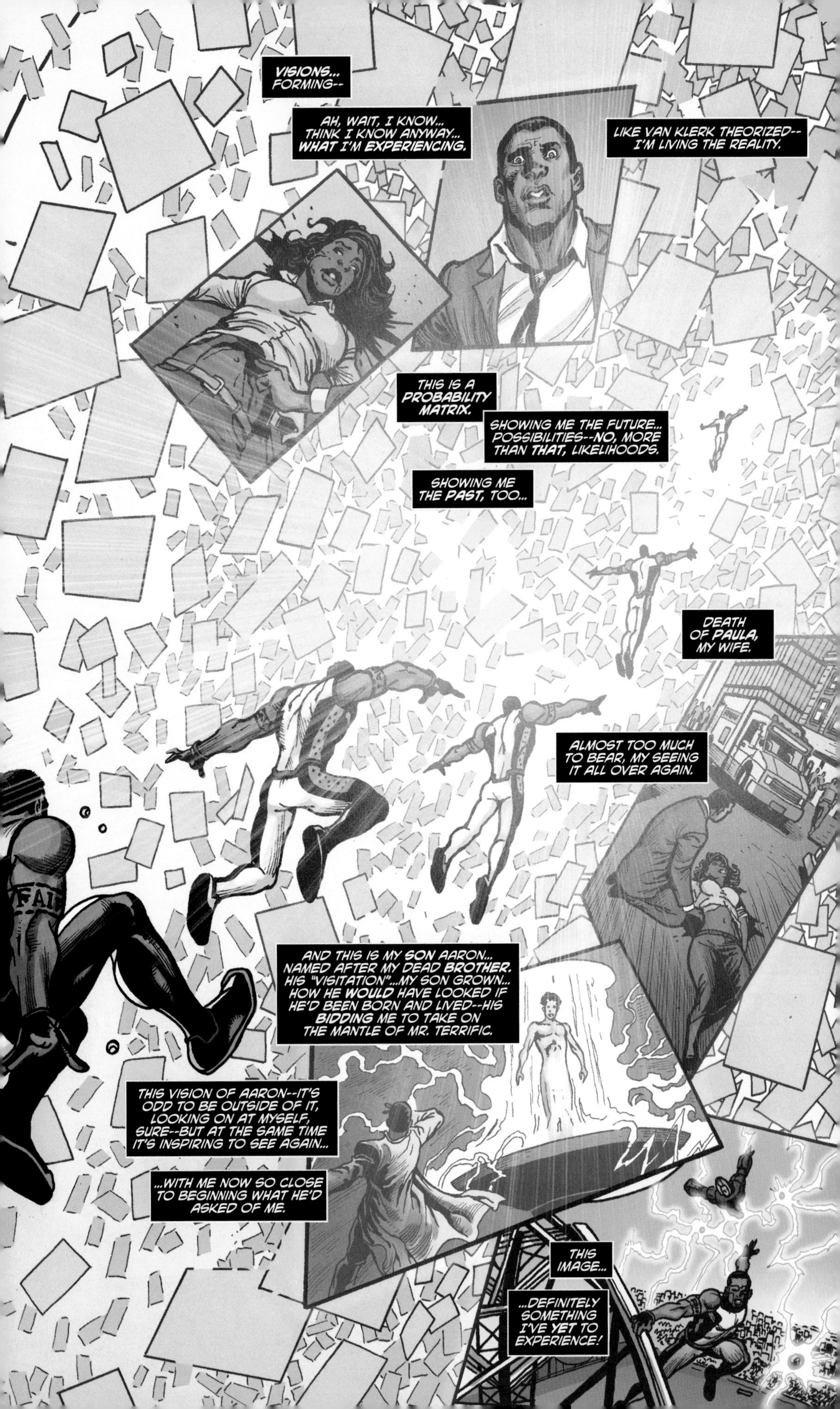
VISIONS... FORMING--
AH, WAIT, I KNOW... THINK I KNOW ANYWAY... WHAT I'M EXPERIENCING.
LIKE VAN KLERK THEORIZED-- I'M LIVING THE REALITY.
THIS IS A PROBABILITY MATRIX.
SHOWING ME THE FUTURE... POSSIBILITIES--NO, MORE THAN THAT, LIKELIHOODS.
SHOWING ME THE PAST, TOO...
DEATH OF PAULA, MY WIFE.
ALMOST TOO MUCH TO BEAR, MY SEEING IT ALL OVER AGAIN.
AND THIS IS MY SON AARON... NAMED AFTER MY DEAD BROTHER. HIS "VISITATION"...MY SON GROWN... HOW HE WOULD HAVE LOOKED IF HE'D BEEN BORN AND LIVED--HIS BIDDING ME TO TAKE ON THE MANTLE OF MR. TERRIFIC.
THIS VISION OF AARON--IT'S ODD TO BE OUTSIDE OF IT, LOOKING ON AT MYSELF, SURE--BUT AT THE SAME TIME IT'S INSPIRING TO SEE AGAIN...
...WITH ME NOW SO CLOSE TO BEGINNING WHAT HE'D ASKED OF ME.
THIS IMAGE...
...DEFINITELY SOMETHING I'VE YET TO EXPERIENCE!

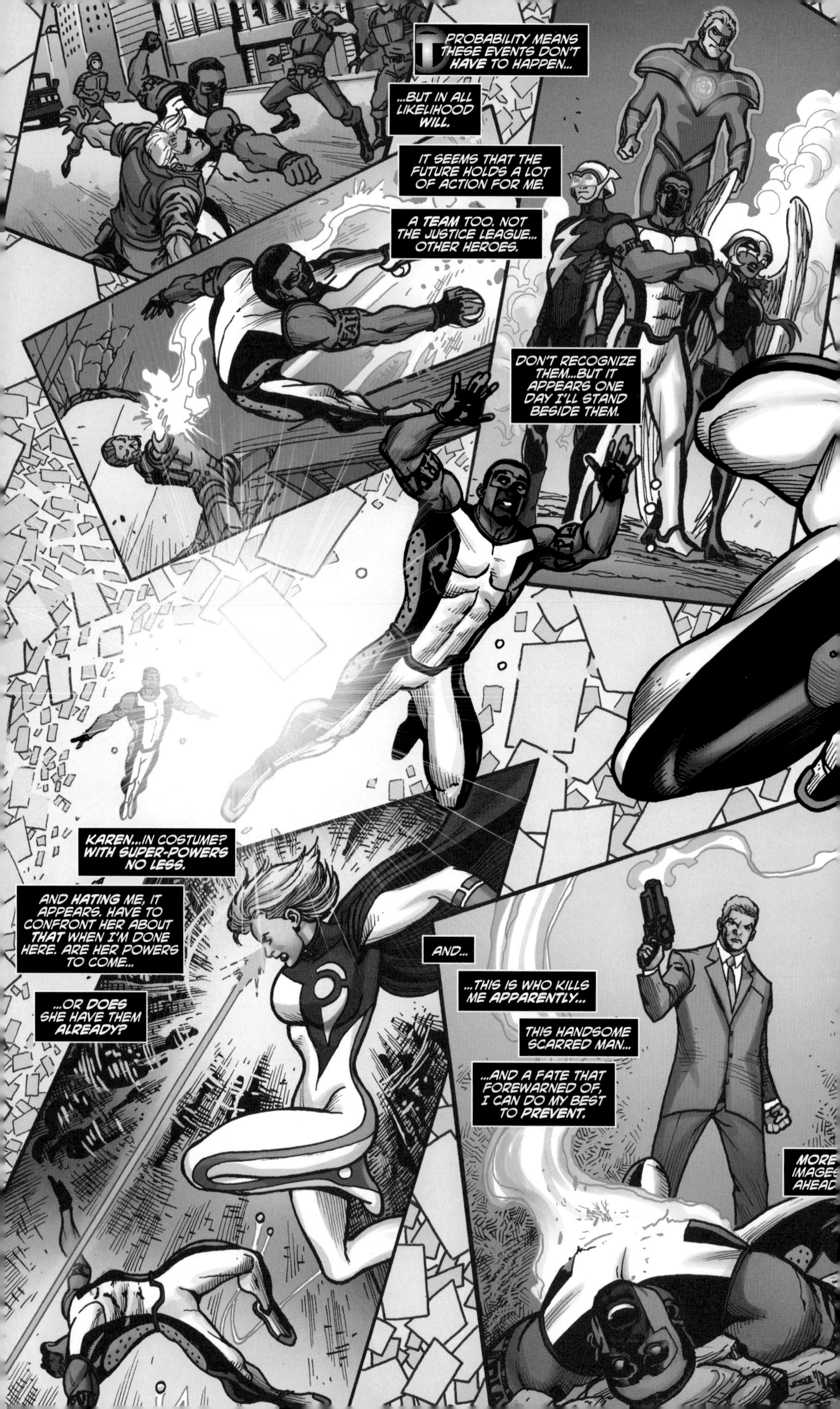
PROBABILITY MEANS THESE EVENTS DON'T HAVE TO HAPPEN...
...BUT IN ALL LIKELIHOOD WILL.
IT SEEMS THAT THE FUTURE HOLDS A LOT OF ACTION FOR ME.
A TEAM TOO. NOT THE JUSTICE LEAGUE... OTHER HEROES.
DON'T RECOGNIZE THEM...BUT IT APPEARS ONE DAY I'LL STAND BESIDE THEM.
KAREN...IN COSTUME? WITH SUPER-POWERS NO LESS.
AND HATING ME, IT APPEARS. HAVE TO CONFRONT HER ABOUT THAT WHEN I'M DONE HERE. ARE HER POWERS TO COME...
...OR DOES SHE HAVE THEM ALREADY?
AND...
...THIS IS WHO KILLS ME APPARENTLY...
THIS HANDSOME SCARRED MAN...
...AND A FATE THAT FOREWARNED OF, I CAN DO MY BEST TO PREVENT.
MORE IMAGES AHEAD

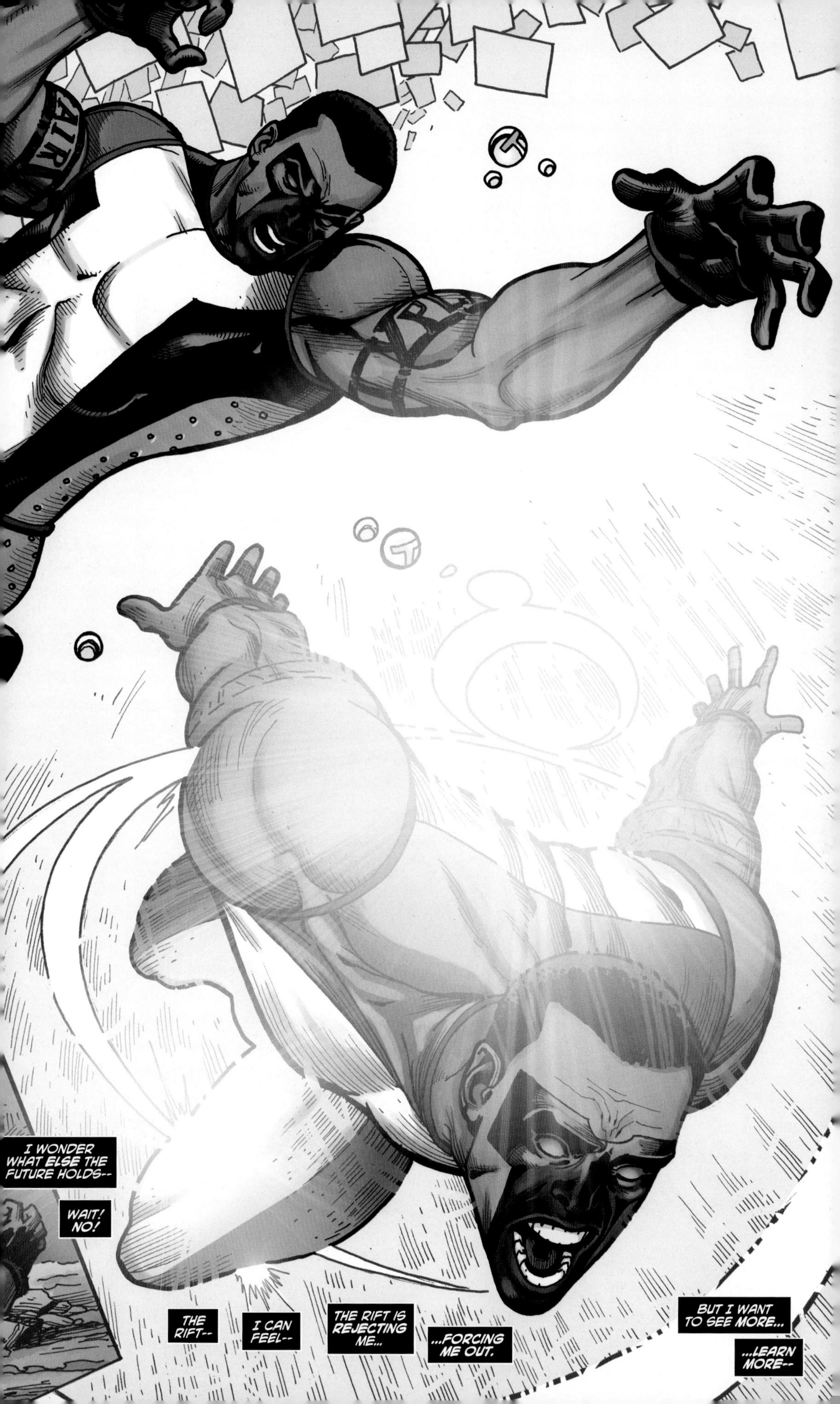
AIR
I WONDER WHAT ELSE THE FUTURE HOLDS--
WAIT! NO!
THE RIFT--
I CAN FEEL--
THE RIFT IS REJECTING ME...
...FORCING ME OUT.
BUT I WANT TO SEE MORE...
...LEARN MORE--

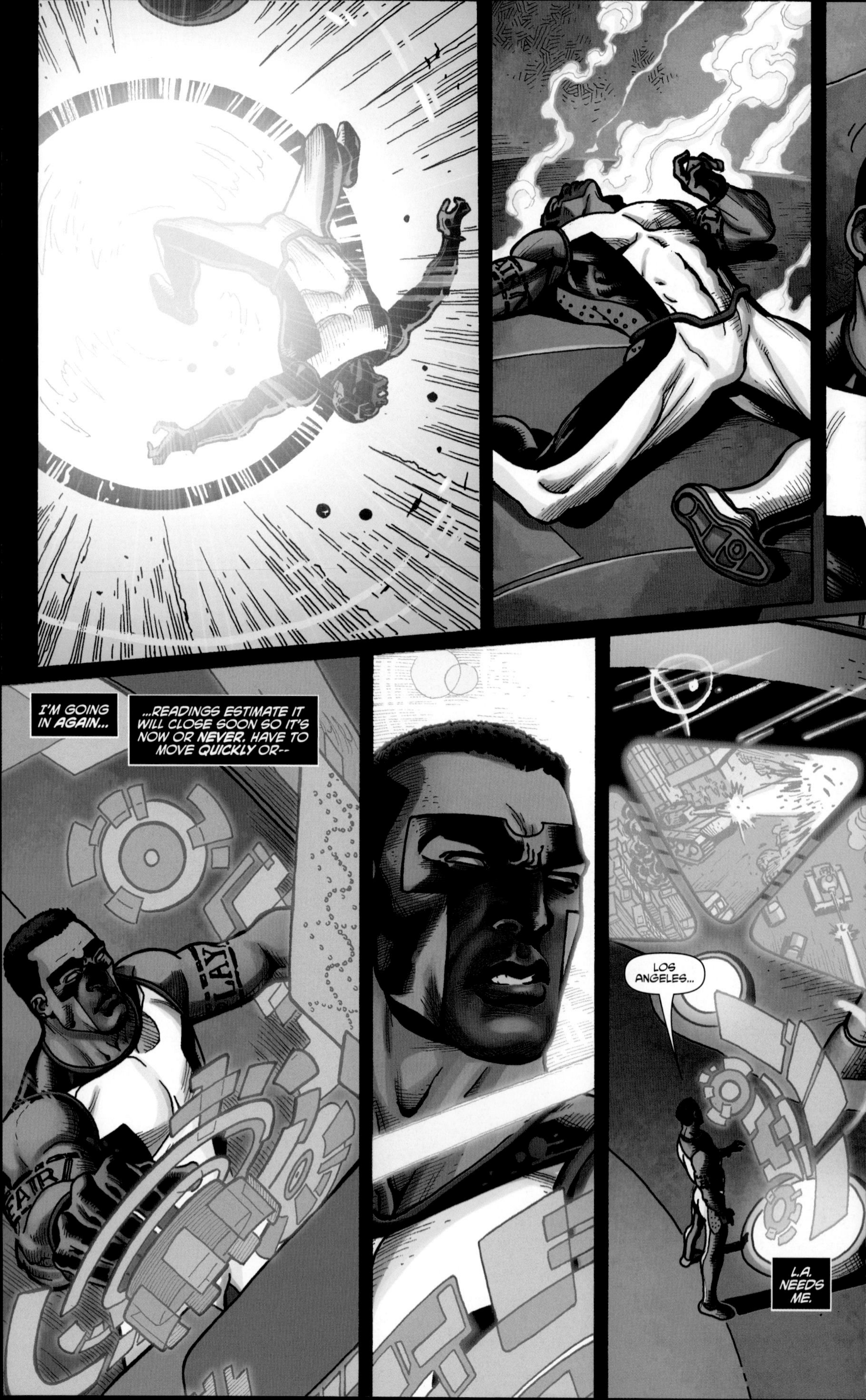
I'M GOING IN AGAIN...
...READINGS ESTIMATE IT WILL CLOSE SOON SO IT'S NOW OR NEVER. HAVE TO MOVE QUICKLY OR--
LOS ANGELES...
L.A. NEEDS ME.

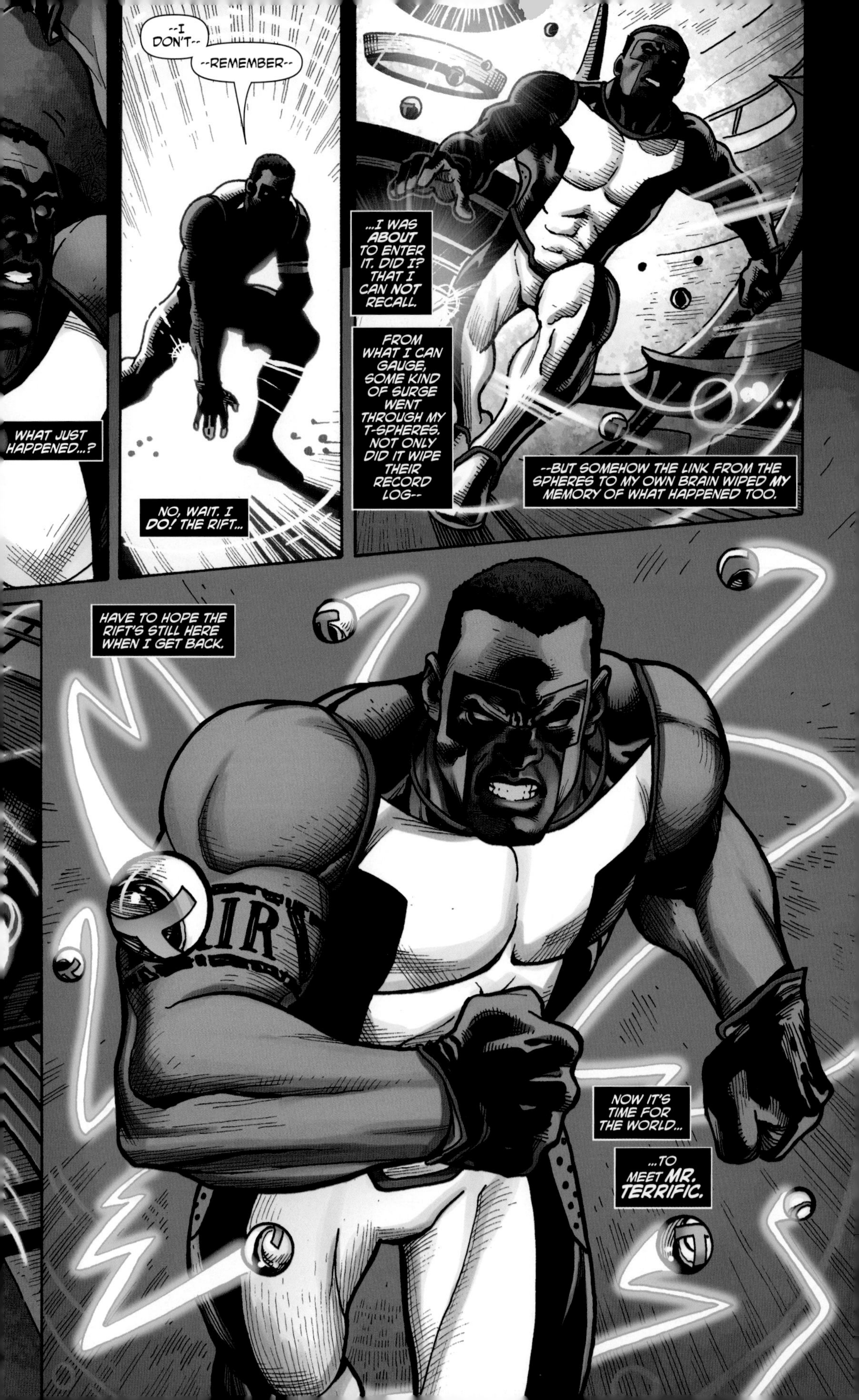

WHAT JUST HAPPENED...?
--I DON'T--
--REMEMBER--
NO, WAIT. I DO! THE RIFT...
...I WAS ABOUT TO ENTER IT. DID I? THAT I CAN NOT RECALL.
FROM WHAT I CAN GAUGE, SOME KIND OF SURGE WENT THROUGH MY T-SPHERES. NOT ONLY DID IT WIPE THEIR RECORD LOG--
--BUT SOMEHOW THE LINK FROM THE SPHERES TO MY OWN BRAIN WIPED MY MEMORY OF WHAT HAPPENED TOO.
HAVE TO HOPE THE RIFT'S STILL HERE WHEN I GET BACK.
NOW IT'S TIME FOR THE WORLD...
...TO MEET MR. TERRIFIC.

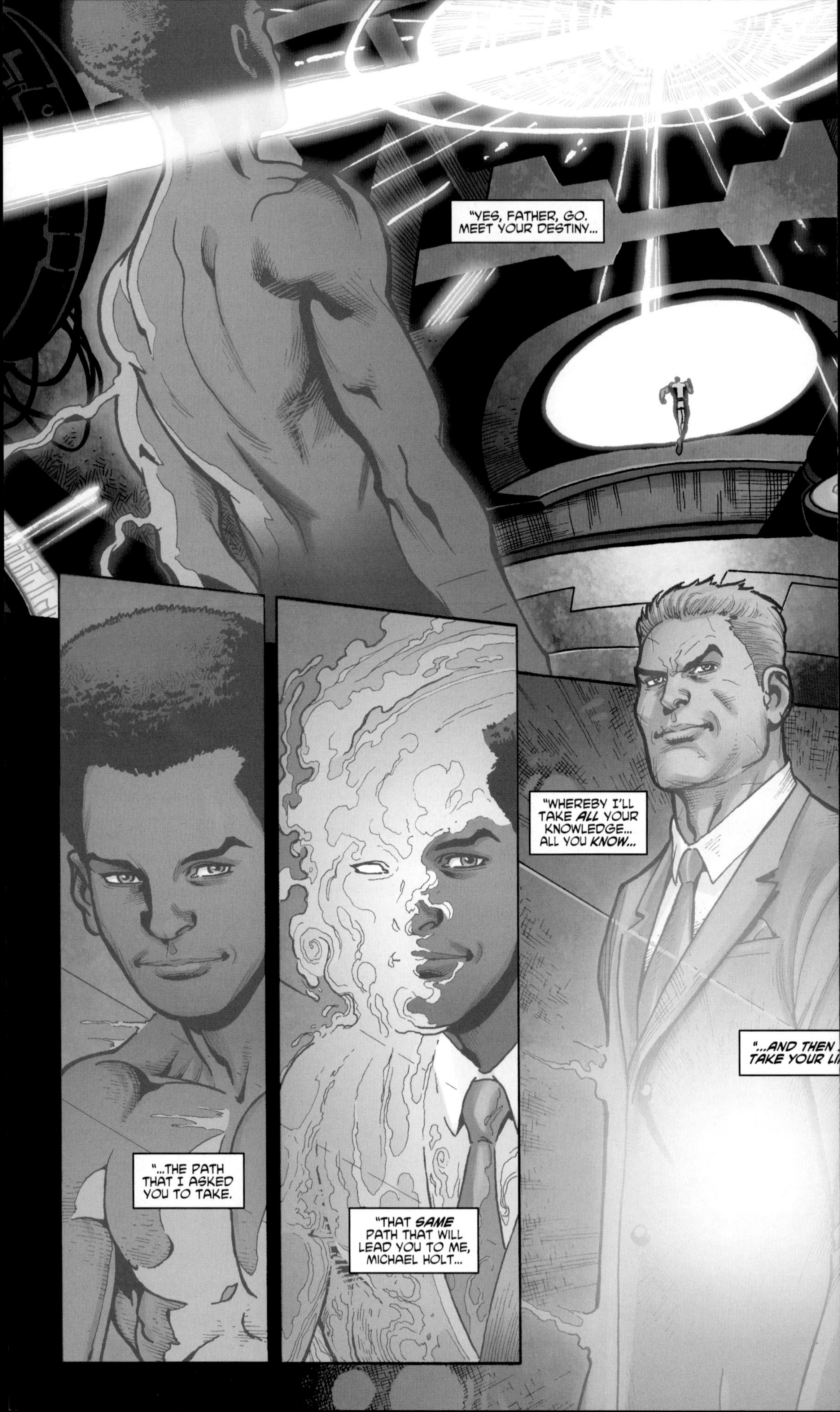
"YES, FATHER, GO. MEET YOUR DESTINY...
"...THE PATH THAT I ASKED YOU TO TAKE.
"THAT SAME PATH THAT WILL LEAD YOU TO ME, MICHAEL HOLT...
"WHEREBY I'LL TAKE ALL YOUR KNOWLEDGE... ALL YOU KNOW...
"...AND THEN TAKE YOUR LI

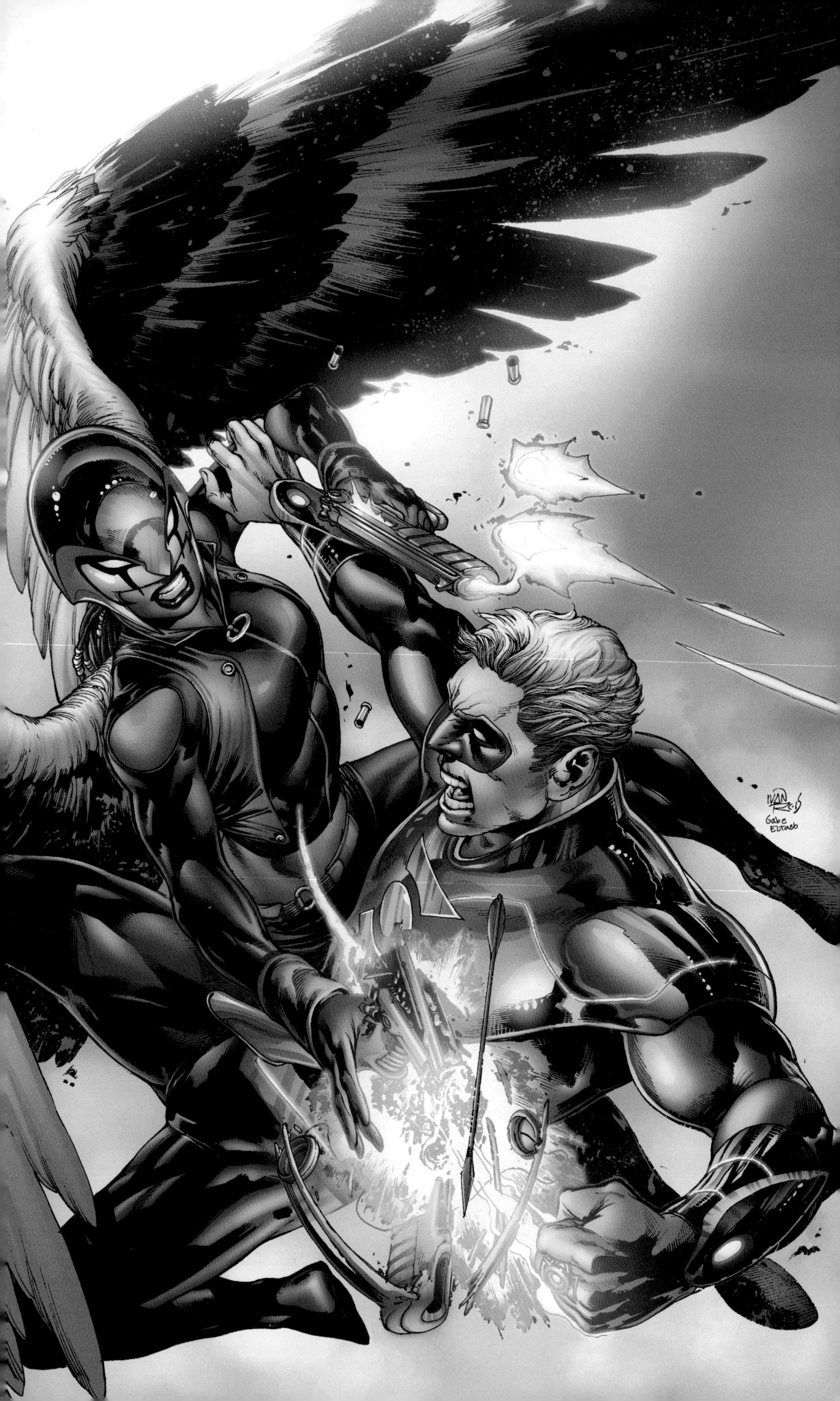

JAMES ROBINSON writer YILDIRAY CINAR penciller TREVOR SCOTT inker cover by IVAN REIS & GABE ELTAEB

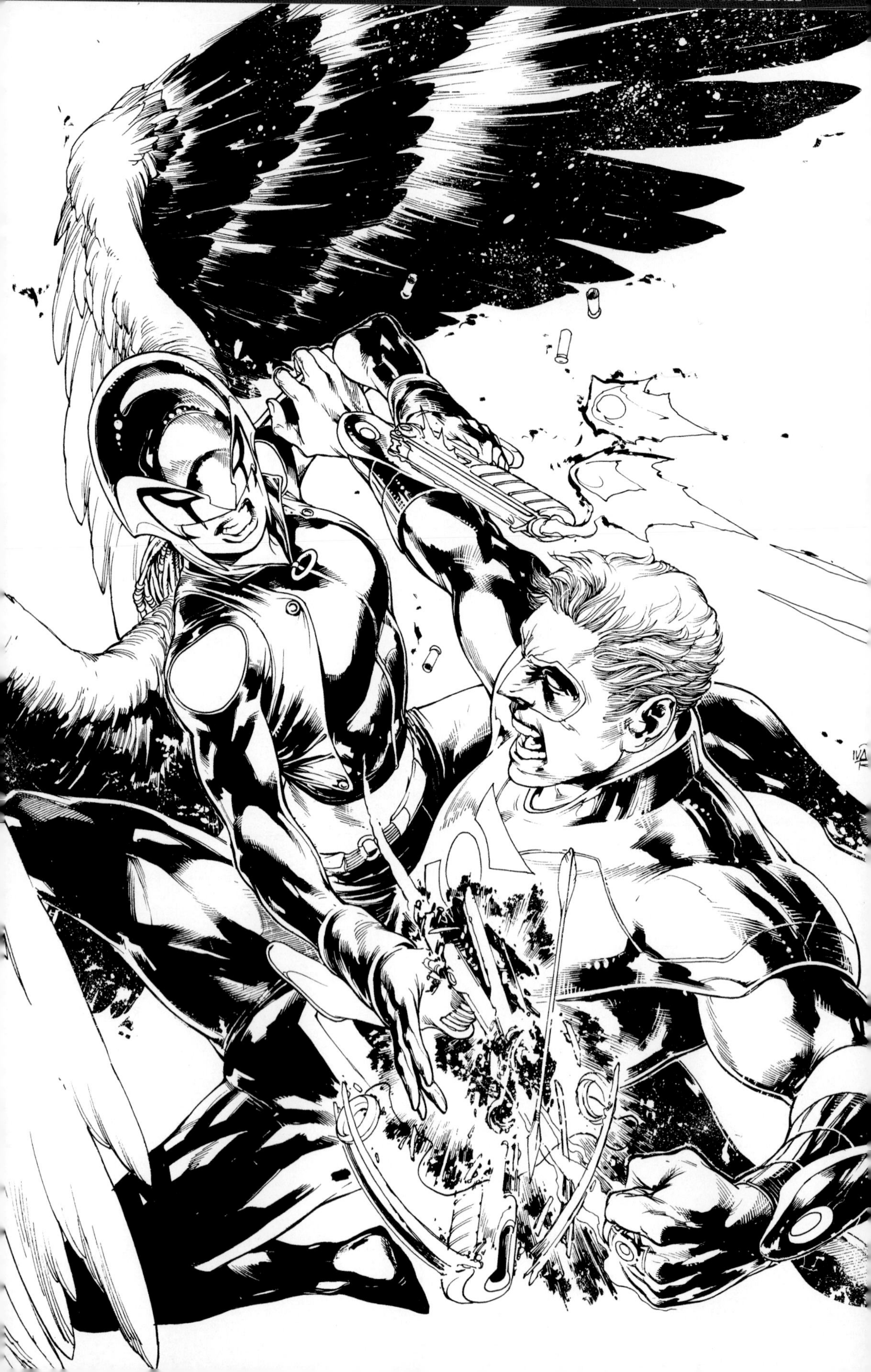

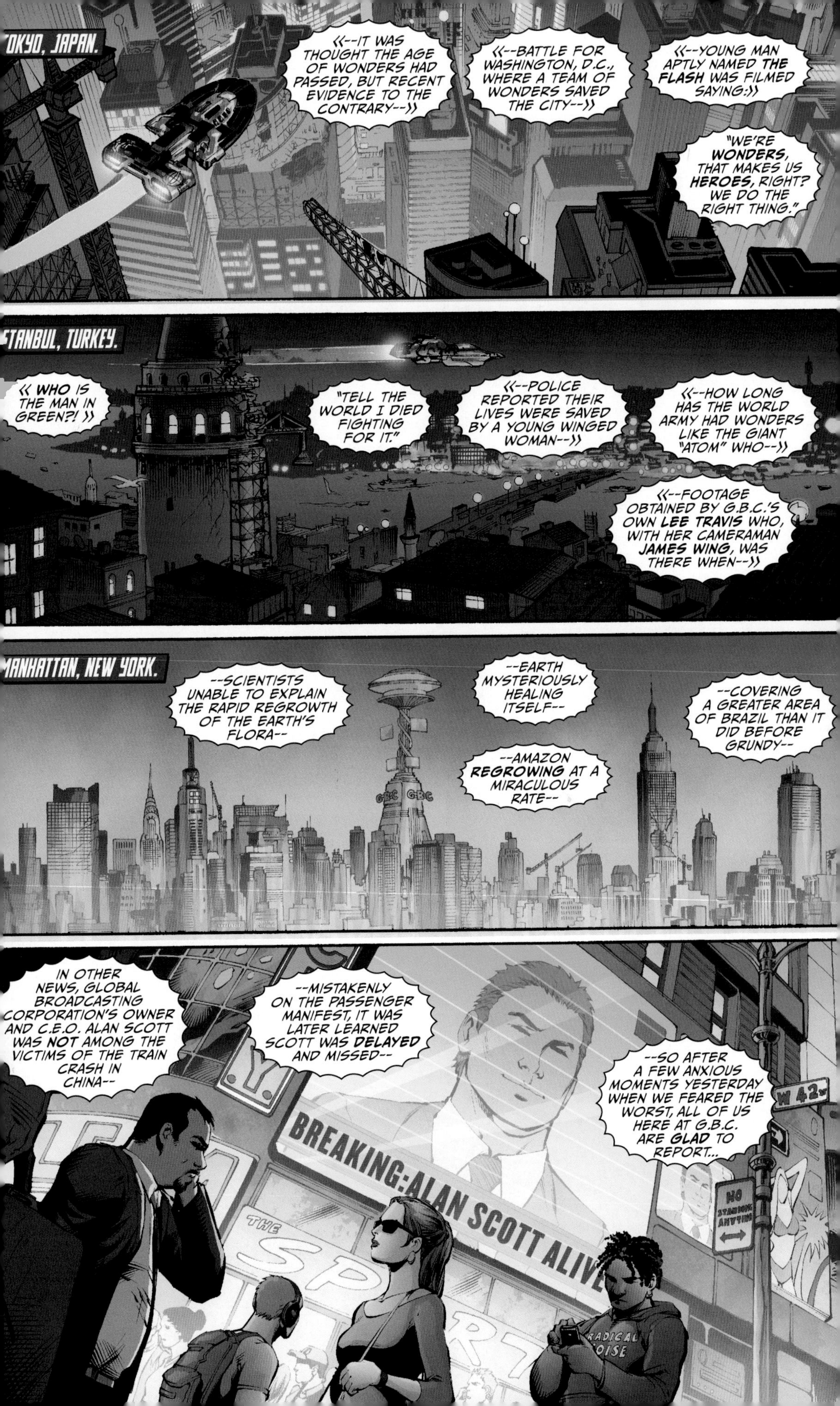

TOKYO, JAPAN.
<<--IT WAS THOUGHT THE AGE OF WONDERS HAD PASSED, BUT RECENT EVIDENCE TO THE CONTRARY-->>
<<--BATTLE FOR WASHINGTON, D.C., WHERE A TEAM OF WONDERS SAVED THE CITY-->>
<<--YOUNG MAN APTLY NAMED THE FLASH WAS FILMED SAYING:>>
"WE'RE WONDERS, THAT MAKES US HEROES, RIGHT? WE DO THE RIGHT THING."
ISTANBUL, TURKEY.
<< WHO IS THE MAN IN GREEN?! >>
"TELL THE WORLD I DIED FIGHTING FOR IT."
<<--POLICE REPORTED THEIR LIVES WERE SAVED BY A YOUNG WINGED WOMAN-->>
<<--HOW LONG HAS THE WORLD ARMY HAD WONDERS LIKE THE GIANT "ATOM" WHO-->>
<<--FOOTAGE OBTAINED BY G.B.C.'S OWN LEE TRAVIS WHO, WITH HER CAMERAMAN JAMES WING, WAS THERE WHEN-->>
MANHATTAN, NEW YORK.
--SCIENTISTS UNABLE TO EXPLAIN THE RAPID REGROWTH OF THE EARTH'S FLORA--
--EARTH MYSTERIOUSLY HEALING ITSELF--
--AMAZON REGROWING AT A MIRACULOUS RATE--
--COVERING A GREATER AREA OF BRAZIL THAN IT DID BEFORE GRUNDY--
GBC GBC
IN OTHER NEWS, GLOBAL BROADCASTING CORPORATION'S OWNER AND C.E.O. ALAN SCOTT WAS NOT AMONG THE VICTIMS OF THE TRAIN CRASH IN CHINA--
--MISTAKENLY ON THE PASSENGER MANIFEST, IT WAS LATER LEARNED SCOTT WAS DELAYED AND MISSED--
--SO AFTER A FEW ANXIOUS MOMENTS YESTERDAY WHEN WE FEARED THE WORST, ALL OF US HERE AT G.B.C. ARE GLAD TO REPORT...
BREAKING: ALAN SCOTT ALIVE
W 42 ST
NO STANDING ANYTIME
RADICAL NOISE

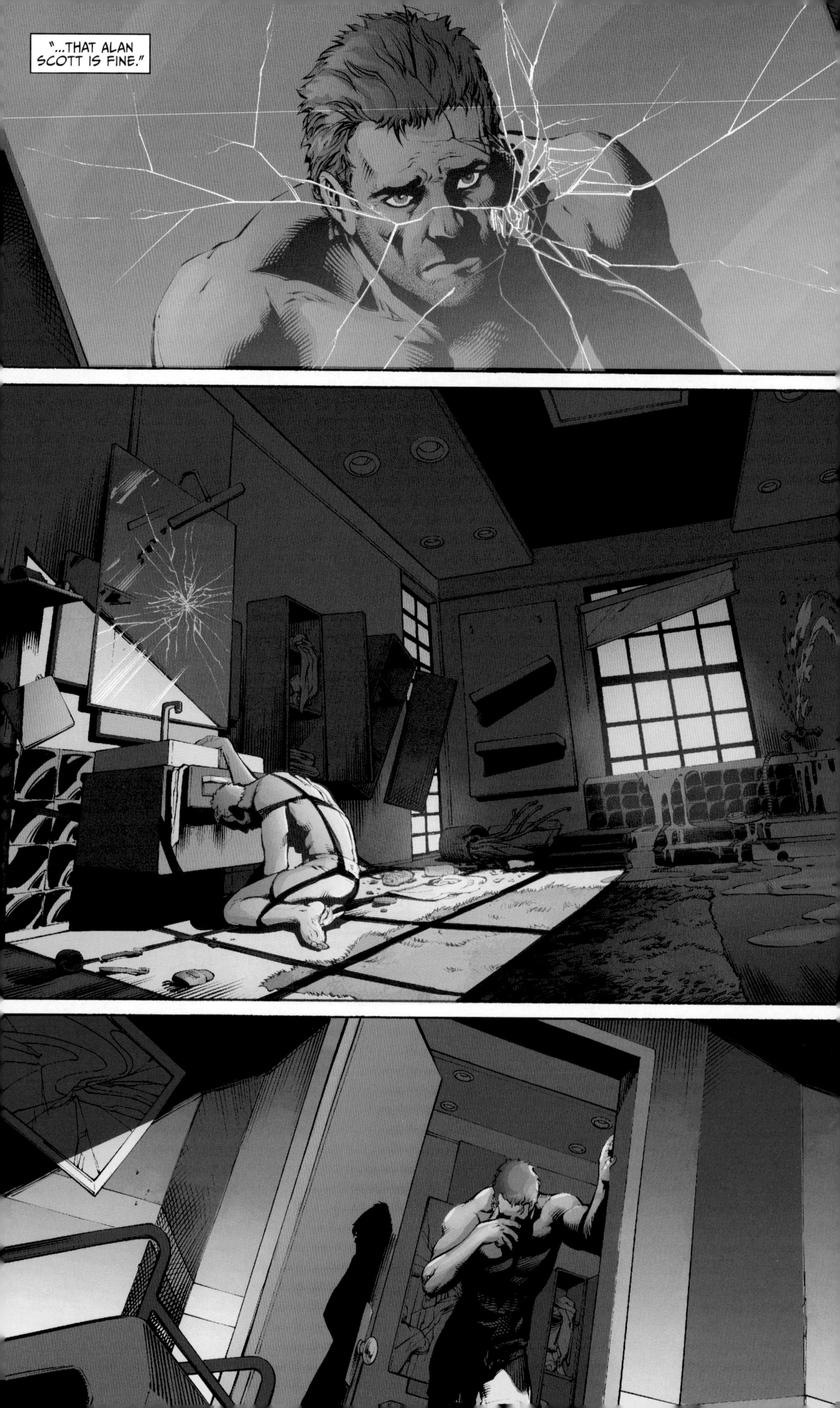
"...THAT ALAN SCOTT IS FINE."

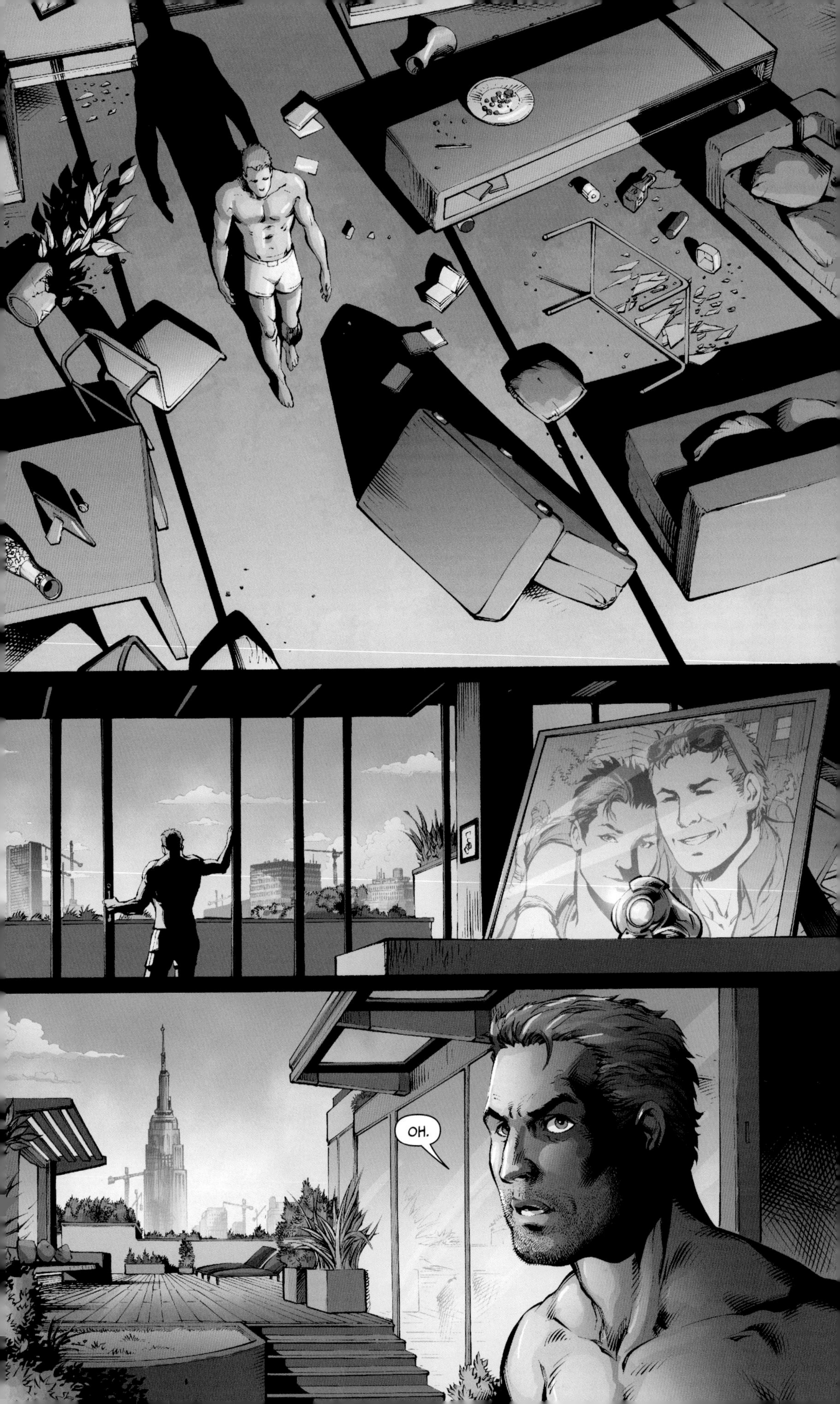
OH.

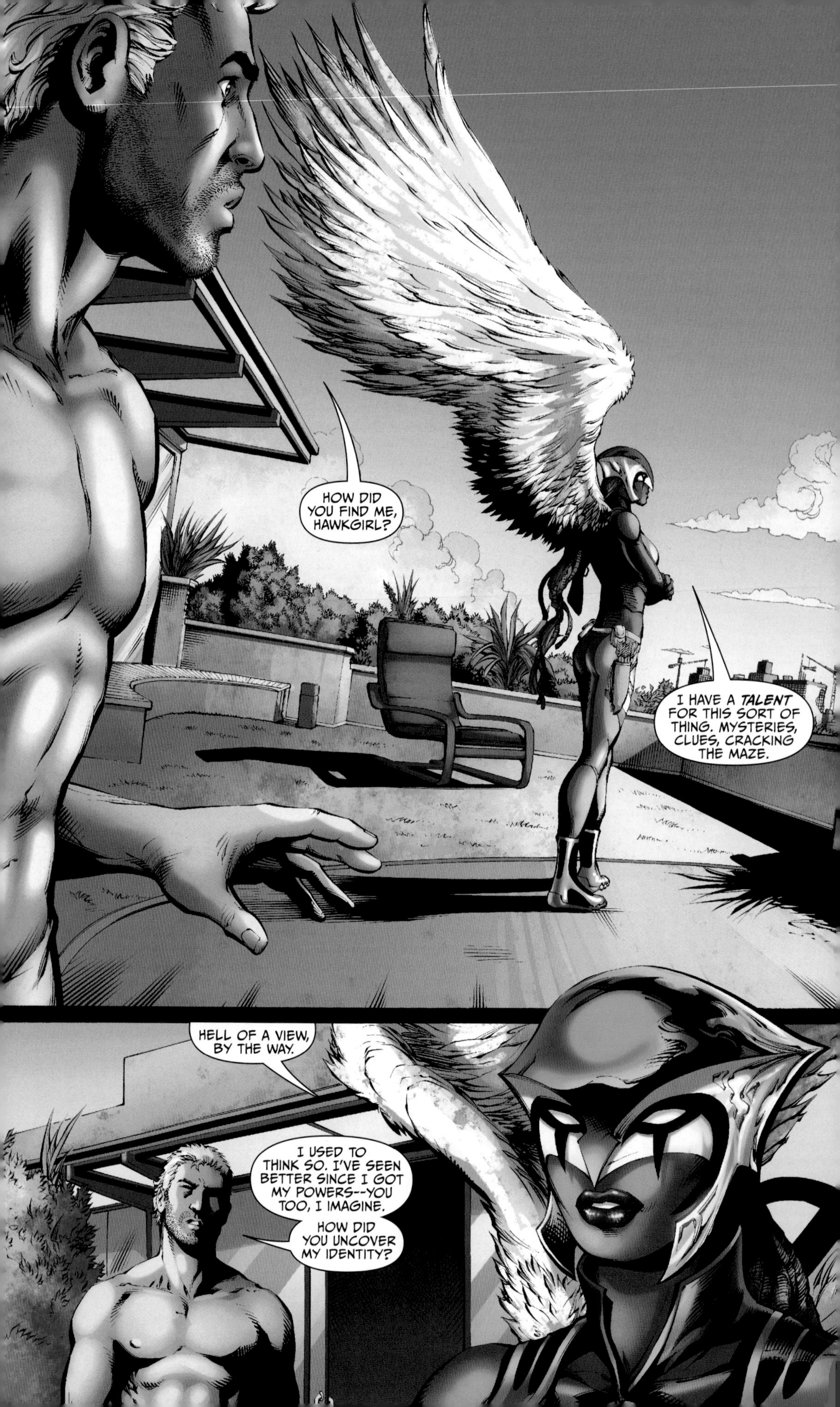
HOW DID YOU FIND ME, HAWKGIRL?
I HAVE A *TALENT* FOR THIS SORT OF THING. MYSTERIES, CLUES, CRACKING THE MAZE.
HELL OF A VIEW, BY THE WAY.
I USED TO THINK SO. I'VE SEEN BETTER SINCE I GOT MY POWERS--YOU TOO, I IMAGINE.
HOW DID YOU UNCOVER MY IDENTITY?

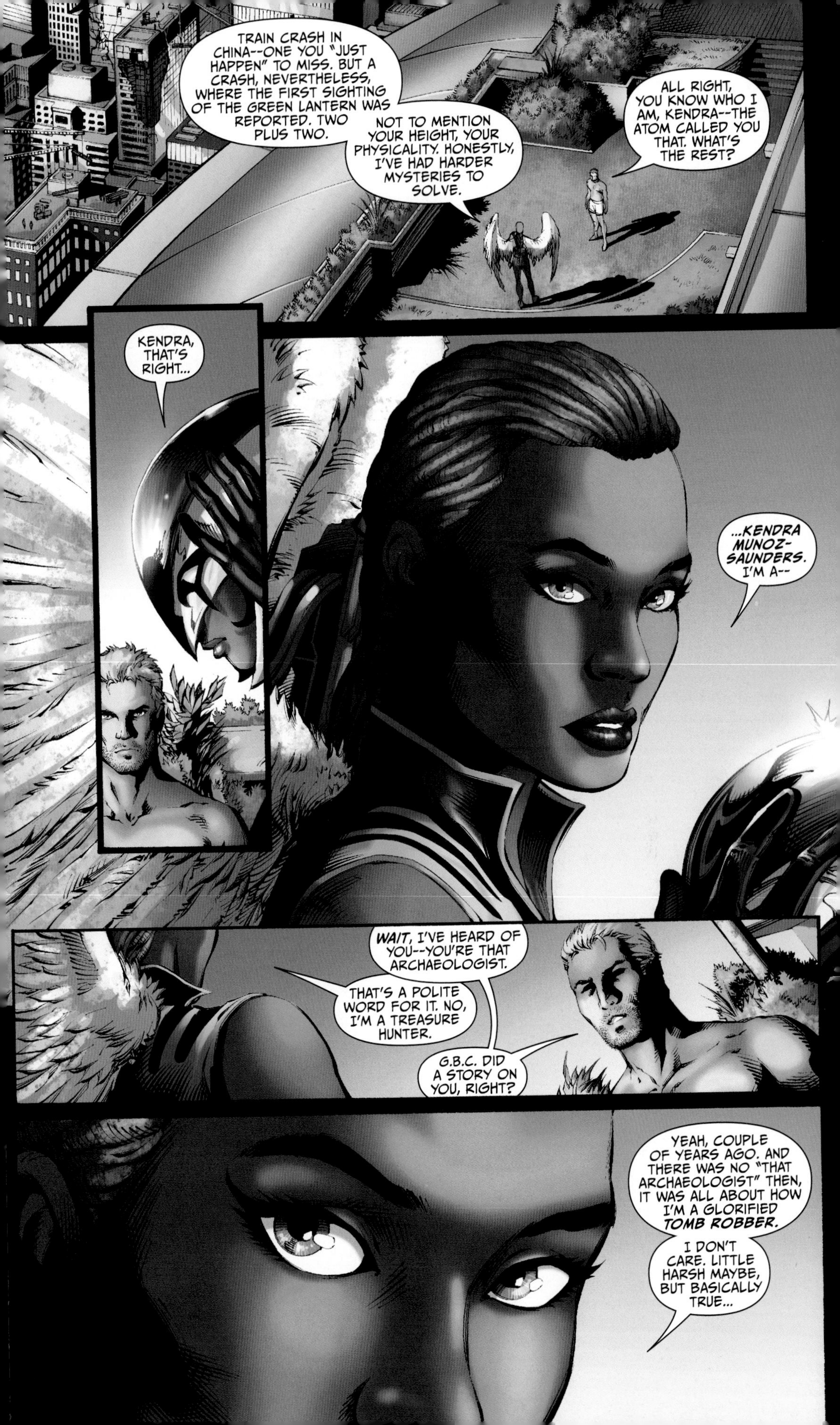
TRAIN CRASH IN CHINA--ONE YOU "JUST HAPPEN" TO MISS. BUT A CRASH, NEVERTHELESS, WHERE THE FIRST SIGHTING OF THE GREEN LANTERN WAS REPORTED. TWO PLUS TWO.
NOT TO MENTION YOUR HEIGHT, YOUR PHYSICALITY. HONESTLY, I'VE HAD HARDER MYSTERIES TO SOLVE.
ALL RIGHT, YOU KNOW WHO I AM, KENDRA--THE ATOM CALLED YOU THAT. WHAT'S THE REST?
KENDRA, THAT'S RIGHT...
...KENDRA MUNOZ-SAUNDERS. I'M A--
WAIT, I'VE HEARD OF YOU--YOU'RE THAT ARCHAEOLOGIST.
THAT'S A POLITE WORD FOR IT. NO, I'M A TREASURE HUNTER.
G.B.C. DID A STORY ON YOU, RIGHT?
YEAH, COUPLE OF YEARS AGO. AND THERE WAS NO "THAT ARCHAEOLOGIST" THEN, IT WAS ALL ABOUT HOW I'M A GLORIFIED TOMB ROBBER.
I DON'T CARE. LITTLE HARSH MAYBE, BUT BASICALLY TRUE...

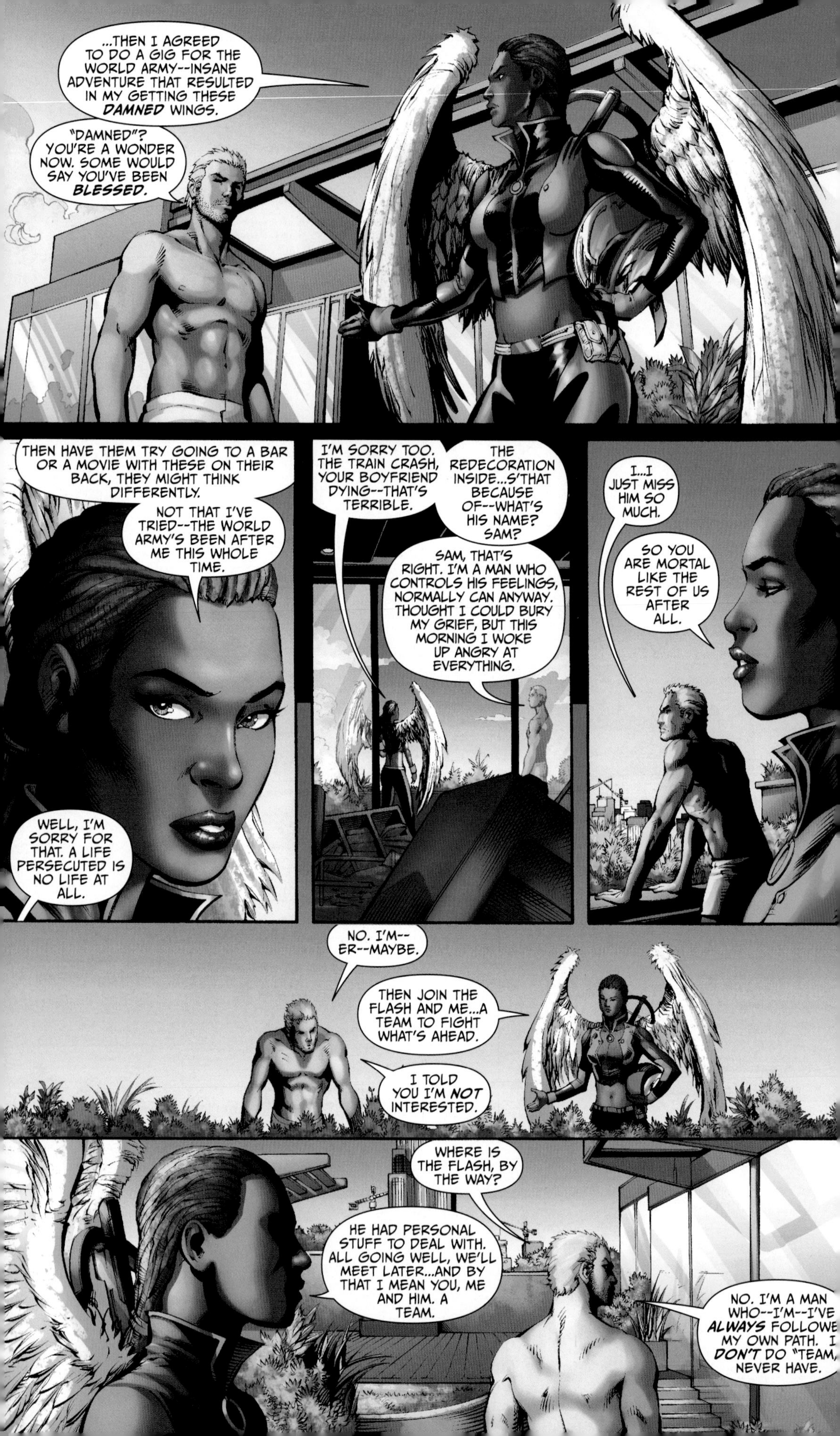
...THEN I AGREED TO DO A GIG FOR THE WORLD ARMY--INSANE ADVENTURE THAT RESULTED IN MY GETTING THESE *DAMNED* WINGS.
"DAMNED"? YOU'RE A WONDER NOW. SOME WOULD SAY YOU'VE BEEN *BLESSED.*
THEN HAVE THEM TRY GOING TO A BAR OR A MOVIE WITH THESE ON THEIR BACK, THEY MIGHT THINK DIFFERENTLY.
NOT THAT I'VE TRIED--THE WORLD ARMY'S BEEN AFTER ME THIS WHOLE TIME.
WELL, I'M SORRY FOR THAT. A LIFE PERSECUTED IS NO LIFE AT ALL.
I'M SORRY TOO. THE TRAIN CRASH, YOUR BOYFRIEND DYING--THAT'S TERRIBLE.
THE REDECORATION INSIDE...S'THAT BECAUSE OF--WHAT'S HIS NAME? SAM?
SAM, THAT'S RIGHT. I'M A MAN WHO CONTROLS HIS FEELINGS, NORMALLY CAN ANYWAY. THOUGHT I COULD BURY MY GRIEF, BUT THIS MORNING I WOKE UP ANGRY AT EVERYTHING.
I...I JUST MISS HIM SO MUCH.
SO YOU ARE MORTAL LIKE THE REST OF US AFTER ALL.
NO. I'M--ER--MAYBE.
THEN JOIN THE FLASH AND ME...A TEAM TO FIGHT WHAT'S AHEAD.
I TOLD YOU I'M *NOT* INTERESTED.
WHERE IS THE FLASH, BY THE WAY?
HE HAD PERSONAL STUFF TO DEAL WITH. ALL GOING WELL, WE'LL MEET LATER...AND BY THAT I MEAN YOU, ME AND HIM. A TEAM.
NO. I'M A MAN WHO--I'M--I'VE *ALWAYS* FOLLOWE MY OWN PATH. I *DON'T* DO "TEAM, NEVER HAVE.

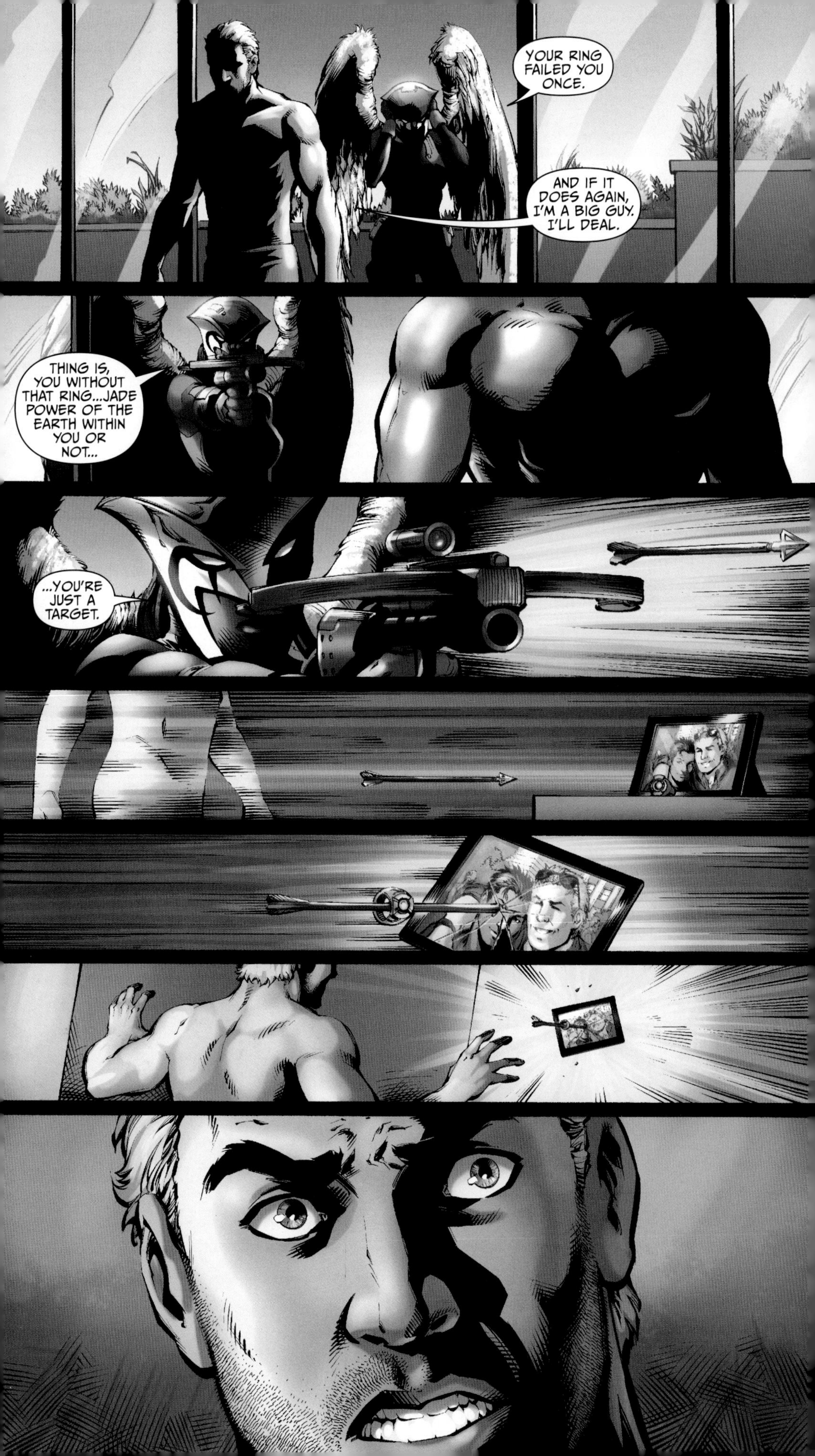
YOUR RING FAILED YOU ONCE.
AND IF IT DOES AGAIN, I'M A BIG GUY. I'LL DEAL.
THING IS, YOU WITHOUT THAT RING...JADE POWER OF THE EARTH WITHIN YOU OR NOT...
...YOU'RE JUST A TARGET.

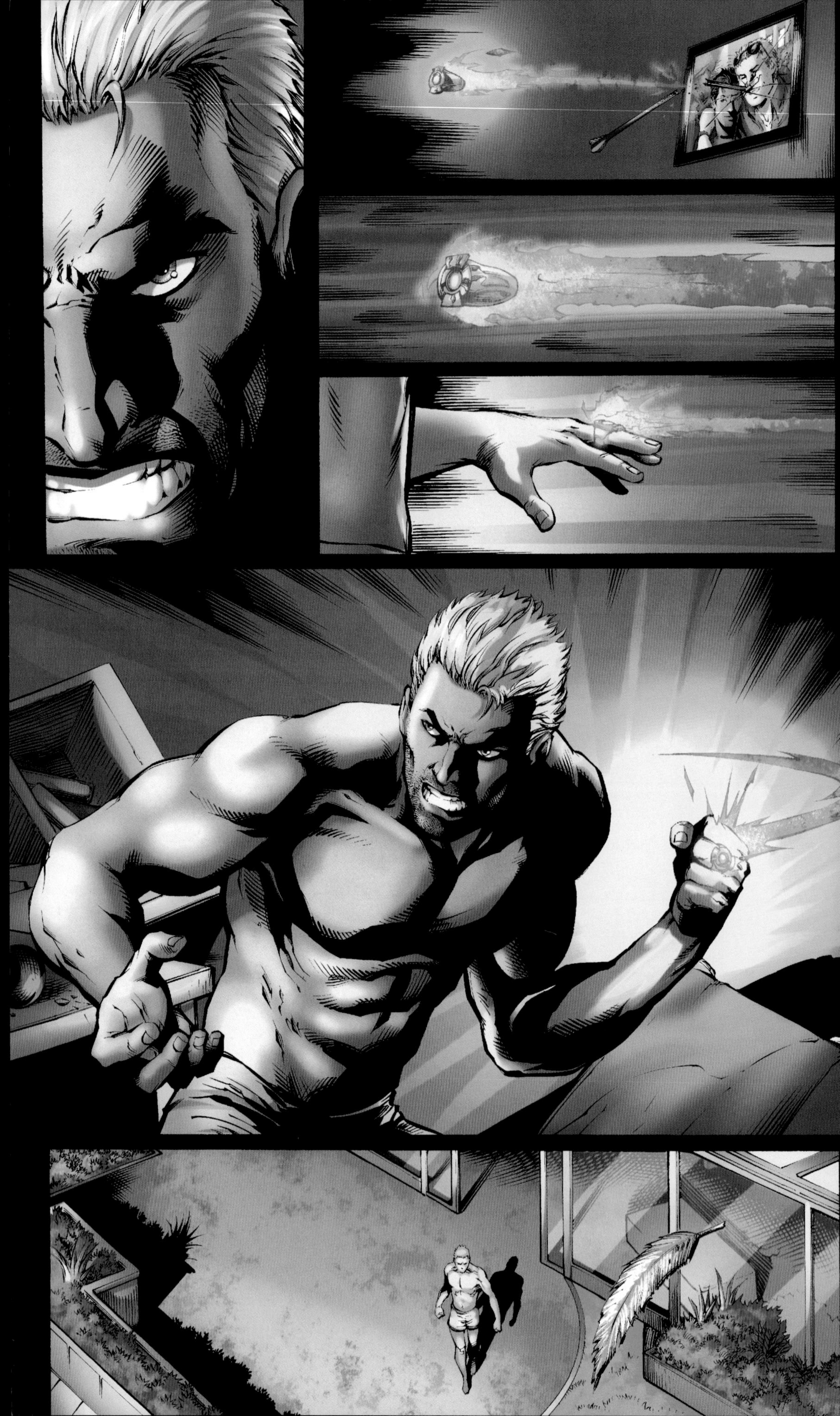

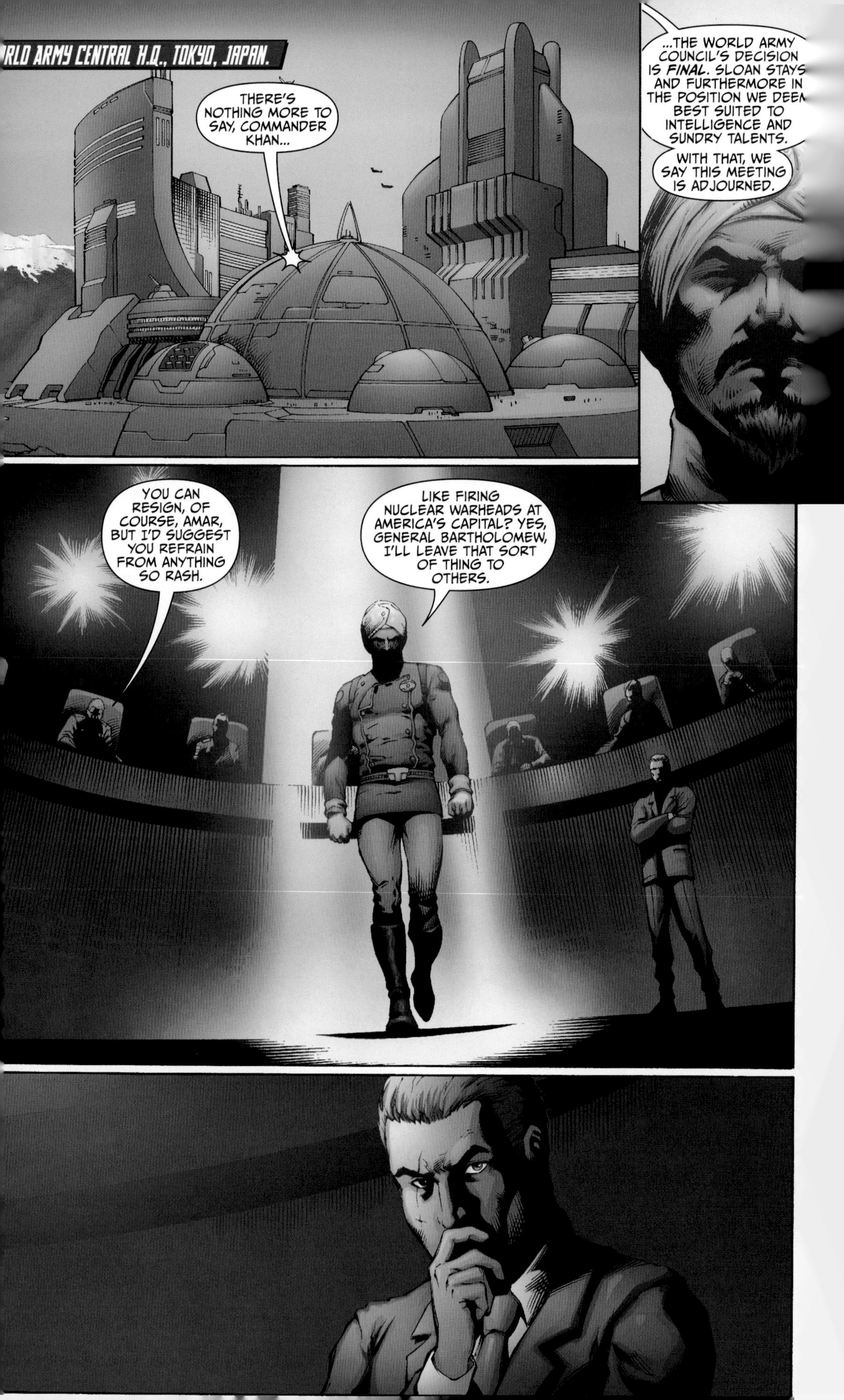
RLD ARMY CENTRAL H.Q., TOKYO, JAPAN.
THERE'S NOTHING MORE TO SAY, COMMANDER KHAN...
...THE WORLD ARMY COUNCIL'S DECISION IS *FINAL*. SLOAN STAYS AND FURTHERMORE IN THE POSITION WE DEEM BEST SUITED TO INTELLIGENCE AND SUNDRY TALENTS.
WITH THAT, WE SAY THIS MEETING IS ADJOURNED.
YOU CAN RESIGN, OF COURSE, AMAR, BUT I'D SUGGEST YOU REFRAIN FROM ANYTHING SO RASH.
LIKE FIRING NUCLEAR WARHEADS AT AMERICA'S CAPITAL? YES, GENERAL BARTHOLOMEW, I'LL LEAVE THAT SORT OF THING TO OTHERS.

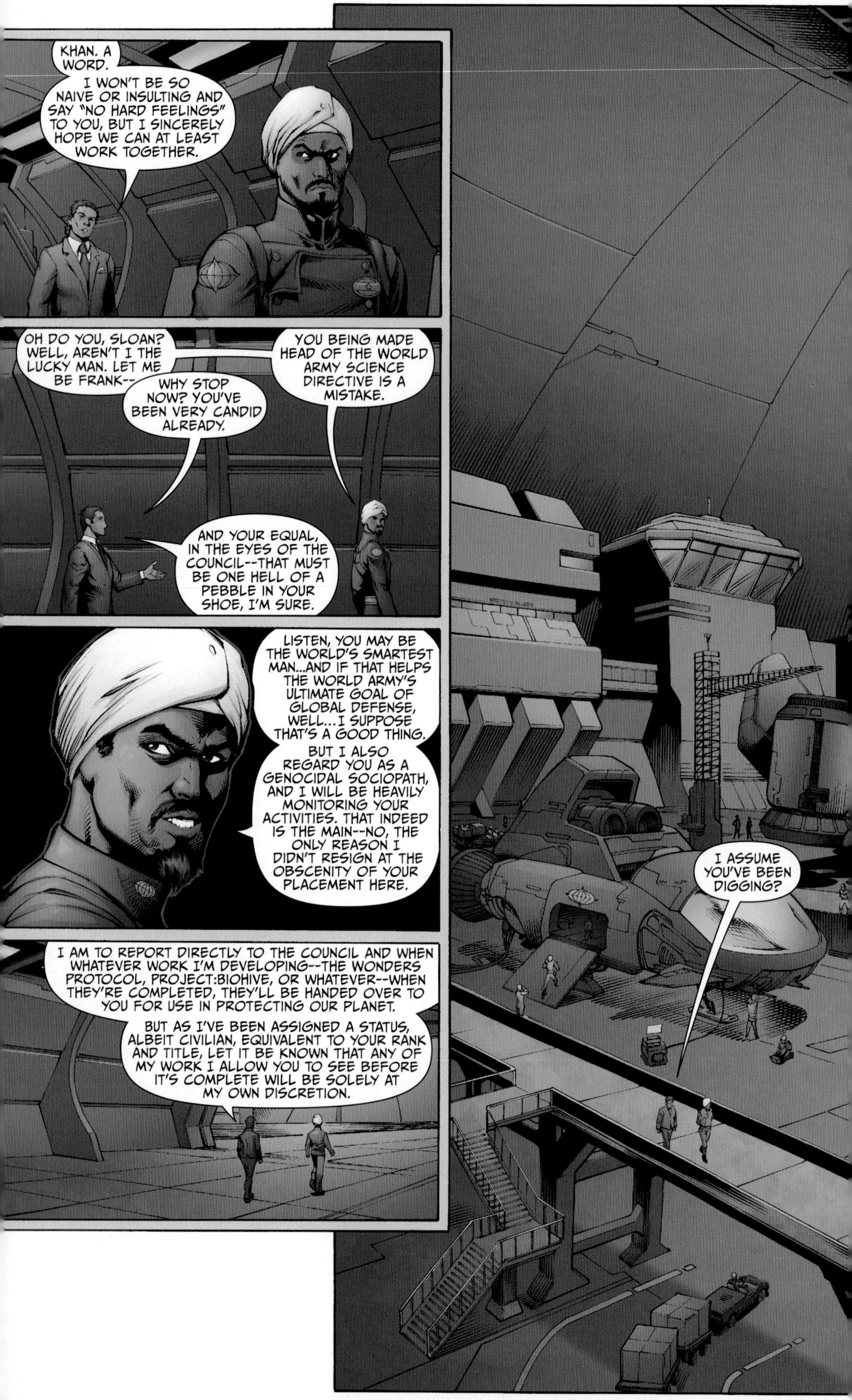
KHAN. A WORD.
I WON'T BE SO NAIVE OR INSULTING AND SAY "NO HARD FEELINGS" TO YOU, BUT I SINCERELY HOPE WE CAN AT LEAST WORK TOGETHER.
OH DO YOU, SLOAN? WELL, AREN'T I THE LUCKY MAN. LET ME BE FRANK--
YOU BEING MADE HEAD OF THE WORLD ARMY SCIENCE DIRECTIVE IS A MISTAKE.
WHY STOP NOW? YOU'VE BEEN VERY CANDID ALREADY.
AND YOUR EQUAL, IN THE EYES OF THE COUNCIL--THAT MUST BE ONE HELL OF A PEBBLE IN YOUR SHOE, I'M SURE.
LISTEN, YOU MAY BE THE WORLD'S SMARTEST MAN...AND IF THAT HELPS THE WORLD ARMY'S ULTIMATE GOAL OF GLOBAL DEFENSE, WELL...I SUPPOSE THAT'S A GOOD THING.
BUT I ALSO REGARD YOU AS A GENOCIDAL SOCIOPATH, AND I WILL BE HEAVILY MONITORING YOUR ACTIVITIES. THAT INDEED IS THE MAIN--NO, THE ONLY REASON I DIDN'T RESIGN AT THE OBSCENITY OF YOUR PLACEMENT HERE.
I ASSUME YOU'VE BEEN DIGGING?
I AM TO REPORT DIRECTLY TO THE COUNCIL AND WHEN WHATEVER WORK I'M DEVELOPING--THE WONDERS PROTOCOL, PROJECT:BIOHIVE, OR WHATEVER--WHEN THEY'RE COMPLETED, THEY'LL BE HANDED OVER TO YOU FOR USE IN PROTECTING OUR PLANET.
BUT AS I'VE BEEN ASSIGNED A STATUS, ALBEIT CIVILIAN, EQUIVALENT TO YOUR RANK AND TITLE, LET IT BE KNOWN THAT ANY OF MY WORK I ALLOW YOU TO SEE BEFORE IT'S COMPLETE WILL BE SOLELY AT MY OWN DISCRETION.

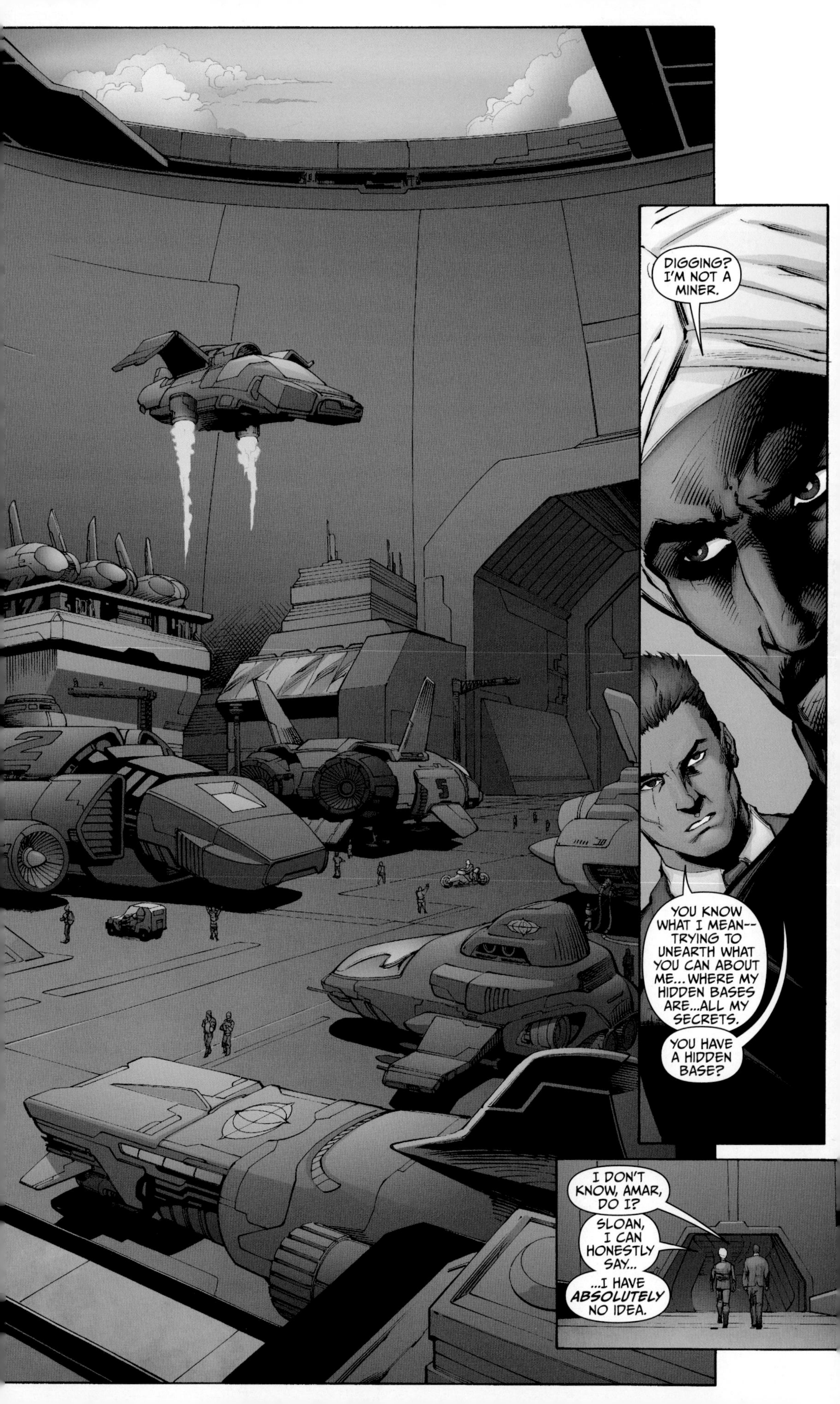
DIGGING? I'M NOT A MINER.
YOU KNOW WHAT I MEAN-- TRYING TO UNEARTH WHAT YOU CAN ABOUT ME...WHERE MY HIDDEN BASES ARE...ALL MY SECRETS.
YOU HAVE A HIDDEN BASE?
I DON'T KNOW, AMAR, DO I?
SLOAN, I CAN HONESTLY SAY...
...I HAVE ABSOLUTELY NO IDEA.

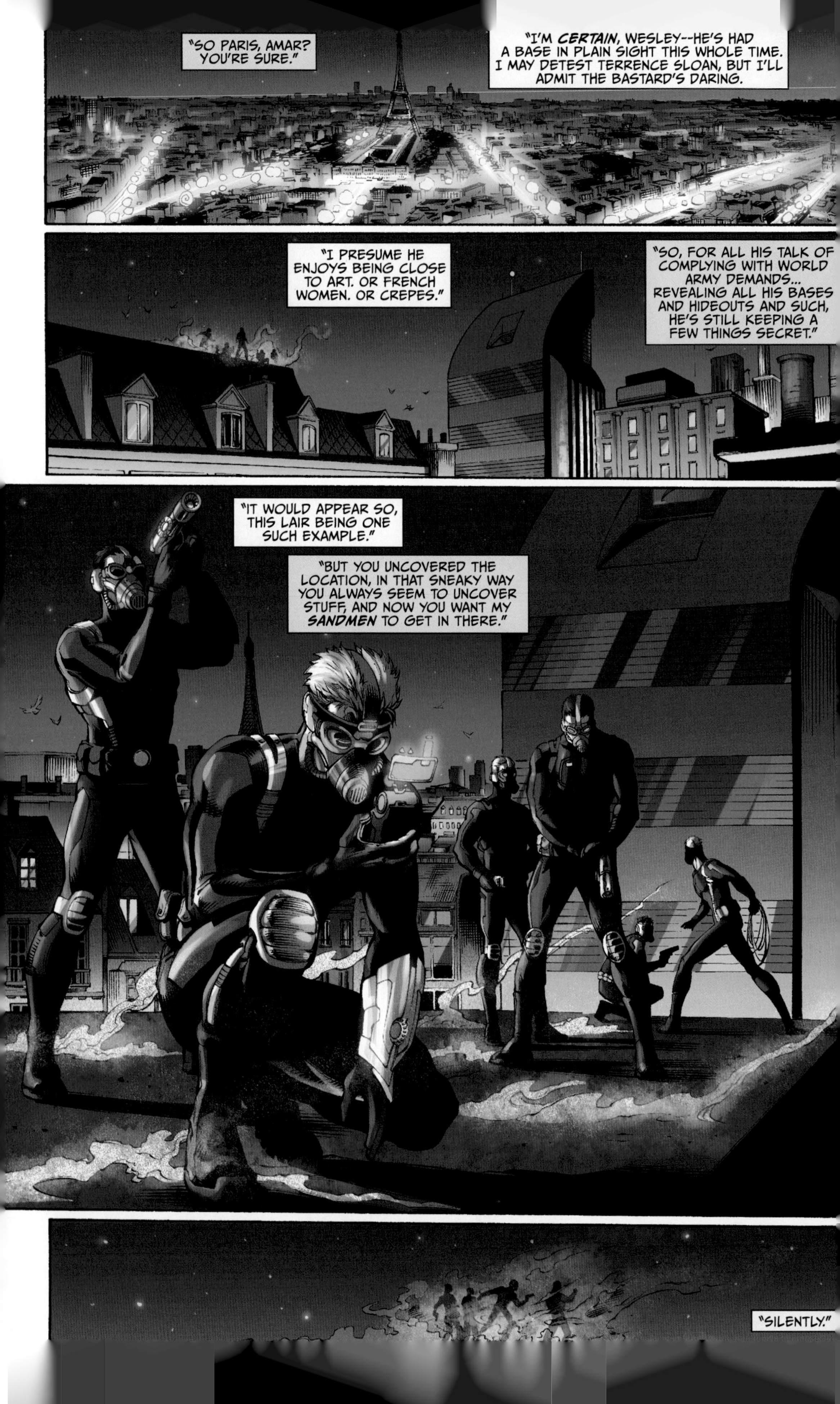
"SO PARIS, AMAR? YOU'RE SURE."
"I'M CERTAIN, WESLEY--HE'S HAD A BASE IN PLAIN SIGHT THIS WHOLE TIME. I MAY DETEST TERRENCE SLOAN, BUT I'LL ADMIT THE BASTARD'S DARING.
"I PRESUME HE ENJOYS BEING CLOSE TO ART. OR FRENCH WOMEN. OR CREPES."
"SO, FOR ALL HIS TALK OF COMPLYING WITH WORLD ARMY DEMANDS... REVEALING ALL HIS BASES AND HIDEOUTS AND SUCH, HE'S STILL KEEPING A FEW THINGS SECRET."
"IT WOULD APPEAR SO, THIS LAIR BEING ONE SUCH EXAMPLE."
"BUT YOU UNCOVERED THE LOCATION, IN THAT SNEAKY WAY YOU ALWAYS SEEM TO UNCOVER STUFF, AND NOW YOU WANT MY SANDMEN TO GET IN THERE."
"SILENTLY."

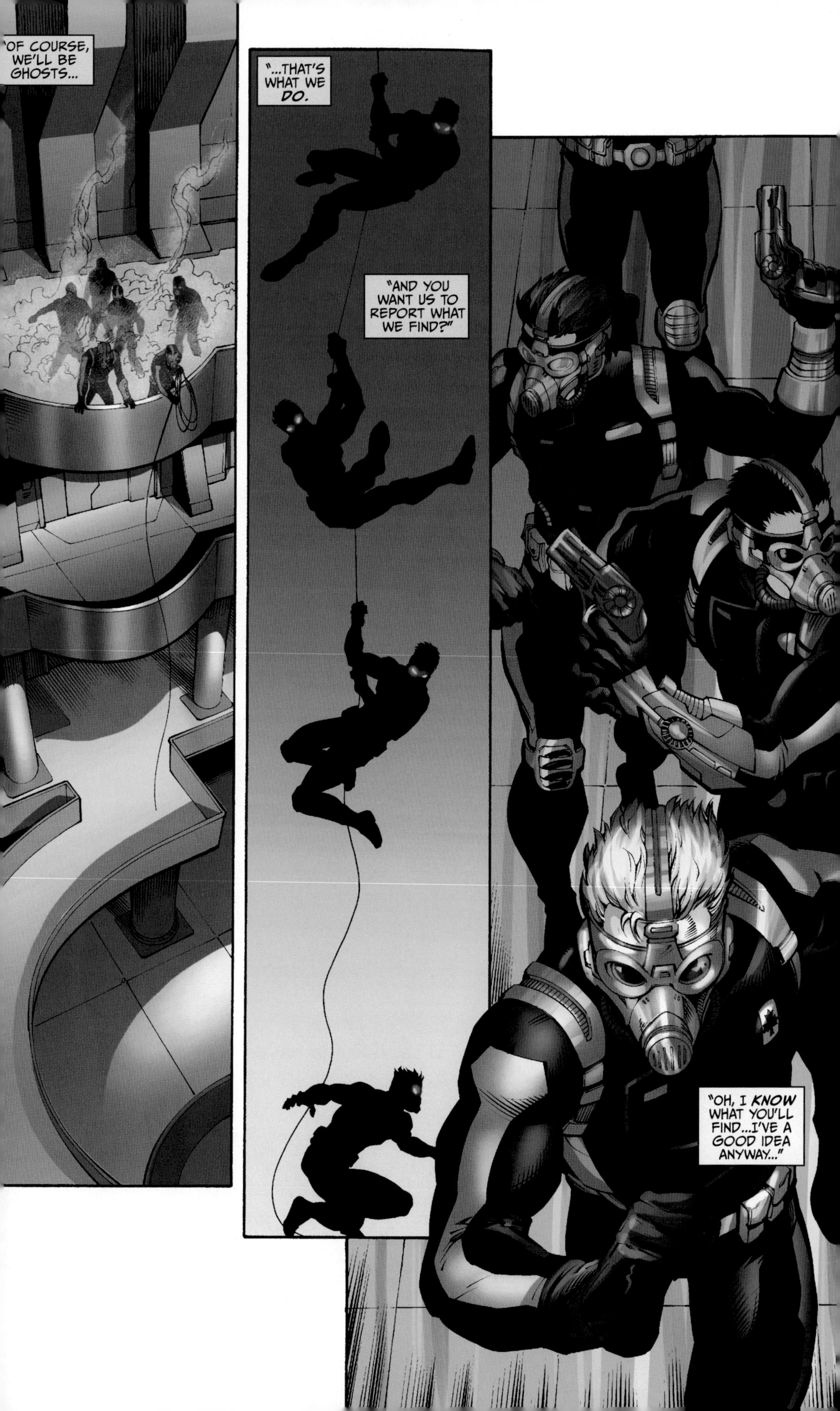

"OF COURSE, WE'LL BE GHOSTS...
"...THAT'S WHAT WE DO.
"AND YOU WANT US TO REPORT WHAT WE FIND?"
"OH, I KNOW WHAT YOU'LL FIND...I'VE A GOOD IDEA ANYWAY..."

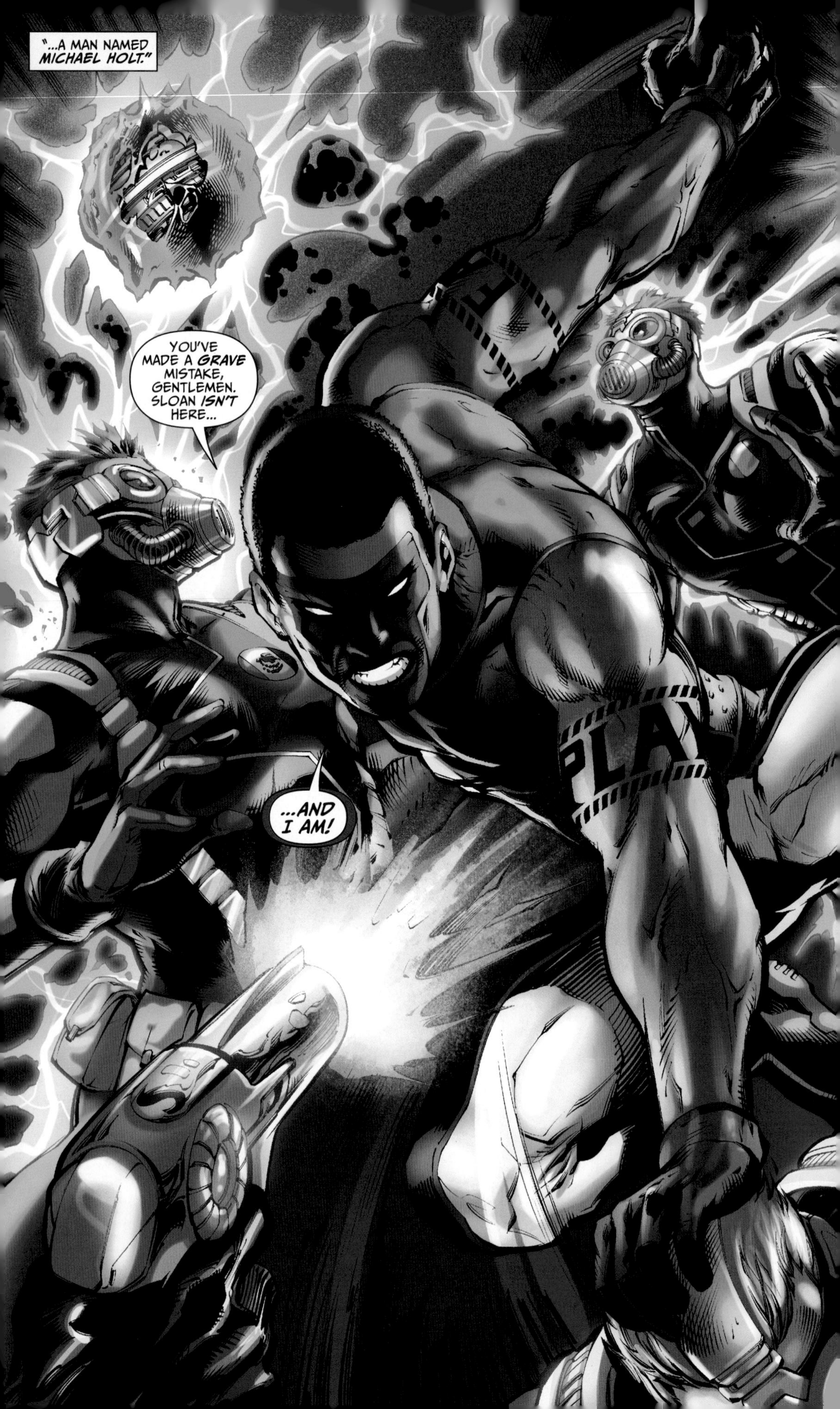
"...A MAN NAMED MICHAEL HOLT."
YOU'VE MADE A GRAVE MISTAKE, GENTLEMEN. SLOAN ISN'T HERE...
...AND I AM!

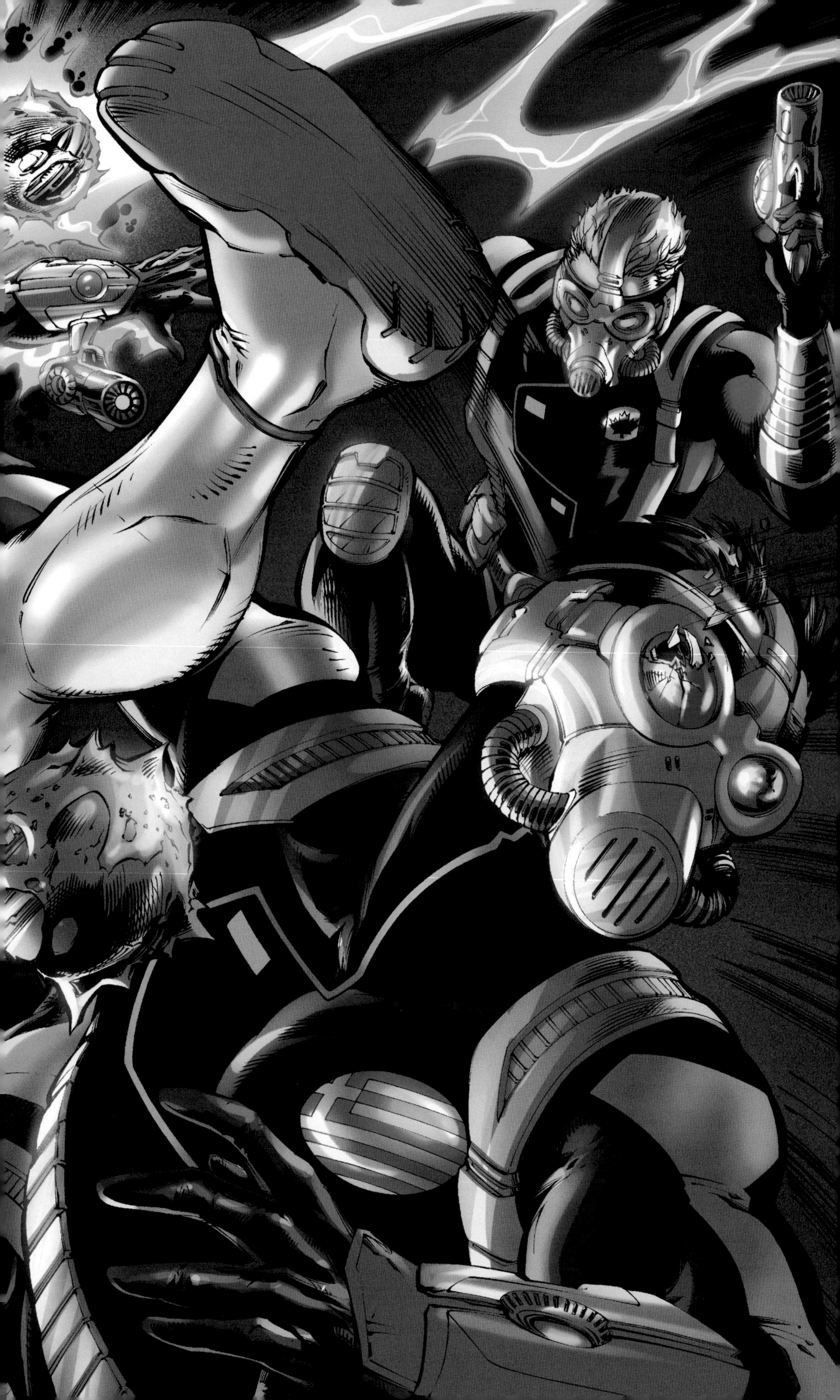

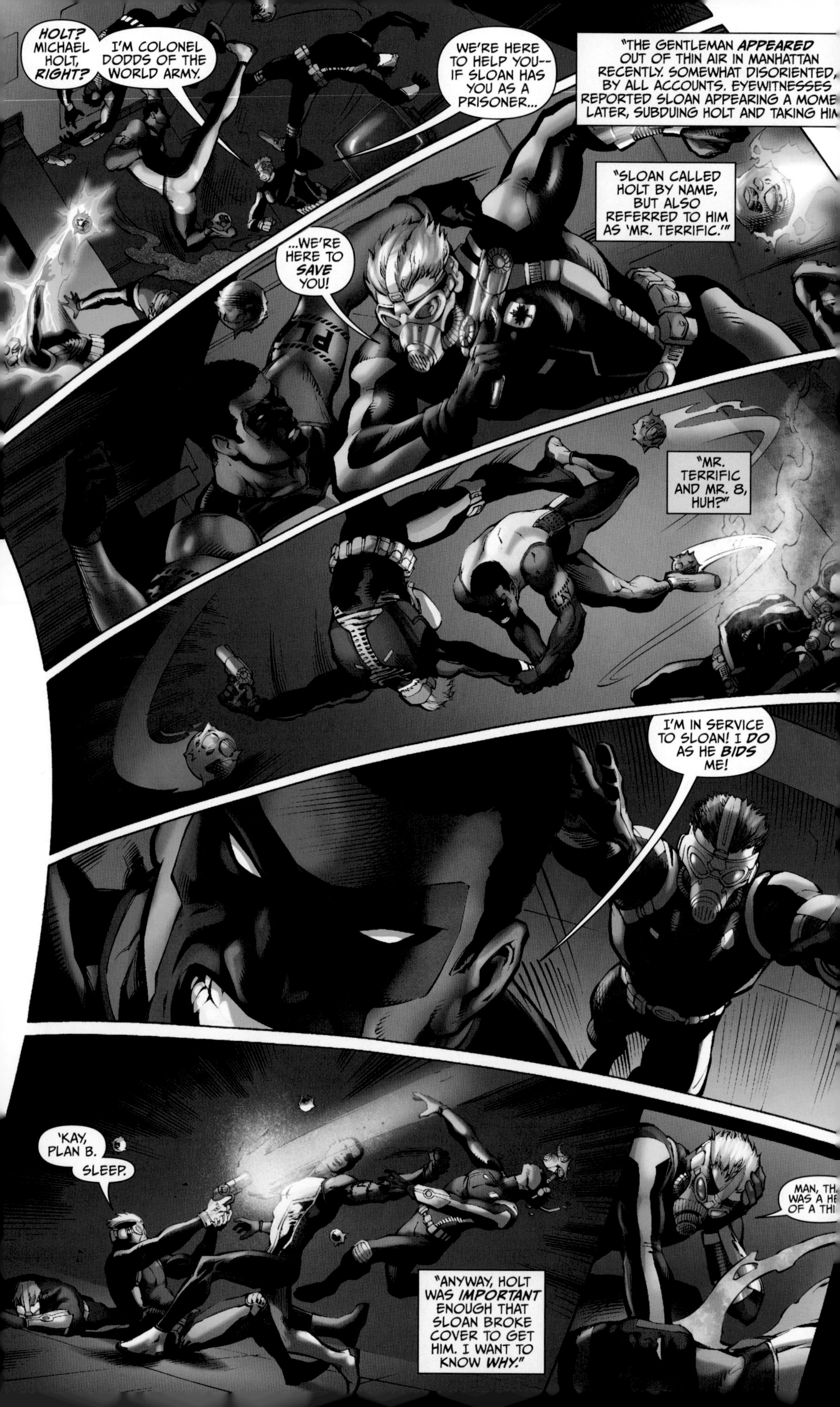

"THE GENTLEMAN APPEARED OUT OF THIN AIR IN MANHATTAN RECENTLY. SOMEWHAT DISORIENTED, BY ALL ACCOUNTS. EYEWITNESSES REPORTED SLOAN APPEARING A MOME LATER, SUBDUING HOLT AND TAKING HI
HOLT? MICHAEL HOLT, RIGHT?
I'M COLONEL DODDS OF THE WORLD ARMY.
WE'RE HERE TO HELP YOU-- IF SLOAN HAS YOU AS A PRISONER...
"SLOAN CALLED HOLT BY NAME, BUT ALSO REFERRED TO HIM AS 'MR. TERRIFIC.'"
...WE'RE HERE TO SAVE YOU!
"MR. TERRIFIC AND MR. 8, HUH?"
I'M IN SERVICE TO SLOAN! I DO AS HE BIDS ME!
'KAY, PLAN B.
SLEEP.
MAN, TH WAS A HE OF A TH
"ANYWAY, HOLT WAS IMPORTANT ENOUGH THAT SLOAN BROKE COVER TO GET HIM. I WANT TO KNOW WHY."

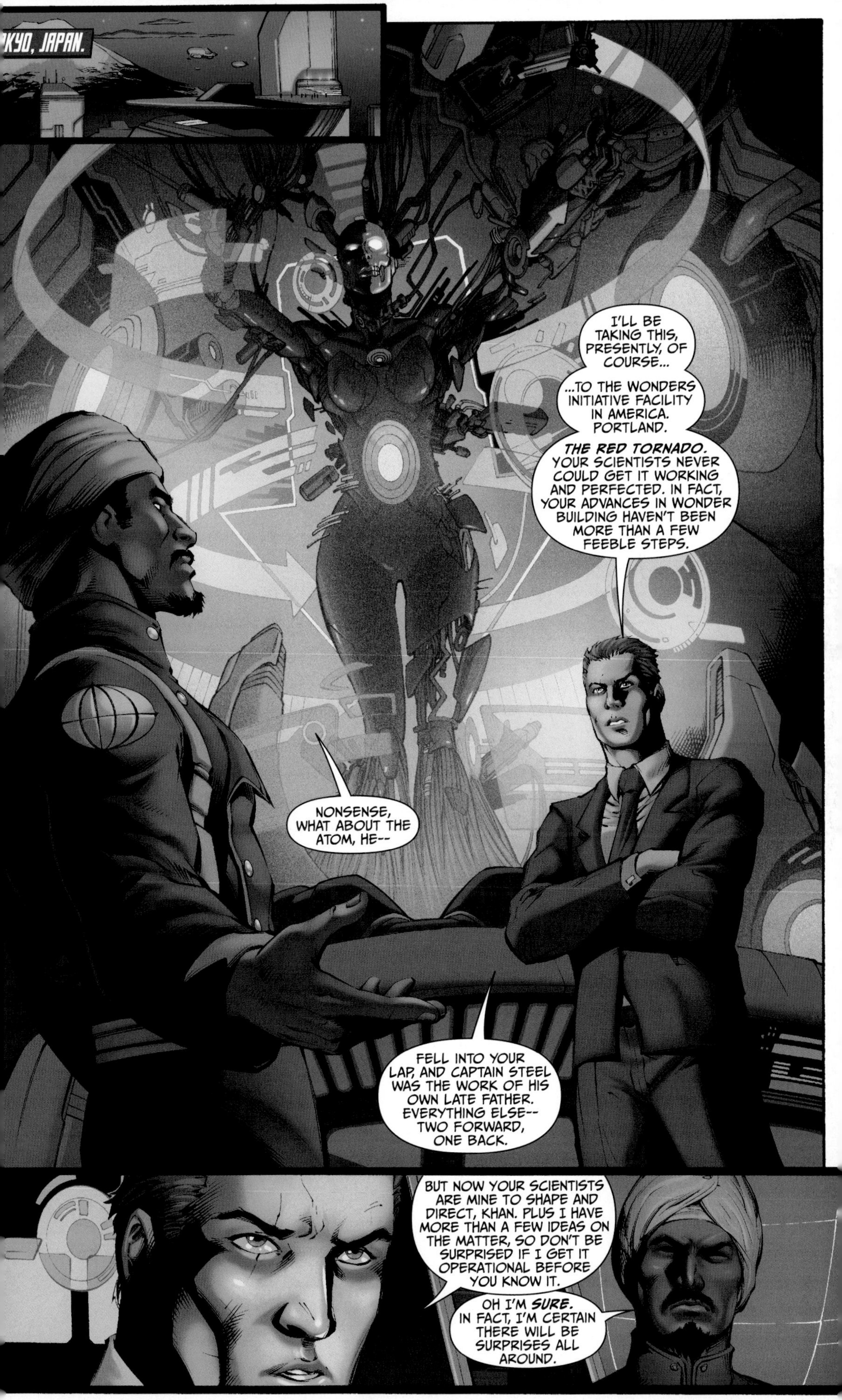

KYO, JAPAN.
I'LL BE TAKING THIS, PRESENTLY, OF COURSE...
...TO THE WONDERS INITIATIVE FACILITY IN AMERICA. PORTLAND.
THE RED TORNADO. YOUR SCIENTISTS NEVER COULD GET IT WORKING AND PERFECTED. IN FACT, YOUR ADVANCES IN WONDER BUILDING HAVEN'T BEEN MORE THAN A FEW FEEBLE STEPS.
NONSENSE, WHAT ABOUT THE ATOM, HE--
FELL INTO YOUR LAP, AND CAPTAIN STEEL WAS THE WORK OF HIS OWN LATE FATHER. EVERYTHING ELSE-- TWO FORWARD, ONE BACK.
BUT NOW YOUR SCIENTISTS ARE MINE TO SHAPE AND DIRECT, KHAN. PLUS I HAVE MORE THAN A FEW IDEAS ON THE MATTER, SO DON'T BE SURPRISED IF I GET IT OPERATIONAL BEFORE YOU KNOW IT.
OH I'M *SURE.* IN FACT, I'M CERTAIN THERE WILL BE SURPRISES ALL AROUND.

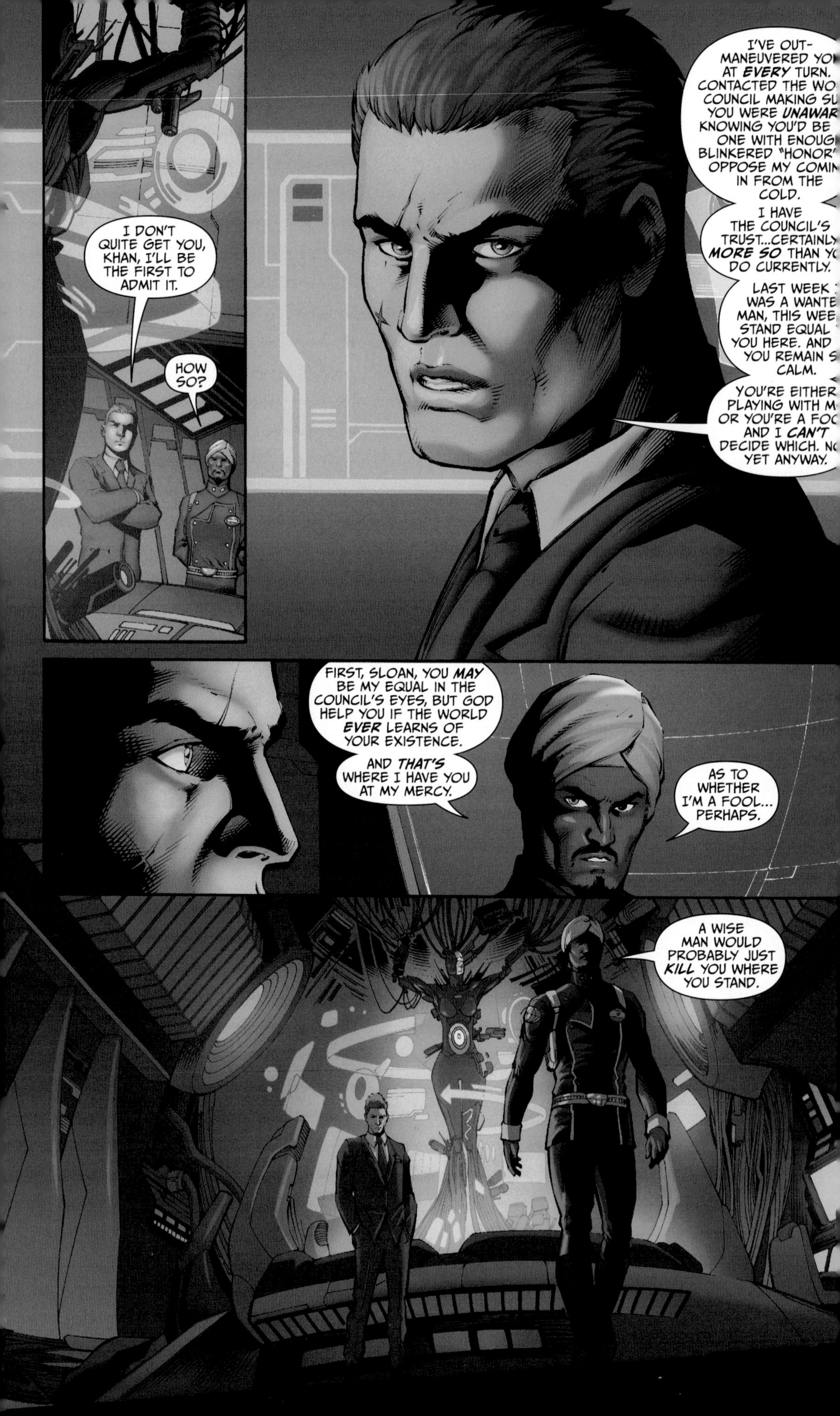
I DON'T QUITE GET YOU, KHAN, I'LL BE THE FIRST TO ADMIT IT.
HOW SO?
I'VE OUT-MANEUVERED YO AT EVERY TURN. CONTACTED THE WO COUNCIL MAKING SU YOU WERE UNAWAR KNOWING YOU'D BE ONE WITH ENOUG BLINKERED "HONOR" OPPOSE MY COMIN IN FROM THE COLD.
I HAVE THE COUNCIL'S TRUST...CERTAINLY MORE SO THAN YO DO CURRENTLY.
LAST WEEK WAS A WANTE MAN, THIS WEE STAND EQUAL YOU HERE. AND YOU REMAIN S CALM.
YOU'RE EITHER PLAYING WITH M OR YOU'RE A FOO AND I CAN'T DECIDE WHICH. N YET ANYWAY.
FIRST, SLOAN, YOU MAY BE MY EQUAL IN THE COUNCIL'S EYES, BUT GOD HELP YOU IF THE WORLD EVER LEARNS OF YOUR EXISTENCE.
AND THAT'S WHERE I HAVE YOU AT MY MERCY.
AS TO WHETHER I'M A FOOL... PERHAPS.
A WISE MAN WOULD PROBABLY JUST KILL YOU WHERE YOU STAND.

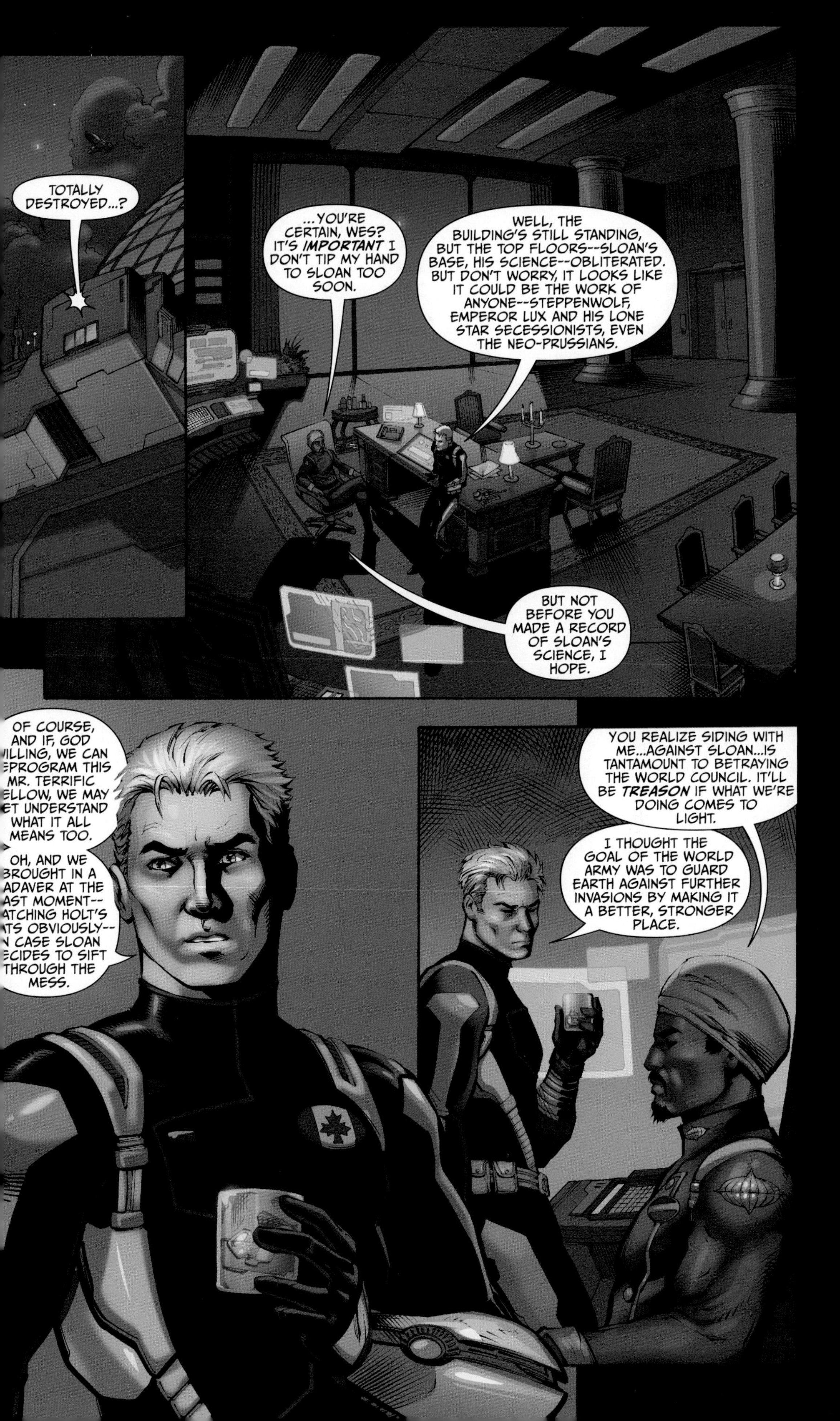

TOTALLY DESTROYED...?
...YOU'RE CERTAIN, WES? IT'S *IMPORTANT* I DON'T TIP MY HAND TO SLOAN TOO SOON.
WELL, THE BUILDING'S STILL STANDING, BUT THE TOP FLOORS--SLOAN'S BASE, HIS SCIENCE--OBLITERATED. BUT DON'T WORRY, IT LOOKS LIKE IT COULD BE THE WORK OF ANYONE--STEPPENWOLF, EMPEROR LUX AND HIS LONE STAR SECESSIONISTS, EVEN THE NEO-PRUSSIANS.
BUT NOT BEFORE YOU MADE A RECORD OF SLOAN'S SCIENCE, I HOPE.
OF COURSE, AND IF, GOD ILLING, WE CAN EPROGRAM THIS MR. TERRIFIC ELLOW, WE MAY ET UNDERSTAND WHAT IT ALL MEANS TOO.
OH, AND WE BROUGHT IN A ADAVER AT THE AST MOMENT-- ATCHING HOLT'S ATS OBVIOUSLY-- N CASE SLOAN ECIDES TO SIFT THROUGH THE MESS.
YOU REALIZE SIDING WITH ME...AGAINST SLOAN...IS TANTAMOUNT TO BETRAYING THE WORLD COUNCIL. IT'LL BE *TREASON* IF WHAT WE'RE DOING COMES TO LIGHT.
I THOUGHT THE GOAL OF THE WORLD ARMY WAS TO GUARD EARTH AGAINST FURTHER INVASIONS BY MAKING IT A BETTER, STRONGER PLACE.

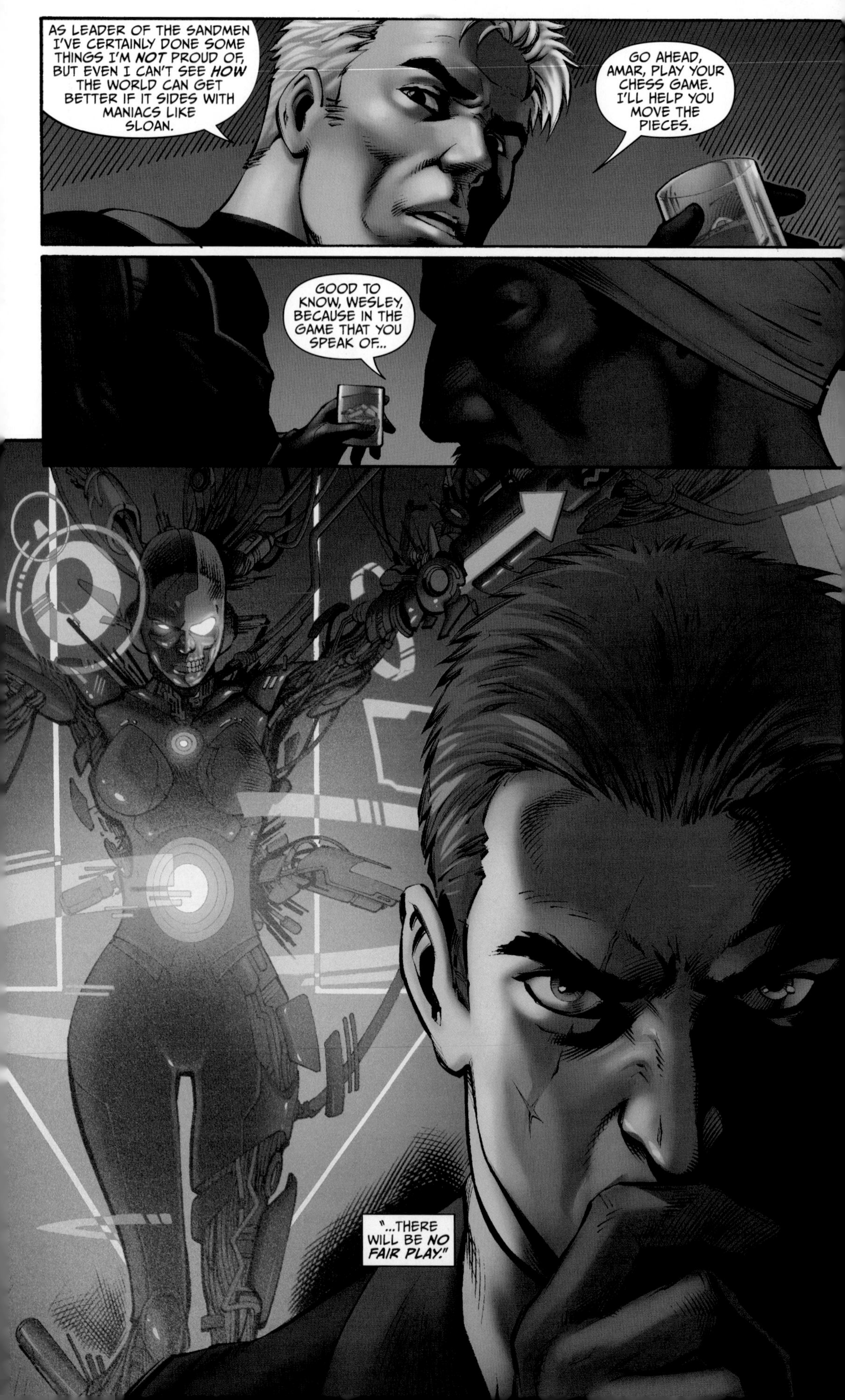

AS LEADER OF THE SANDMEN I'VE CERTAINLY DONE SOME THINGS I'M *NOT* PROUD OF, BUT EVEN I CAN'T SEE *HOW* THE WORLD CAN GET BETTER IF IT SIDES WITH MANIACS LIKE SLOAN.
GO AHEAD, AMAR, PLAY YOUR CHESS GAME. I'LL HELP YOU MOVE THE PIECES.
GOOD TO KNOW, WESLEY, BECAUSE IN THE GAME THAT YOU SPEAK OF...
"...THERE WILL BE *NO FAIR PLAY.*"

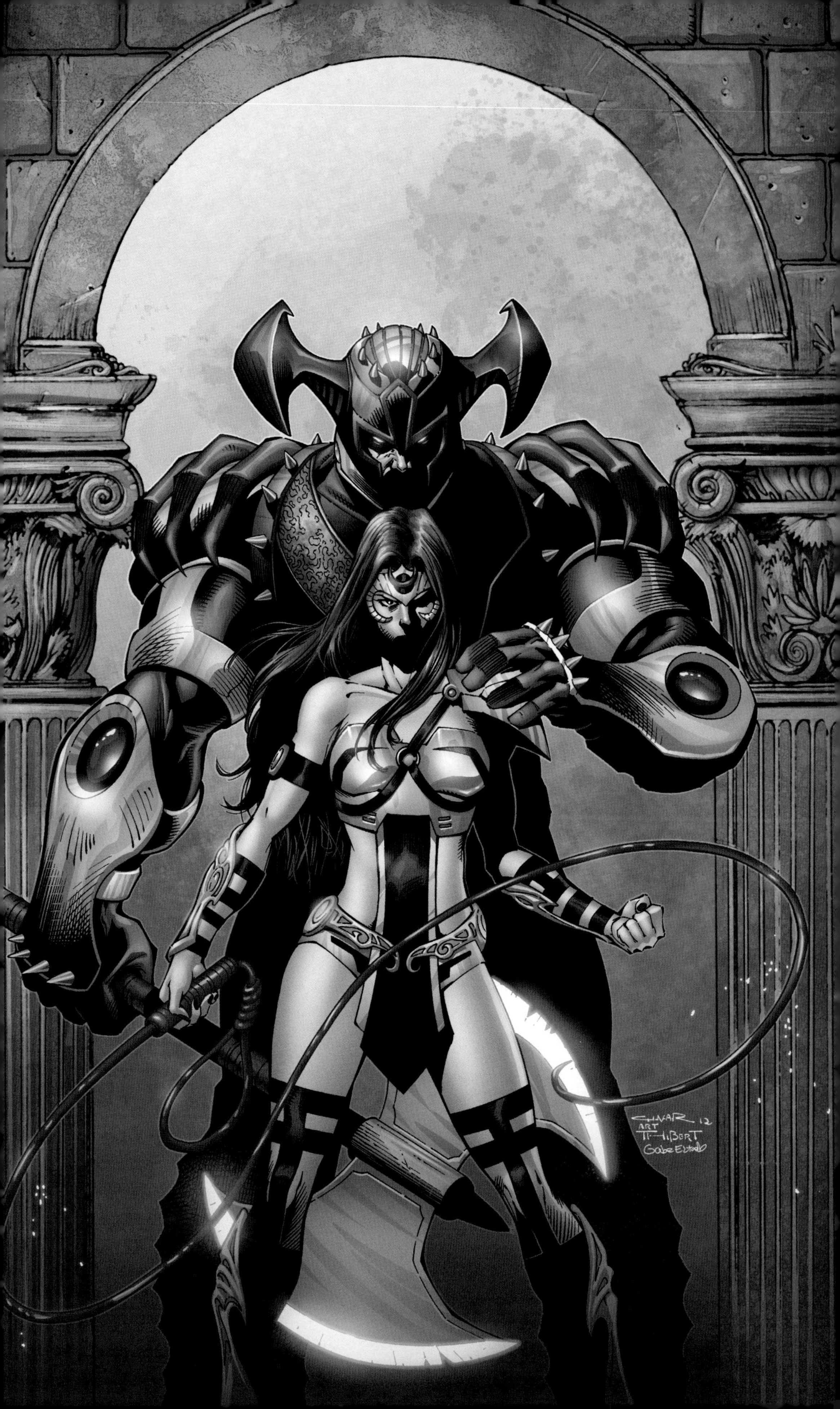
ART THIBERT
Gabe Eltaeb

JAMES ROBINSON writer YILDIRAY CINAR penciller RYAN WINN & ROY JOSE inkers cover by YILDIRAY CINAR, ART THIBERT & GABE ELTAEB

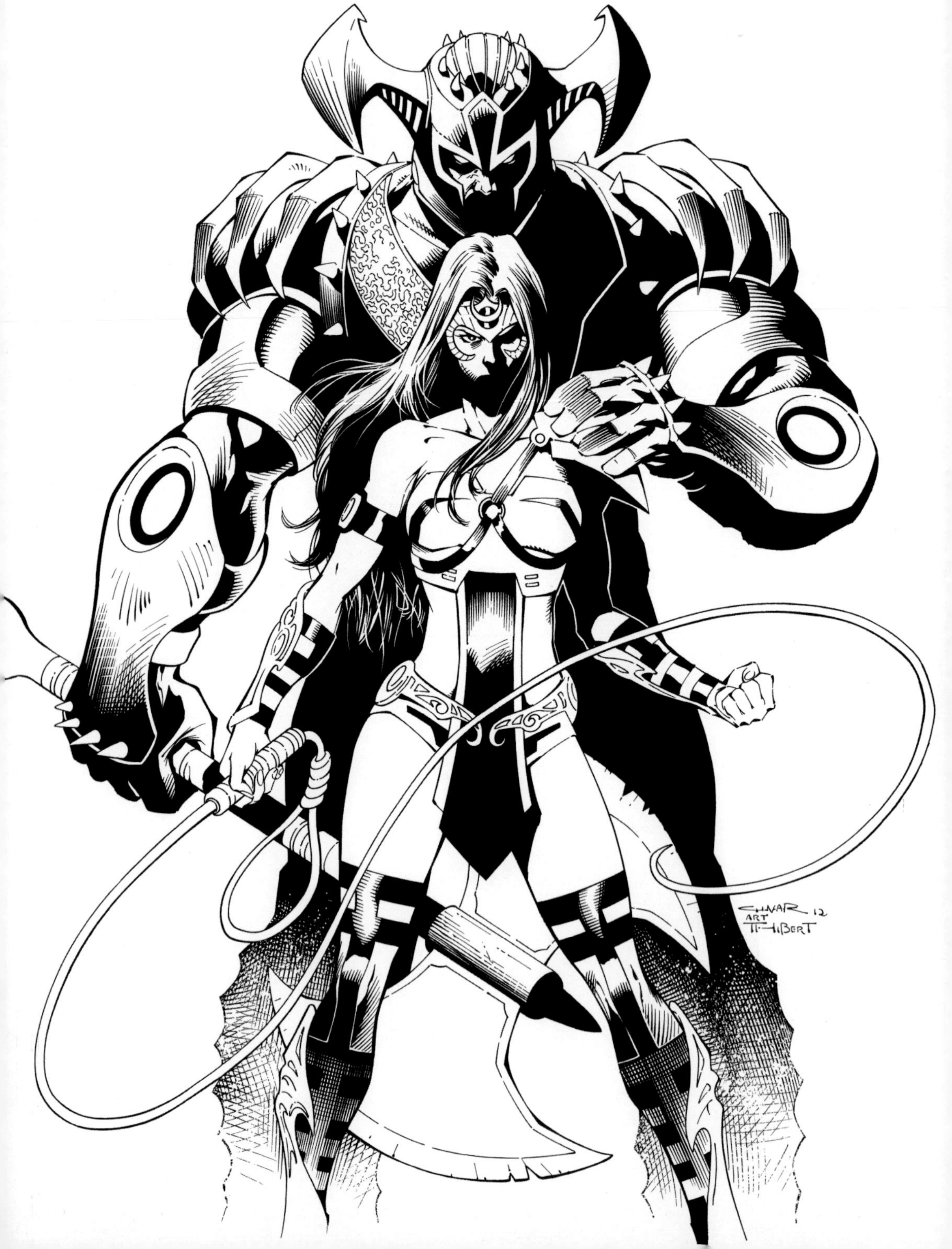
CINAR 12
ART THIBERT

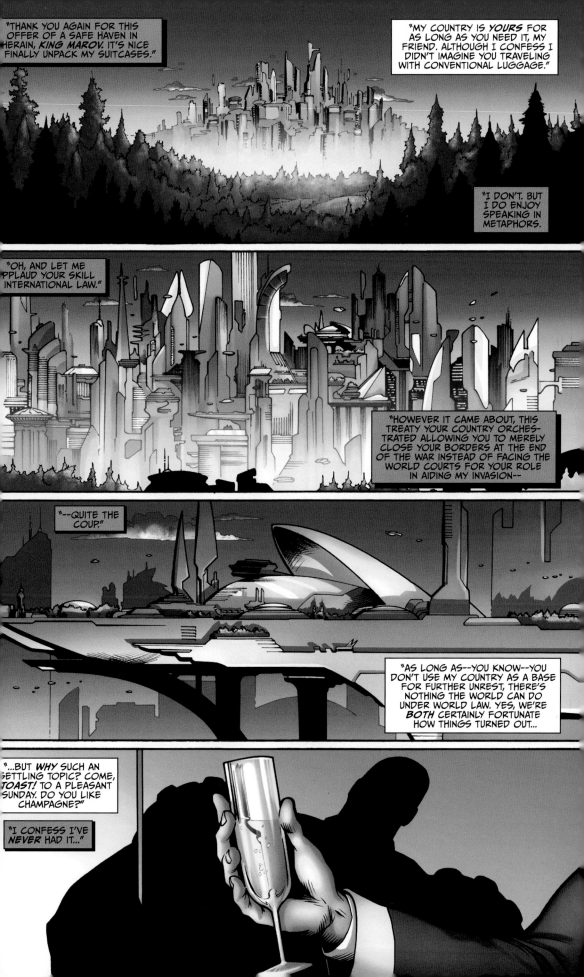

"THANK YOU AGAIN FOR THIS OFFER OF A SAFE HAVEN IN HERAIN, *KING MAROV.* IT'S NICE FINALLY UNPACK MY SUITCASES."

"MY COUNTRY IS *YOURS* FOR AS LONG AS YOU NEED IT, MY FRIEND. ALTHOUGH I CONFESS I DIDN'T IMAGINE YOU TRAVELING WITH CONVENTIONAL LUGGAGE."

"I DON'T. BUT I DO ENJOY SPEAKING IN METAPHORS."

"OH, AND LET ME PPLAUD YOUR SKILL INTERNATIONAL LAW."

"HOWEVER IT CAME ABOUT, THIS TREATY YOUR COUNTRY ORCHES-TRATED ALLOWING YOU TO MERELY CLOSE YOUR BORDERS AT THE END OF THE WAR INSTEAD OF FACING THE WORLD COURTS FOR YOUR ROLE IN AIDING MY INVASION--

"--QUITE THE COUP."

"AS LONG AS--YOU KNOW--YOU DON'T USE MY COUNTRY AS A BASE FOR FURTHER UNREST, THERE'S NOTHING THE WORLD CAN DO UNDER WORLD LAW. YES, WE'RE *BOTH* CERTAINLY FORTUNATE HOW THINGS TURNED OUT..."

"...BUT *WHY* SUCH AN ETTLING TOPIC? COME, *TOAST!* TO A PLEASANT SUNDAY. DO YOU LIKE CHAMPAGNE?"

"I CONFESS I'VE *NEVER* HAD IT..."

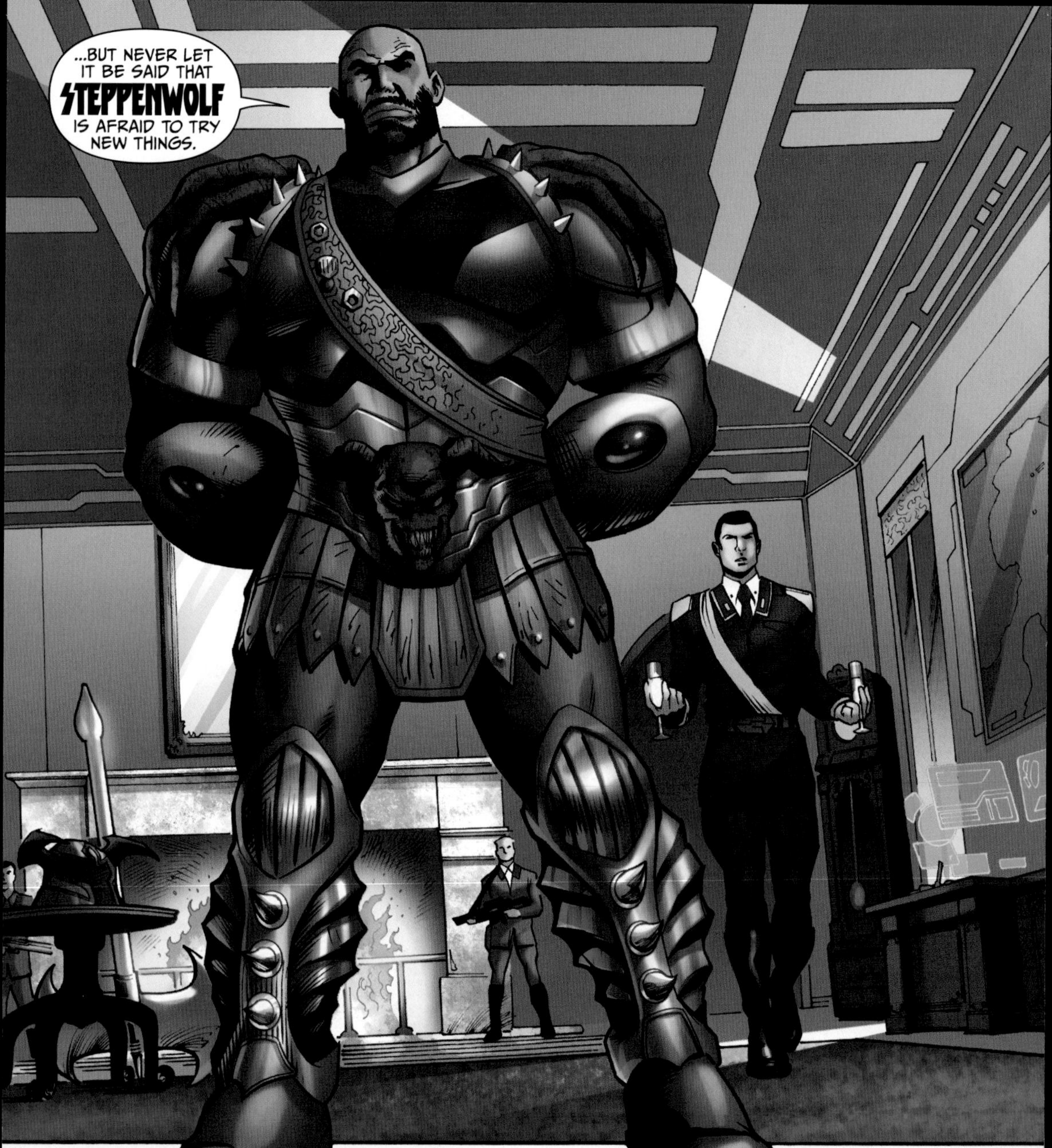
...BUT NEVER LET IT BE SAID THAT STEPPENWOLF IS AFRAID TO TRY NEW THINGS.

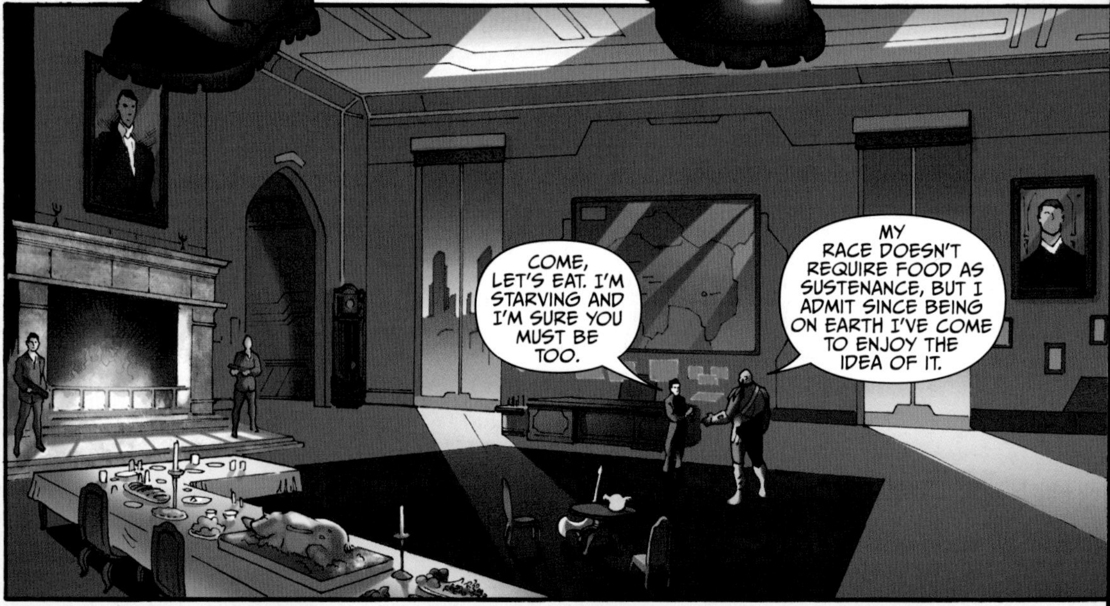
COME, LET'S EAT. I'M STARVING AND I'M SURE YOU MUST BE TOO.
MY RACE DOESN'T REQUIRE FOOD AS SUSTENANCE, BUT I ADMIT SINCE BEING ON EARTH I'VE COME TO ENJOY THE IDEA OF IT.

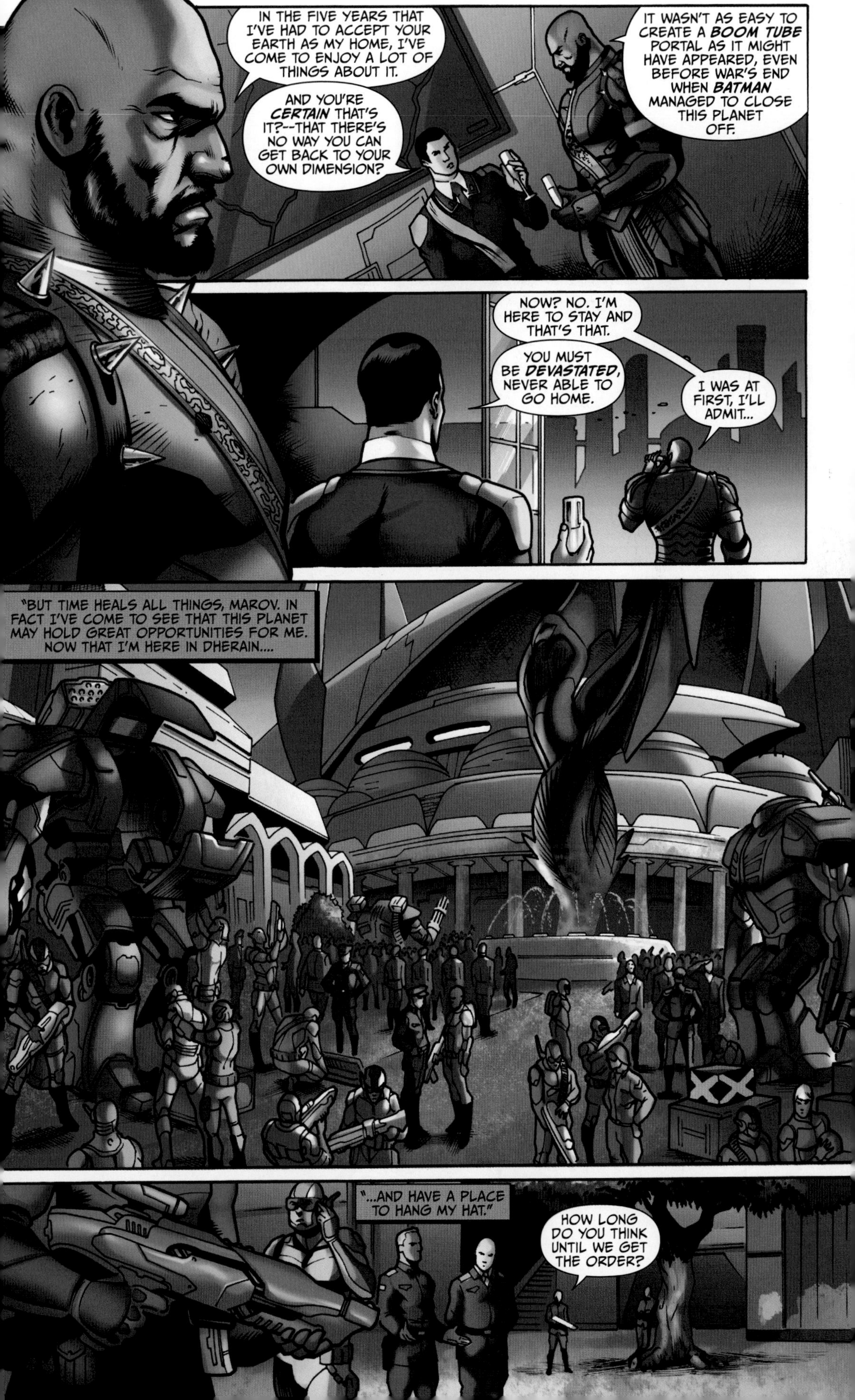
IN THE FIVE YEARS THAT I'VE HAD TO ACCEPT YOUR EARTH AS MY HOME, I'VE COME TO ENJOY A LOT OF THINGS ABOUT IT.
AND YOU'RE CERTAIN THAT'S IT?--THAT THERE'S NO WAY YOU CAN GET BACK TO YOUR OWN DIMENSION?
IT WASN'T AS EASY TO CREATE A BOOM TUBE PORTAL AS IT MIGHT HAVE APPEARED, EVEN BEFORE WAR'S END WHEN BATMAN MANAGED TO CLOSE THIS PLANET OFF.
NOW? NO. I'M HERE TO STAY AND THAT'S THAT.
YOU MUST BE DEVASTATED, NEVER ABLE TO GO HOME.
I WAS AT FIRST, I'LL ADMIT...
"BUT TIME HEALS ALL THINGS, MAROV. IN FACT I'VE COME TO SEE THAT THIS PLANET MAY HOLD GREAT OPPORTUNITIES FOR ME. NOW THAT I'M HERE IN DHERAIN....
"...AND HAVE A PLACE TO HANG MY HAT."
HOW LONG DO YOU THINK UNTIL WE GET THE ORDER?

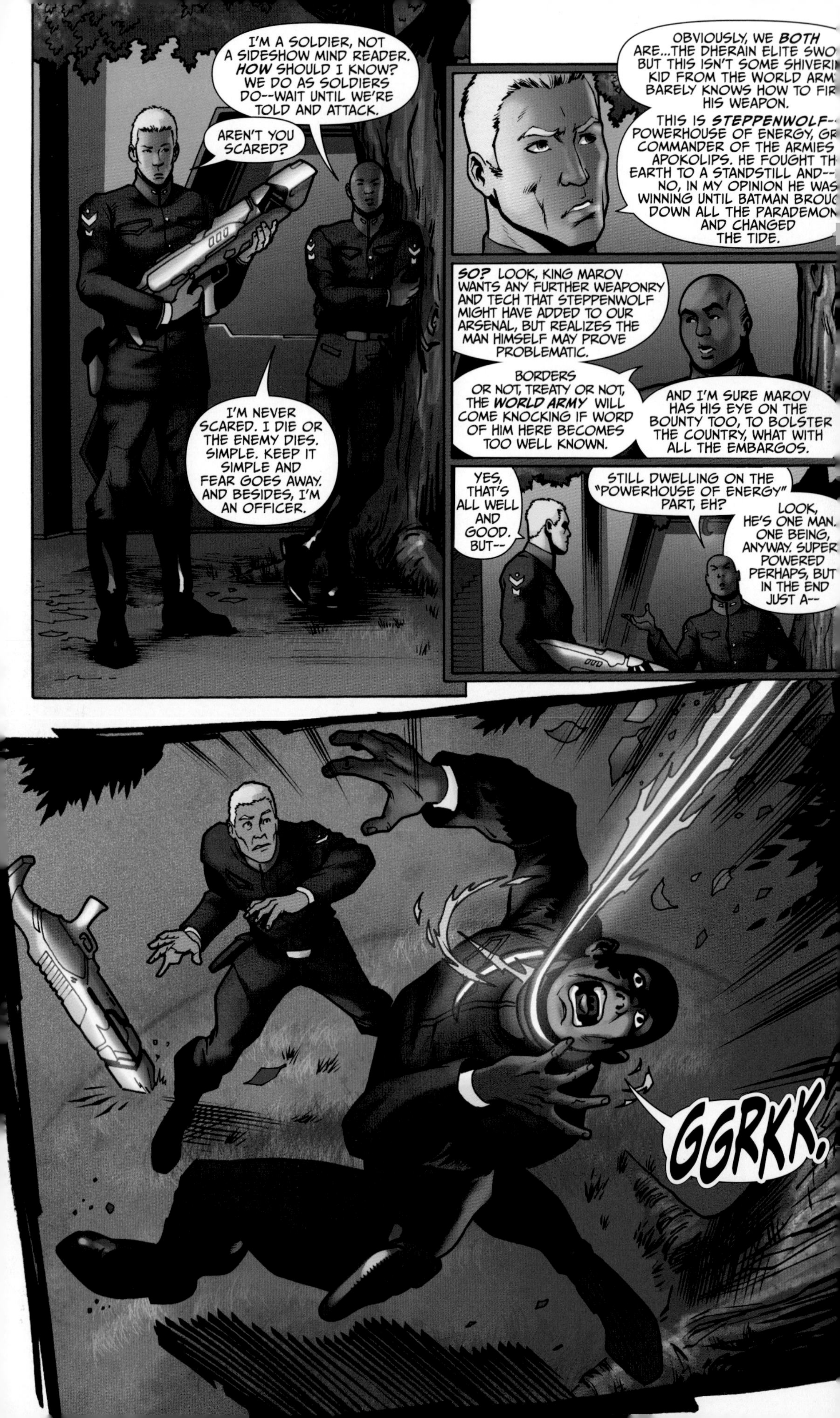
I'M A SOLDIER, NOT A SIDESHOW MIND READER. HOW SHOULD I KNOW? WE DO AS SOLDIERS DO--WAIT UNTIL WE'RE TOLD AND ATTACK.
AREN'T YOU SCARED?
I'M NEVER SCARED. I DIE OR THE ENEMY DIES. SIMPLE. KEEP IT SIMPLE AND FEAR GOES AWAY. AND BESIDES, I'M AN OFFICER.
OBVIOUSLY, WE BOTH ARE...THE DHERAIN ELITE SWO
BUT THIS ISN'T SOME SHIVERI
KID FROM THE WORLD ARM
BARELY KNOWS HOW TO FIR
HIS WEAPON.
THIS IS STEPPENWOLF--
POWERHOUSE OF ENERGY, GR
COMMANDER OF THE ARMIES
APOKOLIPS. HE FOUGHT TH
EARTH TO A STANDSTILL AND--
NO, IN MY OPINION HE WAS
WINNING UNTIL BATMAN BROU
DOWN ALL THE PARADEMON
AND CHANGED THE TIDE.
SO? LOOK, KING MAROV WANTS ANY FURTHER WEAPONRY AND TECH THAT STEPPENWOLF MIGHT HAVE ADDED TO OUR ARSENAL, BUT REALIZES THE MAN HIMSELF MAY PROVE PROBLEMATIC.
BORDERS OR NOT, TREATY OR NOT, THE WORLD ARMY WILL COME KNOCKING IF WORD OF HIM HERE BECOMES TOO WELL KNOWN.
AND I'M SURE MAROV HAS HIS EYE ON THE BOUNTY TOO, TO BOLSTER THE COUNTRY, WHAT WITH ALL THE EMBARGOS.
YES, THAT'S ALL WELL AND GOOD. BUT--
STILL DWELLING ON THE "POWERHOUSE OF ENERGY" PART, EH?
LOOK, HE'S ONE MAN. ONE BEING, ANYWAY. SUPER POWERED PERHAPS, BUT IN THE END JUST A--
GGRKK.

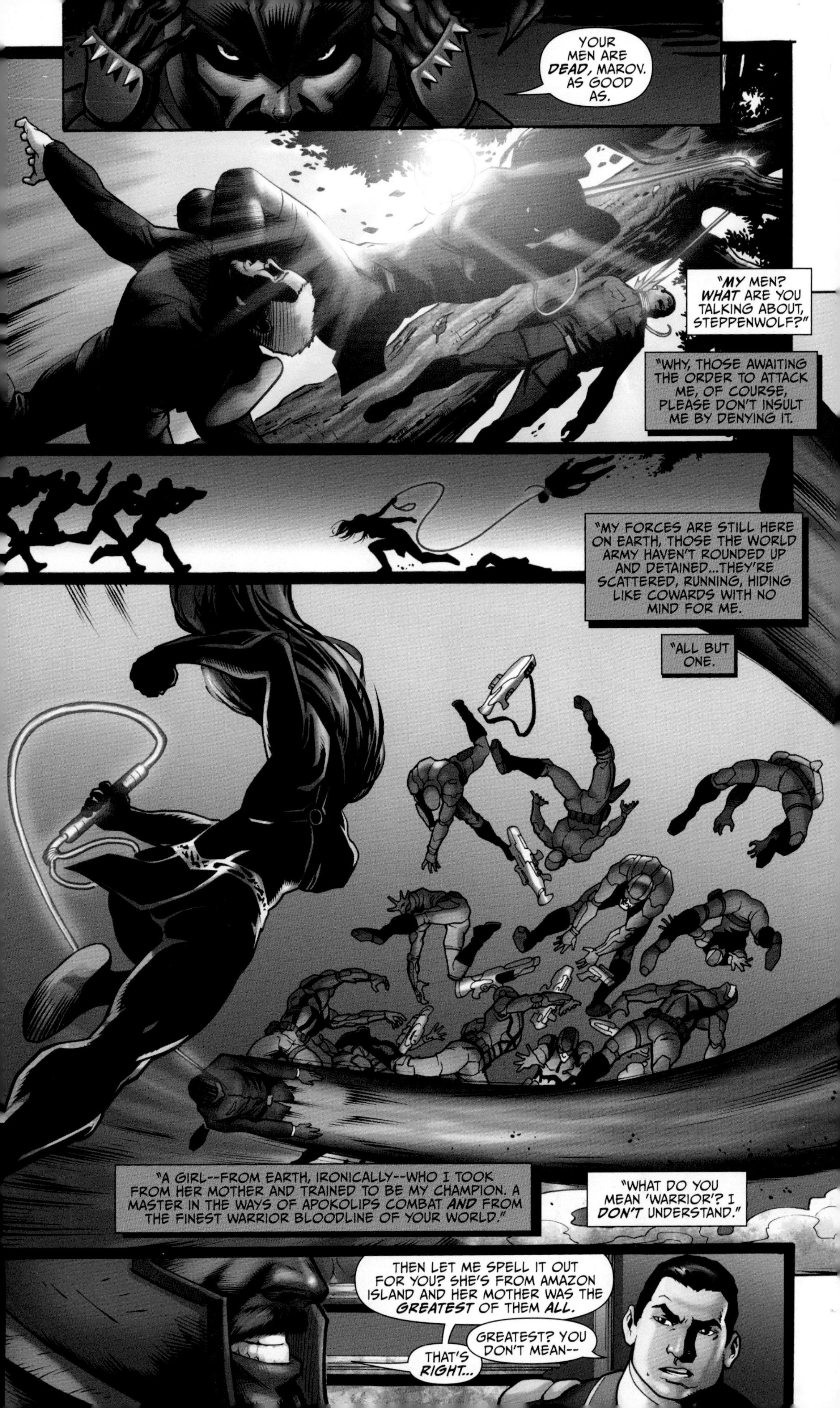
YOUR MEN ARE DEAD, MAROV. AS GOOD AS.
"MY MEN? WHAT ARE YOU TALKING ABOUT, STEPPENWOLF?"
"WHY, THOSE AWAITING THE ORDER TO ATTACK ME, OF COURSE, PLEASE DON'T INSULT ME BY DENYING IT.
"MY FORCES ARE STILL HERE ON EARTH, THOSE THE WORLD ARMY HAVEN'T ROUNDED UP AND DETAINED...THEY'RE SCATTERED, RUNNING, HIDING LIKE COWARDS WITH NO MIND FOR ME.
"ALL BUT ONE.
"A GIRL--FROM EARTH, IRONICALLY--WHO I TOOK FROM HER MOTHER AND TRAINED TO BE MY CHAMPION. A MASTER IN THE WAYS OF APOKOLIPS COMBAT AND FROM THE FINEST WARRIOR BLOODLINE OF YOUR WORLD."
"WHAT DO YOU MEAN 'WARRIOR'? I DON'T UNDERSTAND."
THEN LET ME SPELL IT OUT FOR YOU? SHE'S FROM AMAZON ISLAND AND HER MOTHER WAS THE GREATEST OF THEM ALL.
GREATEST? YOU DON'T MEAN--
THAT'S RIGHT...

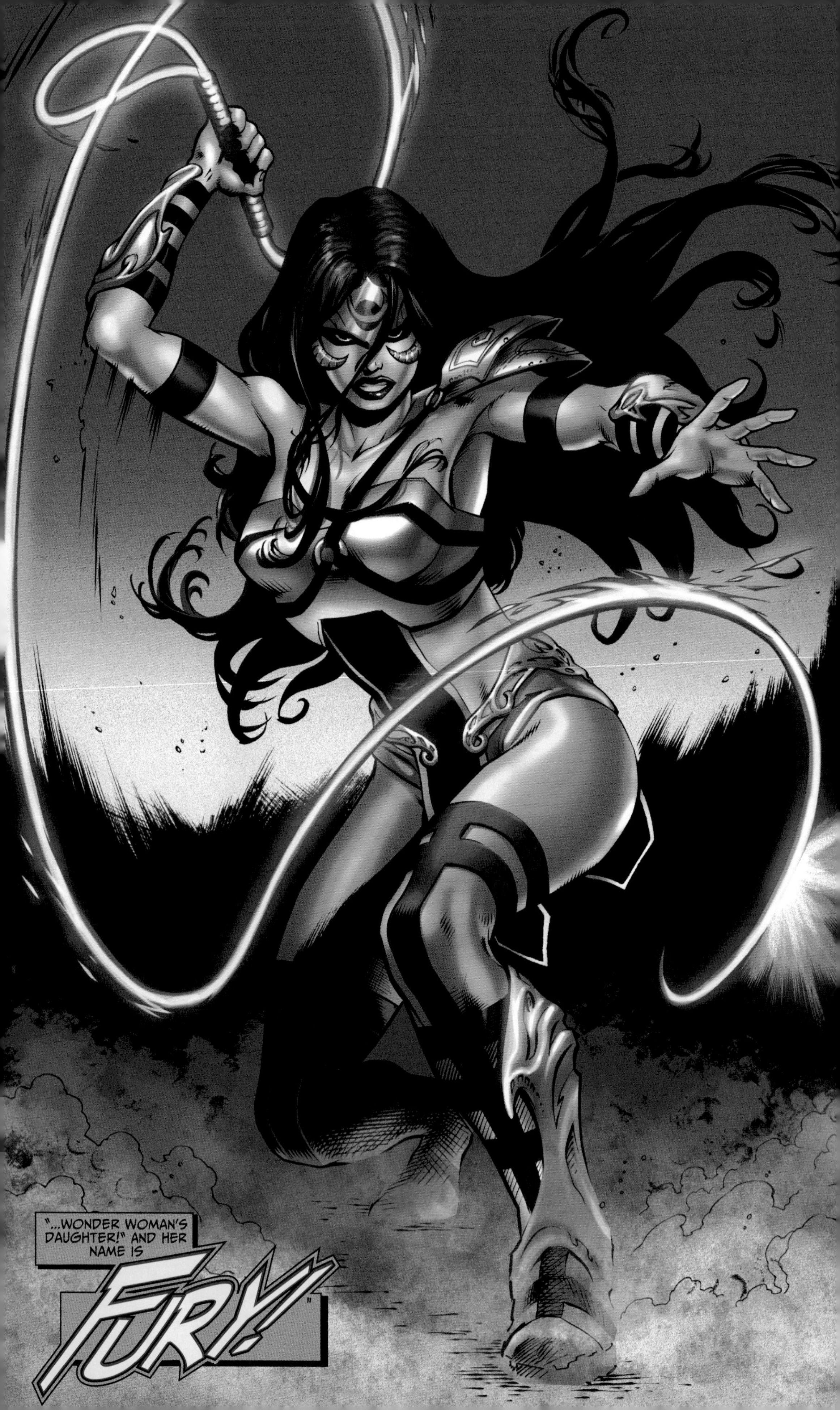
"...WONDER WOMAN'S DAUGHTER!" AND HER NAME IS
FURY!"

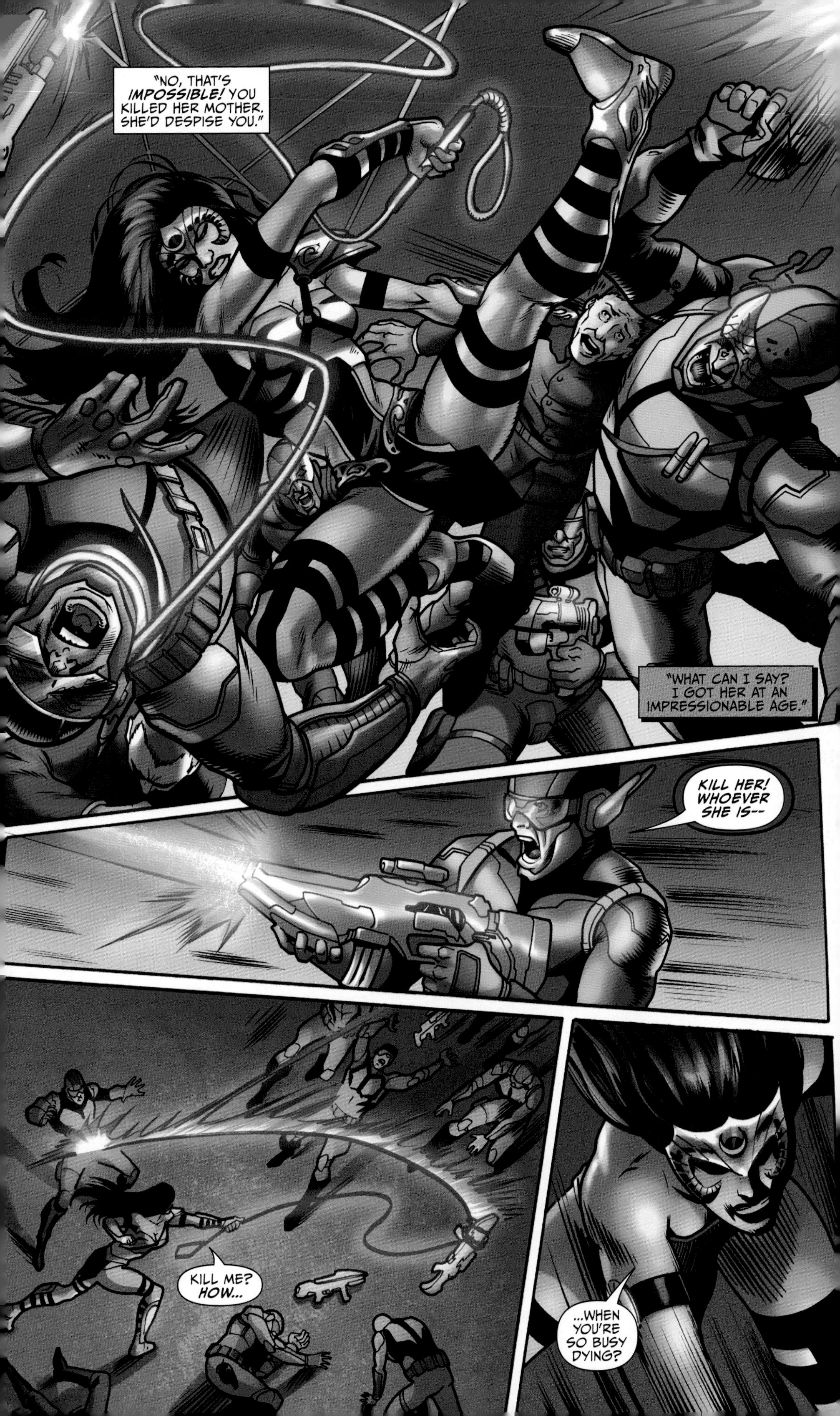
"NO, THAT'S *IMPOSSIBLE!* YOU KILLED HER MOTHER. SHE'D DESPISE YOU."
"WHAT CAN I SAY? I GOT HER AT AN IMPRESSIONABLE AGE."
KILL HER! WHOEVER SHE IS--
KILL ME? *HOW...*
...WHEN YOU'RE SO BUSY DYING?

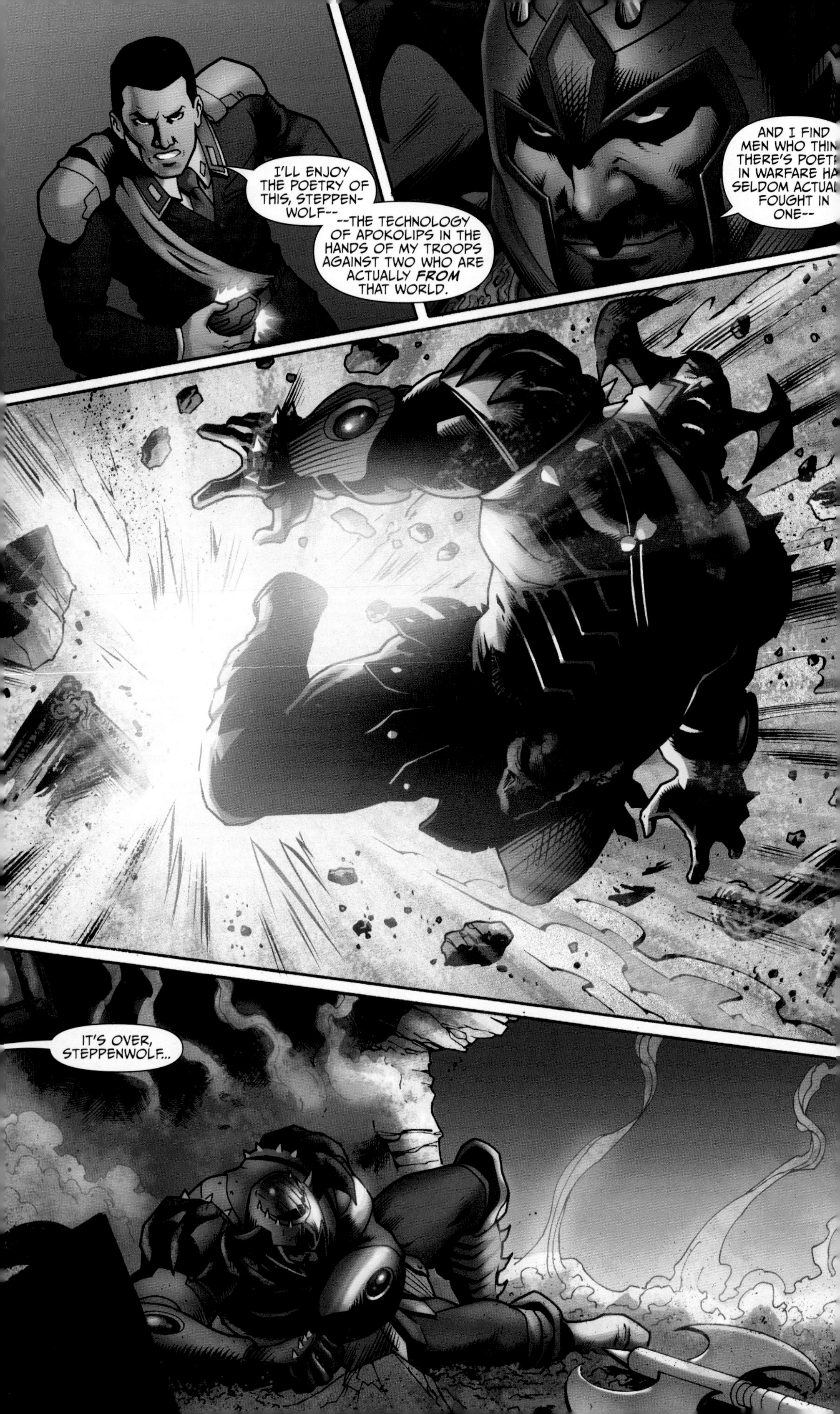
I'LL ENJOY THE POETRY OF THIS, STEPPEN-WOLF--
--THE TECHNOLOGY OF APOKOLIPS IN THE HANDS OF MY TROOPS AGAINST TWO WHO ARE ACTUALLY *FROM* THAT WORLD.
AND I FIND MEN WHO THIN THERE'S POET IN WARFARE HA SELDOM ACTUAL FOUGHT IN ONE--
IT'S OVER, STEPPENWOLF...

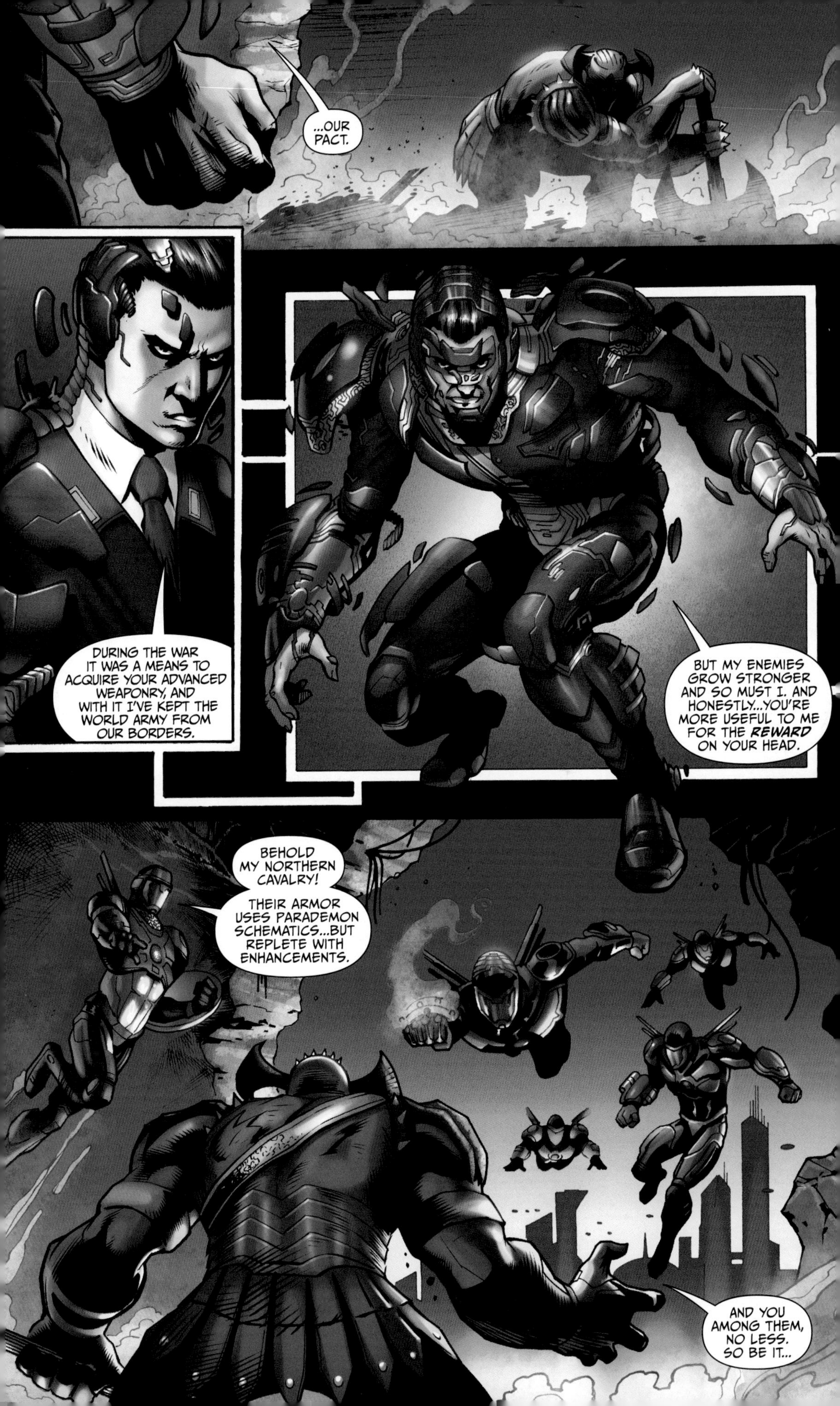
...OUR PACT.
DURING THE WAR IT WAS A MEANS TO ACQUIRE YOUR ADVANCED WEAPONRY, AND WITH IT I'VE KEPT THE WORLD ARMY FROM OUR BORDERS.
BUT MY ENEMIES GROW STRONGER AND SO MUST I. AND HONESTLY...YOU'RE MORE USEFUL TO ME FOR THE *REWARD* ON YOUR HEAD.
BEHOLD MY NORTHERN CAVALRY!
THEIR ARMOR USES PARADEMON SCHEMATICS...BUT REPLETE WITH ENHANCEMENTS.
AND YOU AMONG THEM, NO LESS. SO BE IT...

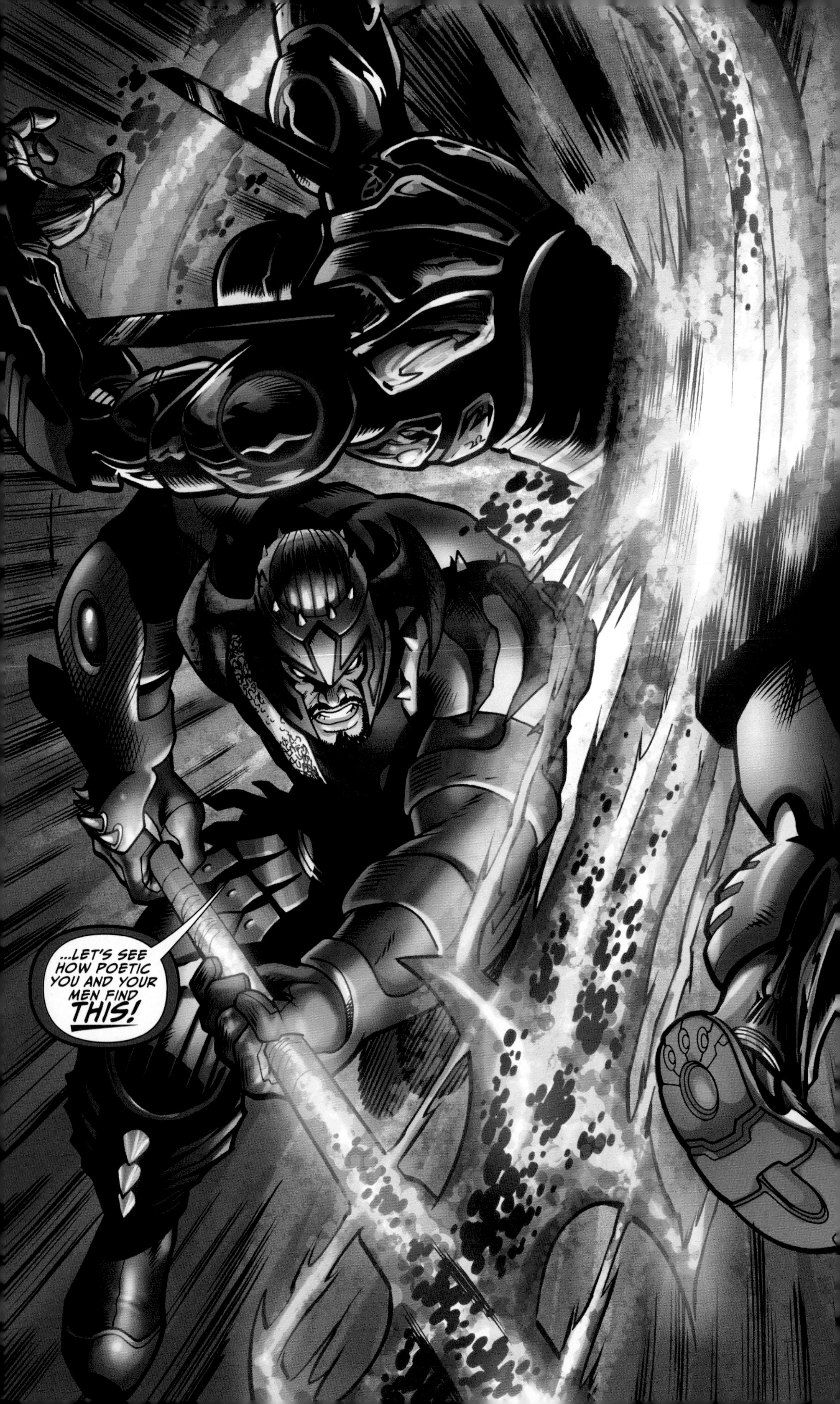
...LET'S SEE HOW POETIC YOU AND YOUR MEN FIND THIS!

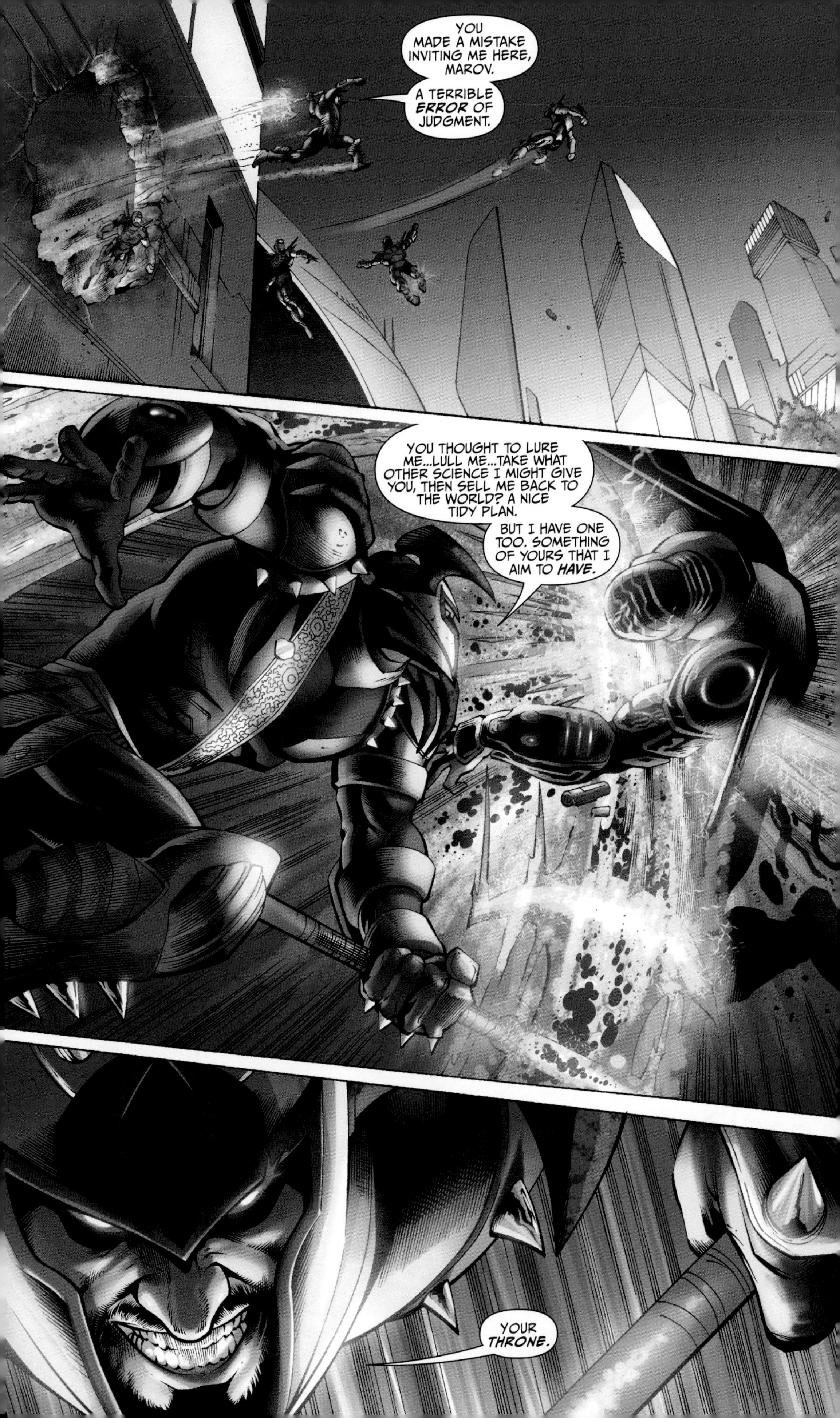

YOU MADE A MISTAKE INVITING ME HERE, MAROV.
A TERRIBLE *ERROR* OF JUDGMENT.
YOU THOUGHT TO LURE ME...LULL ME...TAKE WHAT OTHER SCIENCE I MIGHT GIVE YOU, THEN SELL ME BACK TO THE WORLD? A NICE TIDY PLAN.
BUT I HAVE ONE TOO. SOMETHING OF YOURS THAT I AIM TO *HAVE.*
YOUR *THRONE.*

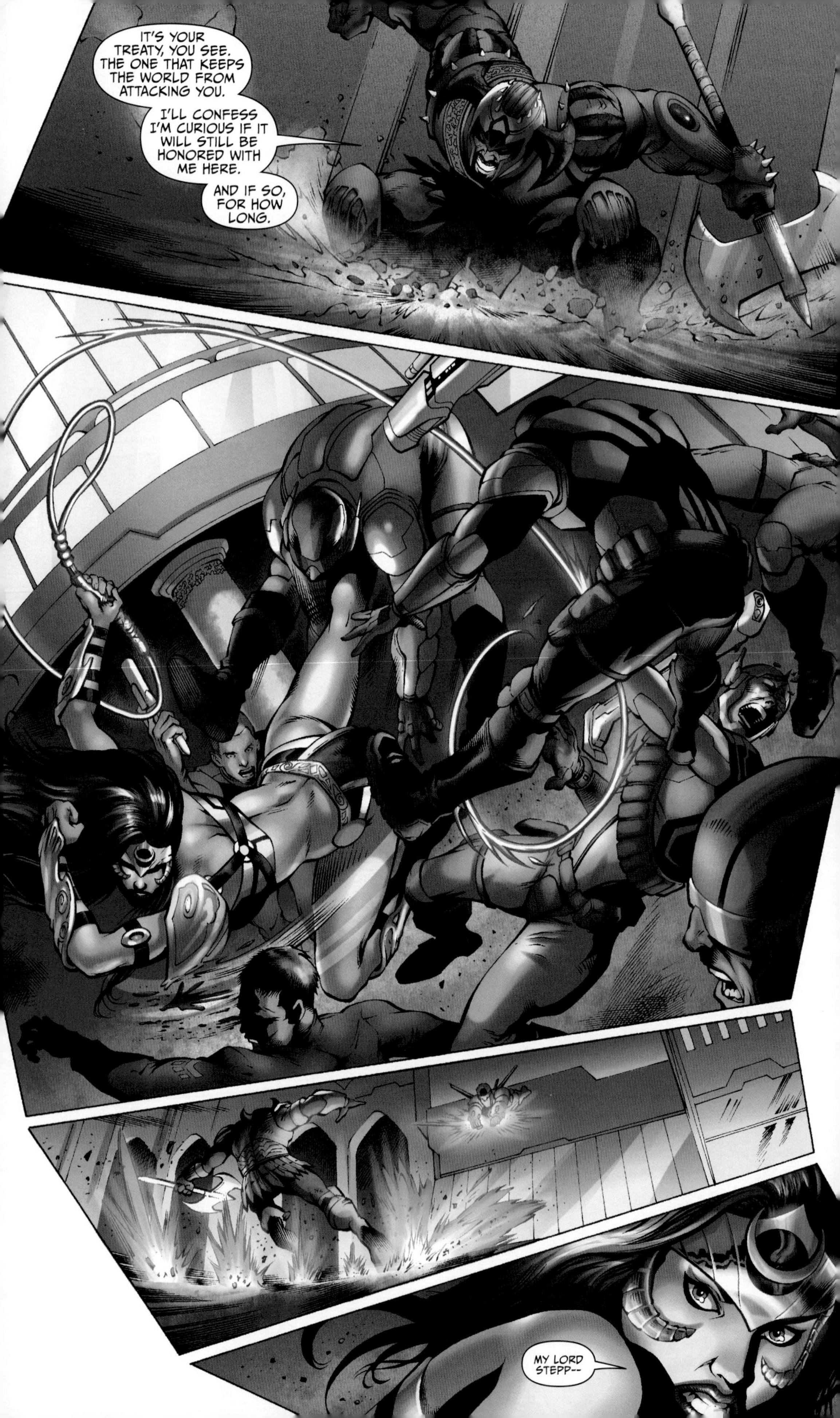
IT'S YOUR TREATY, YOU SEE. THE ONE THAT KEEPS THE WORLD FROM ATTACKING YOU.
I'LL CONFESS I'M CURIOUS IF IT WILL STILL BE HONORED WITH ME HERE.
AND IF SO, FOR HOW LONG.
MY LORD STEPP--

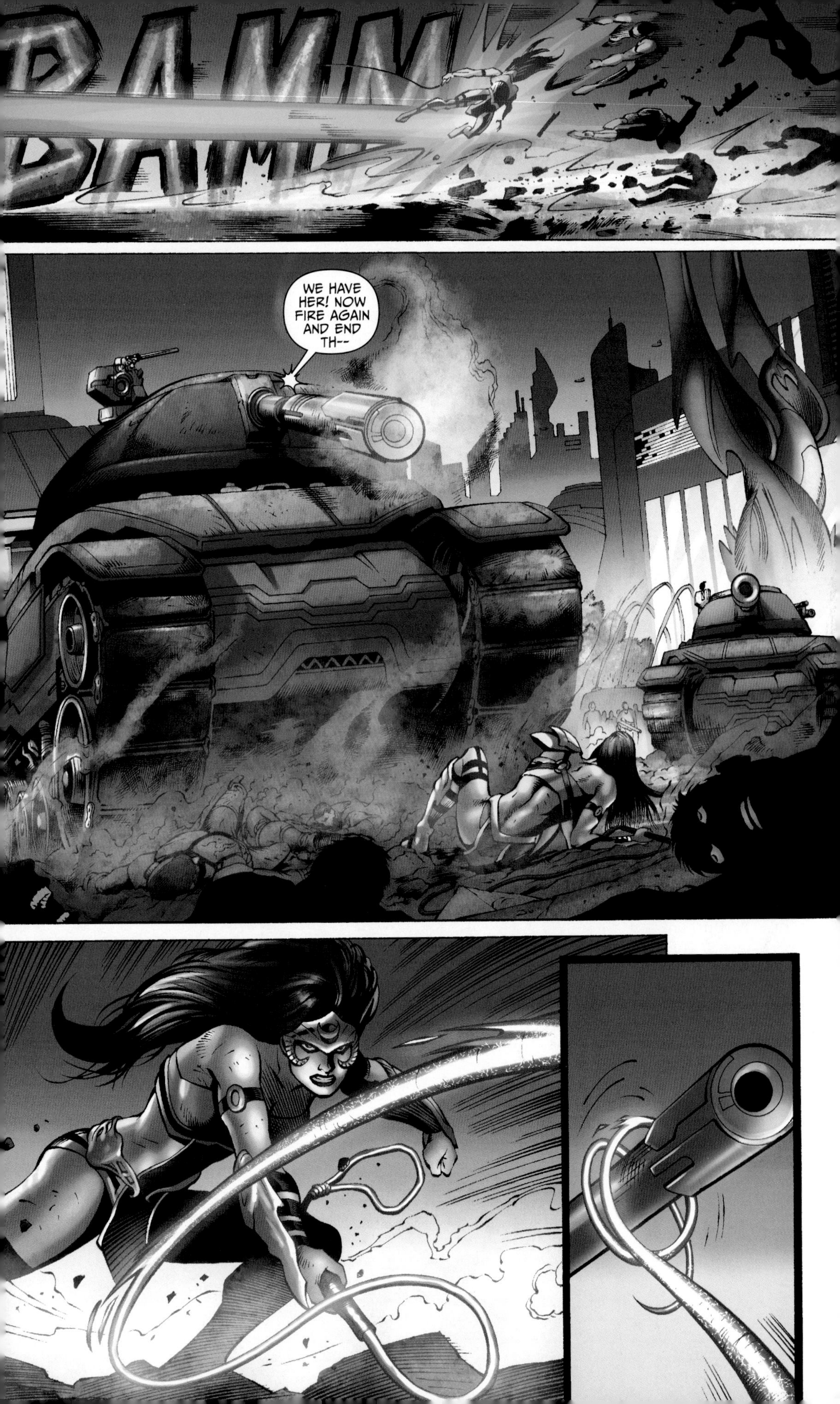
BAMM BAMM
WE HAVE HER! NOW FIRE AGAIN AND END TH--

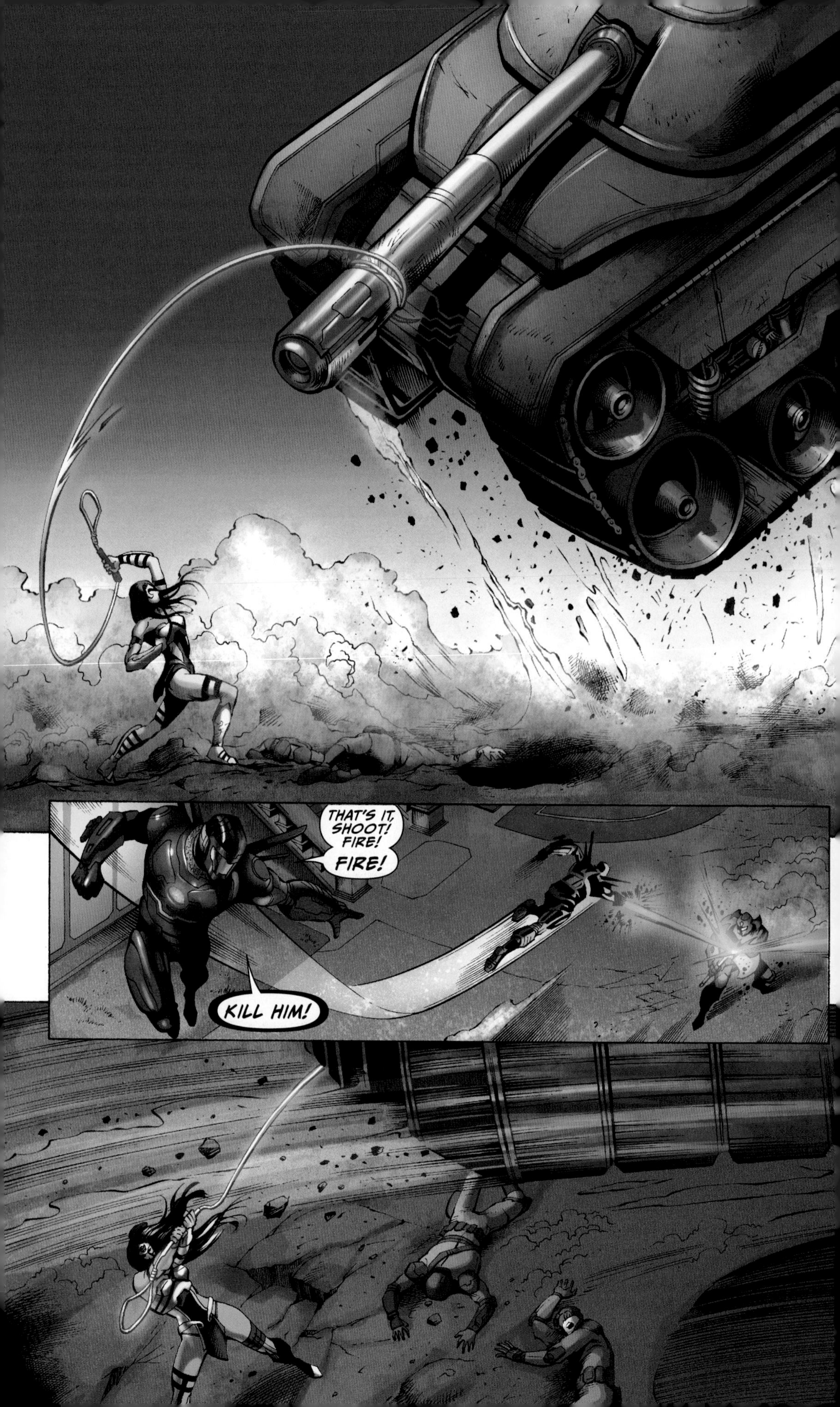
THAT'S IT, SHOOT! FIRE!
FIRE!
KILL HIM!

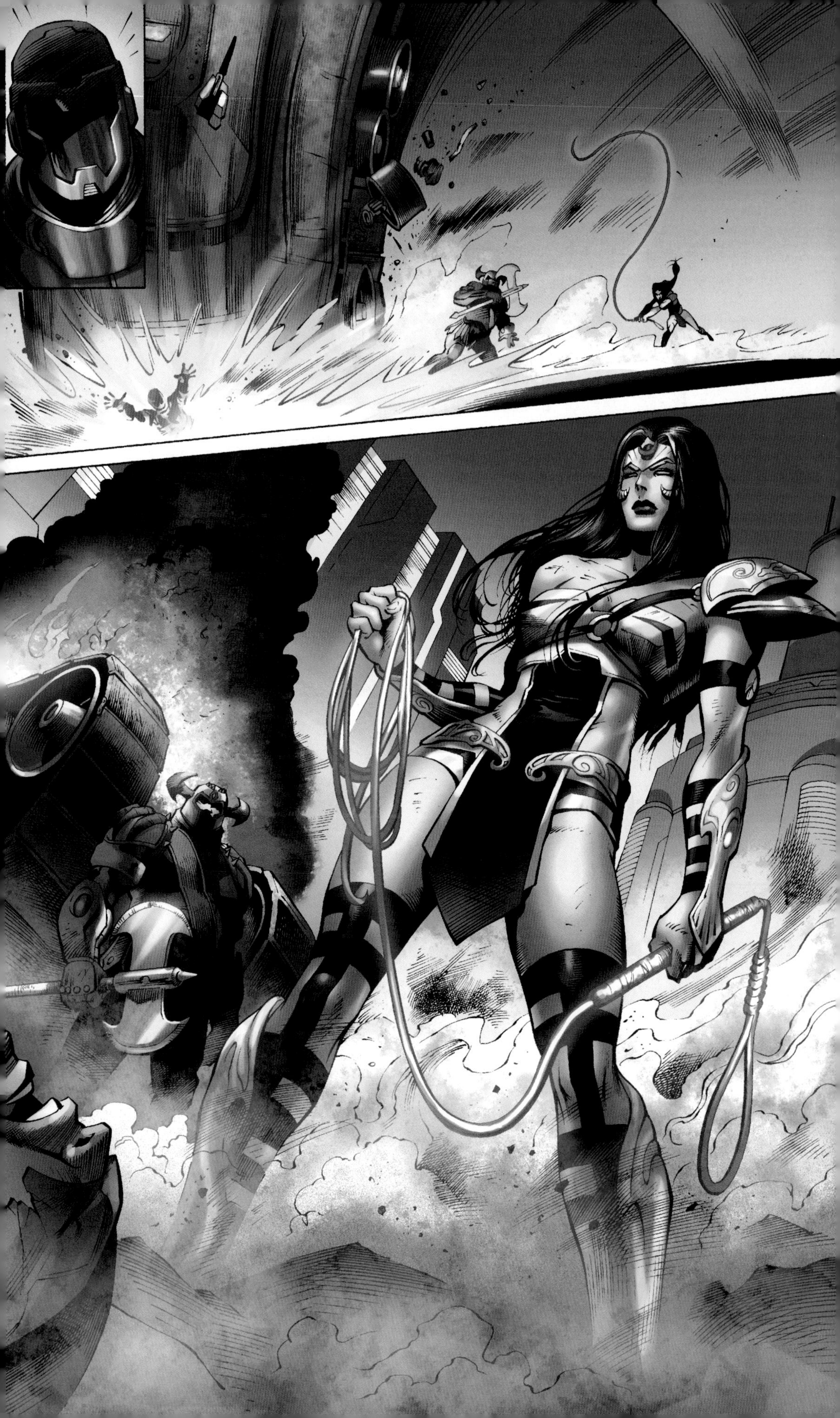

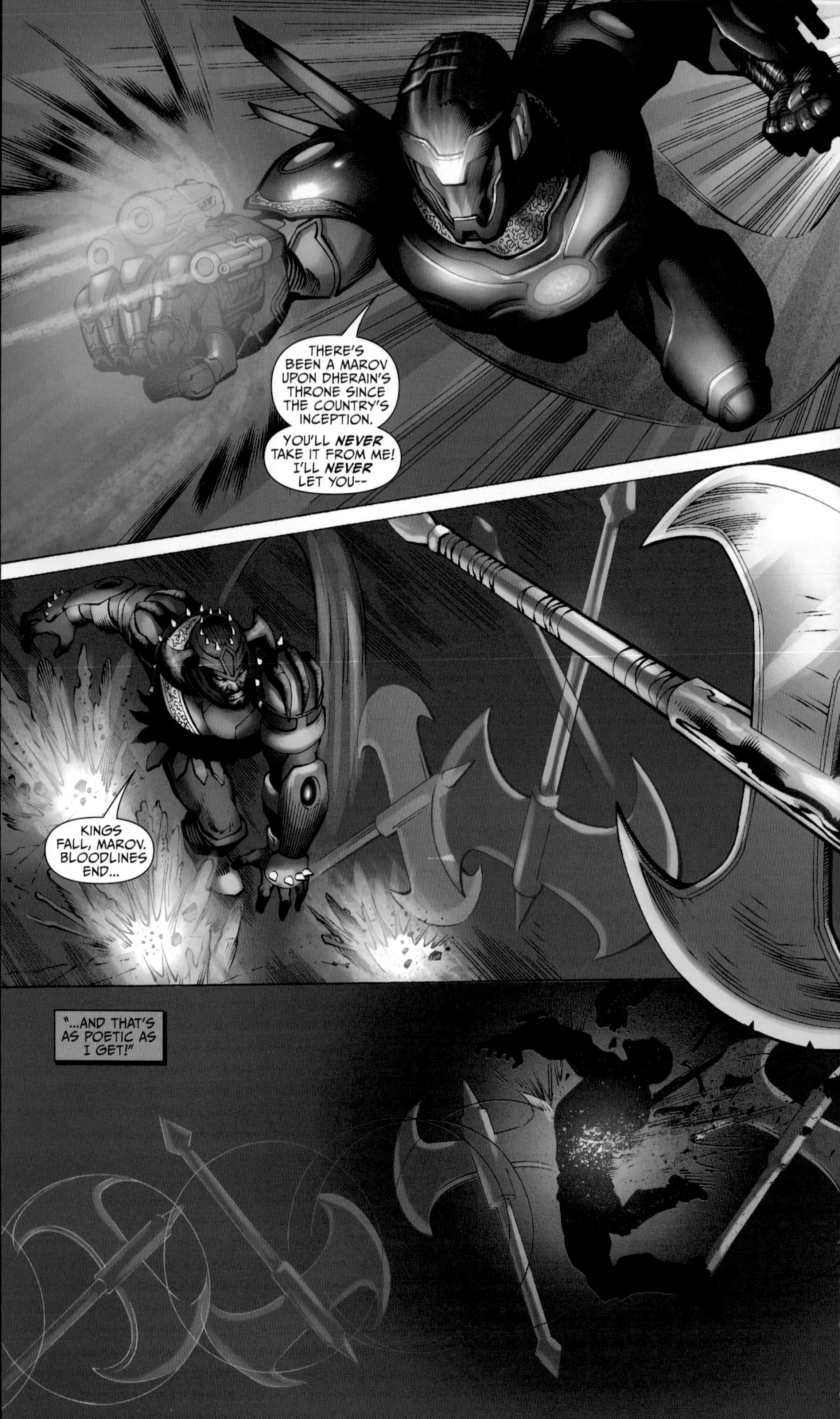

THERE'S BEEN A MAROV UPON DHERAIN'S THRONE SINCE THE COUNTRY'S INCEPTION.
YOU'LL NEVER TAKE IT FROM ME! I'LL NEVER LET YOU--
KINGS FALL, MAROV. BLOODLINES END...
"...AND THAT'S AS POETIC AS I GET!"

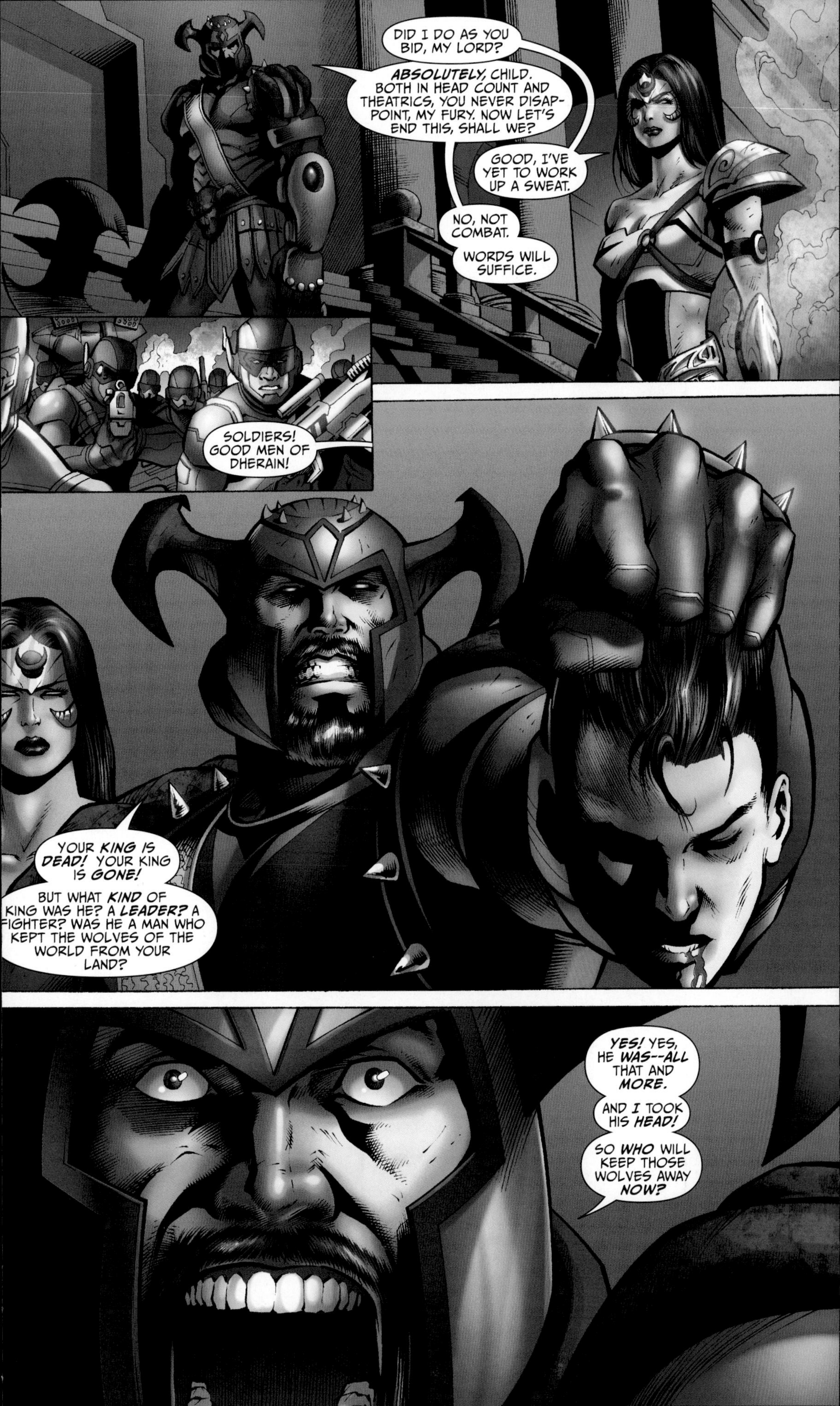

DID I DO AS YOU BID, MY LORD?
ABSOLUTELY, CHILD. BOTH IN HEAD COUNT AND THEATRICS, YOU NEVER DISAP-POINT, MY FURY. NOW LET'S END THIS, SHALL WE?
GOOD, I'VE YET TO WORK UP A SWEAT.
NO, NOT COMBAT.
WORDS WILL SUFFICE.
SOLDIERS! GOOD MEN OF DHERAIN!
YOUR *KING* IS *DEAD!* YOUR KING IS *GONE!*
BUT WHAT *KIND* OF KING WAS HE? A *LEADER?* A FIGHTER? WAS HE A MAN WHO KEPT THE WOLVES OF THE WORLD FROM YOUR LAND?
YES! YES, HE *WAS--ALL* THAT AND *MORE.*
AND *I* TOOK HIS *HEAD!*
SO *WHO* WILL KEEP THOSE WOLVES AWAY *NOW?*

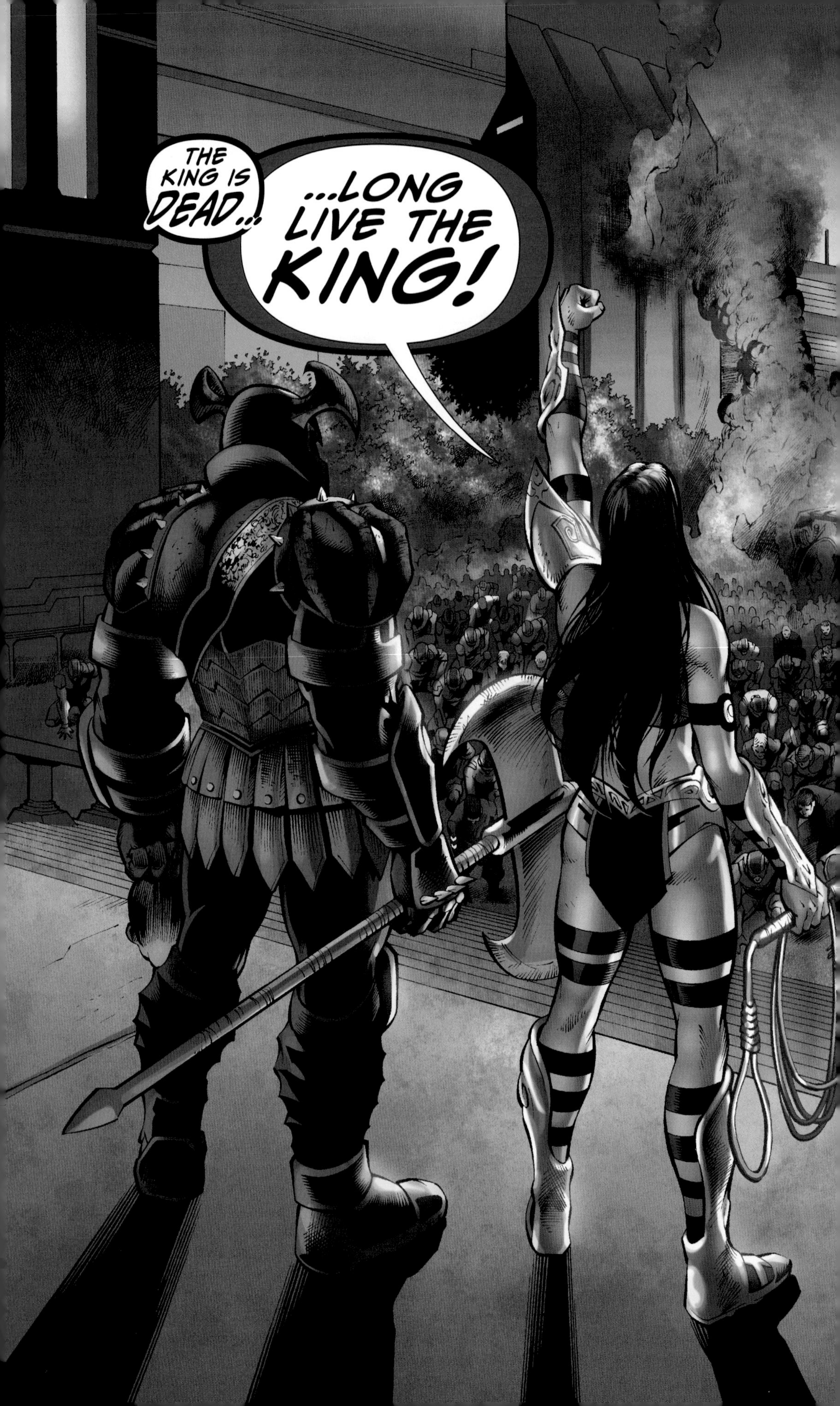
THE KING IS DEAD...
...LONG LIVE THE KING!

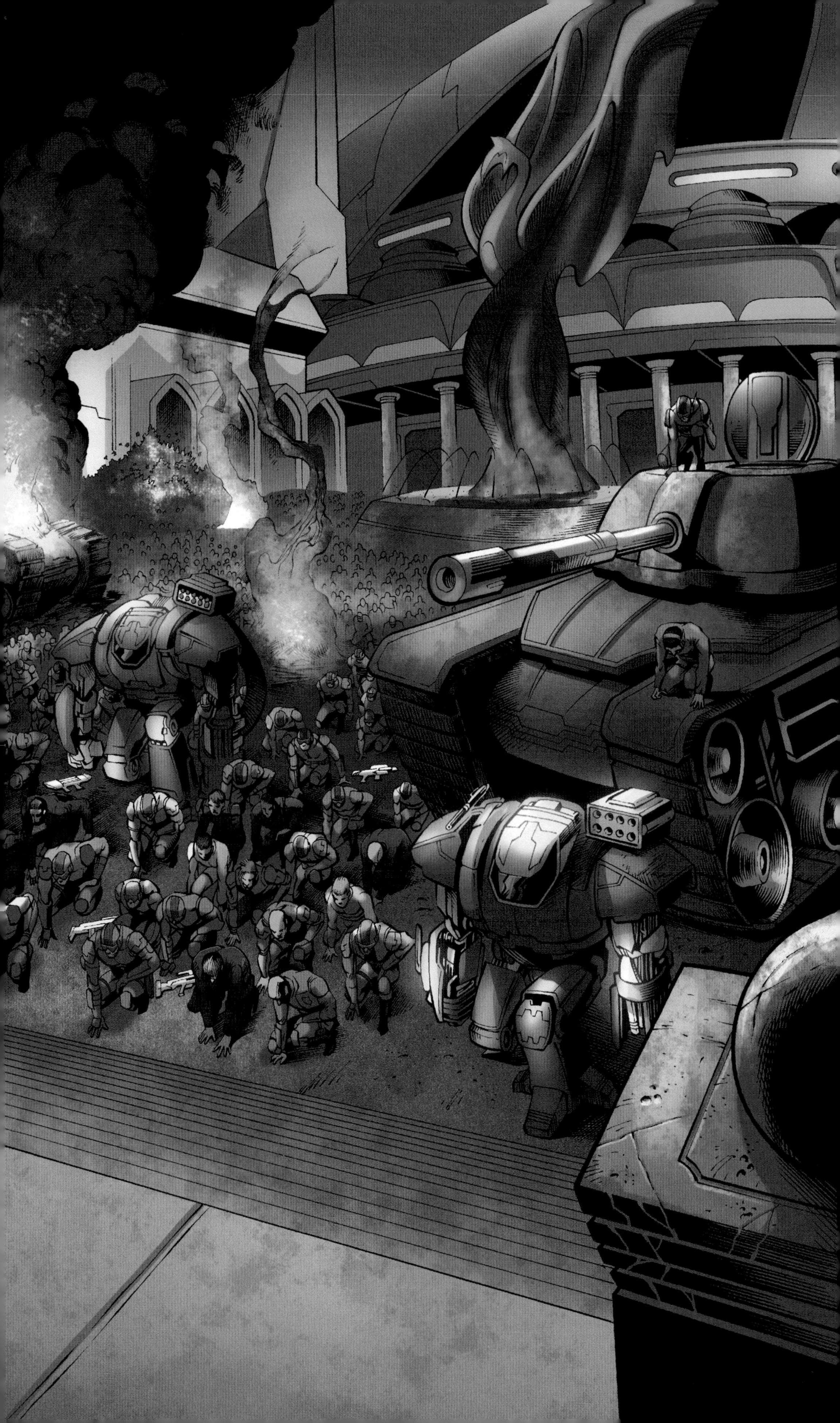

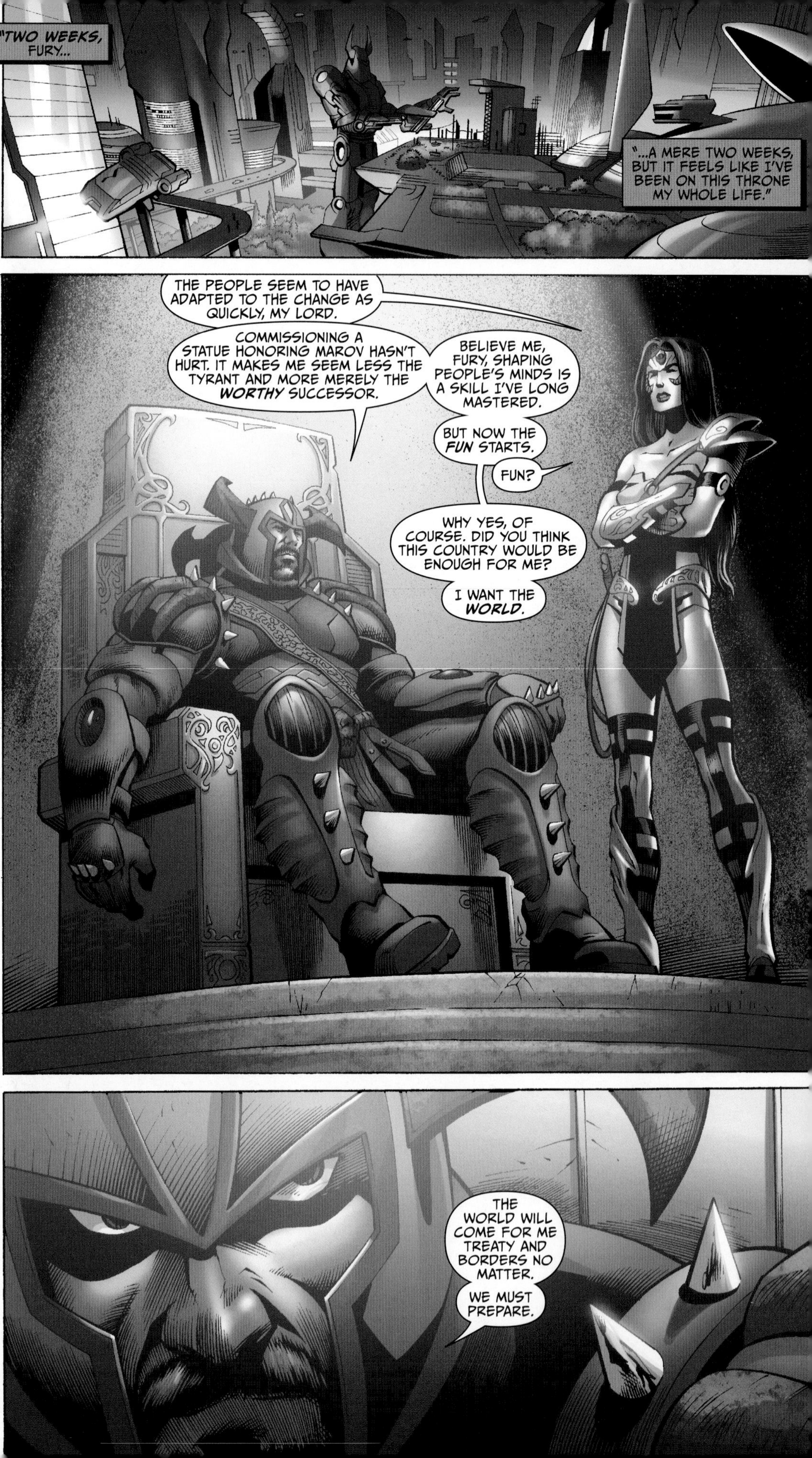
"TWO WEEKS, FURY...
"...A MERE TWO WEEKS, BUT IT FEELS LIKE I'VE BEEN ON THIS THRONE MY WHOLE LIFE."
THE PEOPLE SEEM TO HAVE ADAPTED TO THE CHANGE AS QUICKLY, MY LORD.
COMMISSIONING A STATUE HONORING MAROV HASN'T HURT. IT MAKES ME SEEM LESS THE TYRANT AND MORE MERELY THE WORTHY SUCCESSOR.
BELIEVE ME, FURY, SHAPING PEOPLE'S MINDS IS A SKILL I'VE LONG MASTERED.
BUT NOW THE FUN STARTS.
FUN?
WHY YES, OF COURSE. DID YOU THINK THIS COUNTRY WOULD BE ENOUGH FOR ME?
I WANT THE WORLD.
THE WORLD WILL COME FOR ME TREATY AND BORDERS NO MATTER.
WE MUST PREPARE.

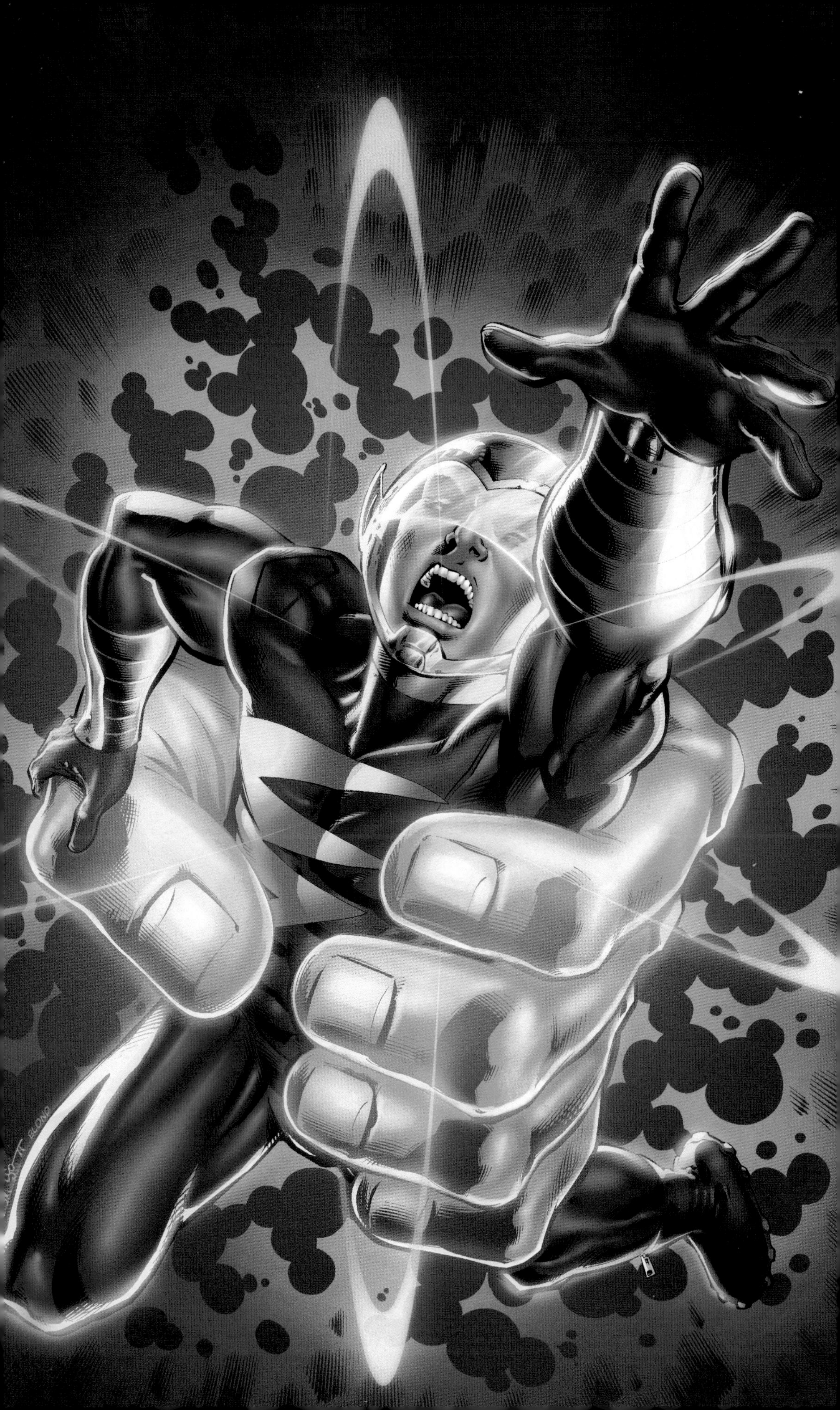

JAMES ROBINSON writer NICOLA SCOTT penciller TREVOR SCOTT inker cover by NICOLA SCOTT, TREVOR SCOTT & BLOND

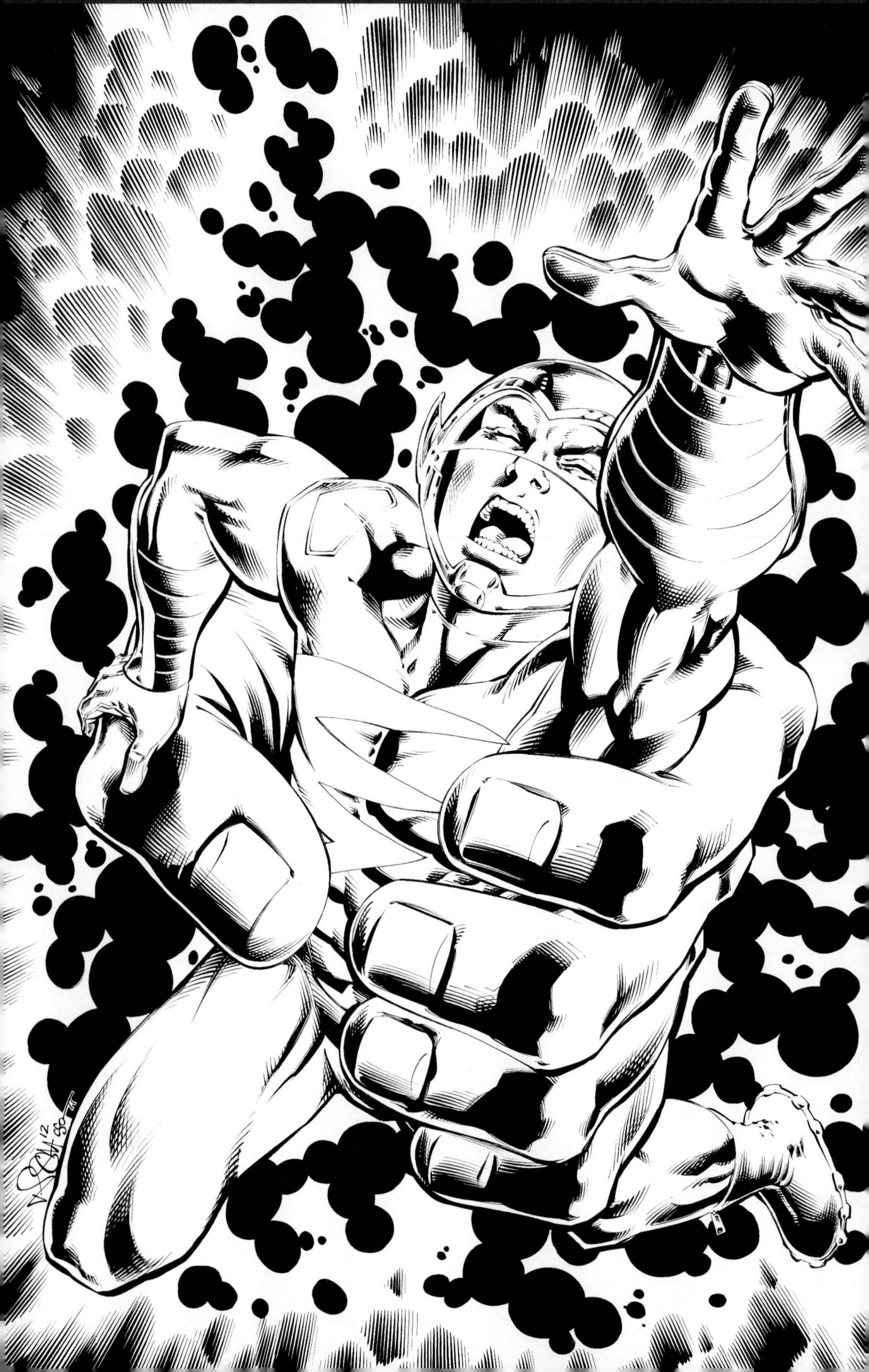

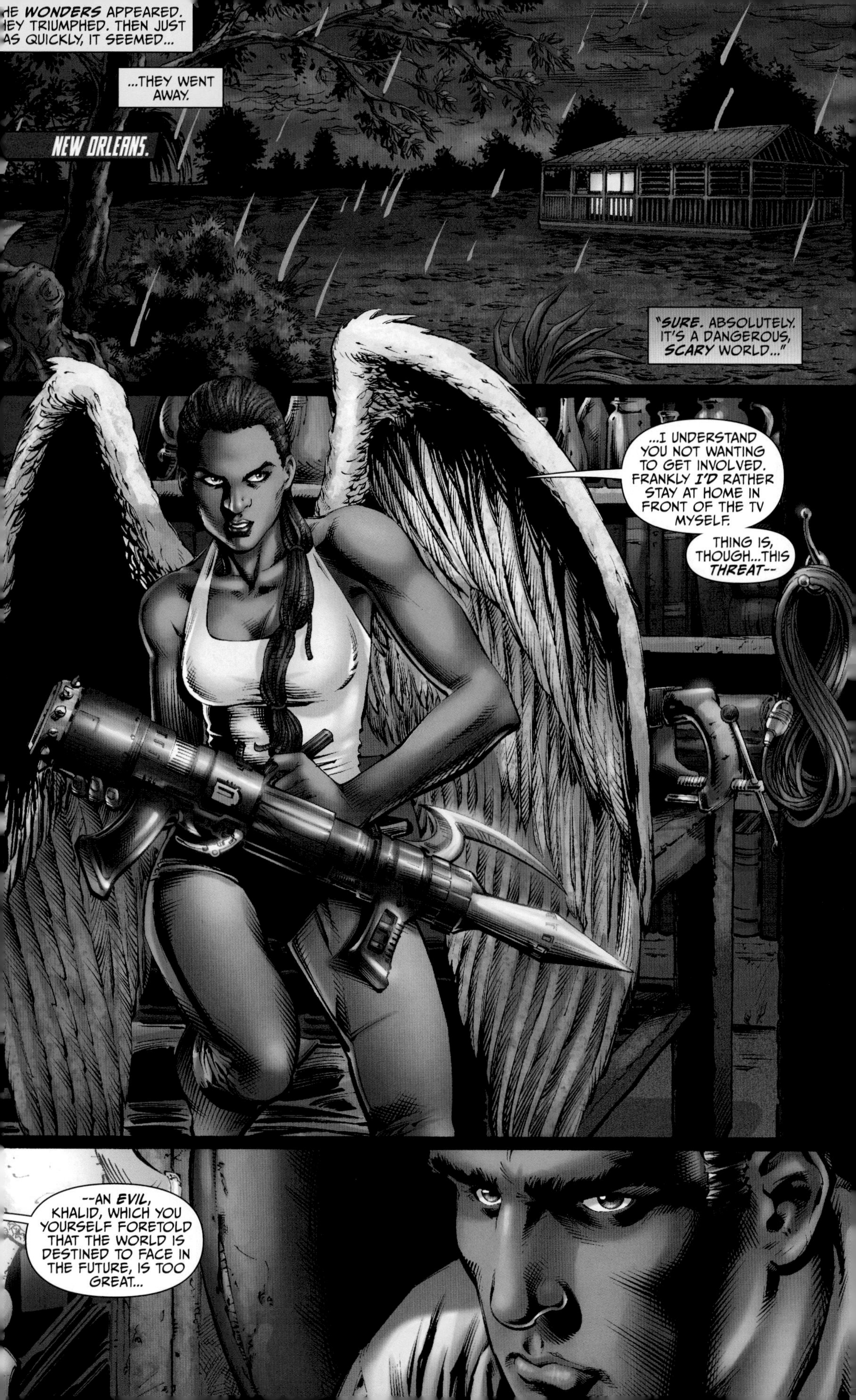

HE WONDERS APPEARED. HEY TRIUMPHED. THEN JUST AS QUICKLY, IT SEEMED...
...THEY WENT AWAY.
NEW ORLEANS.
"SURE. ABSOLUTELY. IT'S A DANGEROUS, SCARY WORLD..."
...I UNDERSTAND YOU NOT WANTING TO GET INVOLVED. FRANKLY I'D RATHER STAY AT HOME IN FRONT OF THE TV MYSELF.
THING IS, THOUGH...THIS THREAT--
--AN EVIL, KHALID, WHICH YOU YOURSELF FORETOLD THAT THE WORLD IS DESTINED TO FACE IN THE FUTURE, IS TOO GREAT...

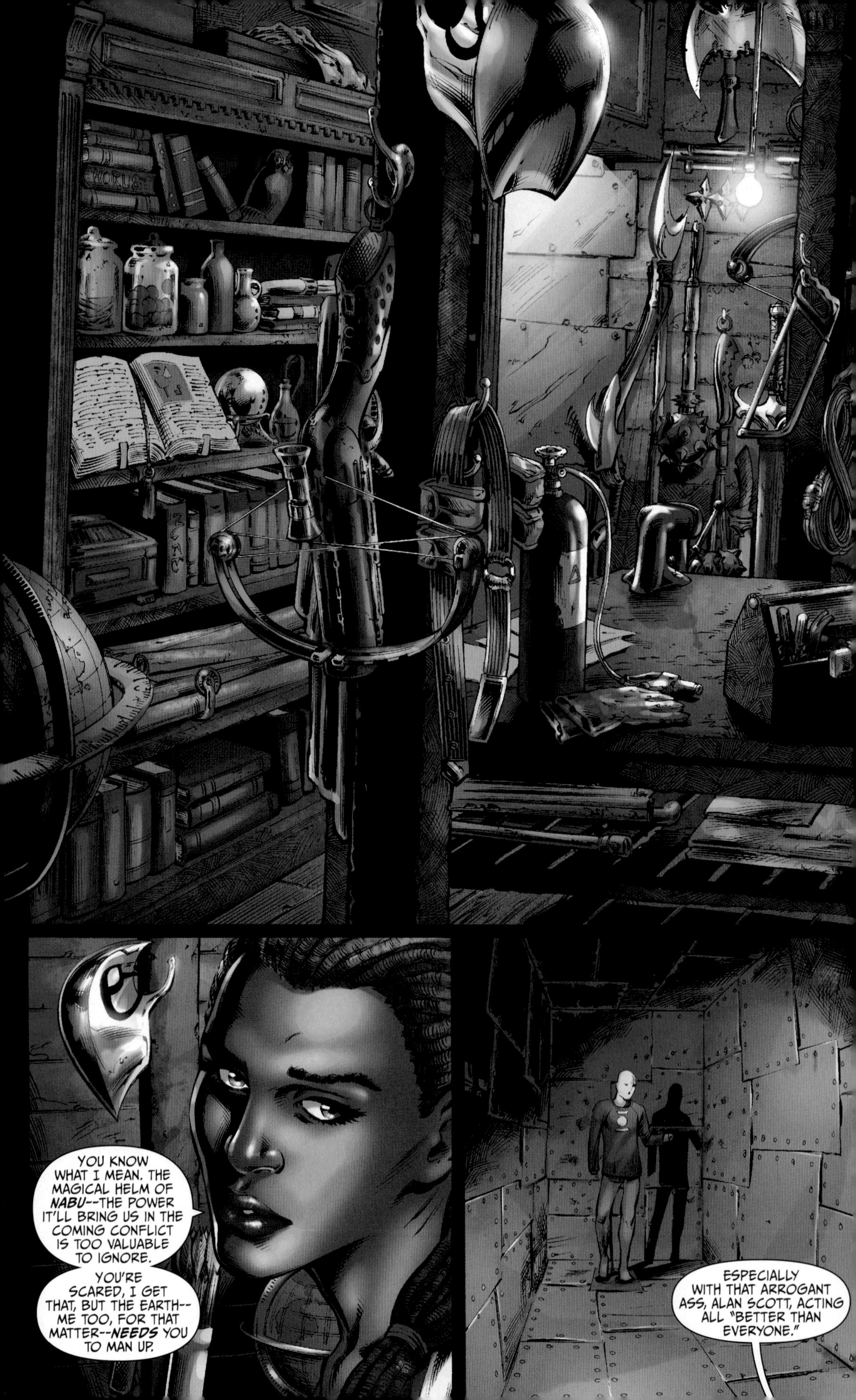

YOU KNOW WHAT I MEAN. THE MAGICAL HELM OF ***NABU***--THE POWER IT'LL BRING US IN THE COMING CONFLICT IS TOO VALUABLE TO IGNORE.
YOU'RE SCARED, I GET THAT, BUT THE EARTH--ME TOO, FOR THAT MATTER--***NEEDS*** YOU TO MAN UP.
ESPECIALLY WITH THAT ARROGANT ASS, ALAN SCOTT, ACTING ALL "BETTER THAN EVERYONE."

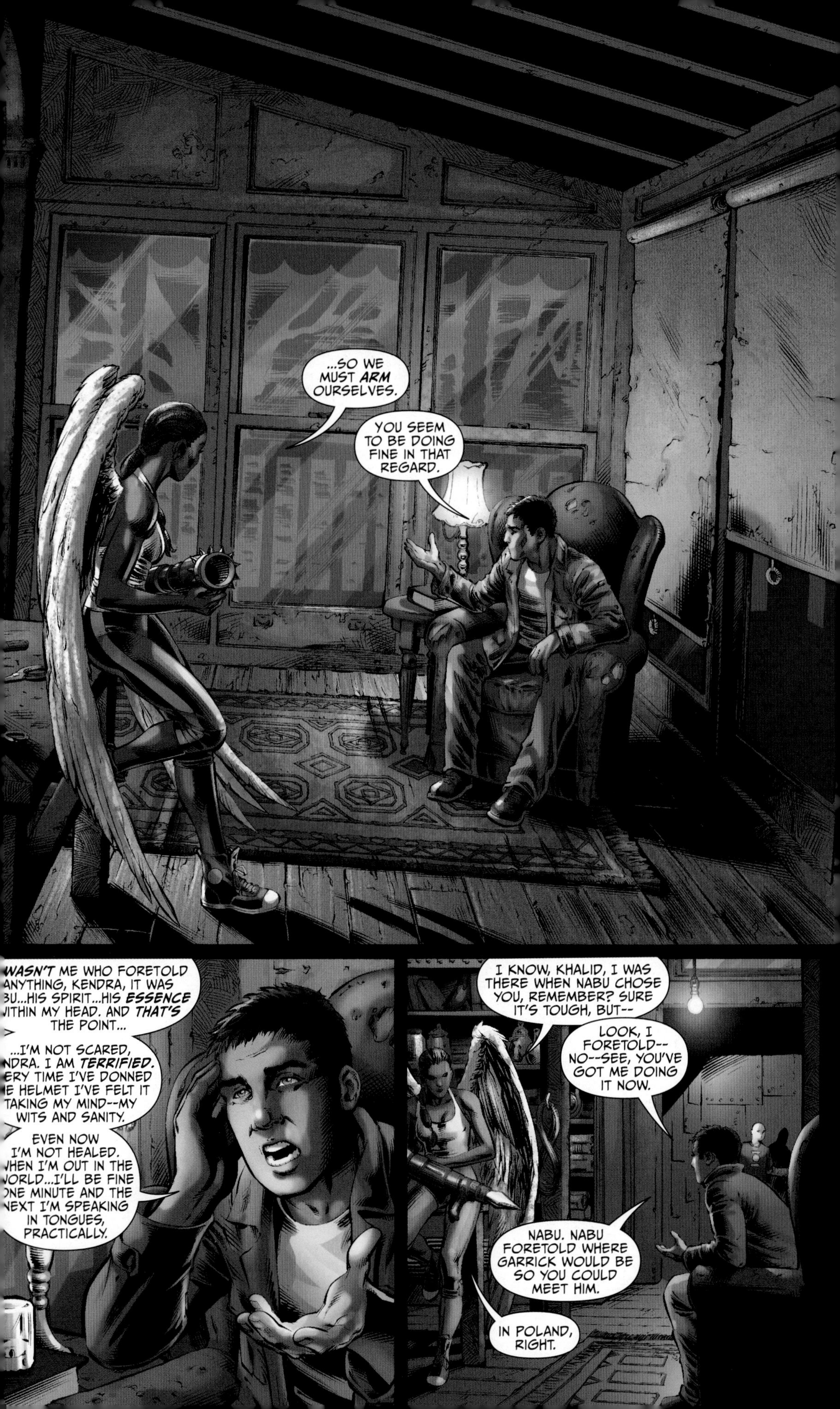

...SO WE MUST ARM OURSELVES.
YOU SEEM TO BE DOING FINE IN THAT REGARD.
WASN'T ME WHO FORETOLD ANYTHING, KENDRA, IT WAS BU...HIS SPIRIT...HIS ESSENCE WITHIN MY HEAD. AND THAT'S THE POINT...
...I'M NOT SCARED, NDRA. I AM TERRIFIED. ERY TIME I'VE DONNED E HELMET I'VE FELT IT TAKING MY MIND--MY WITS AND SANITY.
EVEN NOW I'M NOT HEALED. WHEN I'M OUT IN THE WORLD...I'LL BE FINE ONE MINUTE AND THE NEXT I'M SPEAKING IN TONGUES, PRACTICALLY.
I KNOW, KHALID, I WAS THERE WHEN NABU CHOSE YOU, REMEMBER? SURE IT'S TOUGH, BUT--
LOOK, I FORETOLD-- NO--SEE, YOU'VE GOT ME DOING IT NOW.
NABU. NABU FORETOLD WHERE GARRICK WOULD BE SO YOU COULD MEET HIM.
IN POLAND, RIGHT.

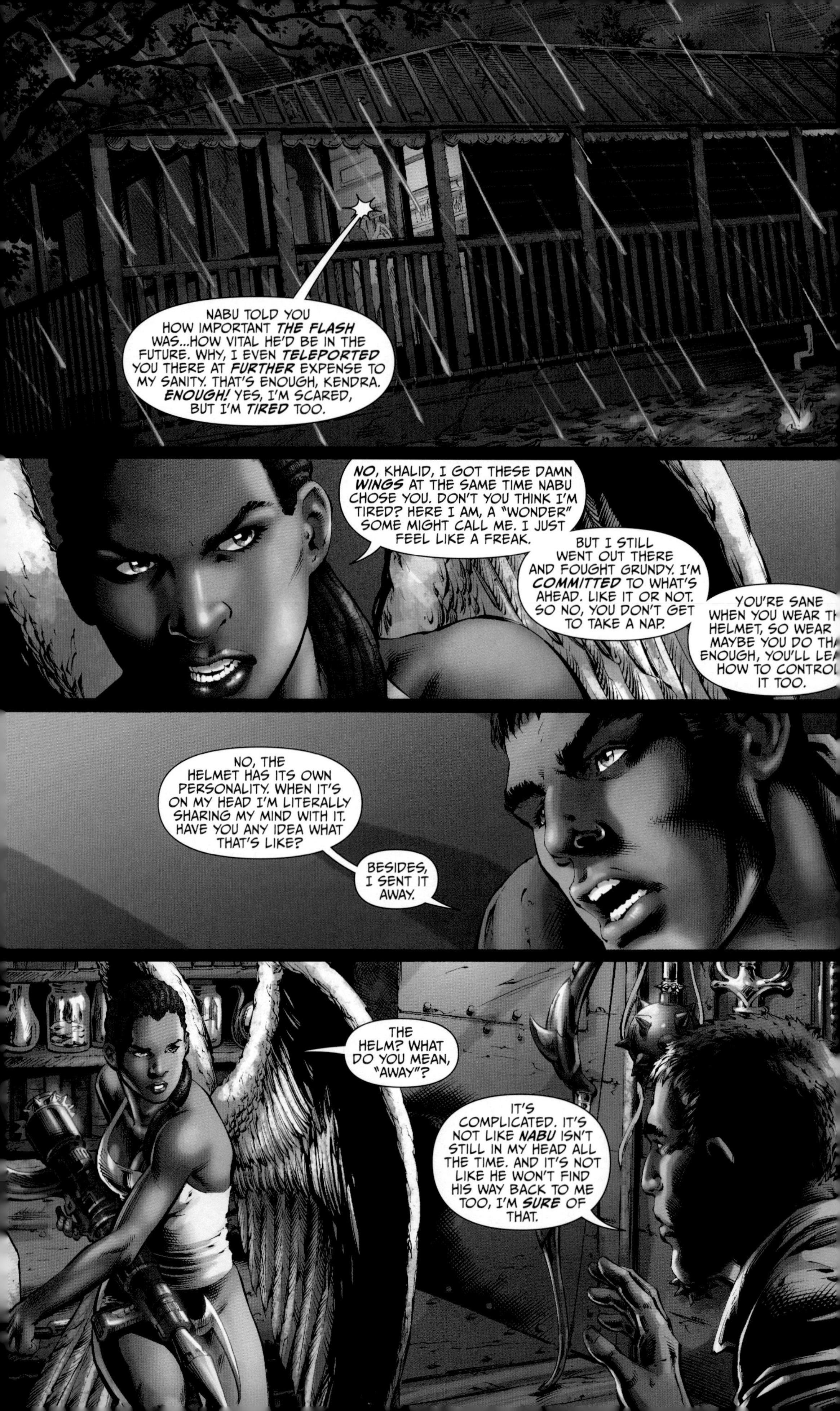
NABU TOLD YOU HOW IMPORTANT THE FLASH WAS...HOW VITAL HE'D BE IN THE FUTURE. WHY, I EVEN TELEPORTED YOU THERE AT FURTHER EXPENSE TO MY SANITY. THAT'S ENOUGH, KENDRA. ENOUGH! YES, I'M SCARED, BUT I'M TIRED TOO.
NO, KHALID, I GOT THESE DAMN WINGS AT THE SAME TIME NABU CHOSE YOU. DON'T YOU THINK I'M TIRED? HERE I AM, A "WONDER" SOME MIGHT CALL ME. I JUST FEEL LIKE A FREAK.
BUT I STILL WENT OUT THERE AND FOUGHT GRUNDY. I'M COMMITTED TO WHAT'S AHEAD. LIKE IT OR NOT. SO NO, YOU DON'T GET TO TAKE A NAP.
YOU'RE SANE WHEN YOU WEAR TH HELMET, SO WEAR MAYBE YOU DO TH ENOUGH, YOU'LL LEA HOW TO CONTRO IT TOO.
NO, THE HELMET HAS ITS OWN PERSONALITY. WHEN IT'S ON MY HEAD I'M LITERALLY SHARING MY MIND WITH IT. HAVE YOU ANY IDEA WHAT THAT'S LIKE?
BESIDES, I SENT IT AWAY.
THE HELM? WHAT DO YOU MEAN, "AWAY"?
IT'S COMPLICATED. IT'S NOT LIKE NABU ISN'T STILL IN MY HEAD ALL THE TIME. AND IT'S NOT LIKE HE WON'T FIND HIS WAY BACK TO ME TOO, I'M SURE OF THAT.

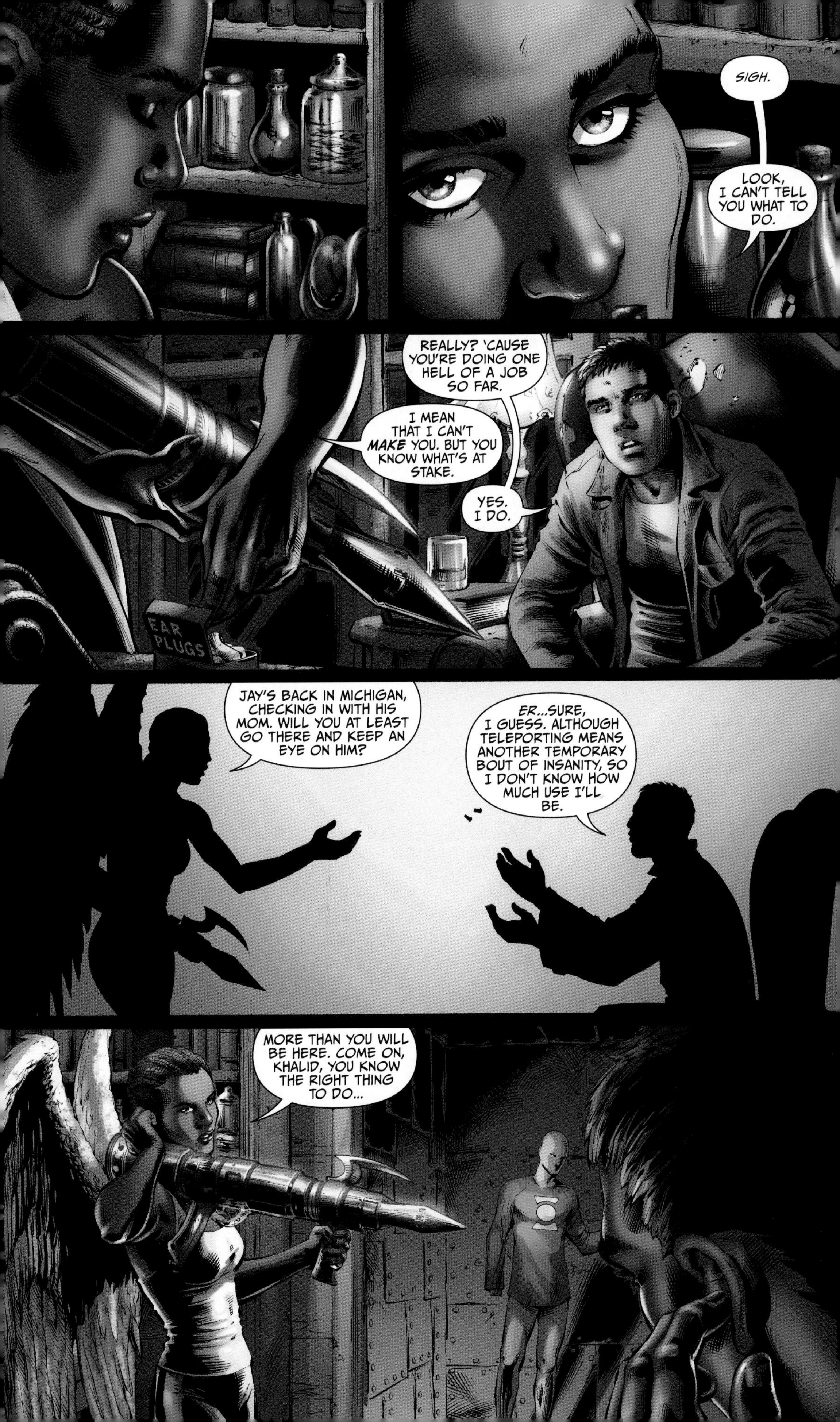
SIGH.
LOOK, I CAN'T TELL YOU WHAT TO DO.
REALLY? 'CAUSE YOU'RE DOING ONE HELL OF A JOB SO FAR.
I MEAN THAT I CAN'T MAKE YOU. BUT YOU KNOW WHAT'S AT STAKE.
YES. I DO.
EAR PLUGS
JAY'S BACK IN MICHIGAN, CHECKING IN WITH HIS MOM. WILL YOU AT LEAST GO THERE AND KEEP AN EYE ON HIM?
ER...SURE, I GUESS. ALTHOUGH TELEPORTING MEANS ANOTHER TEMPORARY BOUT OF INSANITY, SO I DON'T KNOW HOW MUCH USE I'LL BE.
MORE THAN YOU WILL BE HERE. COME ON, KHALID, YOU KNOW THE RIGHT THING TO DO...

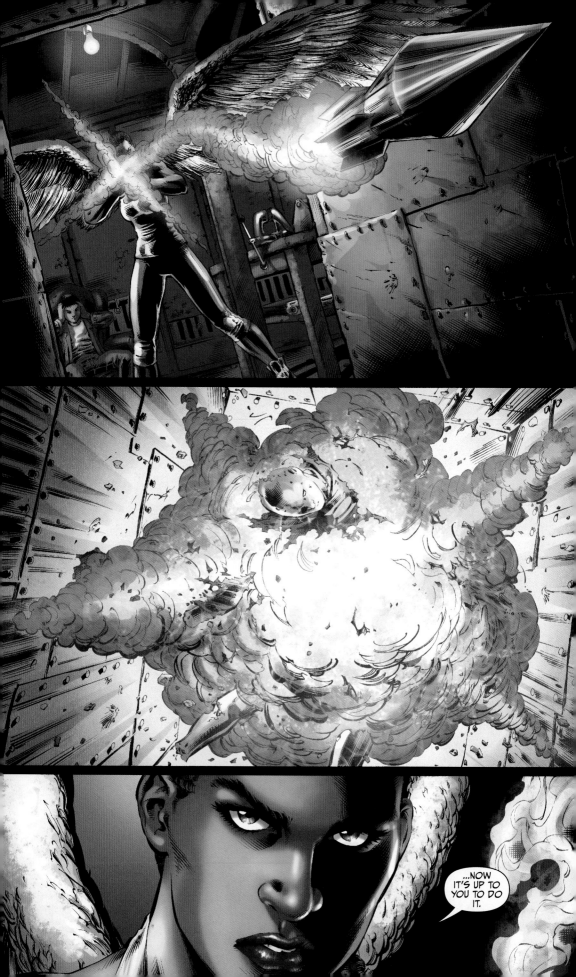

...NOW IT'S UP TO YOU TO DO IT.

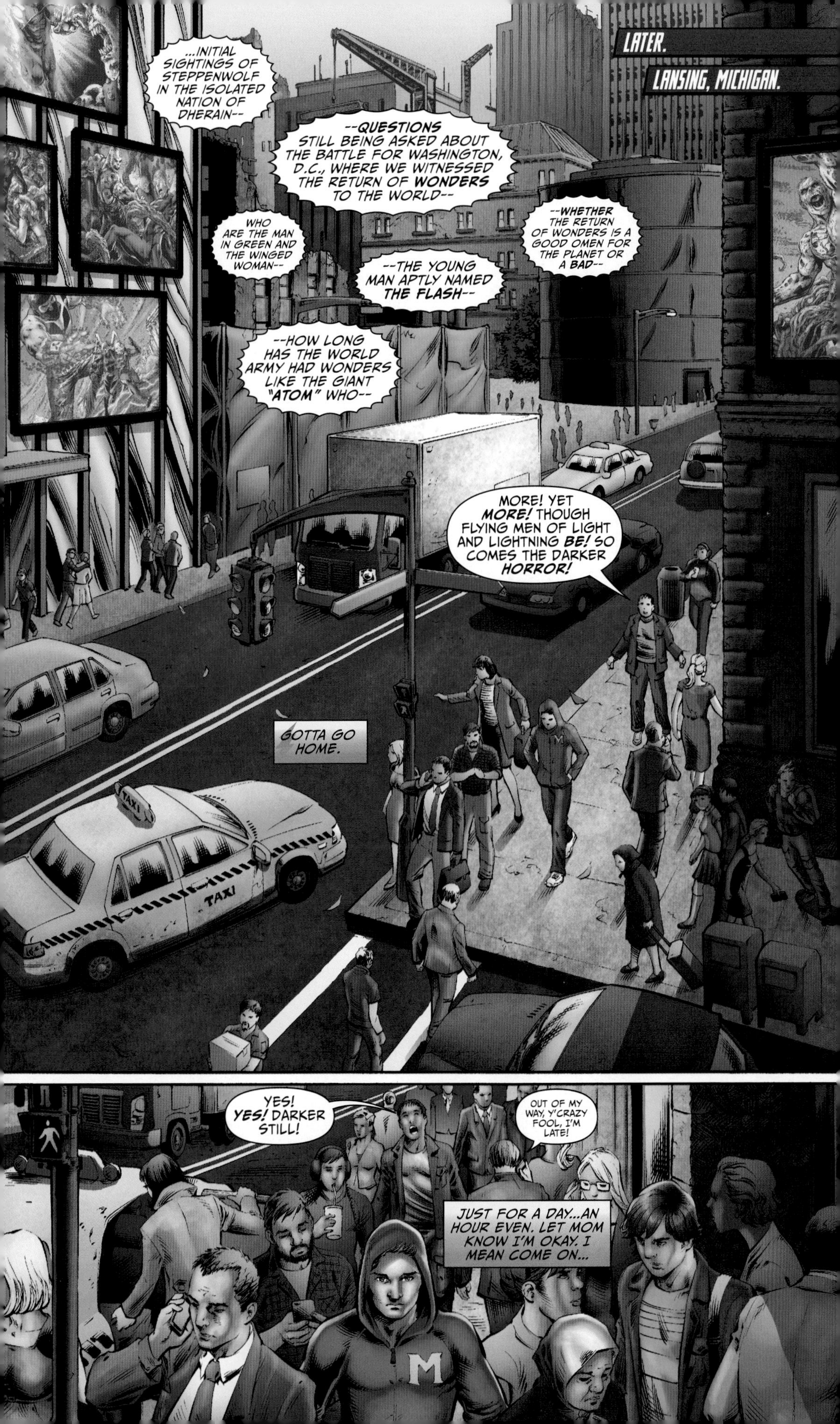
LATER.
LANSING, MICHIGAN.
...INITIAL SIGHTINGS OF STEPPENWOLF IN THE ISOLATED NATION OF DHERAIN--
--QUESTIONS STILL BEING ASKED ABOUT THE BATTLE FOR WASHINGTON, D.C., WHERE WE WITNESSED THE RETURN OF WONDERS TO THE WORLD--
WHO ARE THE MAN IN GREEN AND THE WINGED WOMAN--
--THE YOUNG MAN APTLY NAMED THE FLASH--
--WHETHER THE RETURN OF WONDERS IS A GOOD OMEN FOR THE PLANET OR A BAD--
--HOW LONG HAS THE WORLD ARMY HAD WONDERS LIKE THE GIANT "ATOM" WHO--
MORE! YET MORE! THOUGH FLYING MEN OF LIGHT AND LIGHTNING BE! SO COMES THE DARKER HORROR!
GOTTA GO HOME.
TAXI
TAXI
YES! YES! DARKER STILL!
OUT OF MY WAY, Y'CRAZY FOOL, I'M LATE!
JUST FOR A DAY...AN HOUR EVEN. LET MOM KNOW I'M OKAY. I MEAN COME ON...

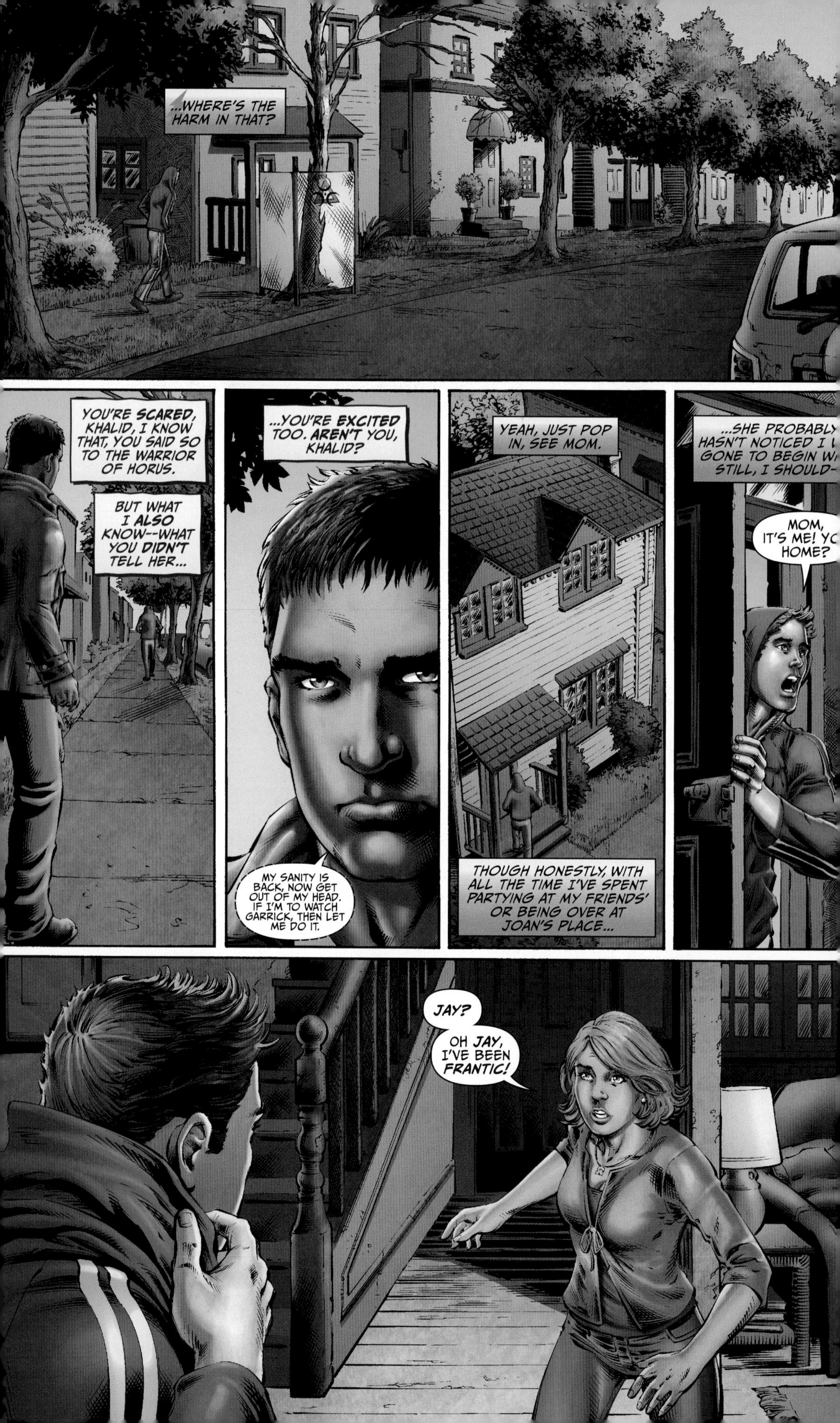
...WHERE'S THE HARM IN THAT?
YOU'RE SCARED, KHALID, I KNOW THAT, YOU SAID SO TO THE WARRIOR OF HORUS.
BUT WHAT I ALSO KNOW--WHAT YOU DIDN'T TELL HER...
...YOU'RE EXCITED TOO. AREN'T YOU, KHALID?
MY SANITY IS BACK, NOW GET OUT OF MY HEAD. IF I'M TO WATCH GARRICK, THEN LET ME DO IT.
YEAH, JUST POP IN, SEE MOM.
THOUGH HONESTLY, WITH ALL THE TIME I'VE SPENT PARTYING AT MY FRIENDS' OR BEING OVER AT JOAN'S PLACE...
...SHE PROBABLY HASN'T NOTICED I
GONE TO BEGIN W
STILL, I SHOULD-
MOM, IT'S ME! YO
HOME?
JAY?
OH JAY, I'VE BEEN FRANTIC!

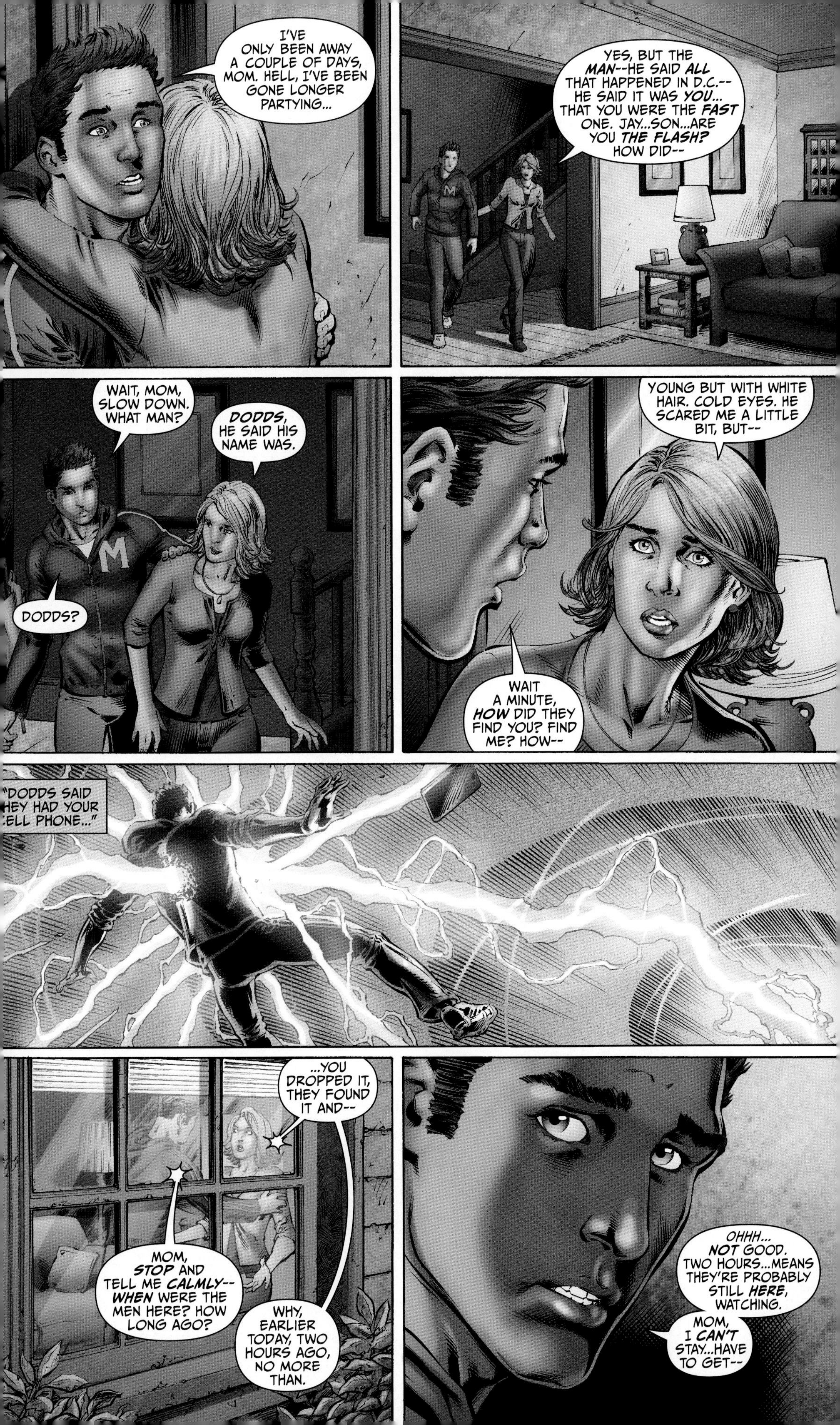
I'VE ONLY BEEN AWAY A COUPLE OF DAYS, MOM. HELL, I'VE BEEN GONE LONGER PARTYING...
YES, BUT THE MAN--HE SAID ALL THAT HAPPENED IN D.C.-- HE SAID IT WAS YOU... THAT YOU WERE THE FAST ONE. JAY...SON...ARE YOU THE FLASH? HOW DID--
WAIT, MOM, SLOW DOWN. WHAT MAN?
DODDS, HE SAID HIS NAME WAS.
DODDS?
YOUNG BUT WITH WHITE HAIR. COLD EYES. HE SCARED ME A LITTLE BIT, BUT--
WAIT A MINUTE, HOW DID THEY FIND YOU? FIND ME? HOW--
"DODDS SAID THEY HAD YOUR CELL PHONE..."
...YOU DROPPED IT, THEY FOUND IT AND--
MOM, STOP AND TELL ME CALMLY-- WHEN WERE THE MEN HERE? HOW LONG AGO?
WHY, EARLIER TODAY, TWO HOURS AGO, NO MORE THAN.
OHHH... NOT GOOD. TWO HOURS...MEANS THEY'RE PROBABLY STILL HERE, WATCHING.
MOM, I CAN'T STAY...HAVE TO GET--

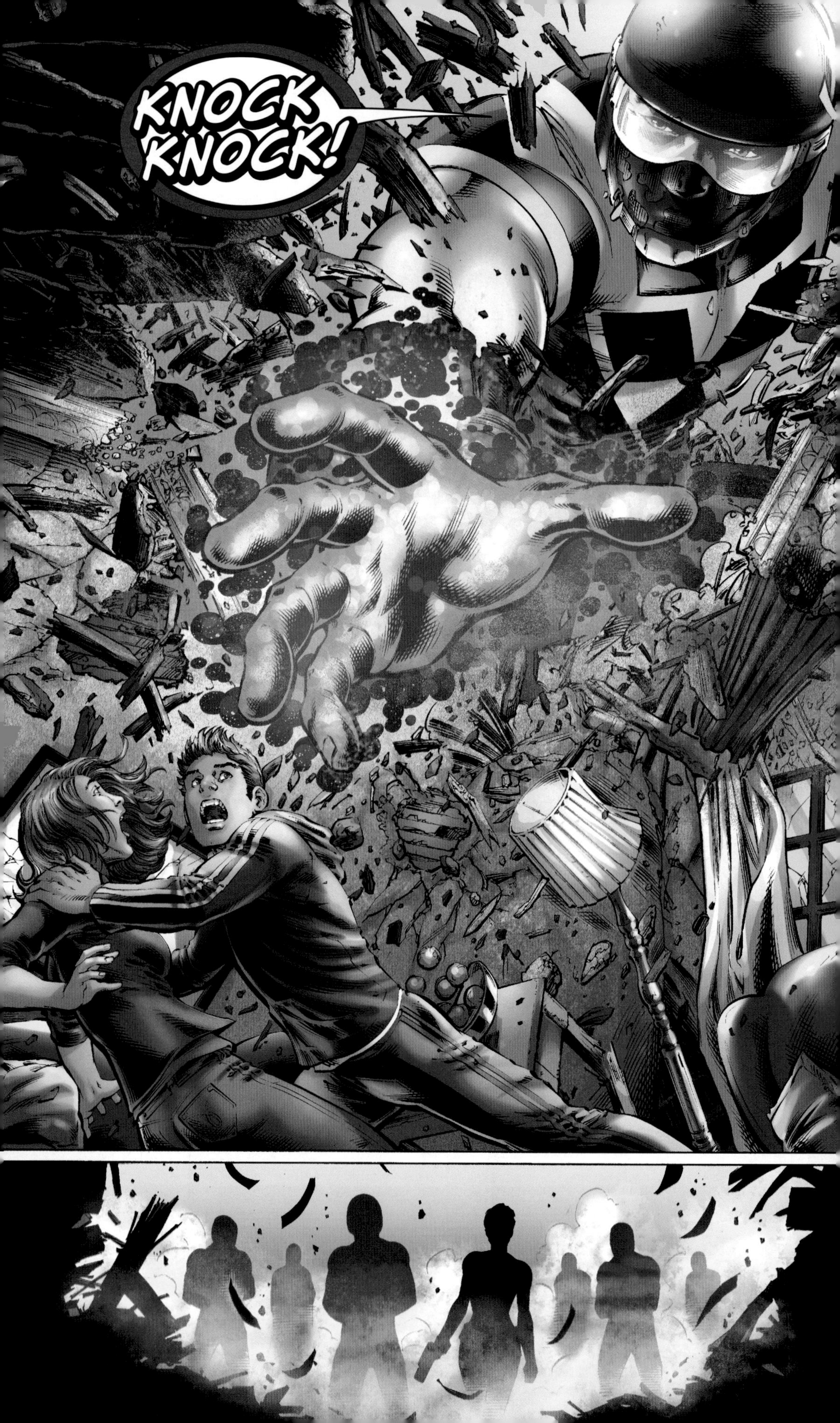
KNOCK KNOCK!

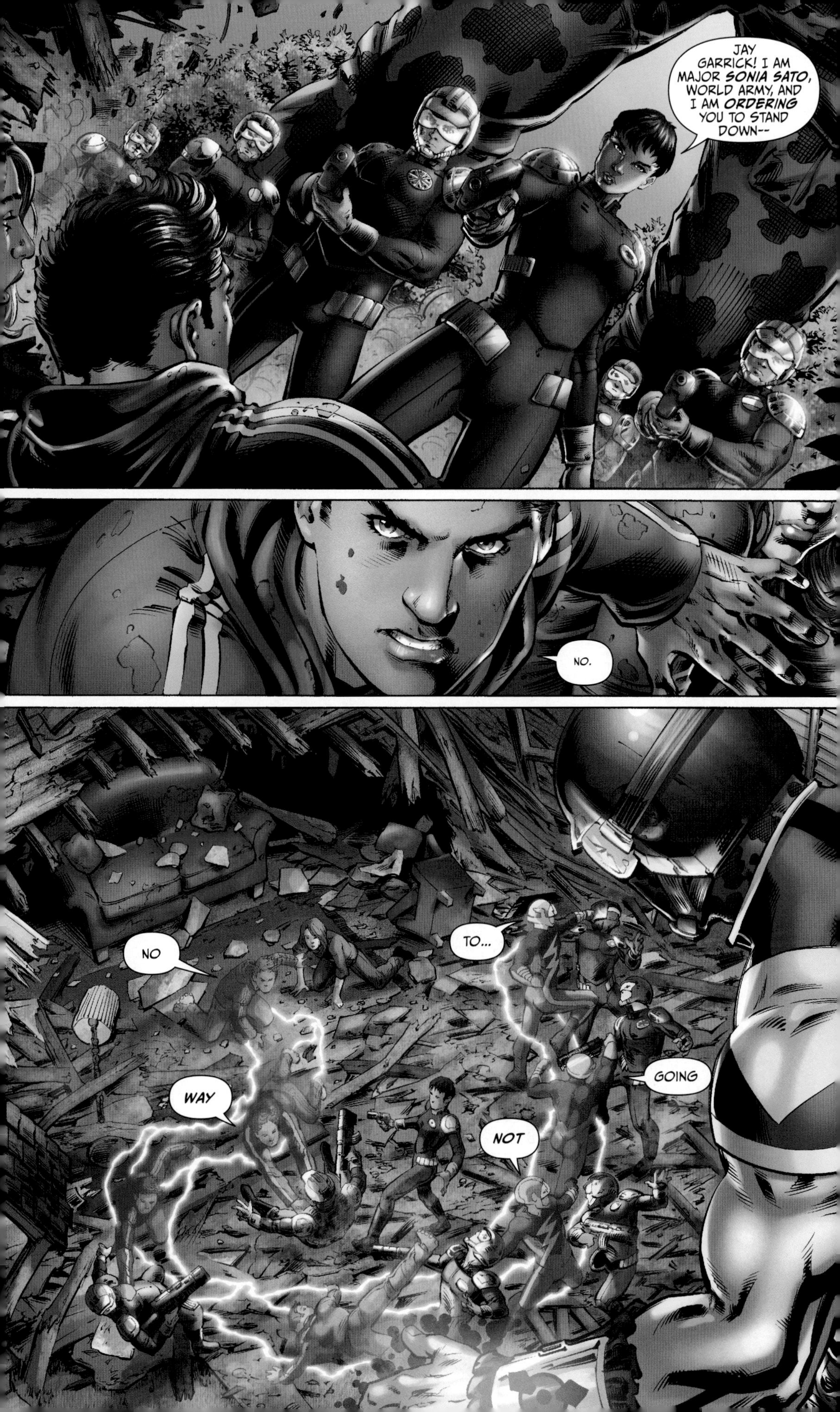
JAY GARRICK! I AM MAJOR SONIA SATO, WORLD ARMY, AND I AM ORDERING YOU TO STAND DOWN--
NO.
NO
WAY
TO...
NOT
GOING

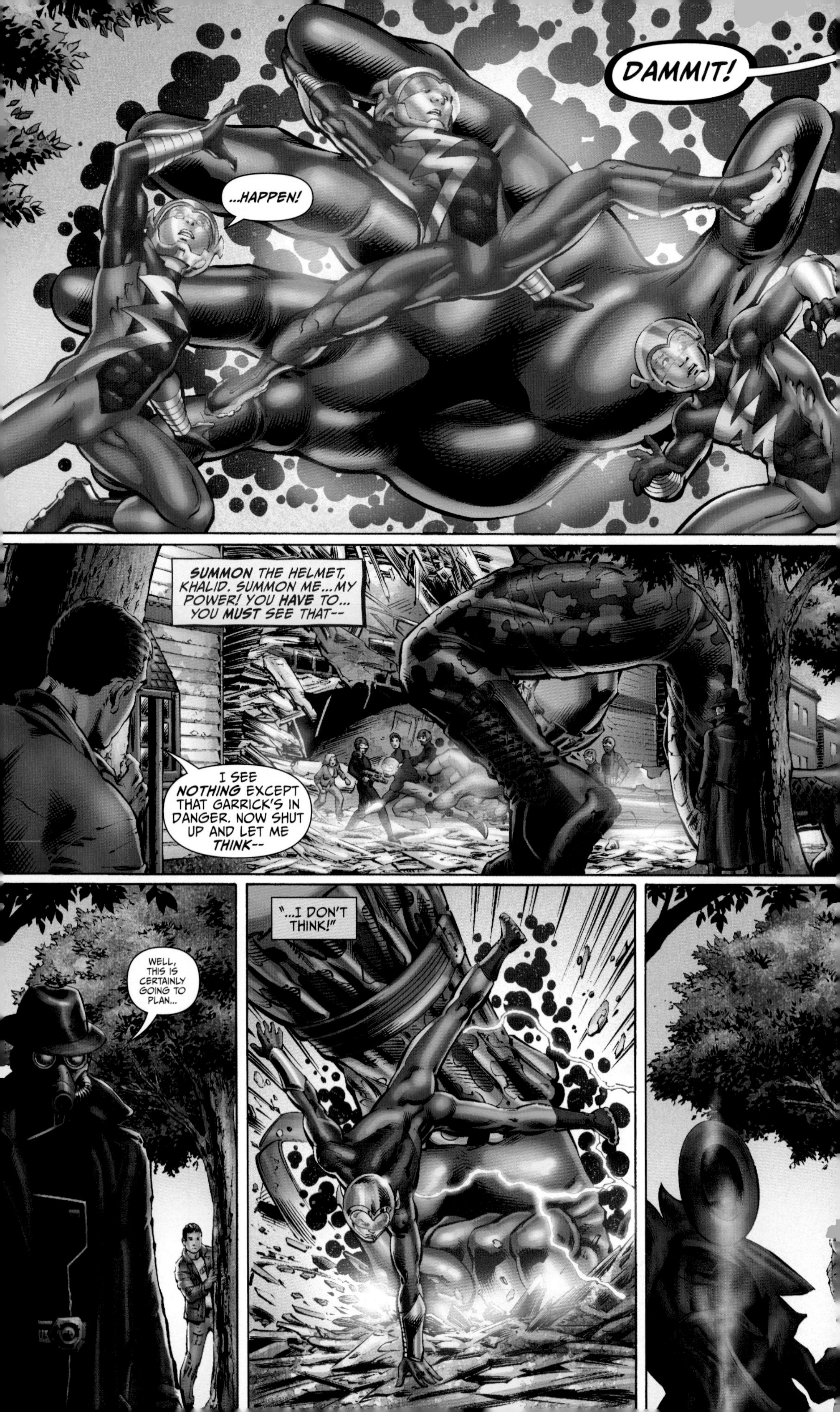
DAMMIT!
...HAPPEN!
SUMMON THE HELMET, KHALID. SUMMON ME...MY POWER! YOU HAVE TO... YOU MUST SEE THAT--
I SEE NOTHING EXCEPT THAT GARRICK'S IN DANGER. NOW SHUT UP AND LET ME THINK--
WELL, THIS IS CERTAINLY GOING TO PLAN...
"...I DON'T THINK!"

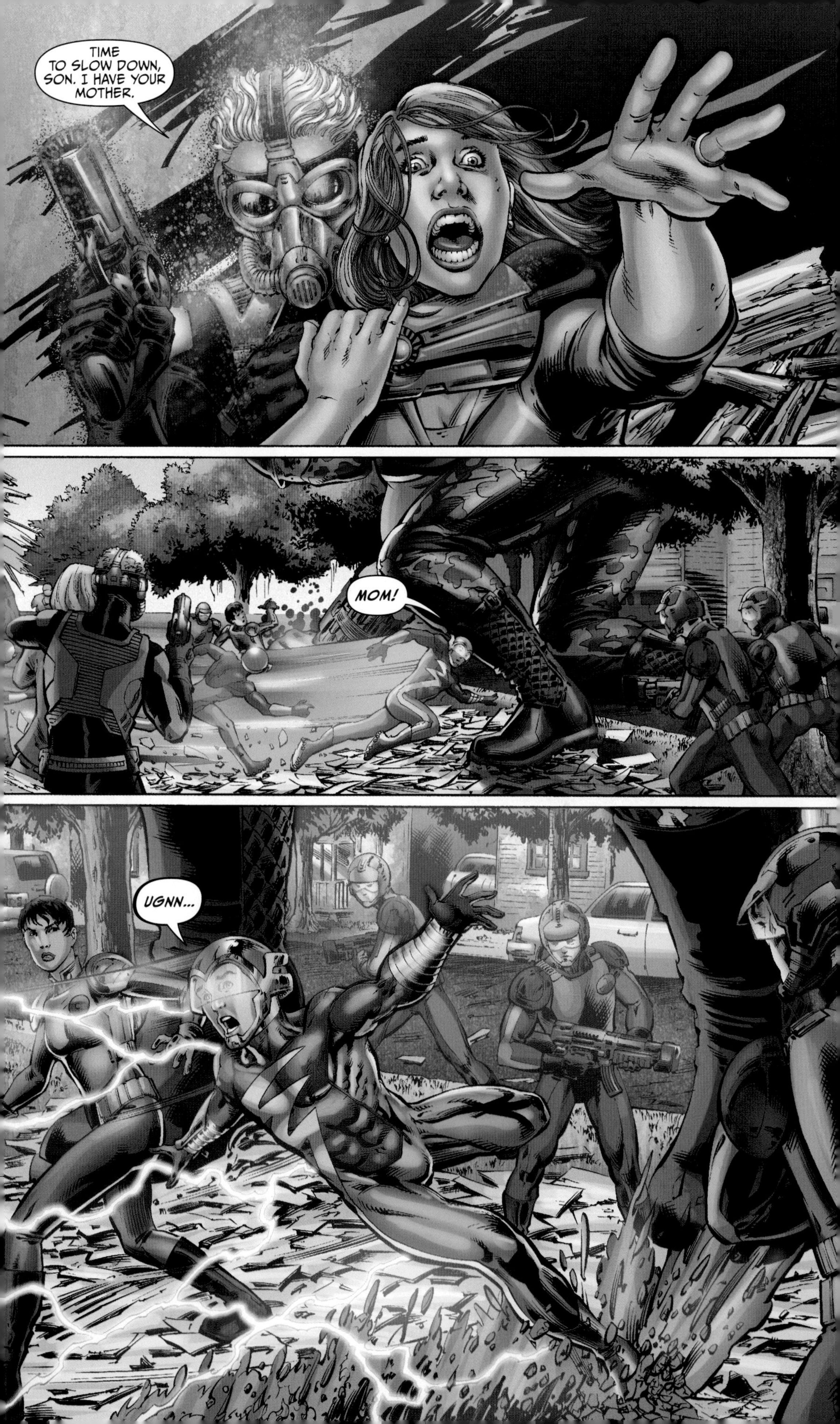
TIME TO SLOW DOWN, SON. I HAVE YOUR MOTHER.
MOM!
UGNN...

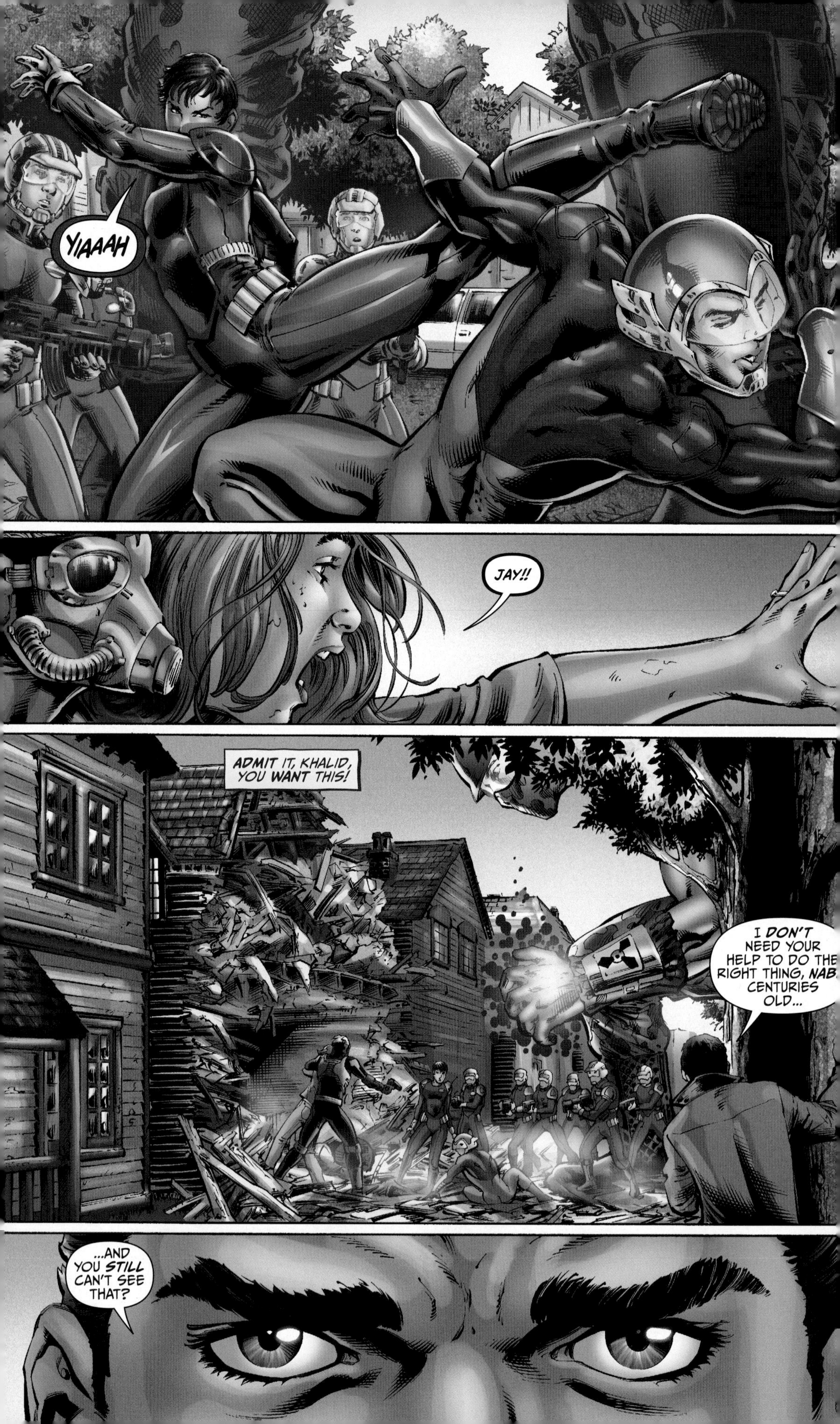
YIAAAH
JAY!!
ADMIT IT, KHALID, YOU WANT THIS!
I DON'T NEED YOUR HELP TO DO THE RIGHT THING, NABU. CENTURIES OLD...
...AND YOU STILL CAN'T SEE THAT?

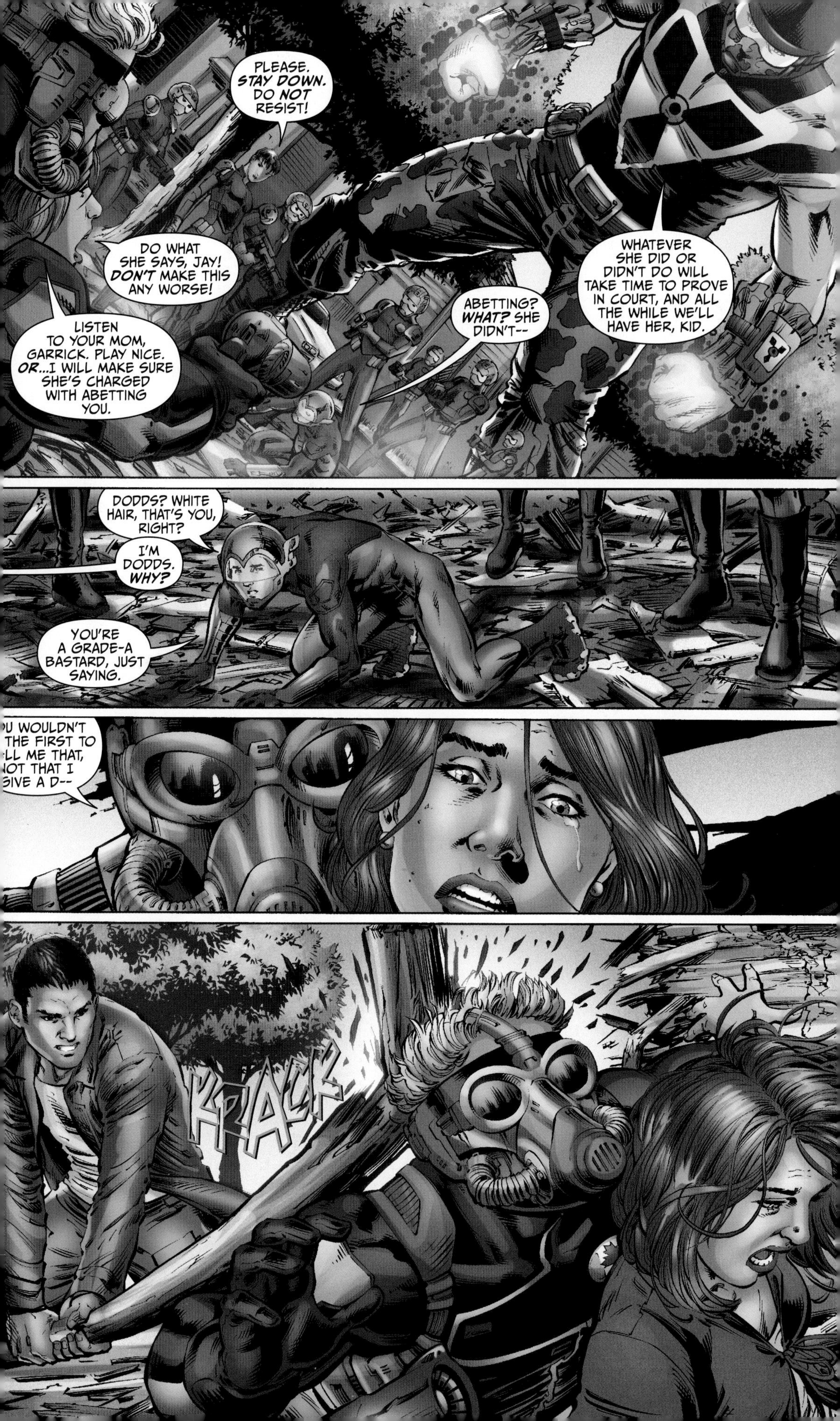
PLEASE. STAY DOWN. DO NOT RESIST!
DO WHAT SHE SAYS, JAY! DON'T MAKE THIS ANY WORSE!
LISTEN TO YOUR MOM, GARRICK. PLAY NICE. OR...I WILL MAKE SURE SHE'S CHARGED WITH ABETTING YOU.
ABETTING? WHAT? SHE DIDN'T--
WHATEVER SHE DID OR DIDN'T DO WILL TAKE TIME TO PROVE IN COURT, AND ALL THE WHILE WE'LL HAVE HER, KID.
DODDS? WHITE HAIR, THAT'S YOU, RIGHT?
I'M DODDS. WHY?
YOU'RE A GRADE-A BASTARD, JUST SAYING.
OU WOULDN'T THE FIRST TO LL ME THAT, NOT THAT I GIVE A D--
KRACK

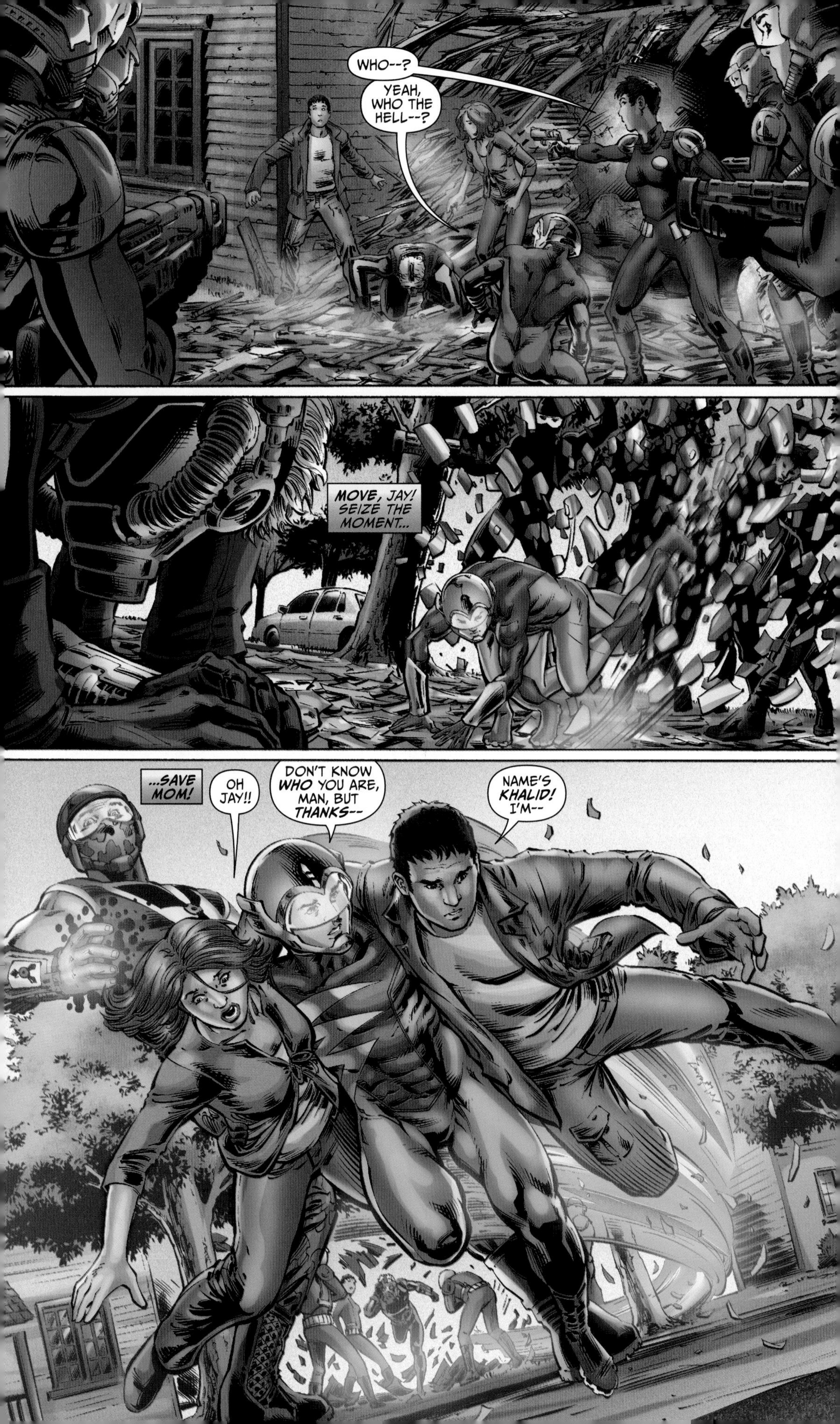
WHO--?
YEAH, WHO THE HELL--?
MOVE, JAY! SEIZE THE MOMENT...
...SAVE MOM!
OH JAY!!
DON'T KNOW WHO YOU ARE, MAN, BUT THANKS--
NAME'S KHALID! I'M--

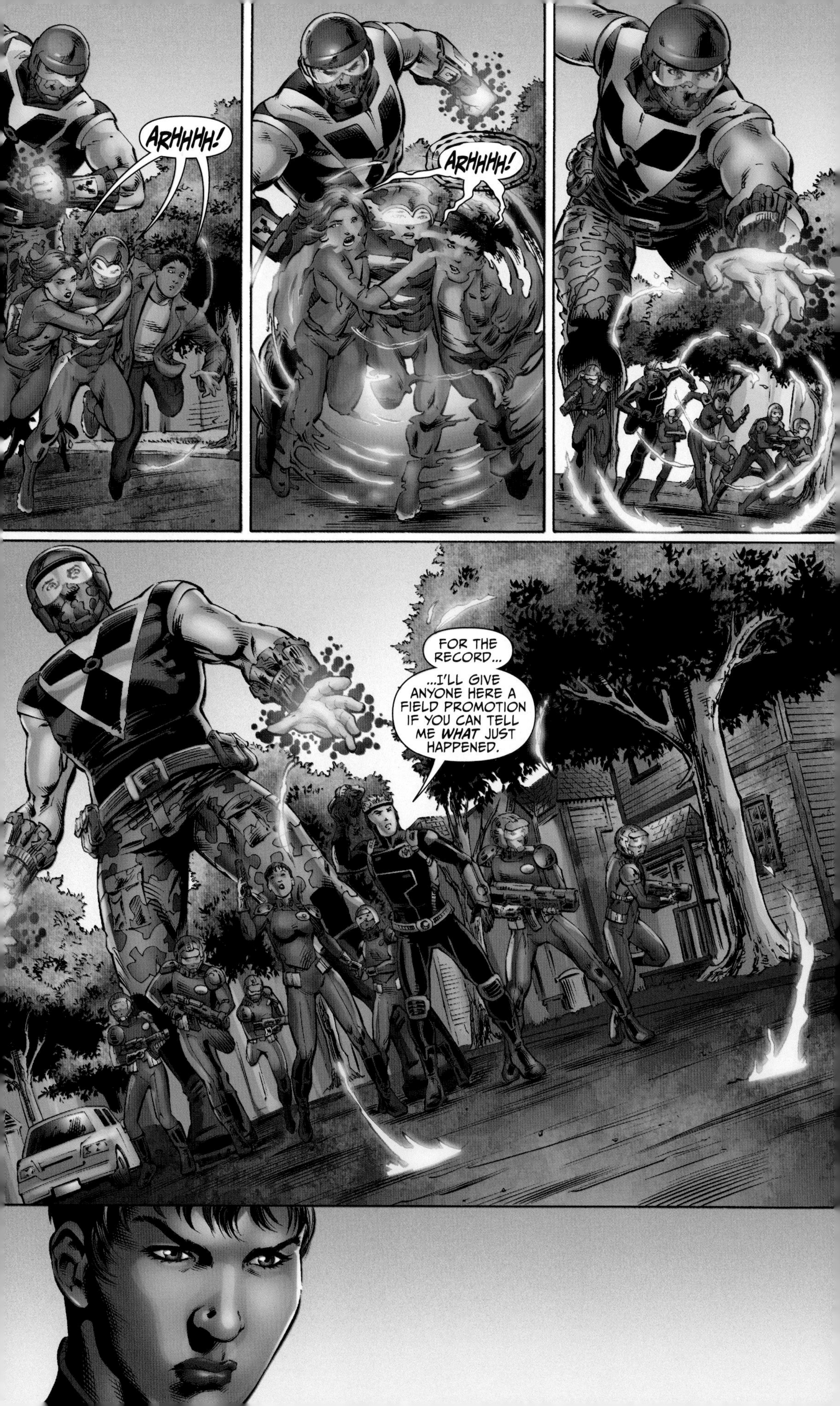
ARHHHH!
ARHHHH!
FOR THE RECORD...
...I'LL GIVE ANYONE HERE A FIELD PROMOTION IF YOU CAN TELL ME *WHAT* JUST HAPPENED.

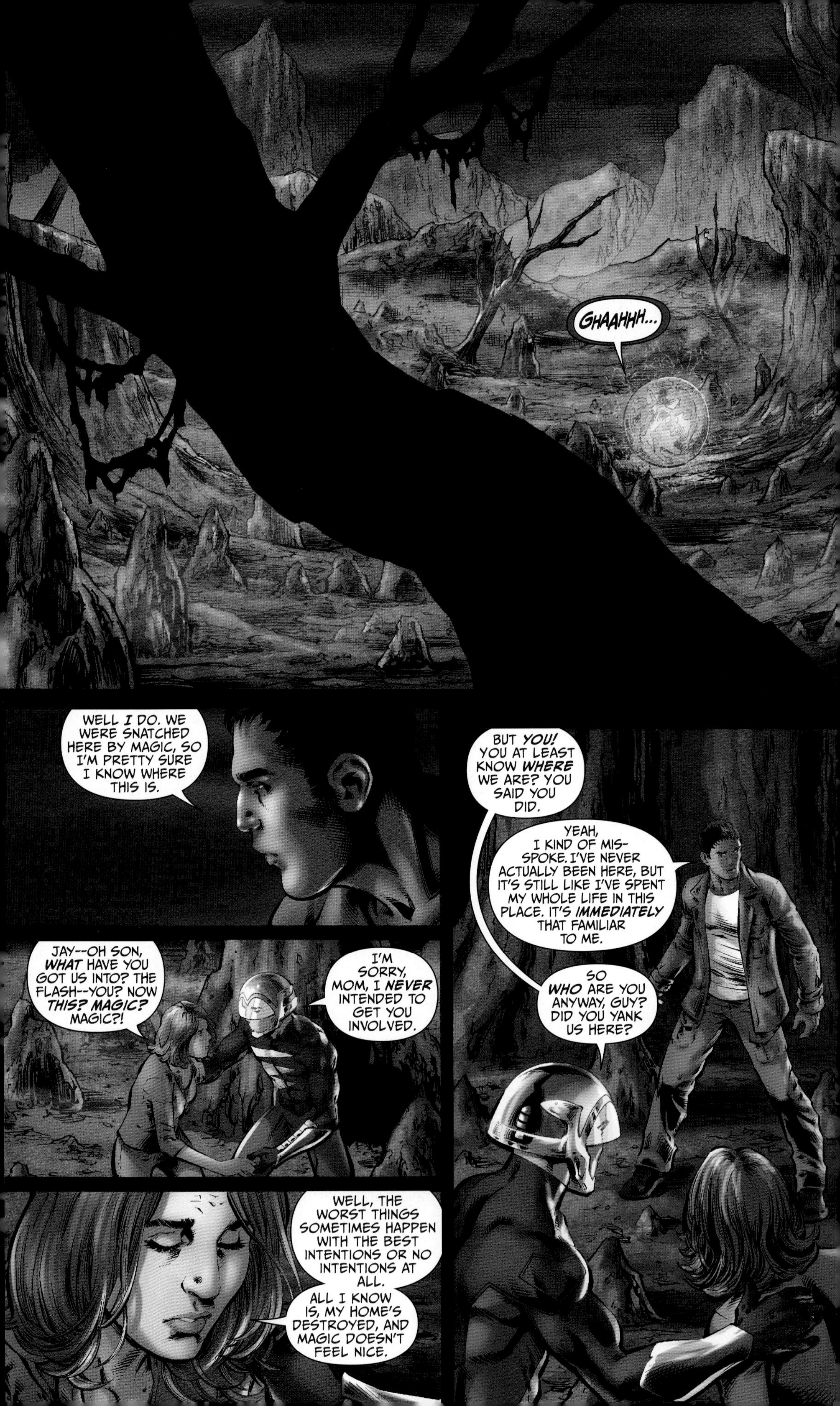
GHAAHHH...
WELL I DO. WE WERE SNATCHED HERE BY MAGIC, SO I'M PRETTY SURE I KNOW WHERE THIS IS.
JAY--OH SON, WHAT HAVE YOU GOT US INTO? THE FLASH--YOU? NOW THIS? MAGIC? MAGIC?!
I'M SORRY, MOM, I NEVER INTENDED TO GET YOU INVOLVED.
WELL, THE WORST THINGS SOMETIMES HAPPEN WITH THE BEST INTENTIONS OR NO INTENTIONS AT ALL.
ALL I KNOW IS, MY HOME'S DESTROYED, AND MAGIC DOESN'T FEEL NICE.
BUT YOU! YOU AT LEAST KNOW WHERE WE ARE? YOU SAID YOU DID.
YEAH, I KIND OF MIS-SPOKE. I'VE NEVER ACTUALLY BEEN HERE, BUT IT'S STILL LIKE I'VE SPENT MY WHOLE LIFE IN THIS PLACE. IT'S IMMEDIATELY THAT FAMILIAR TO ME.
SO WHO ARE YOU ANYWAY, GUY? DID YOU YANK US HERE?

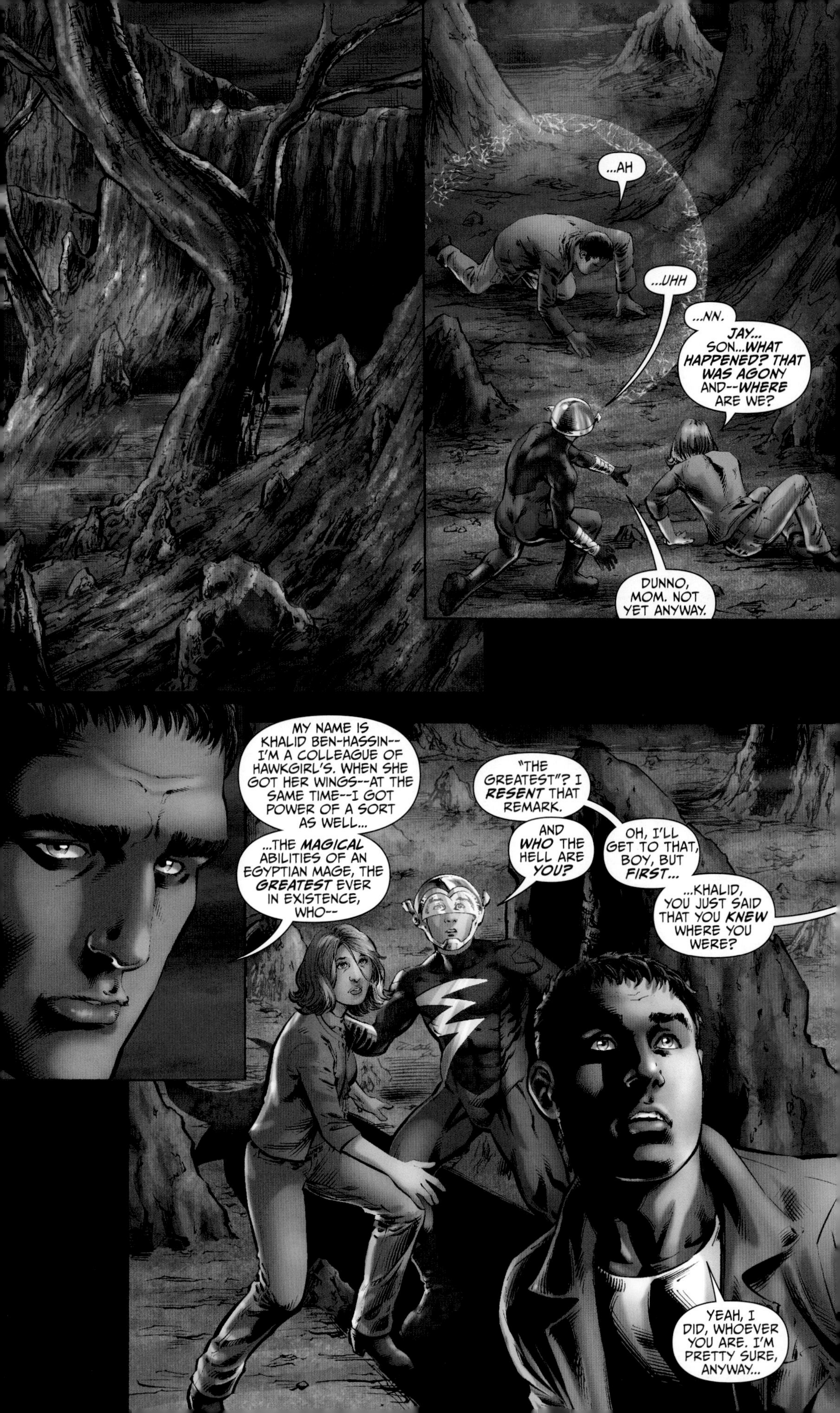
...AH
...UHH
...NN. JAY... SON...WHAT HAPPENED? THAT WAS AGONY AND--WHERE ARE WE?
DUNNO, MOM. NOT YET ANYWAY.
MY NAME IS KHALID BEN-HASSIN-- I'M A COLLEAGUE OF HAWKGIRL'S. WHEN SHE GOT HER WINGS--AT THE SAME TIME--I GOT POWER OF A SORT AS WELL...
...THE MAGICAL ABILITIES OF AN EGYPTIAN MAGE, THE GREATEST EVER IN EXISTENCE, WHO--
"THE GREATEST"? I RESENT THAT REMARK.
AND WHO THE HELL ARE YOU?
OH, I'LL GET TO THAT, BOY, BUT FIRST...
...KHALID, YOU JUST SAID THAT YOU KNEW WHERE YOU WERE?
YEAH, I DID, WHOEVER YOU ARE. I'M PRETTY SURE, ANYWAY...

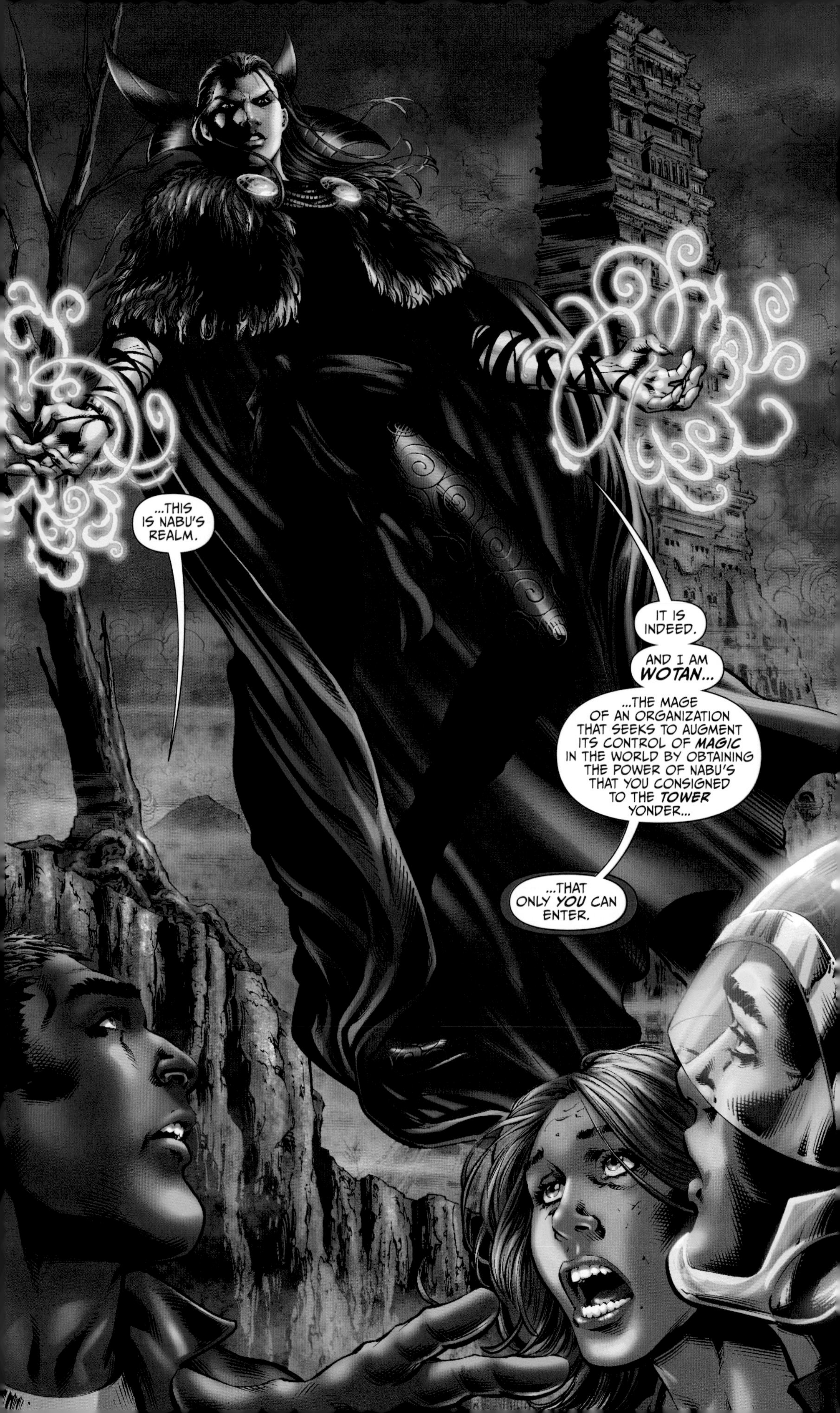
...THIS IS NABU'S REALM.
IT IS INDEED.
AND I AM *WOTAN*...
...THE MAGE OF AN ORGANIZATION THAT SEEKS TO AUGMENT ITS CONTROL OF *MAGIC* IN THE WORLD BY OBTAINING THE POWER OF NABU'S THAT YOU CONSIGNED TO THE *TOWER* YONDER...
...THAT ONLY *YOU* CAN ENTER.

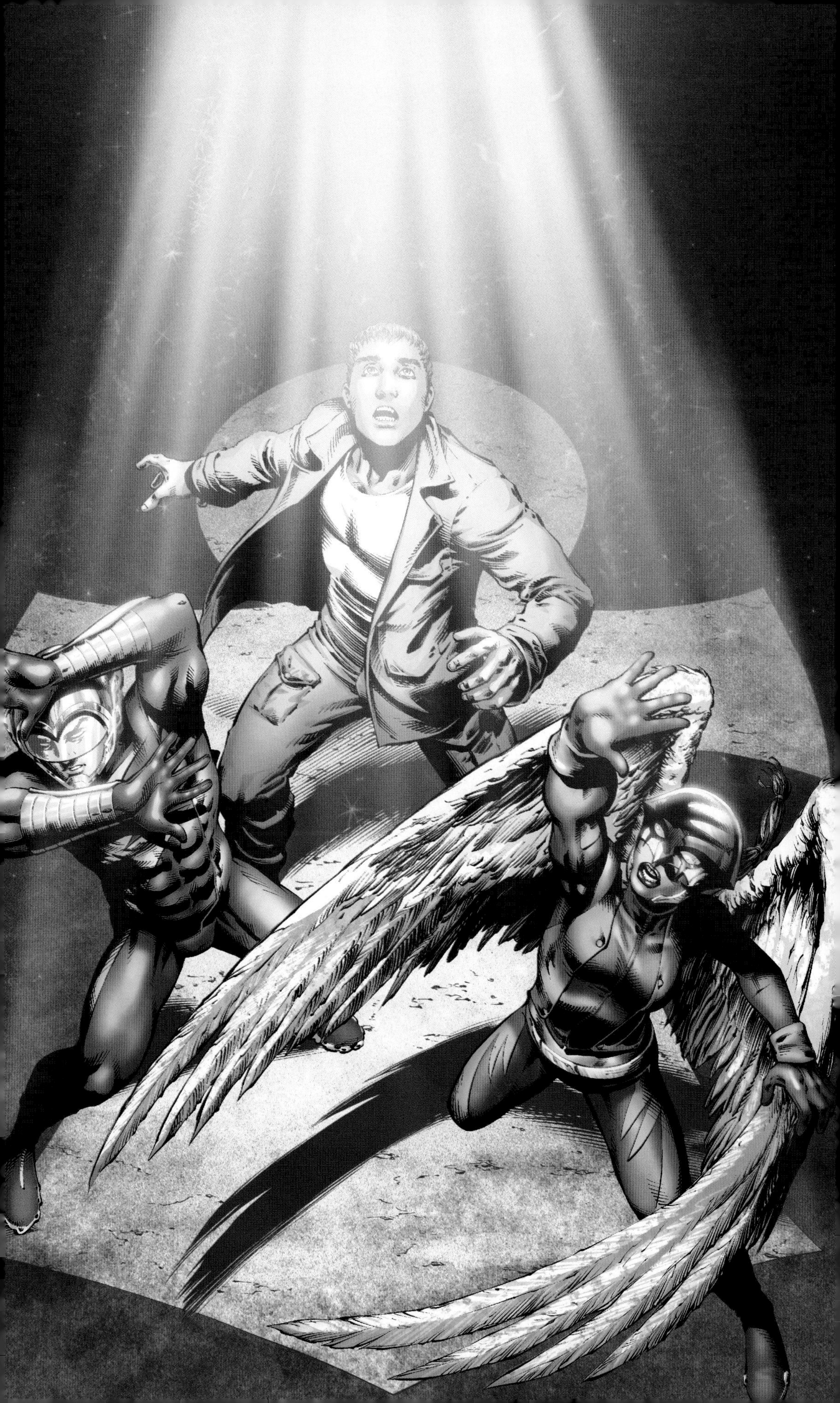

JAMES ROBINSON writer NICOLA SCOTT penciller TREVOR SCOTT inker cover by NICOLA SCOTT, TREVOR SCOTT & ALEX SINCLAIR

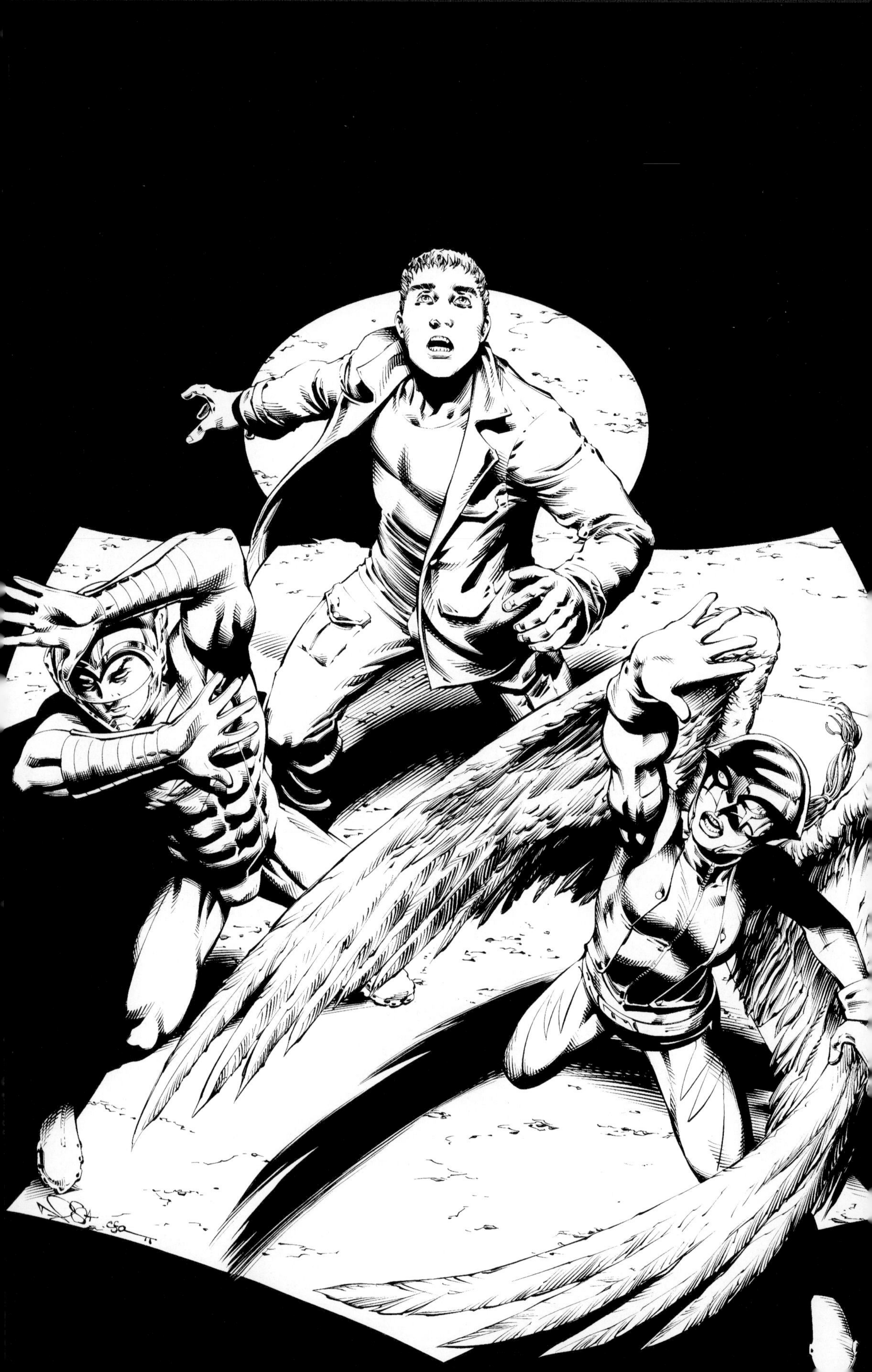

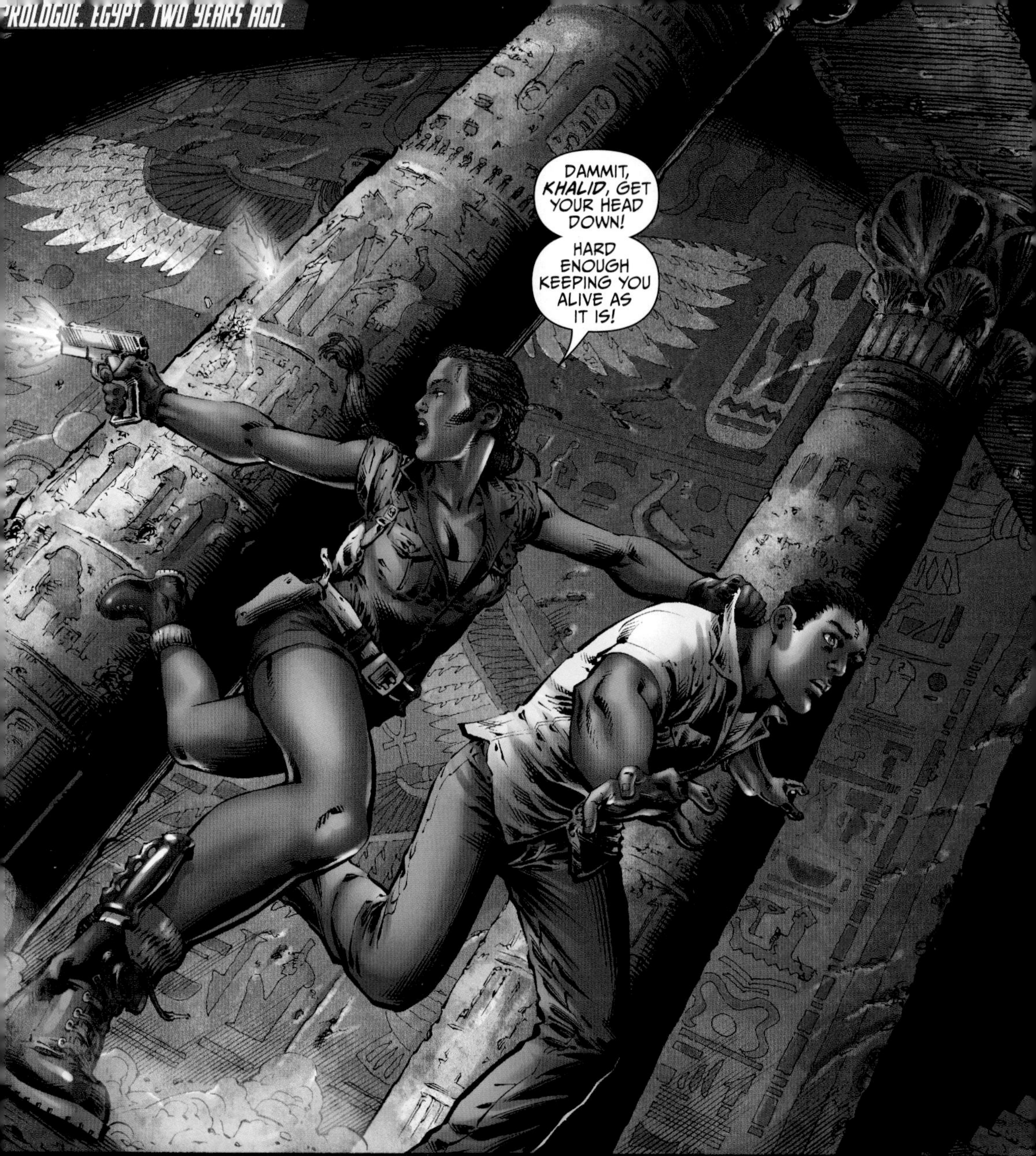
PROLOGUE. EGYPT. TWO YEARS AGO.
DAMMIT, KHALID, GET YOUR HEAD DOWN!
HARD ENOUGH KEEPING YOU ALIVE AS IT IS!

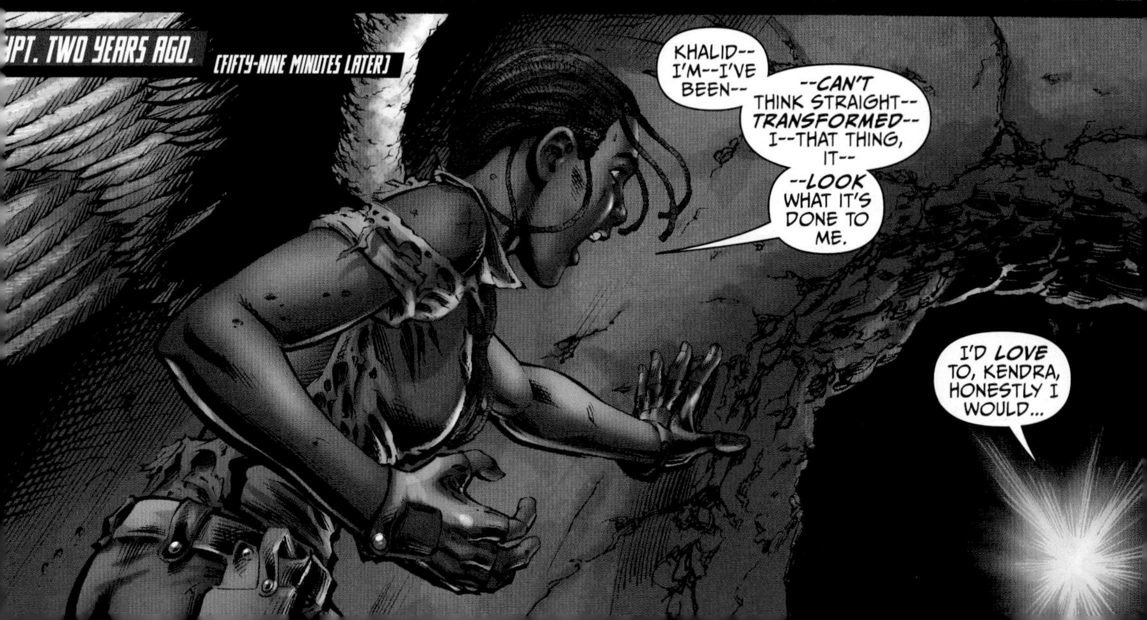
PT. TWO YEARS AGO.
[FIFTY-NINE MINUTES LATER]
KHALID-- I'M--I'VE BEEN--
--CAN'T THINK STRAIGHT-- TRANSFORMED-- I--THAT THING, IT--
--LOOK WHAT IT'S DONE TO ME.
I'D LOVE TO, KENDRA, HONESTLY I WOULD...

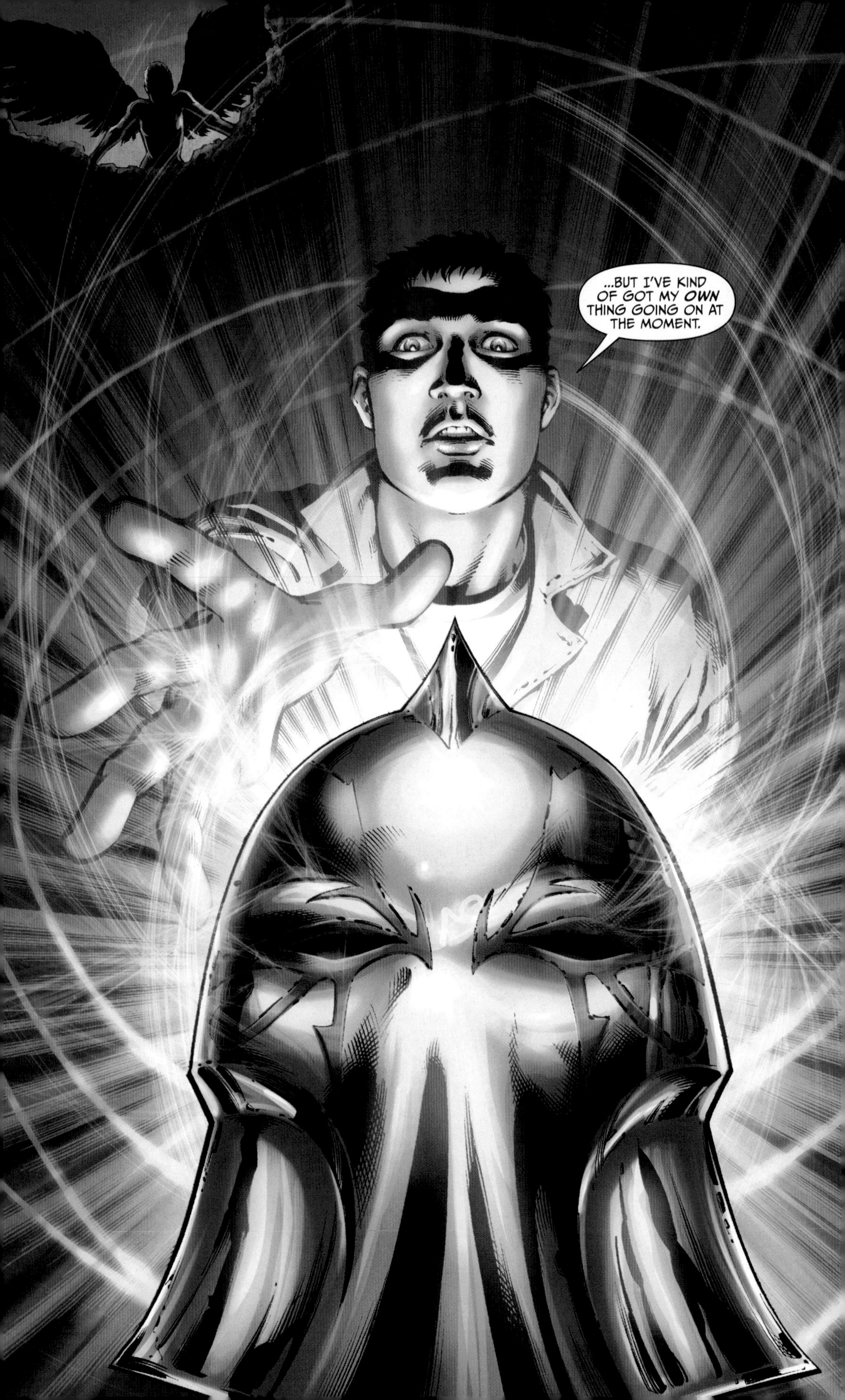
...BUT I'VE KIND OF GOT MY OWN THING GOING ON AT THE MOMENT.

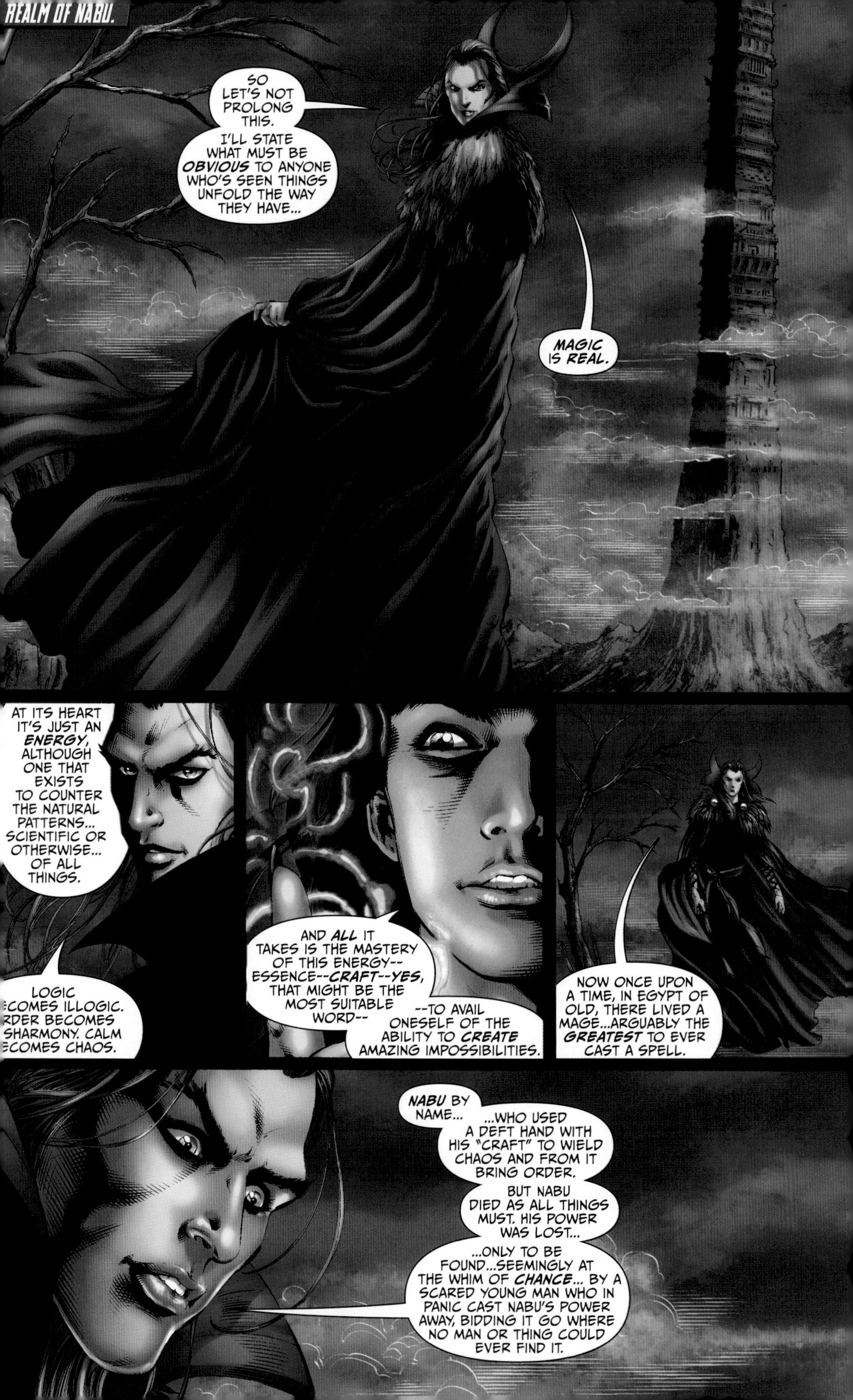
REALM OF NABU.
SO LET'S NOT PROLONG THIS.
I'LL STATE WHAT MUST BE OBVIOUS TO ANYONE WHO'S SEEN THINGS UNFOLD THE WAY THEY HAVE...
MAGIC IS REAL.
AT ITS HEART IT'S JUST AN ENERGY, ALTHOUGH ONE THAT EXISTS TO COUNTER THE NATURAL PATTERNS... SCIENTIFIC OR OTHERWISE... OF ALL THINGS.
LOGIC ECOMES ILLOGIC. RDER BECOMES SHARMONY. CALM ECOMES CHAOS.
AND ALL IT TAKES IS THE MASTERY OF THIS ENERGY--ESSENCE--CRAFT--YES, THAT MIGHT BE THE MOST SUITABLE WORD--
--TO AVAIL ONESELF OF THE ABILITY TO CREATE AMAZING IMPOSSIBILITIES.
NOW ONCE UPON A TIME, IN EGYPT OF OLD, THERE LIVED A MAGE...ARGUABLY THE GREATEST TO EVER CAST A SPELL.
NABU BY NAME...
...WHO USED A DEFT HAND WITH HIS "CRAFT" TO WIELD CHAOS AND FROM IT BRING ORDER.
BUT NABU DIED AS ALL THINGS MUST. HIS POWER WAS LOST...
...ONLY TO BE FOUND...SEEMINGLY AT THE WHIM OF CHANCE... BY A SCARED YOUNG MAN WHO IN PANIC CAST NABU'S POWER AWAY, BIDDING IT GO WHERE NO MAN OR THING COULD EVER FIND IT.

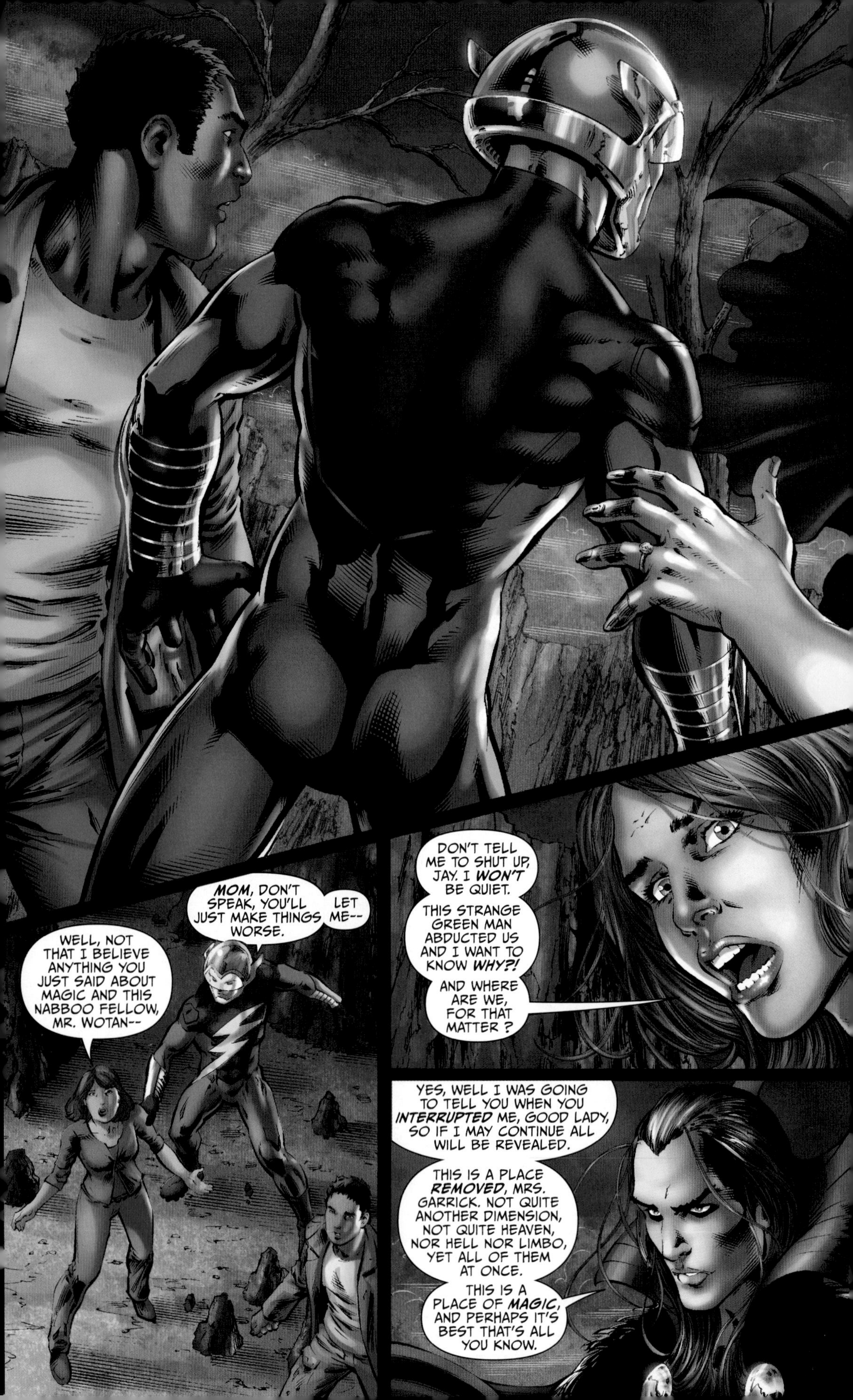

WELL, NOT THAT I BELIEVE ANYTHING YOU JUST SAID ABOUT MAGIC AND THIS NABBOO FELLOW, MR. WOTAN--
MOM, DON'T SPEAK, YOU'LL JUST MAKE THINGS WORSE.
LET ME--
DON'T TELL ME TO SHUT UP, JAY. I WON'T BE QUIET.
THIS STRANGE GREEN MAN ABDUCTED US AND I WANT TO KNOW WHY?!
AND WHERE ARE WE, FOR THAT MATTER ?
YES, WELL I WAS GOING TO TELL YOU WHEN YOU INTERRUPTED ME, GOOD LADY, SO IF I MAY CONTINUE ALL WILL BE REVEALED.
THIS IS A PLACE REMOVED, MRS. GARRICK. NOT QUITE ANOTHER DIMENSION, NOT QUITE HEAVEN, NOR HELL NOR LIMBO, YET ALL OF THEM AT ONCE.
THIS IS A PLACE OF MAGIC, AND PERHAPS IT'S BEST THAT'S ALL YOU KNOW.

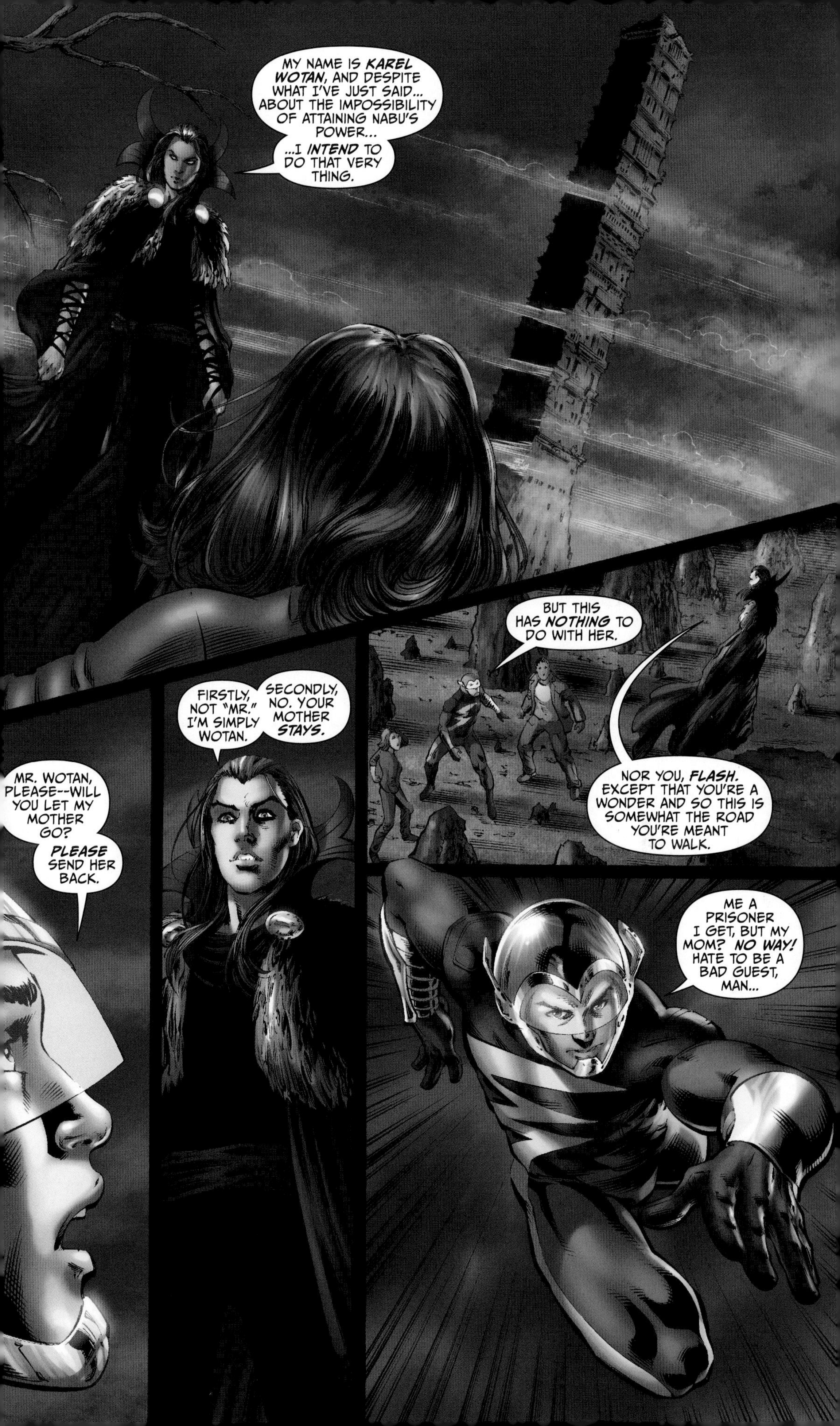
MY NAME IS KAREL WOTAN, AND DESPITE WHAT I'VE JUST SAID... ABOUT THE IMPOSSIBILITY OF ATTAINING NABU'S POWER...
...I INTEND TO DO THAT VERY THING.
BUT THIS HAS NOTHING TO DO WITH HER.
NOR YOU, FLASH. EXCEPT THAT YOU'RE A WONDER AND SO THIS IS SOMEWHAT THE ROAD YOU'RE MEANT TO WALK.
MR. WOTAN, PLEASE--WILL YOU LET MY MOTHER GO?
PLEASE SEND HER BACK.
FIRSTLY, NOT "MR." I'M SIMPLY WOTAN.
SECONDLY, NO. YOUR MOTHER STAYS.
ME A PRISONER I GET, BUT MY MOM? NO WAY! HATE TO BE A BAD GUEST, MAN...

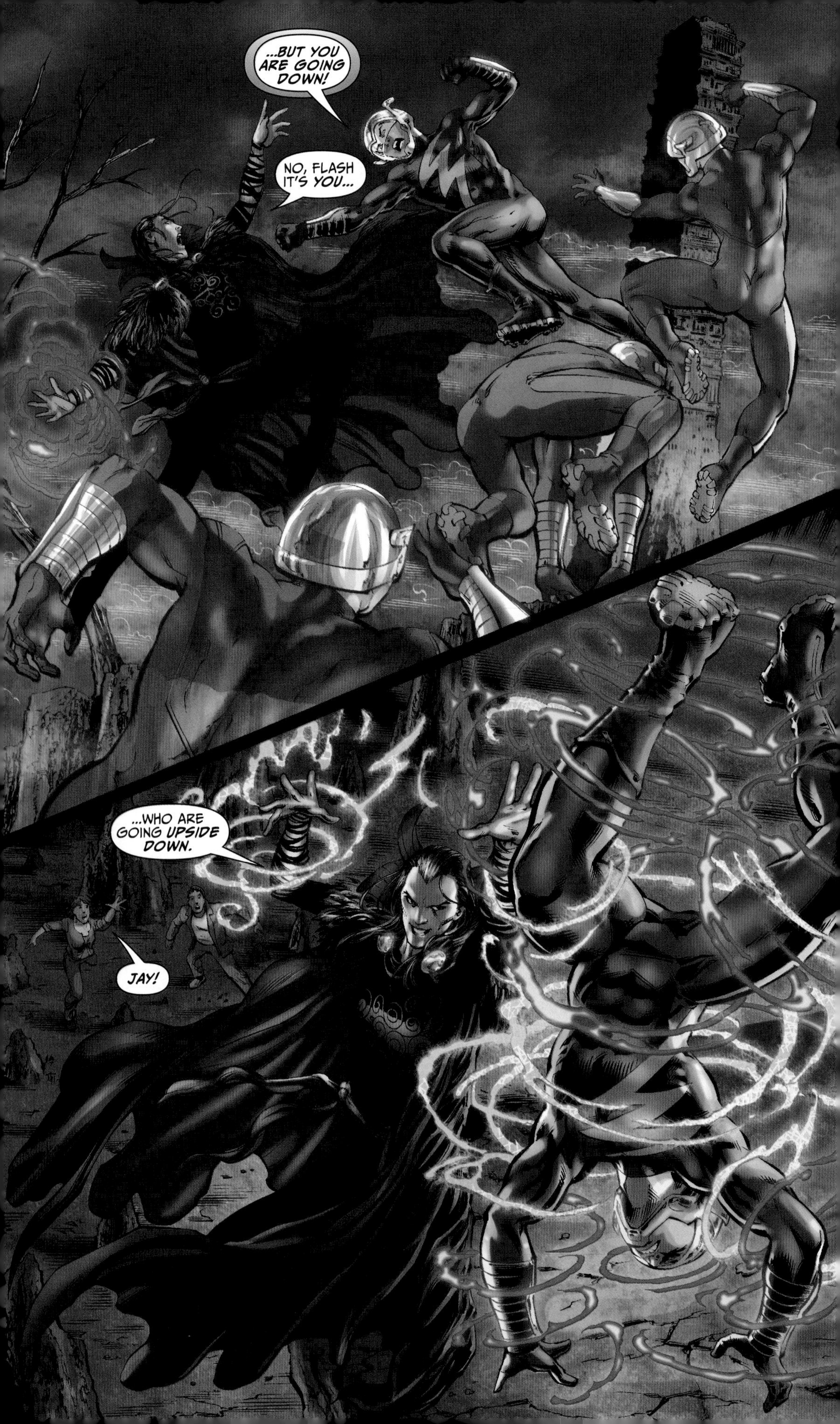
...BUT YOU ARE GOING DOWN!
NO, FLASH IT'S YOU...
...WHO ARE GOING UPSIDE DOWN.
JAY!

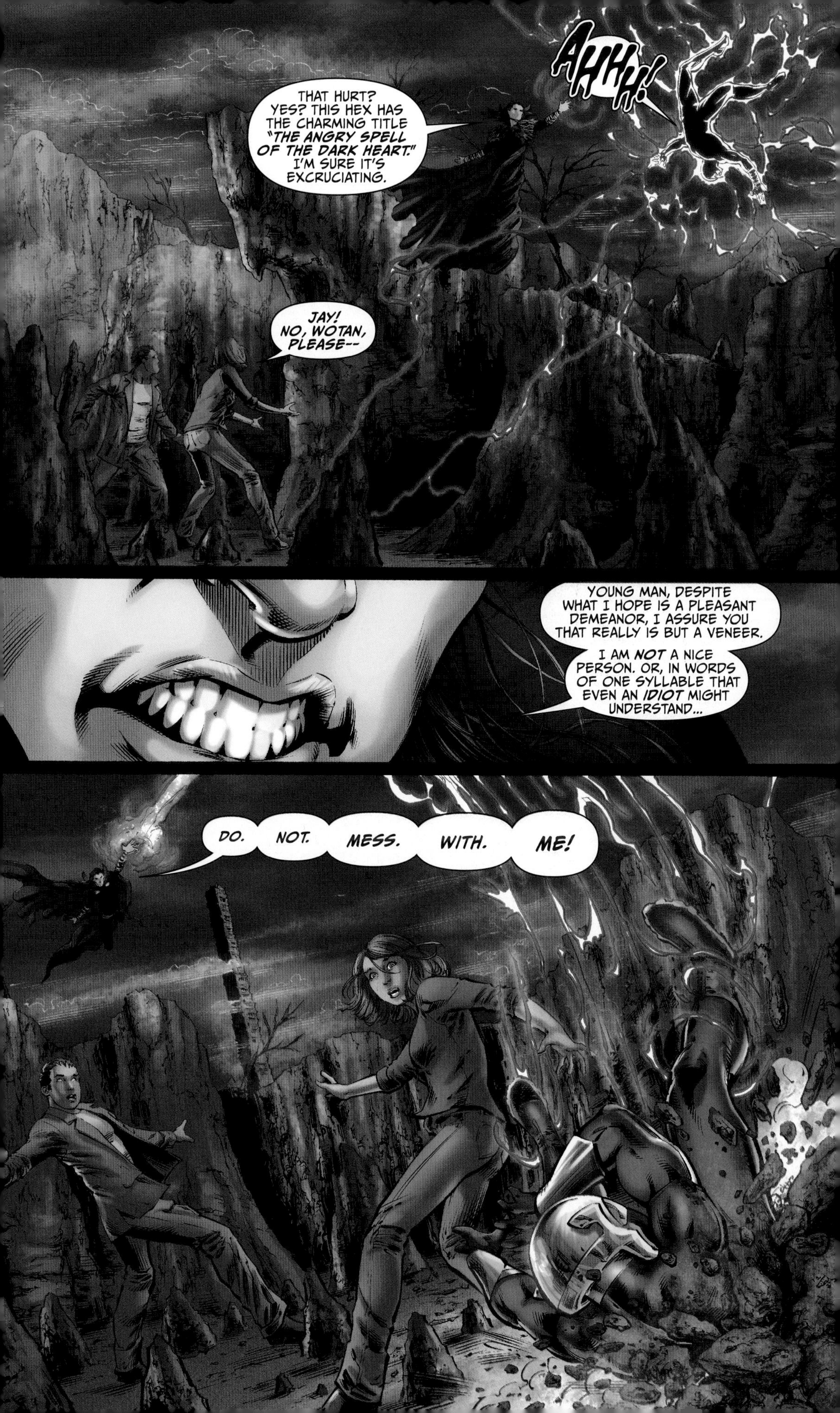
AHHH!
THAT HURT? YES? THIS HEX HAS THE CHARMING TITLE *"THE ANGRY SPELL OF THE DARK HEART."* I'M SURE IT'S EXCRUCIATING.
JAY! NO, WOTAN, PLEASE--
YOUNG MAN, DESPITE WHAT I HOPE IS A PLEASANT DEMEANOR, I ASSURE YOU THAT REALLY IS BUT A VENEER.
I AM ***NOT*** A NICE PERSON. OR, IN WORDS OF ONE SYLLABLE THAT EVEN AN *IDIOT* MIGHT UNDERSTAND...
DO.
NOT.
MESS.
WITH.
ME!

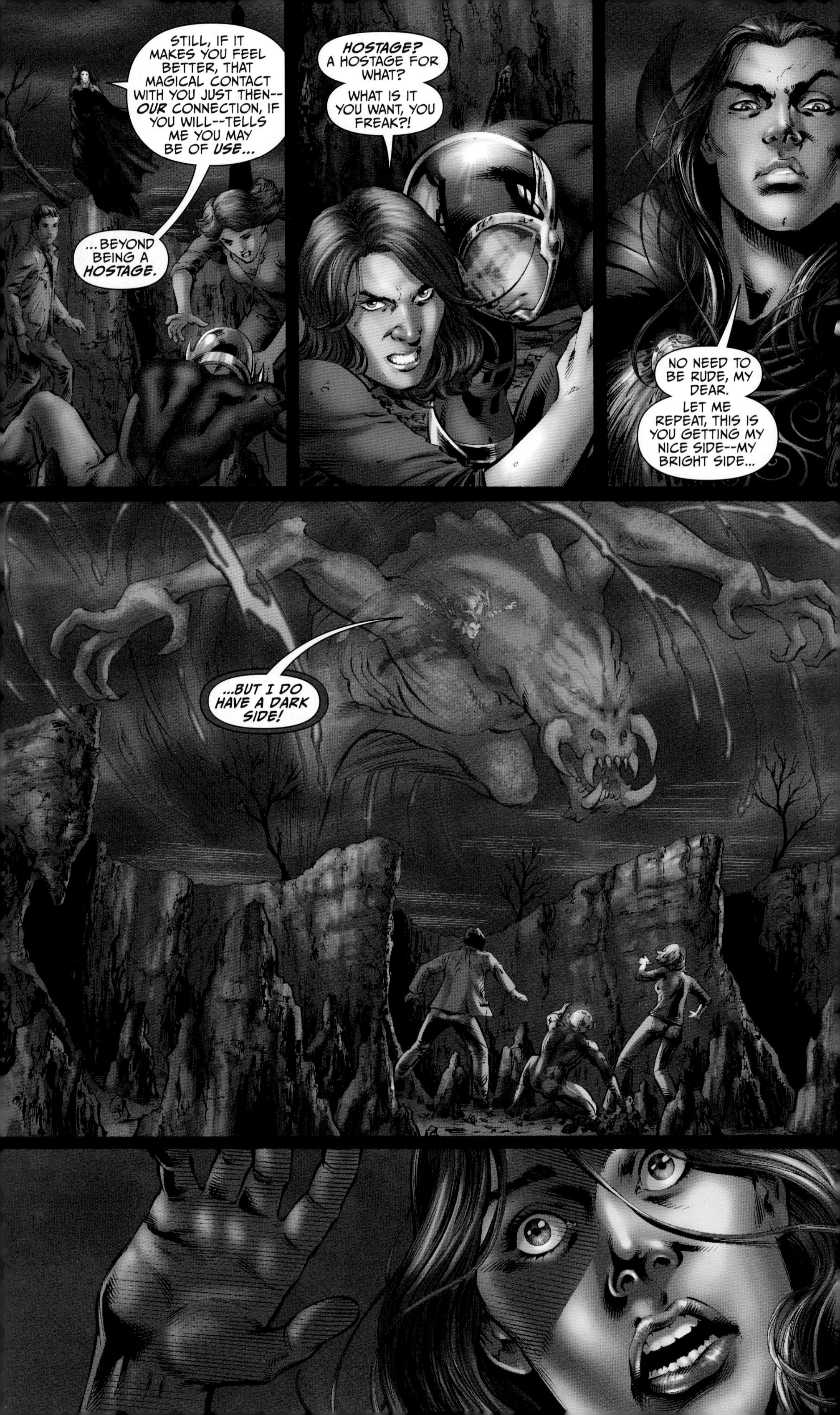
STILL, IF IT MAKES YOU FEEL BETTER, THAT MAGICAL CONTACT WITH YOU JUST THEN--OUR CONNECTION, IF YOU WILL--TELLS ME YOU MAY BE OF USE...
...BEYOND BEING A HOSTAGE.
HOSTAGE? A HOSTAGE FOR WHAT?
WHAT IS IT YOU WANT, YOU FREAK?!
NO NEED TO BE RUDE, MY DEAR.
LET ME REPEAT, THIS IS YOU GETTING MY NICE SIDE--MY BRIGHT SIDE...
...BUT I DO HAVE A DARK SIDE!

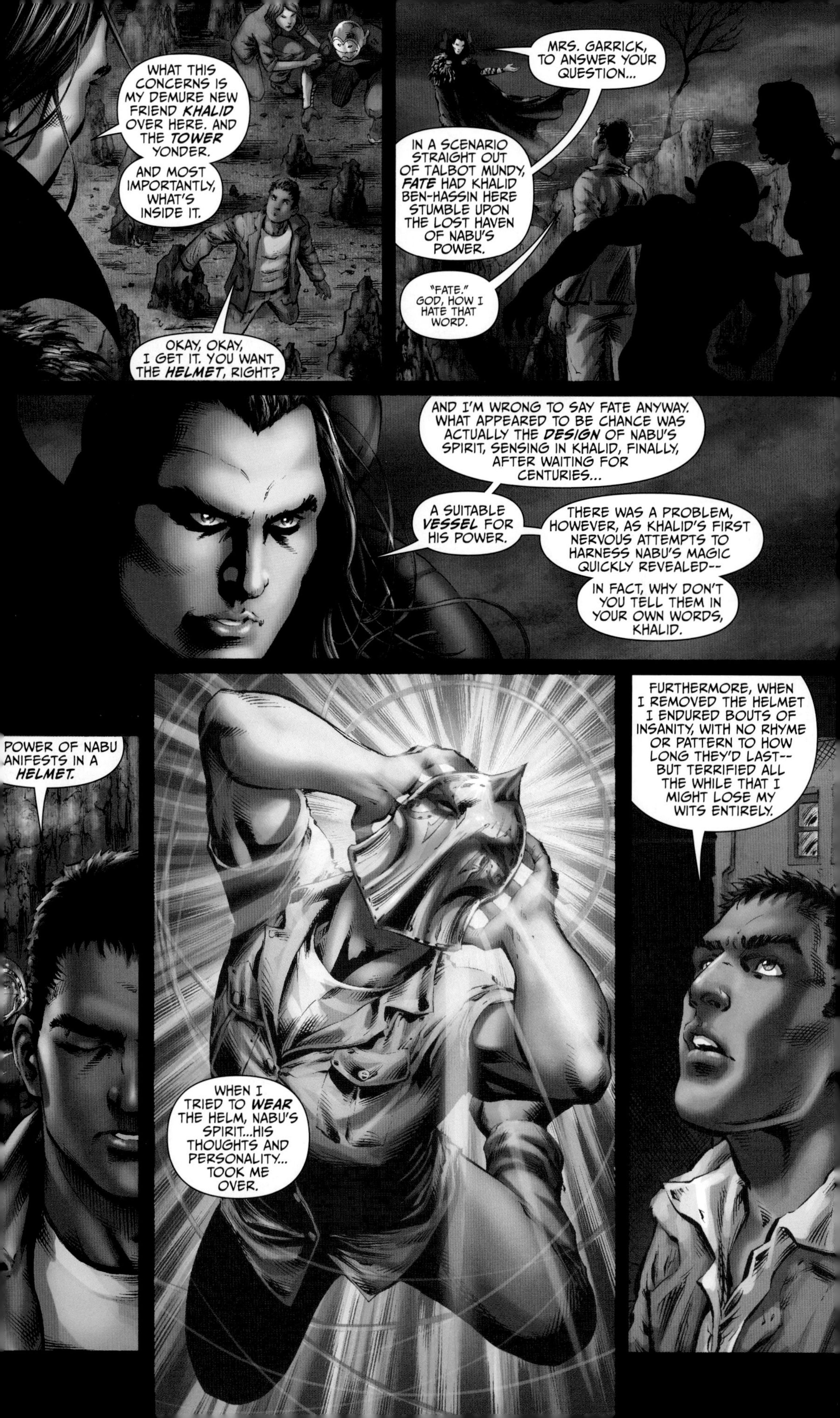
WHAT THIS CONCERNS IS MY DEMURE NEW FRIEND KHALID OVER HERE. AND THE TOWER YONDER.
AND MOST IMPORTANTLY, WHAT'S INSIDE IT.
OKAY, OKAY, I GET IT. YOU WANT THE HELMET, RIGHT?
MRS. GARRICK, TO ANSWER YOUR QUESTION...
IN A SCENARIO STRAIGHT OUT OF TALBOT MUNDY, FATE HAD KHALID BEN-HASSIN HERE STUMBLE UPON THE LOST HAVEN OF NABU'S POWER.
"FATE." GOD, HOW I HATE THAT WORD.
AND I'M WRONG TO SAY FATE ANYWAY. WHAT APPEARED TO BE CHANCE WAS ACTUALLY THE DESIGN OF NABU'S SPIRIT, SENSING IN KHALID, FINALLY, AFTER WAITING FOR CENTURIES...
A SUITABLE VESSEL FOR HIS POWER.
THERE WAS A PROBLEM, HOWEVER, AS KHALID'S FIRST NERVOUS ATTEMPTS TO HARNESS NABU'S MAGIC QUICKLY REVEALED--
IN FACT, WHY DON'T YOU TELL THEM IN YOUR OWN WORDS, KHALID.
POWER OF NABU ANIFESTS IN A HELMET.
WHEN I TRIED TO WEAR THE HELM, NABU'S SPIRIT...HIS THOUGHTS AND PERSONALITY... TOOK ME OVER.
FURTHERMORE, WHEN I REMOVED THE HELMET I ENDURED BOUTS OF INSANITY, WITH NO RHYME OR PATTERN TO HOW LONG THEY'D LAST-- BUT TERRIFIED ALL THE WHILE THAT I MIGHT LOSE MY WITS ENTIRELY.

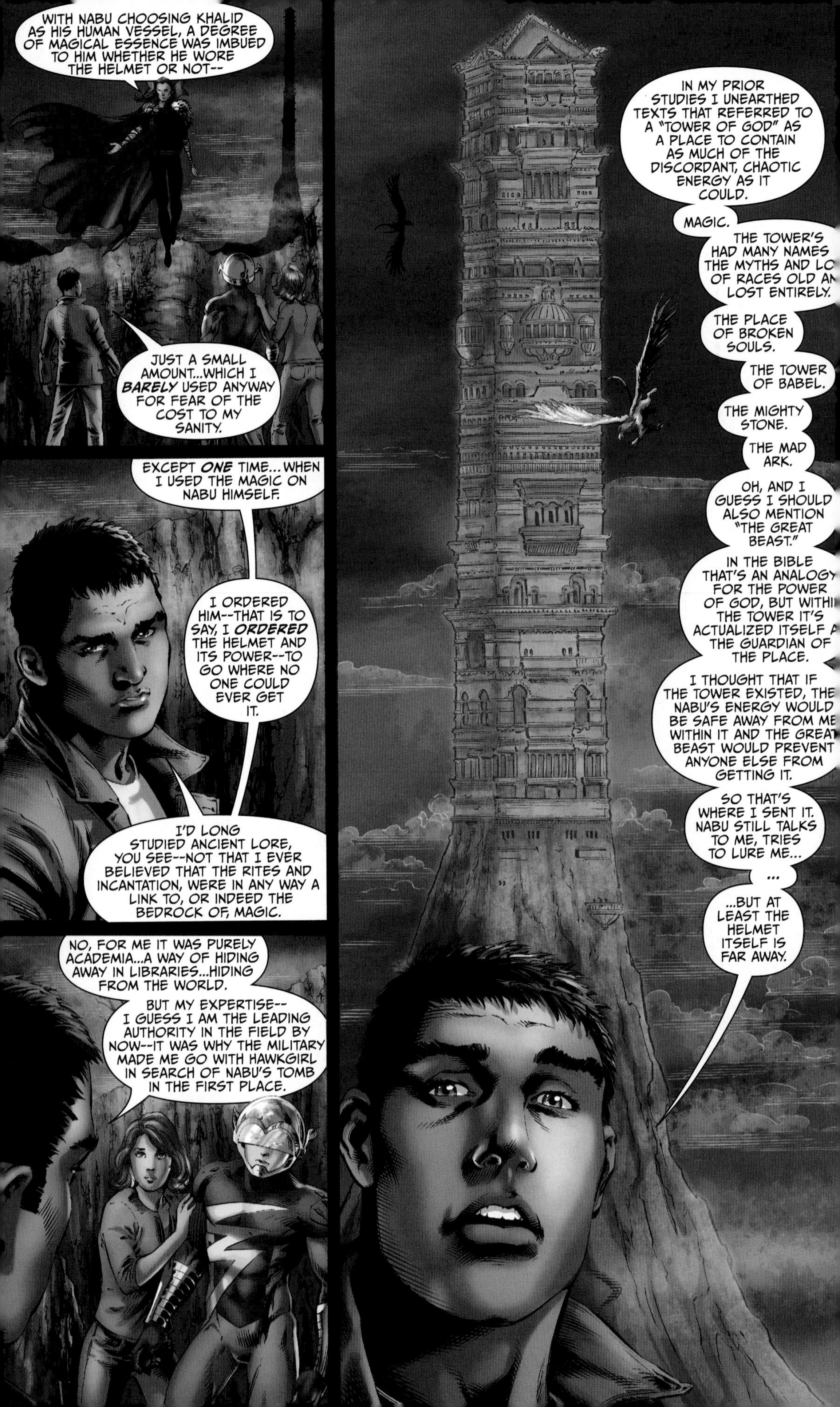

WITH NABU CHOOSING KHALID AS HIS HUMAN VESSEL, A DEGREE OF MAGICAL ESSENCE WAS IMBUED TO HIM WHETHER HE WORE THE HELMET OR NOT--
JUST A SMALL AMOUNT...WHICH I BARELY USED ANYWAY FOR FEAR OF THE COST TO MY SANITY.
EXCEPT ONE TIME...WHEN I USED THE MAGIC ON NABU HIMSELF.
I ORDERED HIM--THAT IS TO SAY, I ORDERED THE HELMET AND ITS POWER--TO GO WHERE NO ONE COULD EVER GET IT.
I'D LONG STUDIED ANCIENT LORE, YOU SEE--NOT THAT I EVER BELIEVED THAT THE RITES AND INCANTATION, WERE IN ANY WAY A LINK TO, OR INDEED THE BEDROCK OF, MAGIC.
NO, FOR ME IT WAS PURELY ACADEMIA...A WAY OF HIDING AWAY IN LIBRARIES...HIDING FROM THE WORLD.
BUT MY EXPERTISE--I GUESS I AM THE LEADING AUTHORITY IN THE FIELD BY NOW--IT WAS WHY THE MILITARY MADE ME GO WITH HAWKGIRL IN SEARCH OF NABU'S TOMB IN THE FIRST PLACE.
IN MY PRIOR STUDIES I UNEARTHED TEXTS THAT REFERRED TO A "TOWER OF GOD" AS A PLACE TO CONTAIN AS MUCH OF THE DISCORDANT, CHAOTIC ENERGY AS IT COULD.
MAGIC.
THE TOWER'S HAD MANY NAMES THE MYTHS AND LO OF RACES OLD A LOST ENTIRELY.
THE PLACE OF BROKEN SOULS.
THE TOWER OF BABEL.
THE MIGHTY STONE.
THE MAD ARK.
OH, AND I GUESS I SHOULD ALSO MENTION "THE GREAT BEAST."
IN THE BIBLE THAT'S AN ANALOG FOR THE POWER OF GOD, BUT WITHI THE TOWER IT'S ACTUALIZED ITSELF A THE GUARDIAN OF THE PLACE.
I THOUGHT THAT IF THE TOWER EXISTED, THE NABU'S ENERGY WOULD BE SAFE AWAY FROM ME WITHIN IT AND THE GREAT BEAST WOULD PREVENT ANYONE ELSE FROM GETTING IT.
SO THAT'S WHERE I SENT IT. NABU STILL TALKS TO ME, TRIES TO LURE ME...
...
...BUT AT LEAST THE HELMET ITSELF IS FAR AWAY.

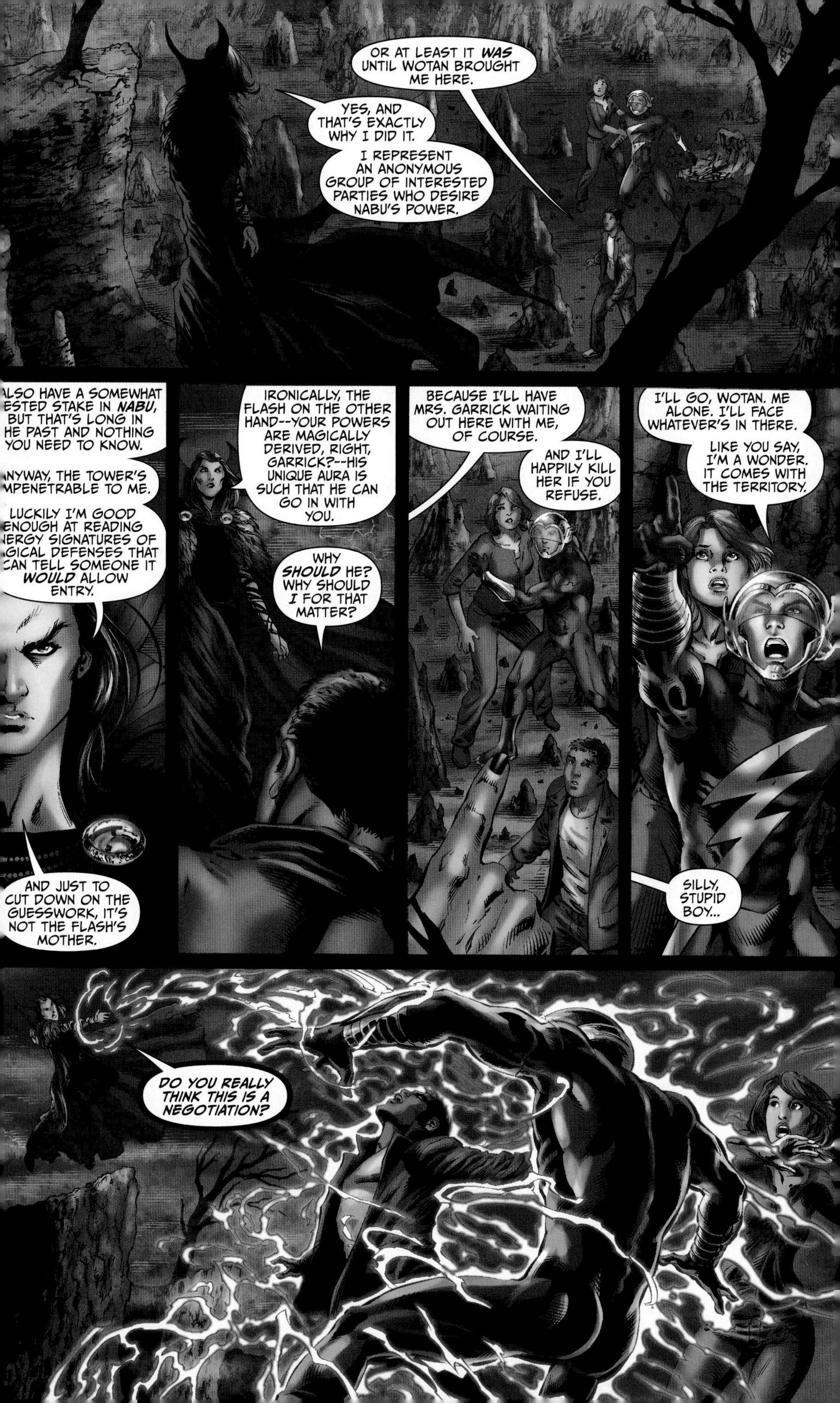

OR AT LEAST IT *WAS* UNTIL WOTAN BROUGHT ME HERE.
YES, AND THAT'S EXACTLY WHY I DID IT.
I REPRESENT AN ANONYMOUS GROUP OF INTERESTED PARTIES WHO DESIRE NABU'S POWER.
ALSO HAVE A SOMEWHAT ESTED STAKE IN *NABU*, BUT THAT'S LONG IN HE PAST AND NOTHING YOU NEED TO KNOW.
NYWAY, THE TOWER'S MPENETRABLE TO ME.
LUCKILY I'M GOOD ENOUGH AT READING NERGY SIGNATURES OF GICAL DEFENSES THAT CAN TELL SOMEONE IT *WOULD* ALLOW ENTRY.
AND JUST TO CUT DOWN ON THE GUESSWORK, IT'S NOT THE FLASH'S MOTHER.
IRONICALLY, THE FLASH ON THE OTHER HAND--YOUR POWERS ARE MAGICALLY DERIVED, RIGHT, GARRICK?--HIS UNIQUE AURA IS SUCH THAT HE CAN GO IN WITH YOU.
WHY *SHOULD* HE? WHY SHOULD *I* FOR THAT MATTER?
BECAUSE I'LL HAVE MRS. GARRICK WAITING OUT HERE WITH ME, OF COURSE.
AND I'LL HAPPILY KILL HER IF YOU REFUSE.
I'LL GO, WOTAN. ME ALONE. I'LL FACE WHATEVER'S IN THERE.
LIKE YOU SAY, I'M A WONDER. IT COMES WITH THE TERRITORY.
SILLY, STUPID BOY...
DO YOU REALLY THINK THIS IS A NEGOTIATION?

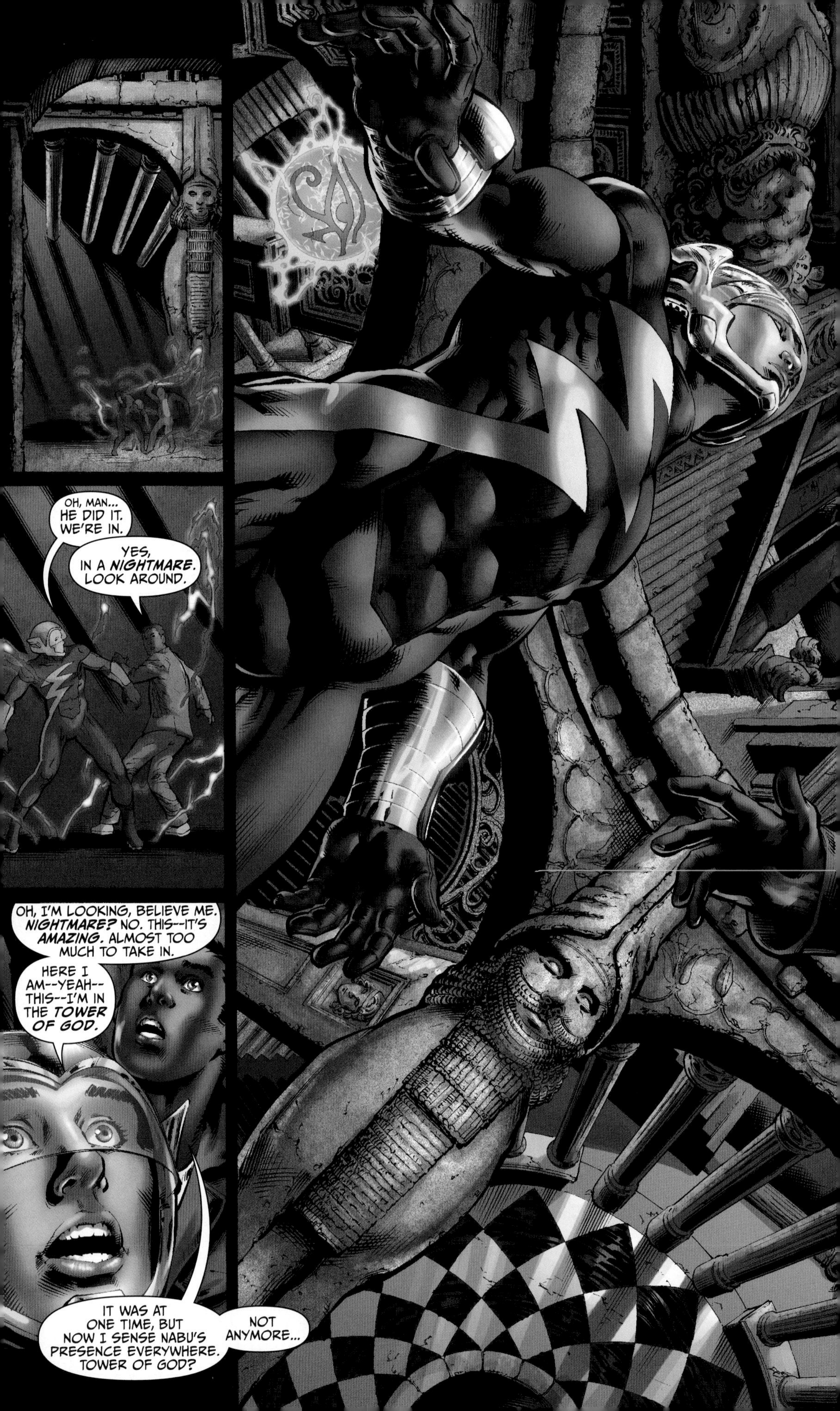
OH, MAN... HE DID IT. WE'RE IN.
YES, IN A NIGHTMARE. LOOK AROUND.
OH, I'M LOOKING, BELIEVE ME. NIGHTMARE? NO. THIS--IT'S AMAZING. ALMOST TOO MUCH TO TAKE IN.
HERE I AM--YEAH--THIS--I'M IN THE TOWER OF GOD.
IT WAS AT ONE TIME, BUT NOW I SENSE NABU'S PRESENCE EVERYWHERE. TOWER OF GOD?
NOT ANYMORE...

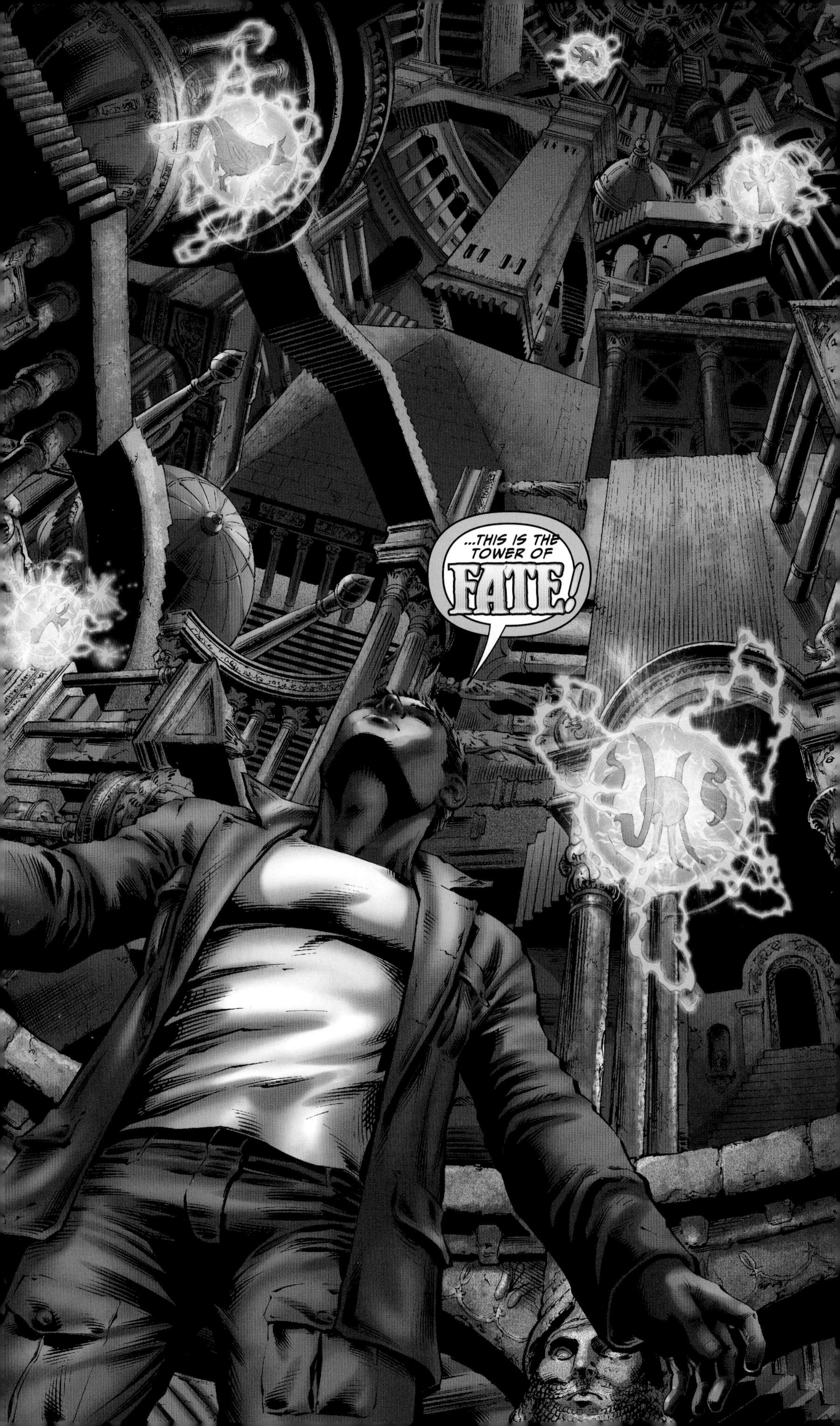
...THIS IS THE TOWER OF FATE!

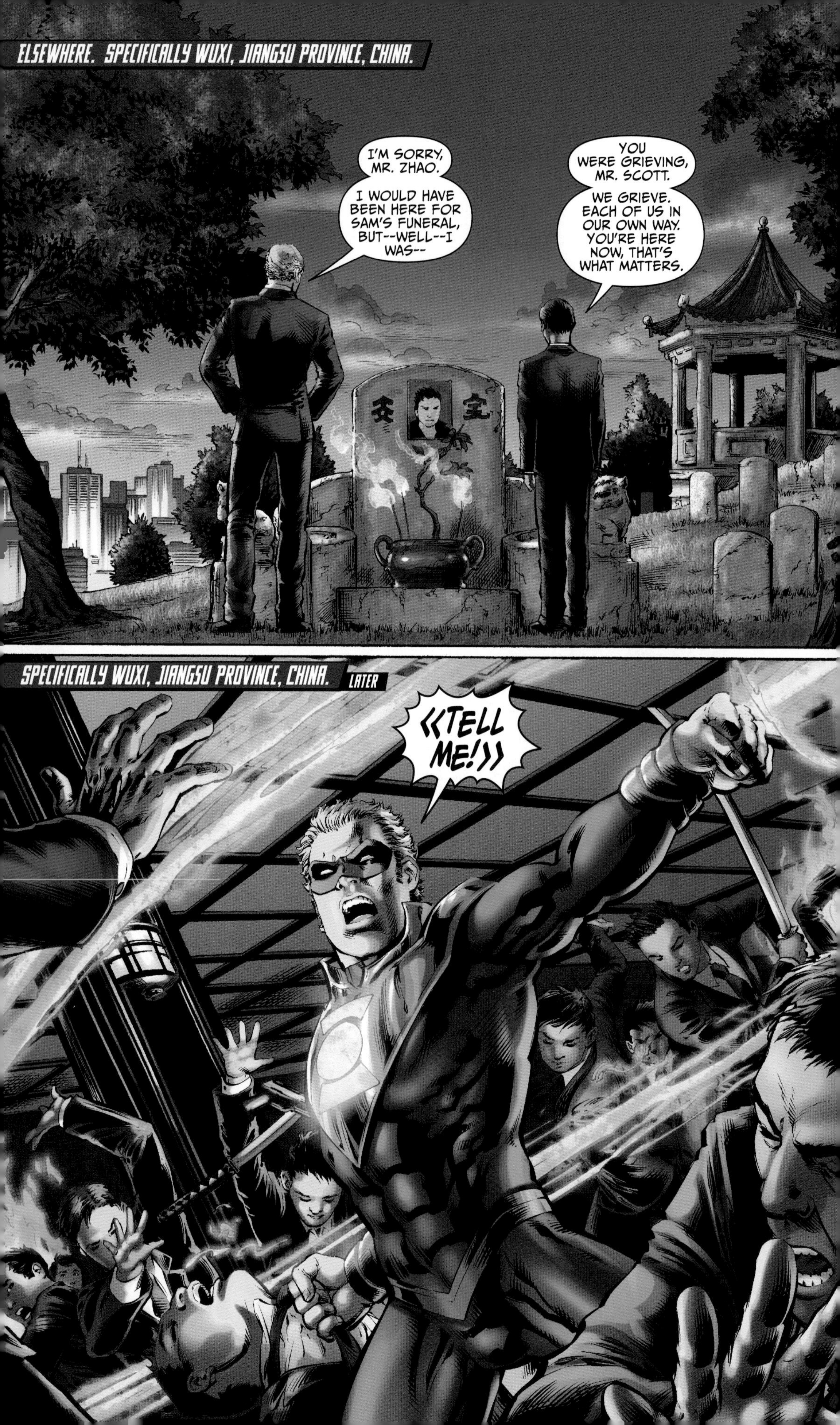
ELSEWHERE. SPECIFICALLY WUXI, JIANGSU PROVINCE, CHINA.
I'M SORRY, MR. ZHAO.
I WOULD HAVE BEEN HERE FOR SAM'S FUNERAL, BUT--WELL--I WAS--
YOU WERE GRIEVING, MR. SCOTT.
WE GRIEVE. EACH OF US IN OUR OWN WAY. YOU'RE HERE NOW, THAT'S WHAT MATTERS.
SPECIFICALLY WUXI, JIANGSU PROVINCE, CHINA. LATER
<<TELL ME!>>

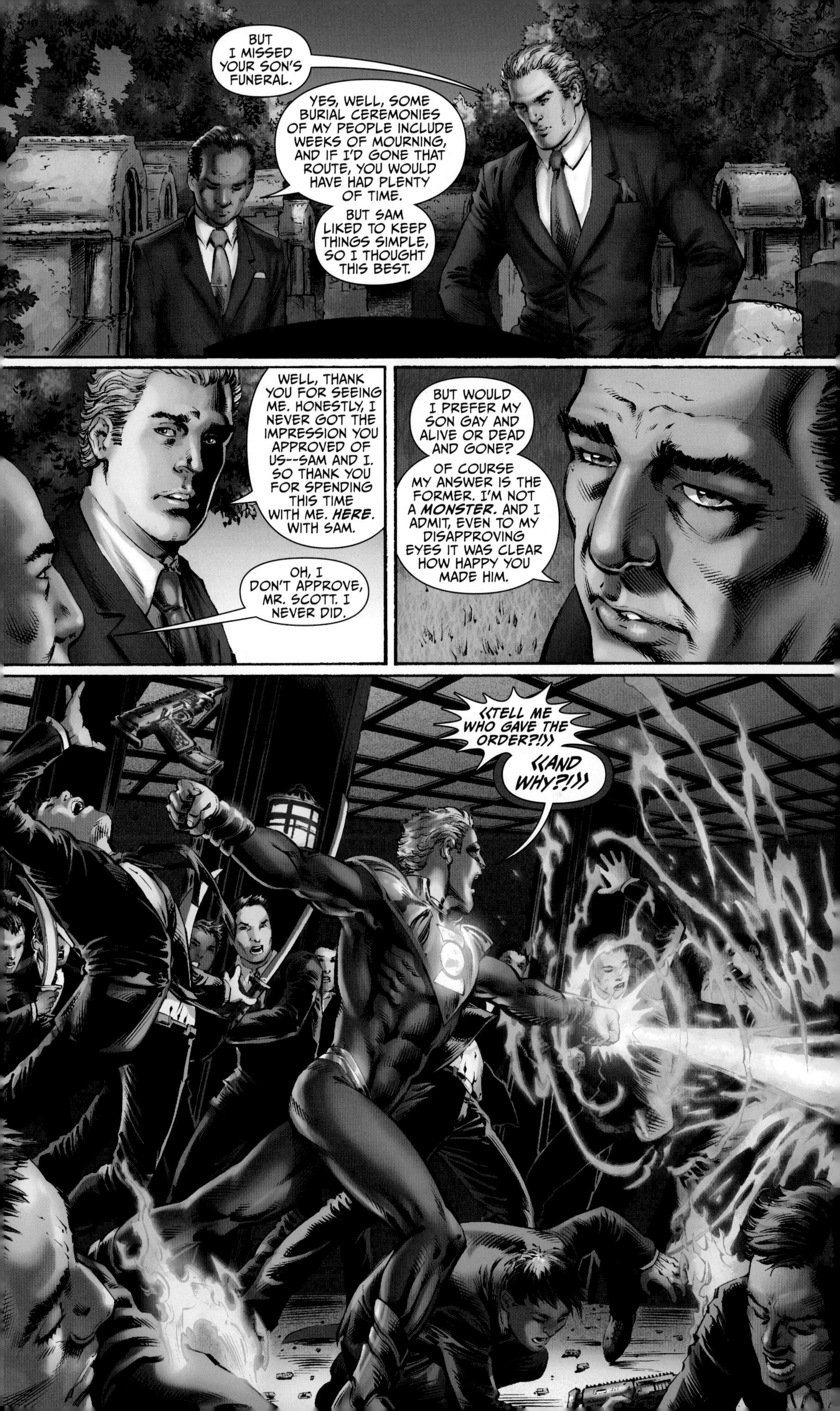
BUT I MISSED YOUR SON'S FUNERAL.
YES, WELL, SOME BURIAL CEREMONIES OF MY PEOPLE INCLUDE WEEKS OF MOURNING, AND IF I'D GONE THAT ROUTE, YOU WOULD HAVE HAD PLENTY OF TIME.
BUT SAM LIKED TO KEEP THINGS SIMPLE, SO I THOUGHT THIS BEST.
WELL, THANK YOU FOR SEEING ME. HONESTLY, I NEVER GOT THE IMPRESSION YOU APPROVED OF US--SAM AND I. SO THANK YOU FOR SPENDING THIS TIME WITH ME. *HERE*. WITH SAM.
OH, I DON'T APPROVE, MR. SCOTT. I NEVER DID.
BUT WOULD I PREFER MY SON GAY AND ALIVE OR DEAD AND GONE?
OF COURSE MY ANSWER IS THE FORMER. I'M NOT A *MONSTER*. AND I ADMIT, EVEN TO MY DISAPPROVING EYES IT WAS CLEAR HOW HAPPY YOU MADE HIM.
«TELL ME WHO GAVE THE ORDER?!»
«AND WHY?!»

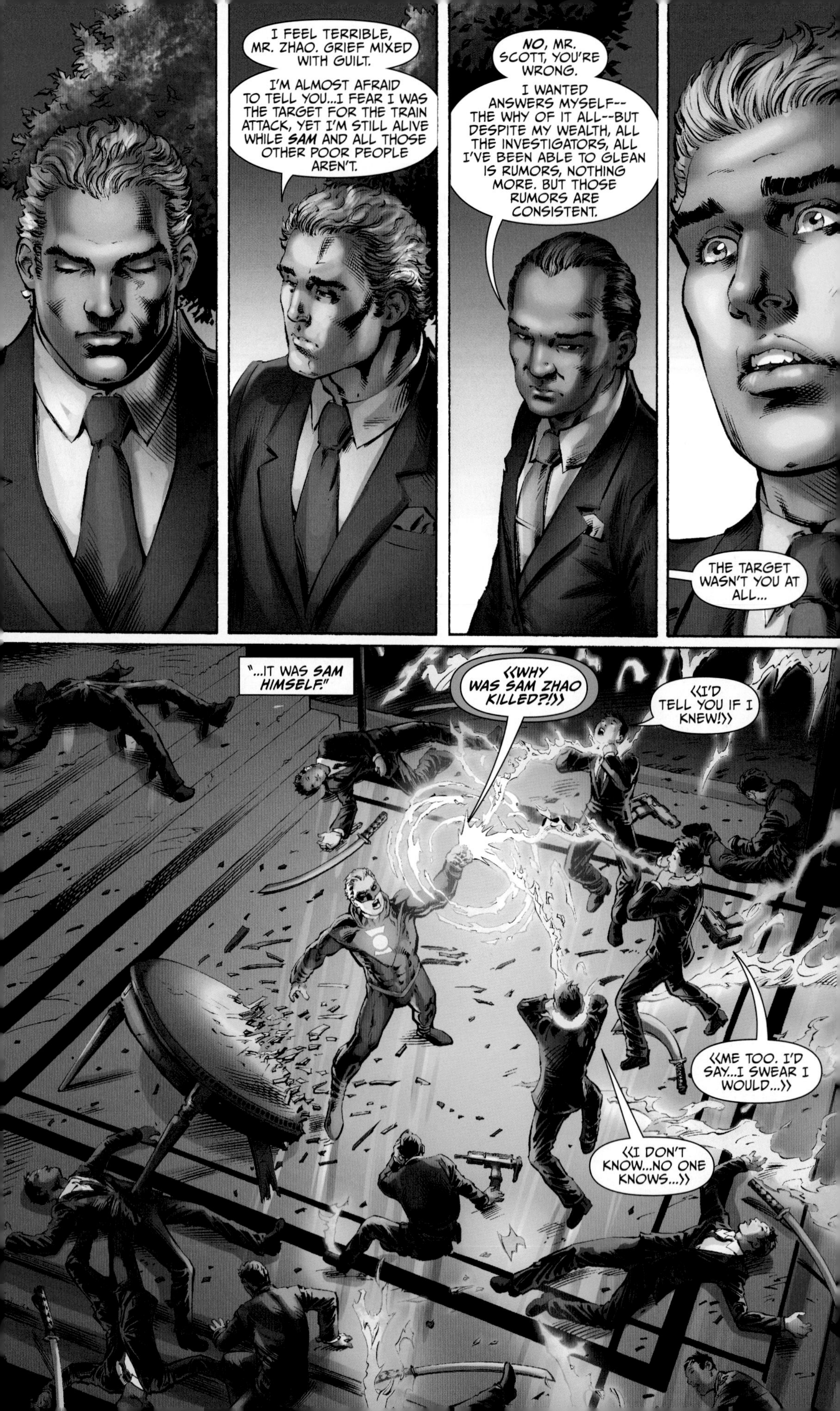
I FEEL TERRIBLE, MR. ZHAO. GRIEF MIXED WITH GUILT.
I'M ALMOST AFRAID TO TELL YOU...I FEAR I WAS THE TARGET FOR THE TRAIN ATTACK, YET I'M STILL ALIVE WHILE SAM AND ALL THOSE OTHER POOR PEOPLE AREN'T.
NO, MR. SCOTT, YOU'RE WRONG.
I WANTED ANSWERS MYSELF-- THE WHY OF IT ALL--BUT DESPITE MY WEALTH, ALL THE INVESTIGATORS, ALL I'VE BEEN ABLE TO GLEAN IS RUMORS, NOTHING MORE. BUT THOSE RUMORS ARE CONSISTENT.
THE TARGET WASN'T YOU AT ALL...
"...IT WAS SAM HIMSELF."
<<WHY WAS SAM ZHAO KILLED?!>>
<<I'D TELL YOU IF I KNEW!>>
<<ME TOO. I'D SAY...I SWEAR I WOULD...>>
<<I DON'T KNOW...NO ONE KNOWS...>>

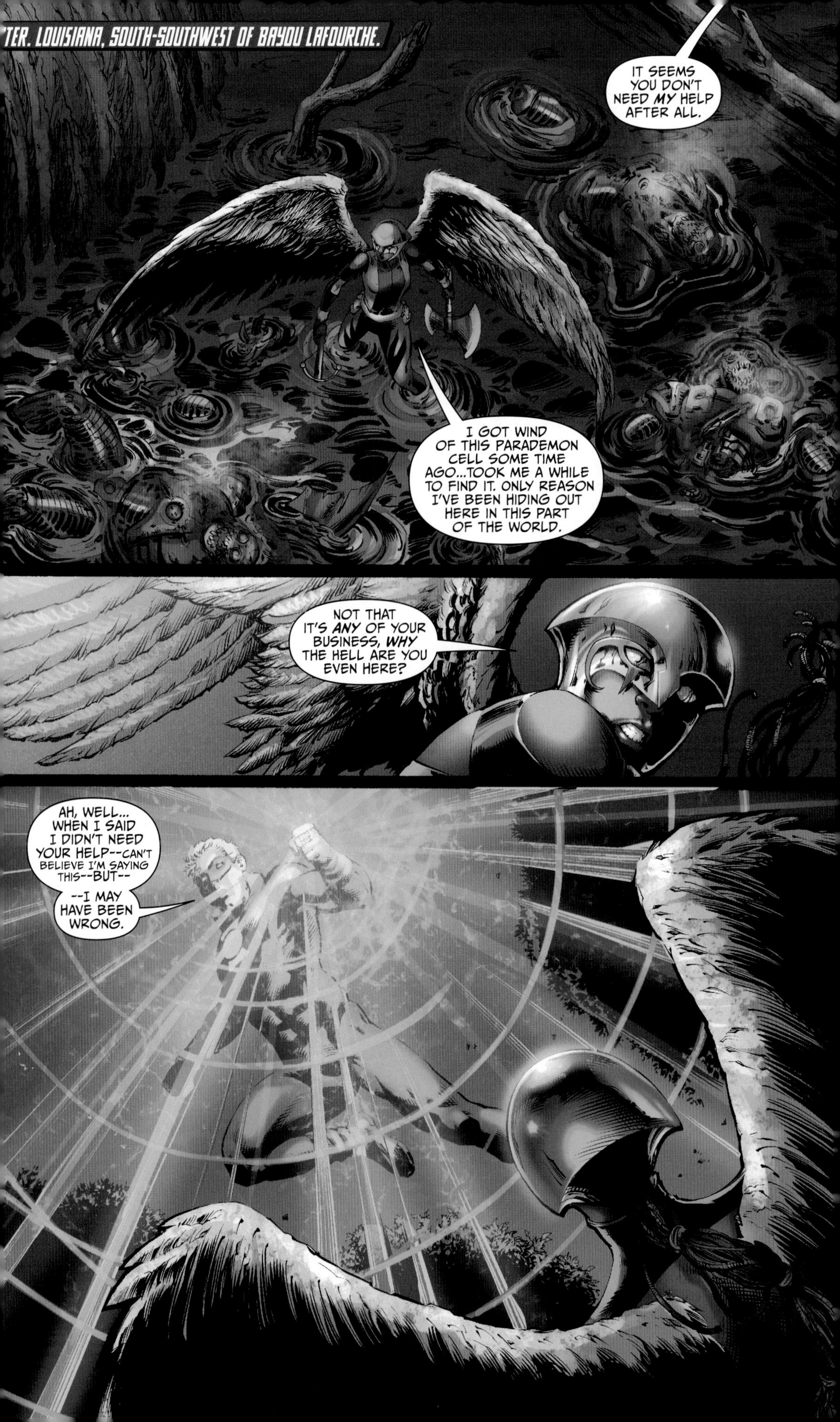
TER. LOUISIANA, SOUTH-SOUTHWEST OF BAYOU LAFOURCHE.
IT SEEMS YOU DON'T NEED MY HELP AFTER ALL.
I GOT WIND OF THIS PARADEMON CELL SOME TIME AGO...TOOK ME A WHILE TO FIND IT. ONLY REASON I'VE BEEN HIDING OUT HERE IN THIS PART OF THE WORLD.
NOT THAT IT'S ANY OF YOUR BUSINESS, WHY THE HELL ARE YOU EVEN HERE?
AH, WELL... WHEN I SAID I DIDN'T NEED YOUR HELP--CAN'T BELIEVE I'M SAYING THIS--BUT--
--I MAY HAVE BEEN WRONG.

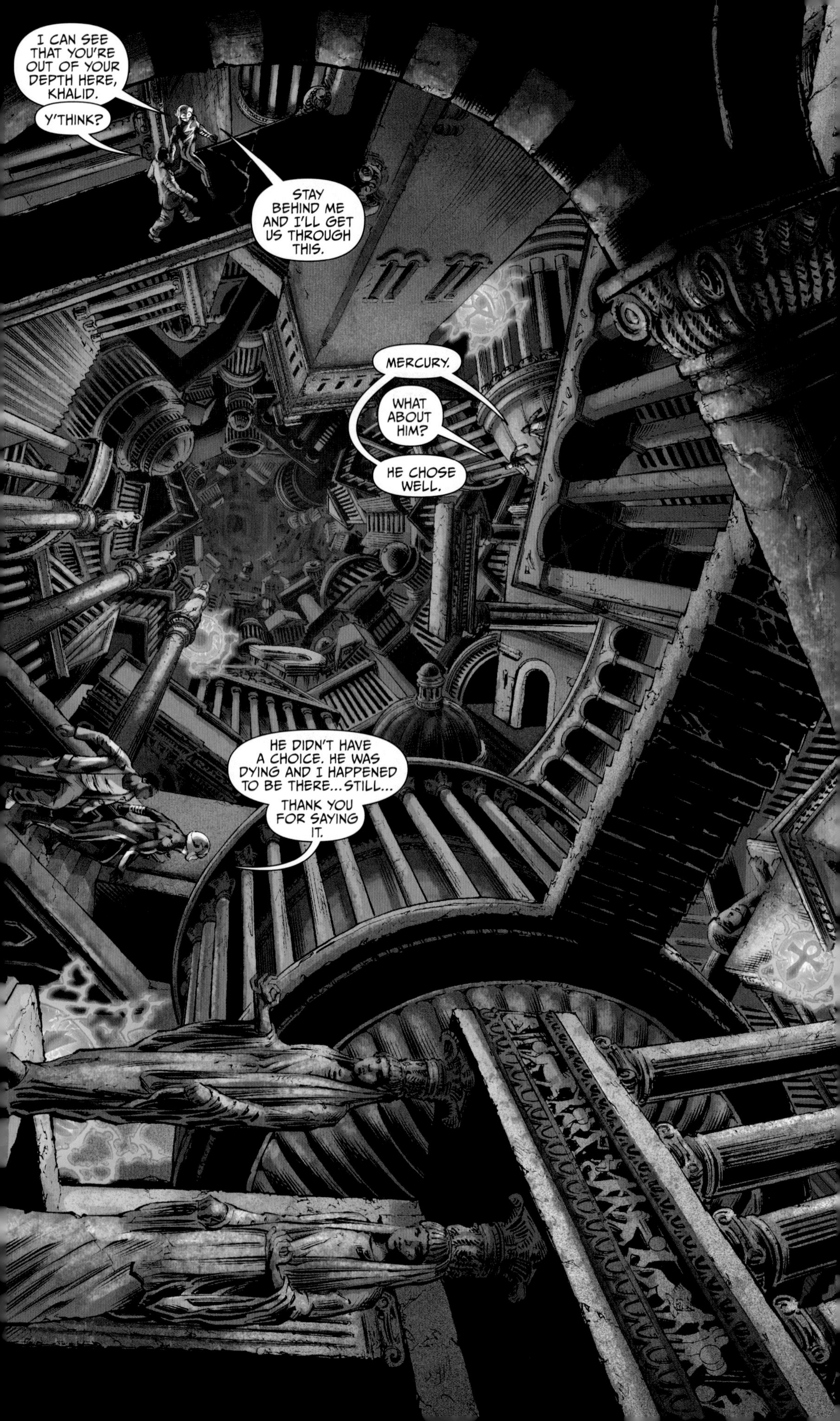
I CAN SEE THAT YOU'RE OUT OF YOUR DEPTH HERE, KHALID.
Y'THINK?
STAY BEHIND ME AND I'LL GET US THROUGH THIS.
MERCURY.
WHAT ABOUT HIM?
HE CHOSE WELL.
HE DIDN'T HAVE A CHOICE. HE WAS DYING AND I HAPPENED TO BE THERE...STILL...
THANK YOU FOR SAYING IT.

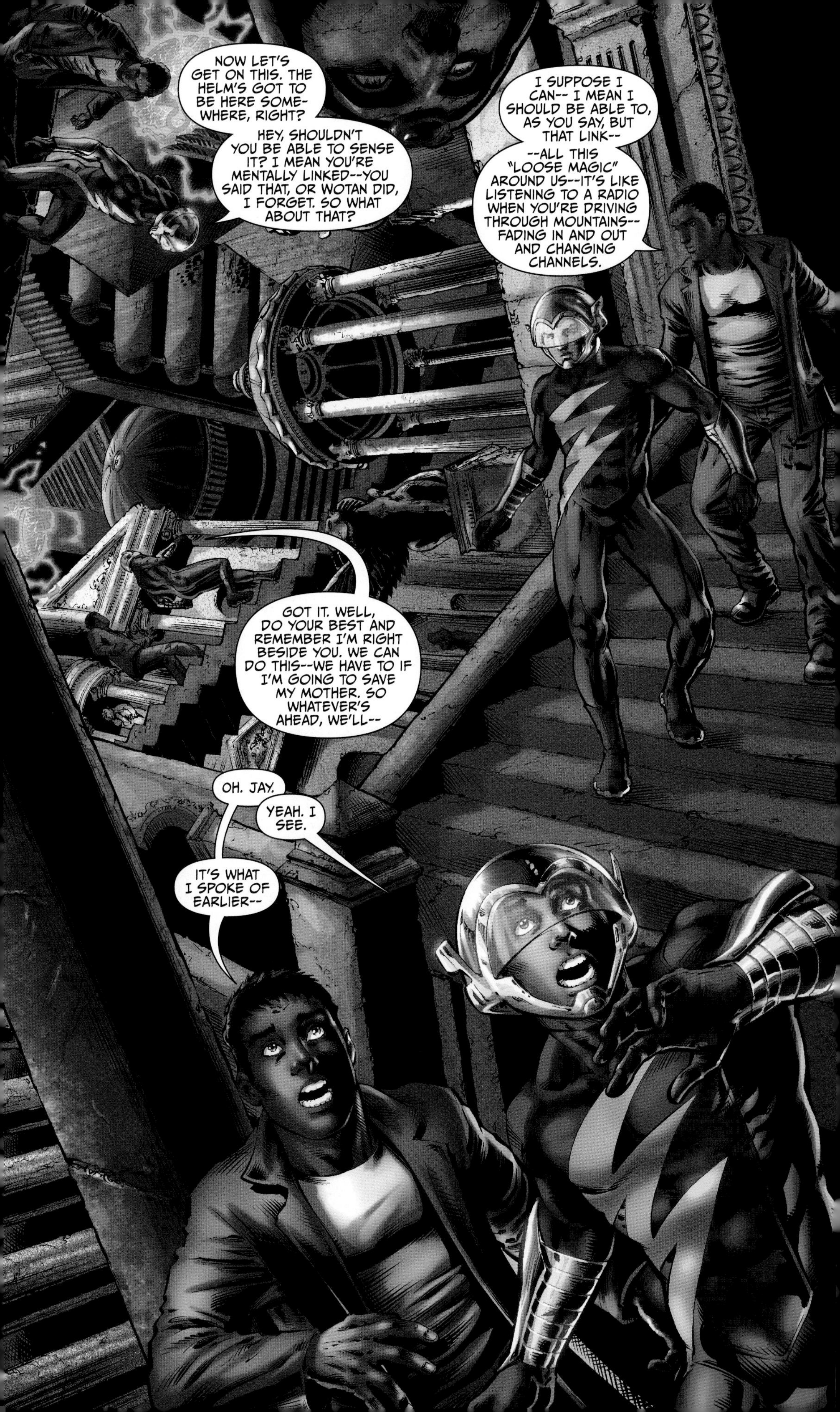
NOW LET'S GET ON THIS. THE HELM'S GOT TO BE HERE SOME-WHERE, RIGHT?
HEY, SHOULDN'T YOU BE ABLE TO SENSE IT? I MEAN YOU'RE MENTALLY LINKED--YOU SAID THAT, OR WOTAN DID, I FORGET. SO WHAT ABOUT THAT?
I SUPPOSE I CAN-- I MEAN I SHOULD BE ABLE TO, AS YOU SAY, BUT THAT LINK--
--ALL THIS "LOOSE MAGIC" AROUND US--IT'S LIKE LISTENING TO A RADIO WHEN YOU'RE DRIVING THROUGH MOUNTAINS-- FADING IN AND OUT AND CHANGING CHANNELS.
GOT IT. WELL, DO YOUR BEST AND REMEMBER I'M RIGHT BESIDE YOU. WE CAN DO THIS--WE HAVE TO IF I'M GOING TO SAVE MY MOTHER. SO WHATEVER'S AHEAD, WE'LL--
OH. JAY.
YEAH. I SEE.
IT'S WHAT I SPOKE OF EARLIER--

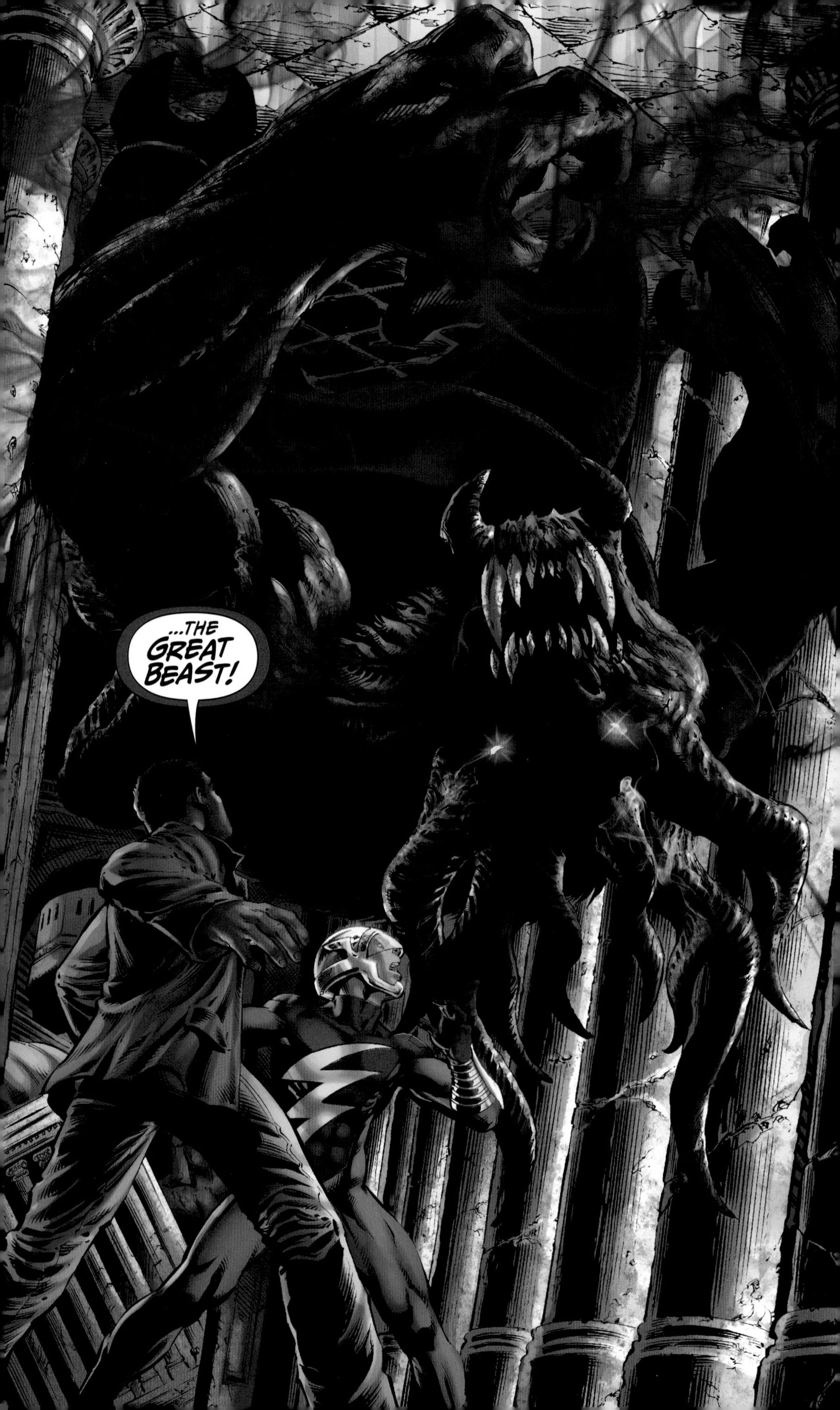
...THE GREAT BEAST!

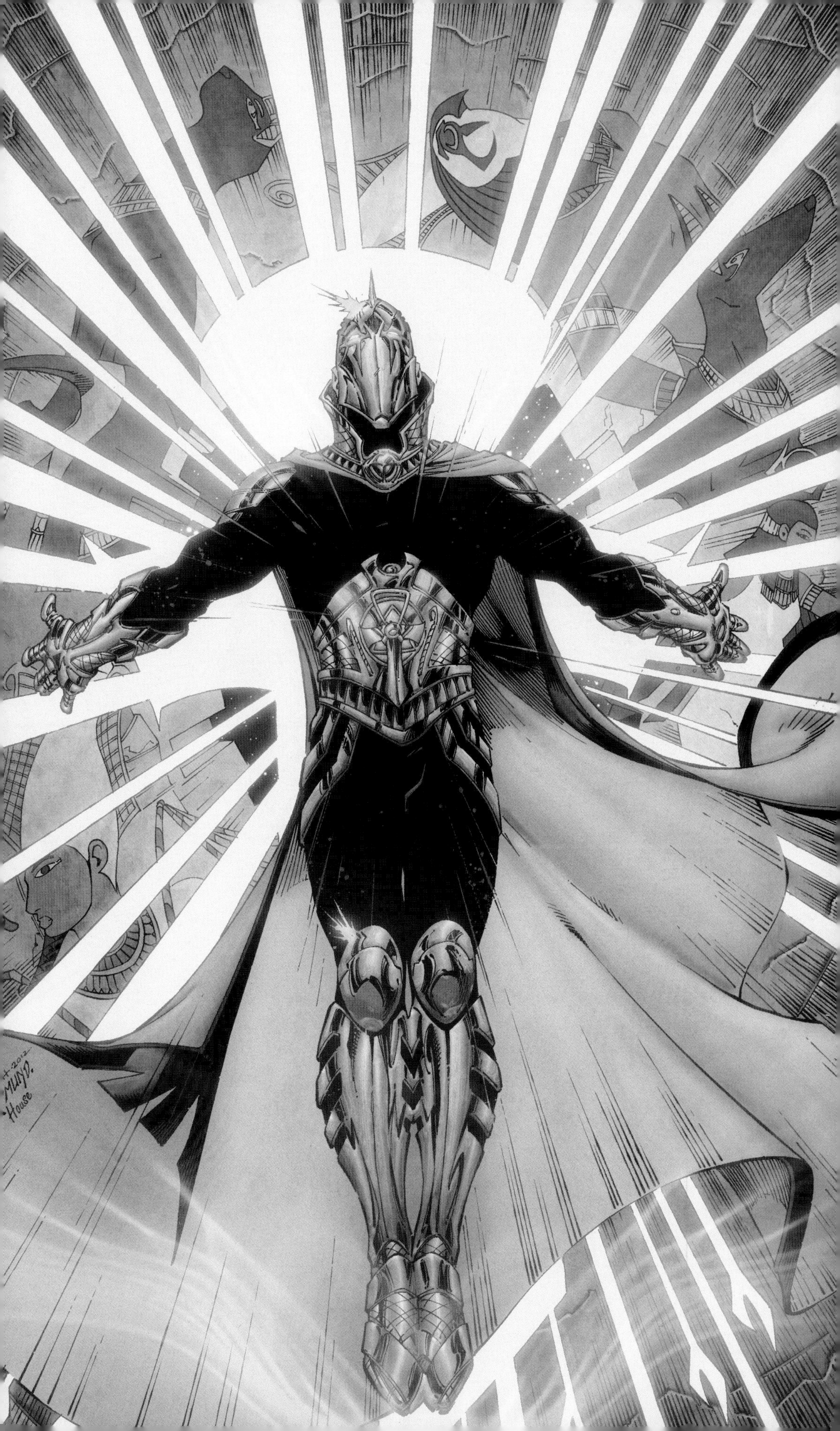

JAMES ROBINSON writer NICOLA SCOTT penciller TREVOR SCOTT inker cover by BRETT BOOTH, NORM RAPMUND & ANDREW DALHO

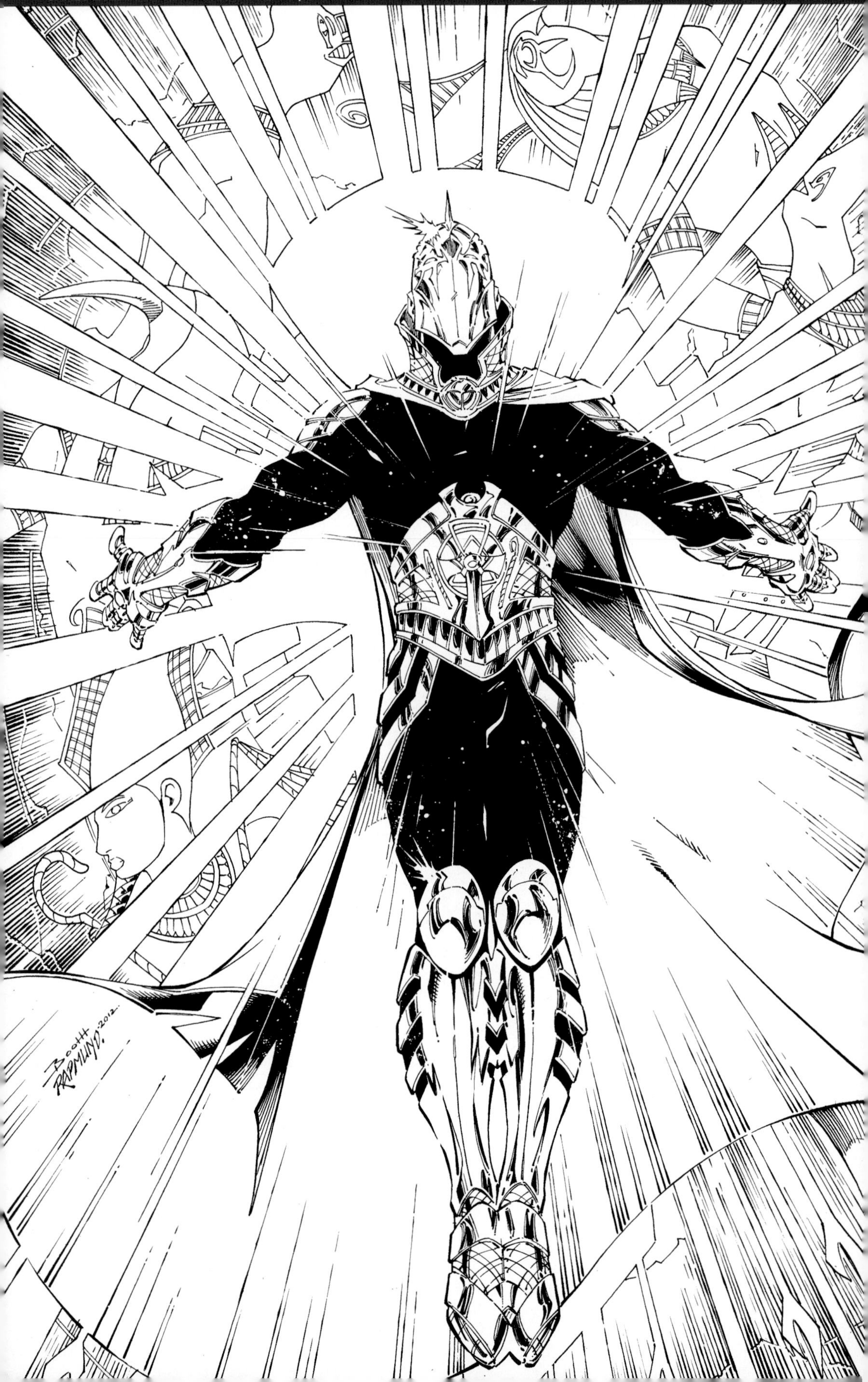
Booth
RAPMUND
2012

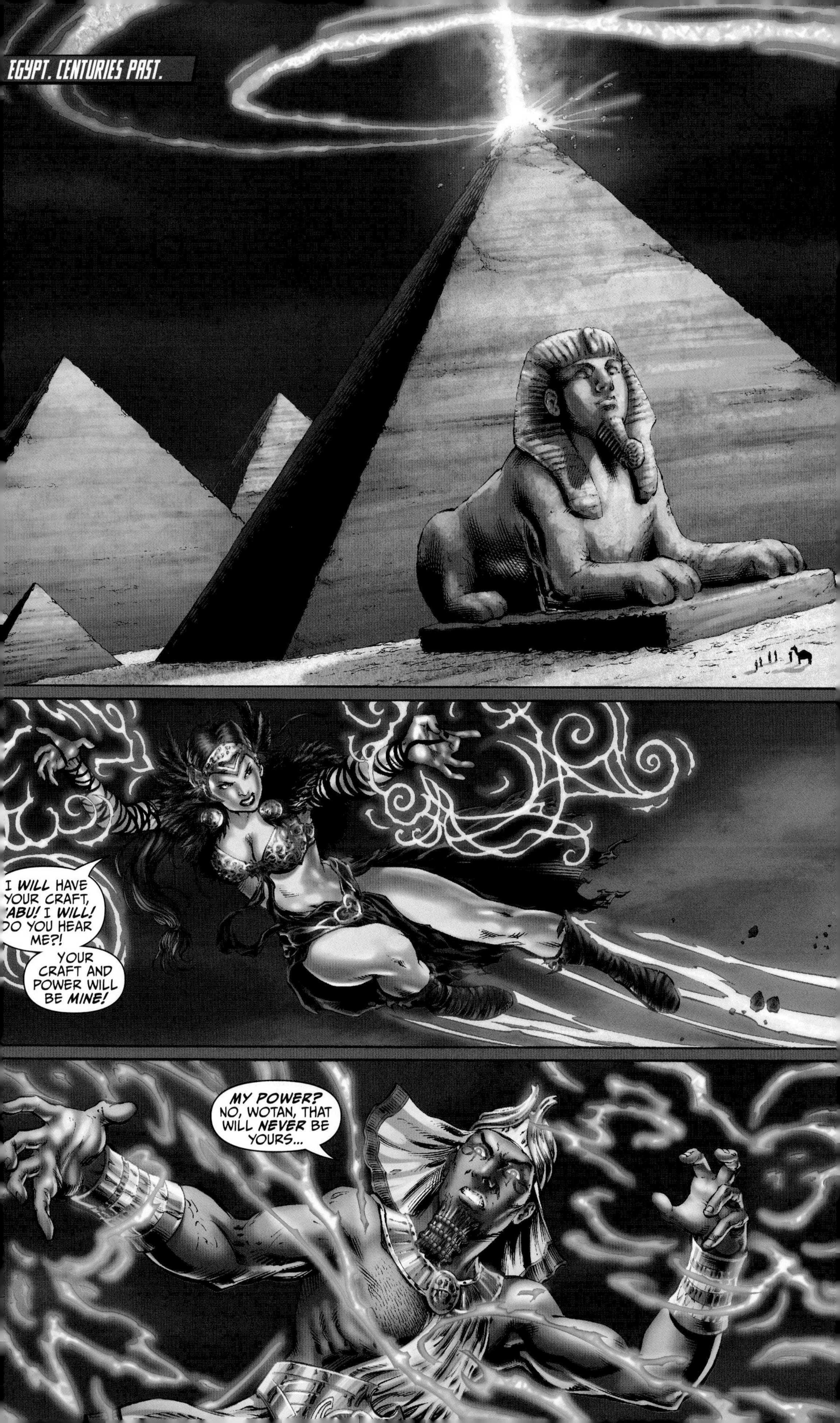
EGYPT. CENTURIES PAST.
I WILL HAVE YOUR CRAFT, ABU! I WILL! DO YOU HEAR ME?!
YOUR CRAFT AND POWER WILL BE MINE!
MY POWER? NO, WOTAN, THAT WILL NEVER BE YOURS...

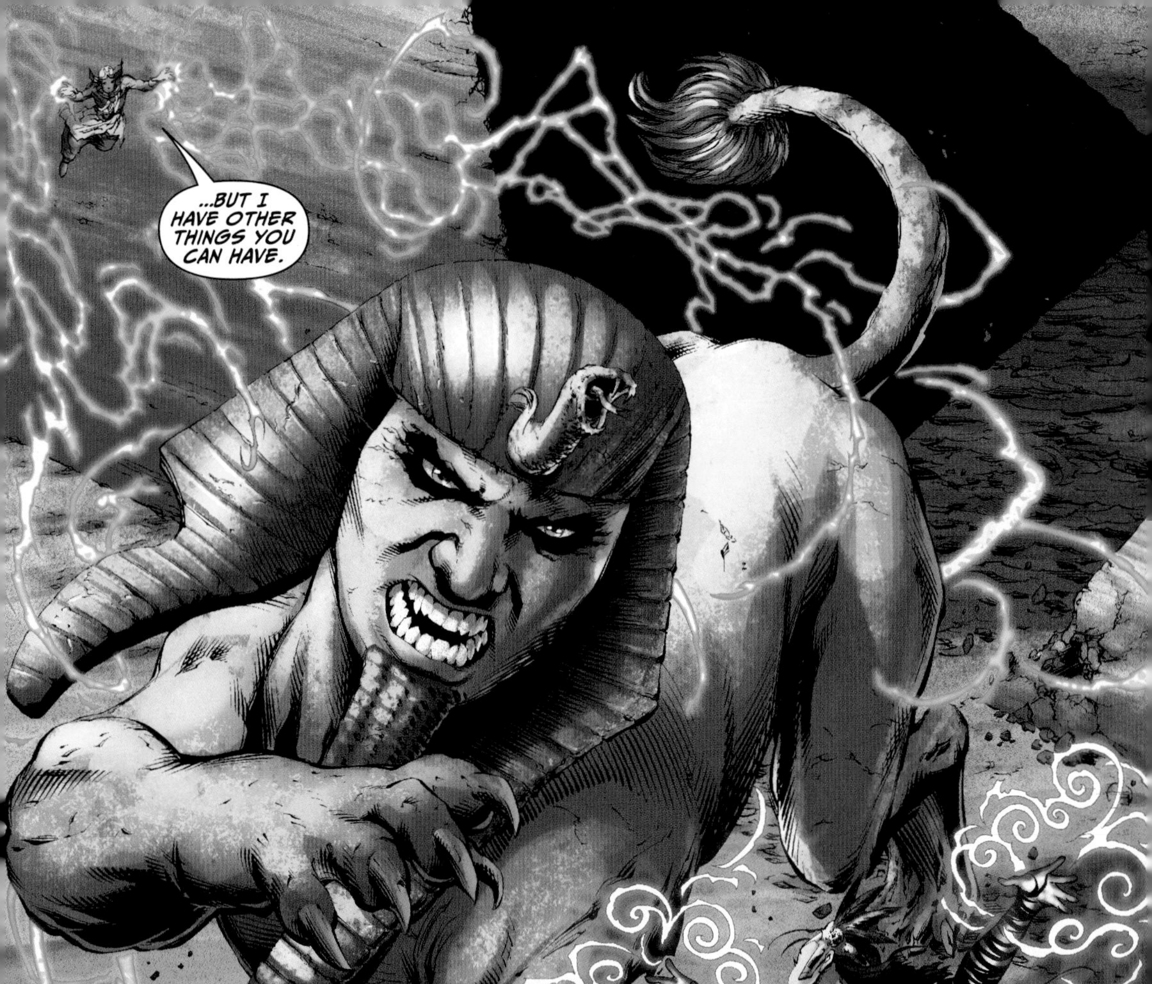
...BUT I HAVE OTHER THINGS YOU CAN HAVE.

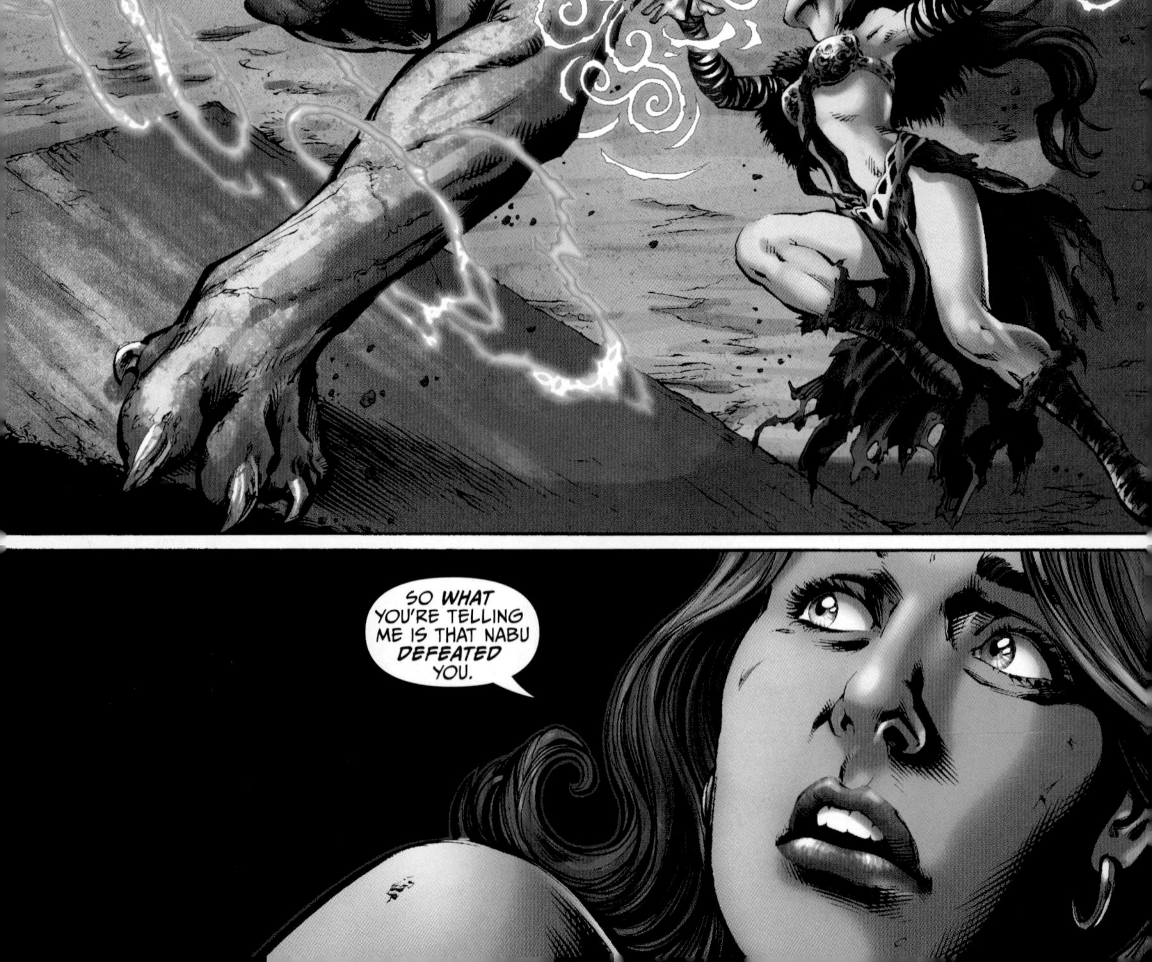
SO WHAT YOU'RE TELLING ME IS THAT NABU DEFEATED YOU.

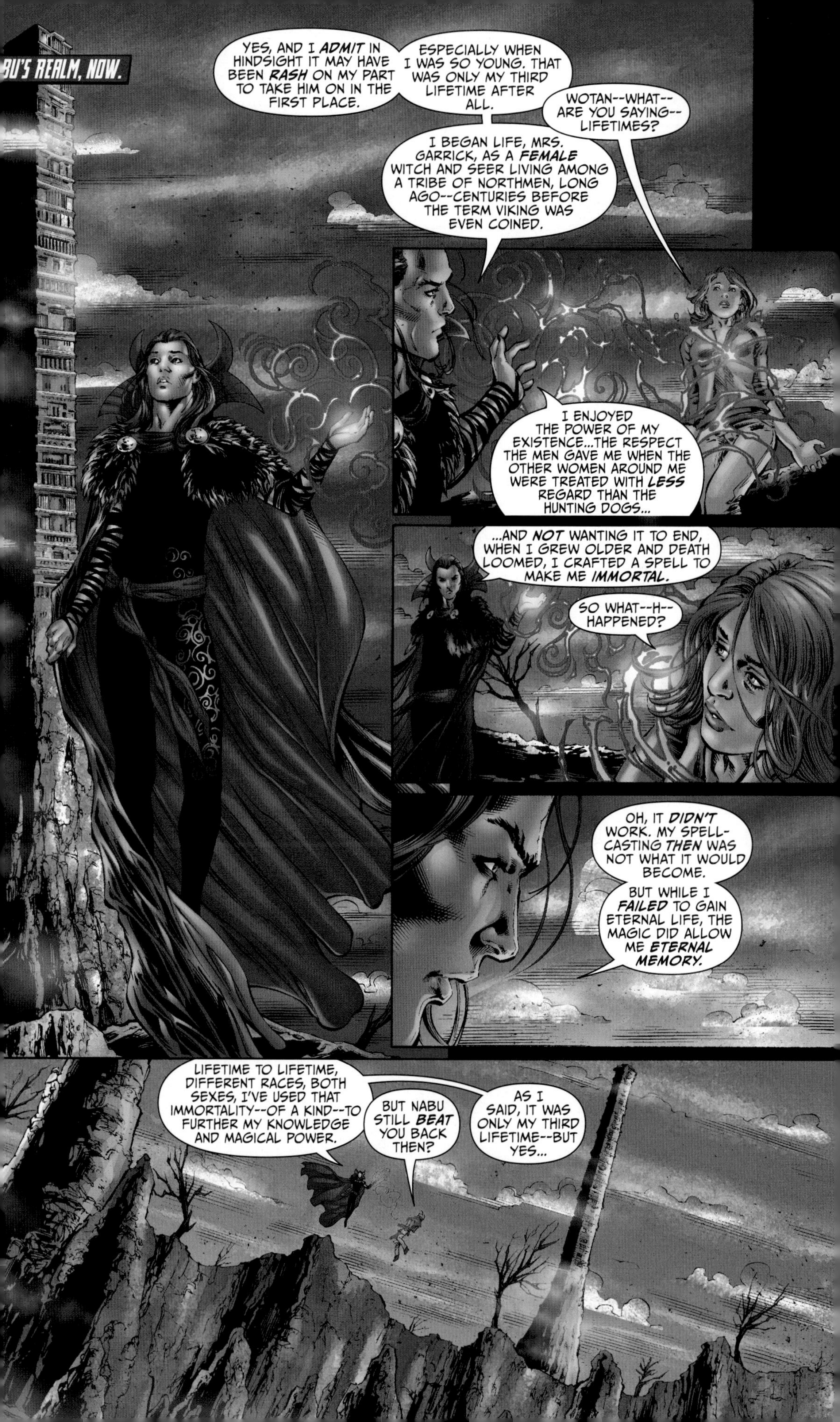

BU'S REALM, NOW.
YES, AND I ADMIT IN HINDSIGHT IT MAY HAVE BEEN RASH ON MY PART TO TAKE HIM ON IN THE FIRST PLACE.
ESPECIALLY WHEN I WAS SO YOUNG. THAT WAS ONLY MY THIRD LIFETIME AFTER ALL.
WOTAN--WHAT--ARE YOU SAYING--LIFETIMES?
I BEGAN LIFE, MRS. GARRICK, AS A FEMALE WITCH AND SEER LIVING AMONG A TRIBE OF NORTHMEN, LONG AGO--CENTURIES BEFORE THE TERM VIKING WAS EVEN COINED.
I ENJOYED THE POWER OF MY EXISTENCE...THE RESPECT THE MEN GAVE ME WHEN THE OTHER WOMEN AROUND ME WERE TREATED WITH LESS REGARD THAN THE HUNTING DOGS...
...AND NOT WANTING IT TO END, WHEN I GREW OLDER AND DEATH LOOMED, I CRAFTED A SPELL TO MAKE ME IMMORTAL.
SO WHAT--H--HAPPENED?
OH, IT DIDN'T WORK. MY SPELL-CASTING THEN WAS NOT WHAT IT WOULD BECOME.
BUT WHILE I FAILED TO GAIN ETERNAL LIFE, THE MAGIC DID ALLOW ME ETERNAL MEMORY.
LIFETIME TO LIFETIME, DIFFERENT RACES, BOTH SEXES, I'VE USED THAT IMMORTALITY--OF A KIND--TO FURTHER MY KNOWLEDGE AND MAGICAL POWER.
BUT NABU STILL BEAT YOU BACK THEN?
AS I SAID, IT WAS ONLY MY THIRD LIFETIME--BUT YES...

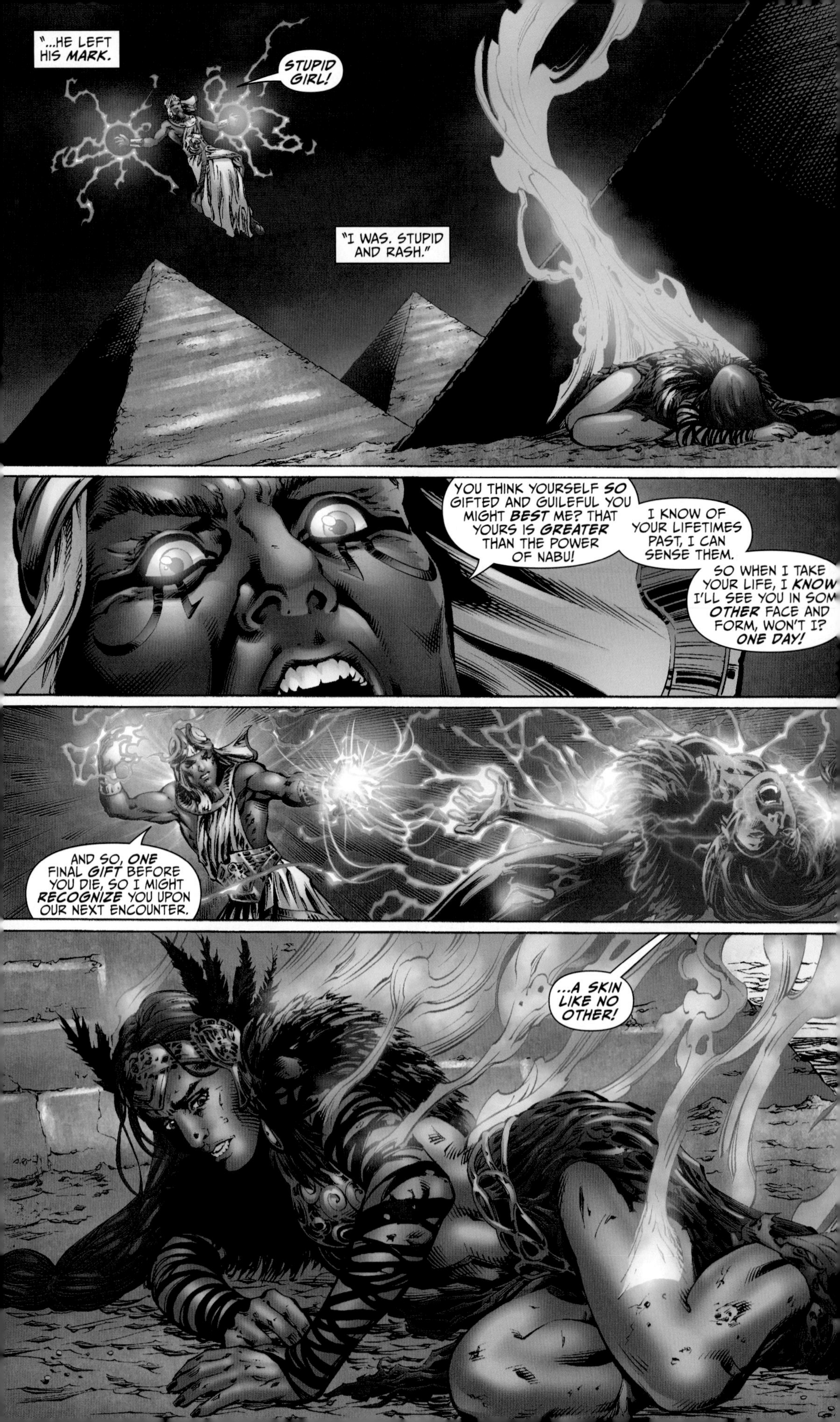
"...HE LEFT HIS MARK.
STUPID GIRL!
"I WAS. STUPID AND RASH."
YOU THINK YOURSELF SO GIFTED AND GUILEFUL YOU MIGHT BEST ME? THAT YOURS IS GREATER THAN THE POWER OF NABU!
I KNOW OF YOUR LIFETIMES PAST, I CAN SENSE THEM.
SO WHEN I TAKE YOUR LIFE, I KNOW I'LL SEE YOU IN SOM OTHER FACE AND FORM, WON'T I? ONE DAY!
AND SO, ONE FINAL GIFT BEFORE YOU DIE, SO I MIGHT RECOGNIZE YOU UPON OUR NEXT ENCOUNTER.
...A SKIN LIKE NO OTHER!

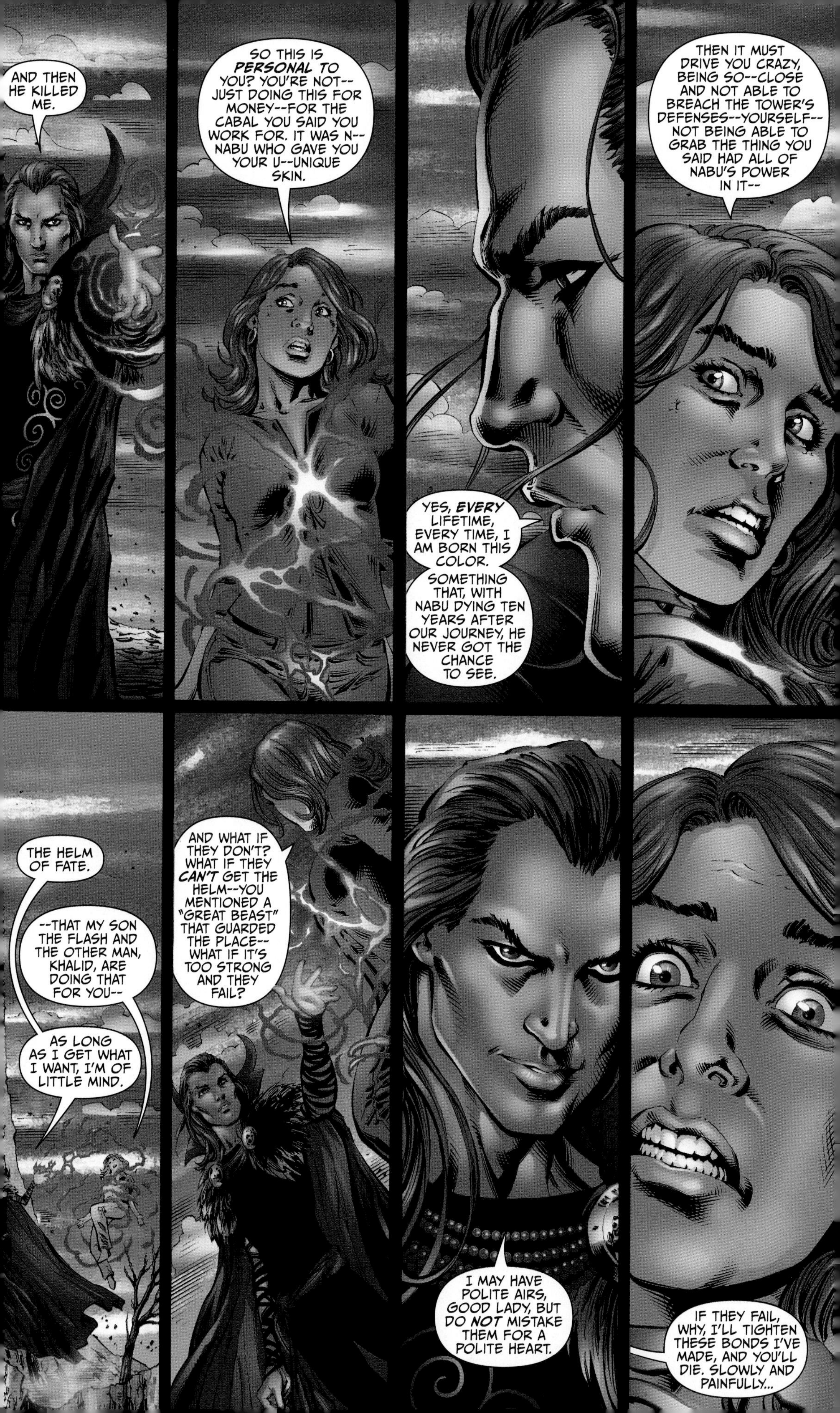
AND THEN HE KILLED ME.
SO THIS IS PERSONAL TO YOU? YOU'RE NOT--JUST DOING THIS FOR MONEY--FOR THE CABAL YOU SAID YOU WORK FOR. IT WAS N--NABU WHO GAVE YOU YOUR U--UNIQUE SKIN.
YES, EVERY LIFETIME, EVERY TIME, I AM BORN THIS COLOR.
SOMETHING THAT, WITH NABU DYING TEN YEARS AFTER OUR JOURNEY, HE NEVER GOT THE CHANCE TO SEE.
THEN IT MUST DRIVE YOU CRAZY, BEING SO--CLOSE AND NOT ABLE TO BREACH THE TOWER'S DEFENSES--YOURSELF--NOT BEING ABLE TO GRAB THE THING YOU SAID HAD ALL OF NABU'S POWER IN IT--
THE HELM OF FATE.
--THAT MY SON THE FLASH AND THE OTHER MAN, KHALID, ARE DOING THAT FOR YOU--
AS LONG AS I GET WHAT I WANT, I'M OF LITTLE MIND.
AND WHAT IF THEY DON'T? WHAT IF THEY CAN'T GET THE HELM--YOU MENTIONED A "GREAT BEAST" THAT GUARDED THE PLACE--WHAT IF IT'S TOO STRONG AND THEY FAIL?
I MAY HAVE POLITE AIRS, GOOD LADY, BUT DO NOT MISTAKE THEM FOR A POLITE HEART.
IF THEY FAIL, WHY, I'LL TIGHTEN THESE BONDS I'VE MADE, AND YOU'LL DIE. SLOWLY AND PAINFULLY...

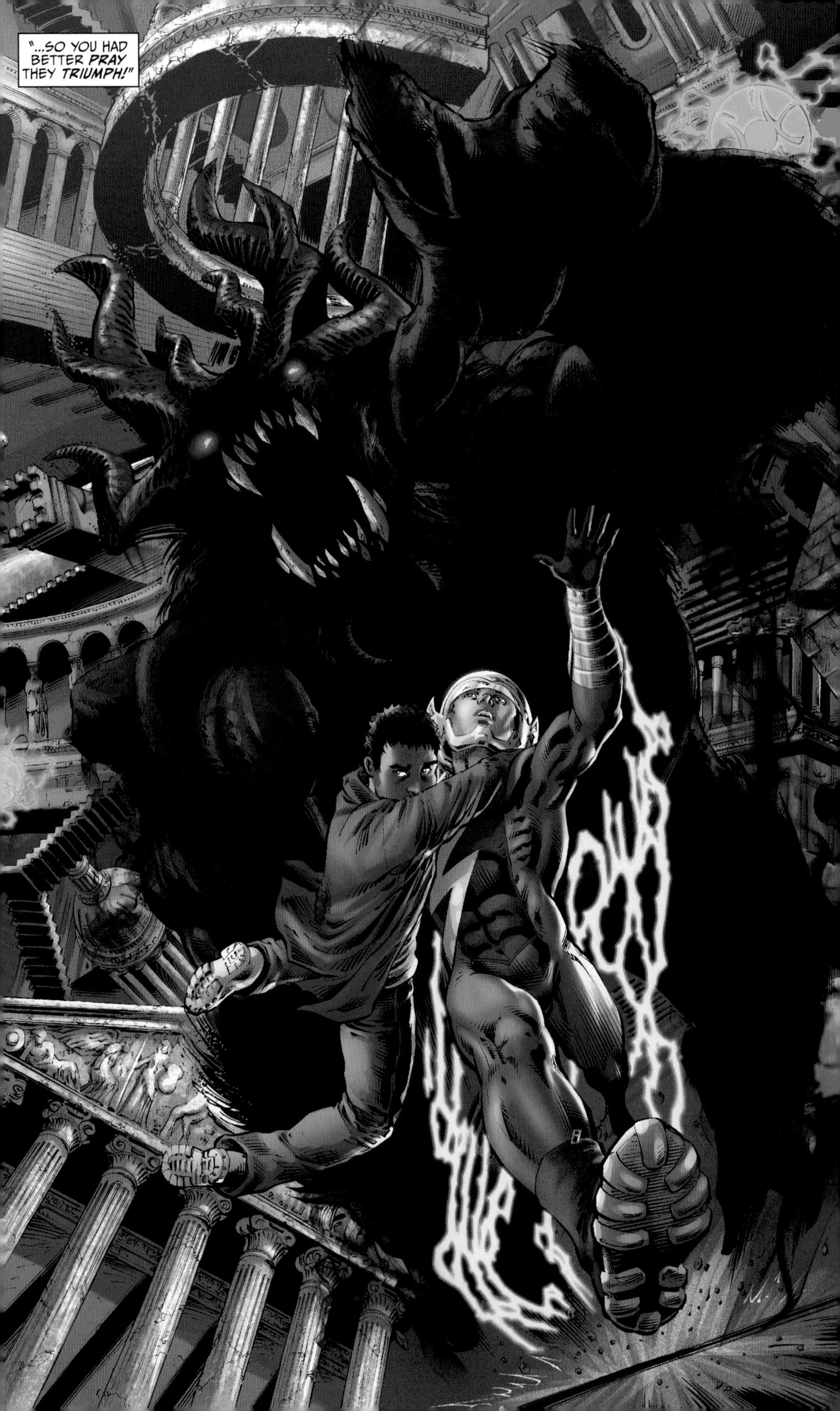
"...SO YOU HAD BETTER PRAY THEY TRIUMPH!"

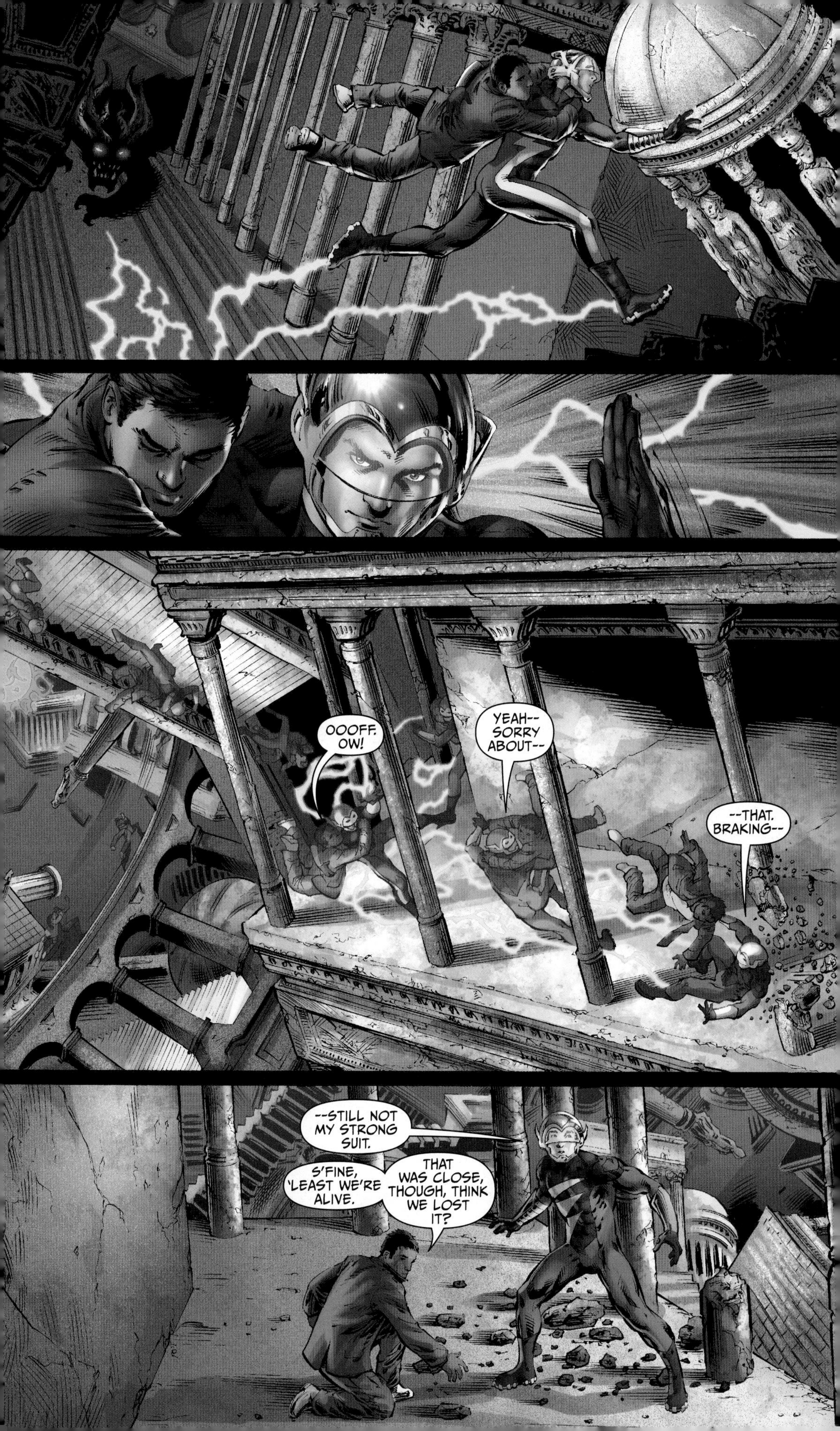
OOOFF. OW!
YEAH-- SORRY ABOUT--
--THAT. BRAKING--
--STILL NOT MY STRONG SUIT.
S'FINE, 'LEAST WE'RE ALIVE.
THAT WAS CLOSE, THOUGH, THINK WE LOST IT?

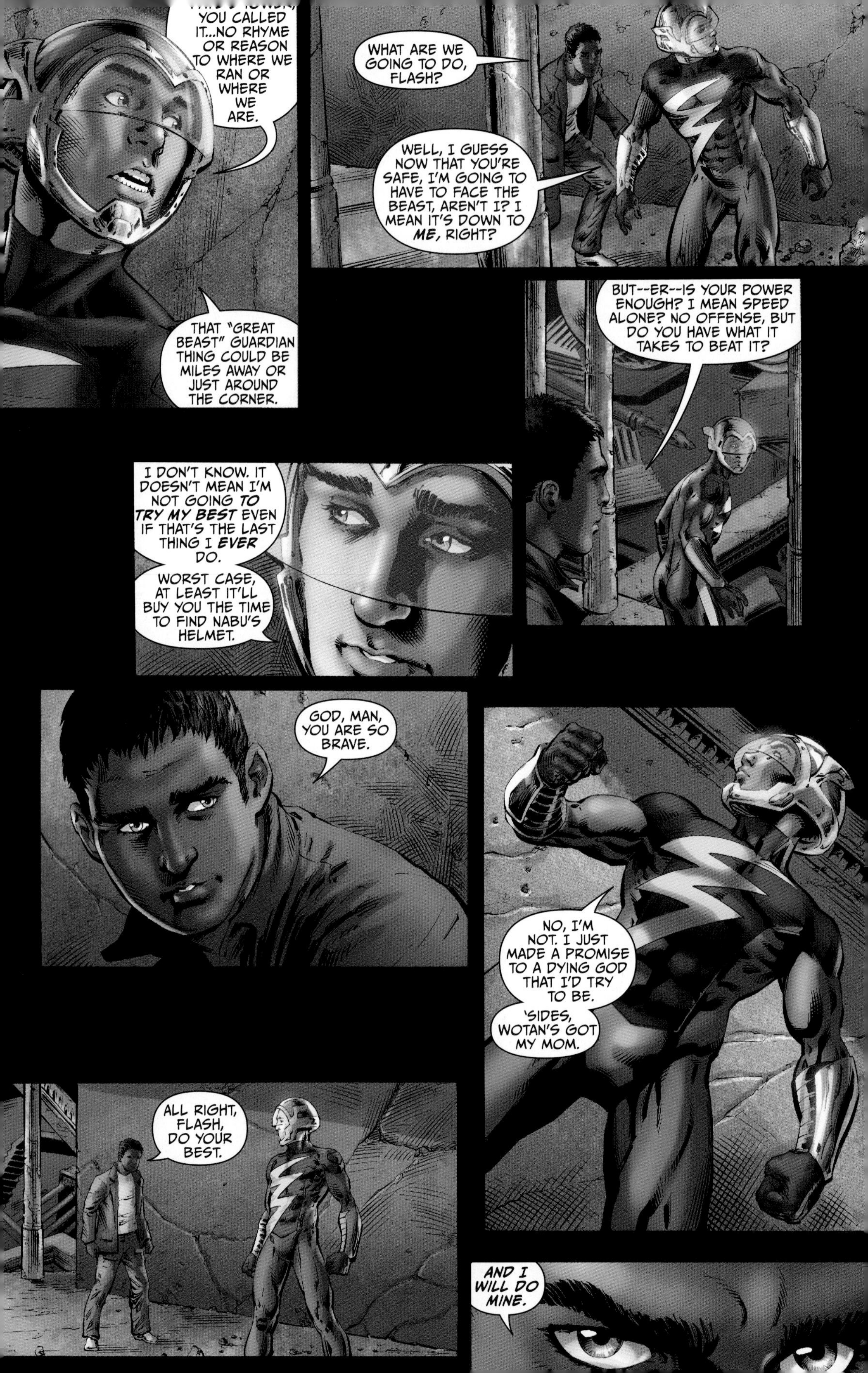
YOU CALLED IT...NO RHYME OR REASON TO WHERE WE RAN OR WHERE WE ARE.
THAT "GREAT BEAST" GUARDIAN THING COULD BE MILES AWAY OR JUST AROUND THE CORNER.
WHAT ARE WE GOING TO DO, FLASH?
WELL, I GUESS NOW THAT YOU'RE SAFE, I'M GOING TO HAVE TO FACE THE BEAST, AREN'T I? I MEAN IT'S DOWN TO *ME*, RIGHT?
BUT--ER--IS YOUR POWER ENOUGH? I MEAN SPEED ALONE? NO OFFENSE, BUT DO YOU HAVE WHAT IT TAKES TO BEAT IT?
I DON'T KNOW. IT DOESN'T MEAN I'M NOT GOING ***TO TRY MY BEST*** EVEN IF THAT'S THE LAST THING I ***EVER*** DO.
WORST CASE, AT LEAST IT'LL BUY YOU THE TIME TO FIND NABU'S HELMET.
GOD, MAN, YOU ARE SO BRAVE.
NO, I'M NOT. I JUST MADE A PROMISE TO A DYING GOD THAT I'D TRY TO BE.
'SIDES, WOTAN'S GOT MY MOM.
ALL RIGHT, FLASH, DO YOUR BEST.
AND I WILL DO MINE.

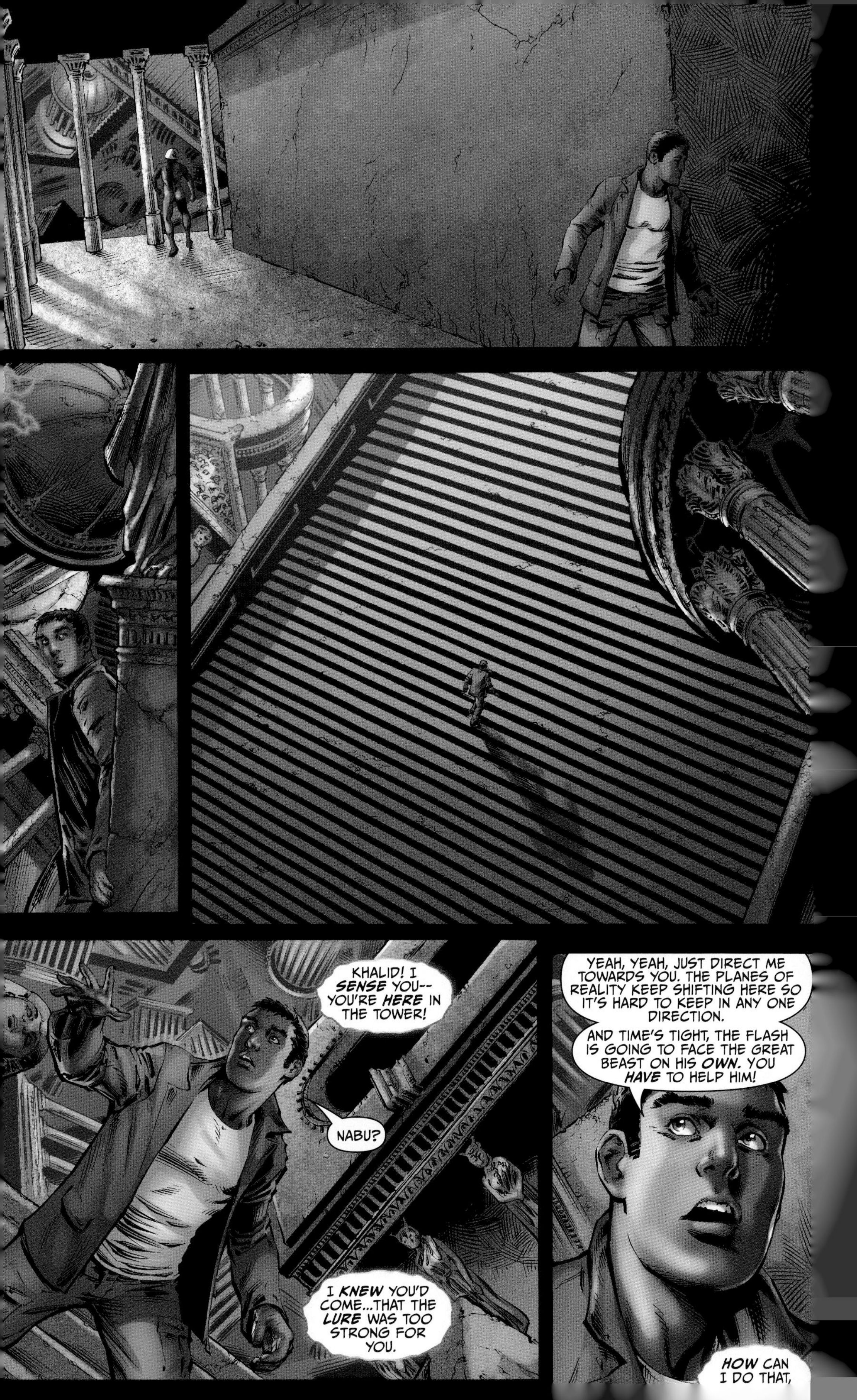
KHALID! I SENSE YOU-- YOU'RE HERE IN THE TOWER!
NABU?
I KNEW YOU'D COME...THAT THE LURE WAS TOO STRONG FOR YOU.
YEAH, YEAH, JUST DIRECT ME TOWARDS YOU. THE PLANES OF REALITY KEEP SHIFTING HERE SO IT'S HARD TO KEEP IN ANY ONE DIRECTION.
AND TIME'S TIGHT, THE FLASH IS GOING TO FACE THE GREAT BEAST ON HIS OWN. YOU HAVE TO HELP HIM!
HOW CAN I DO THAT,

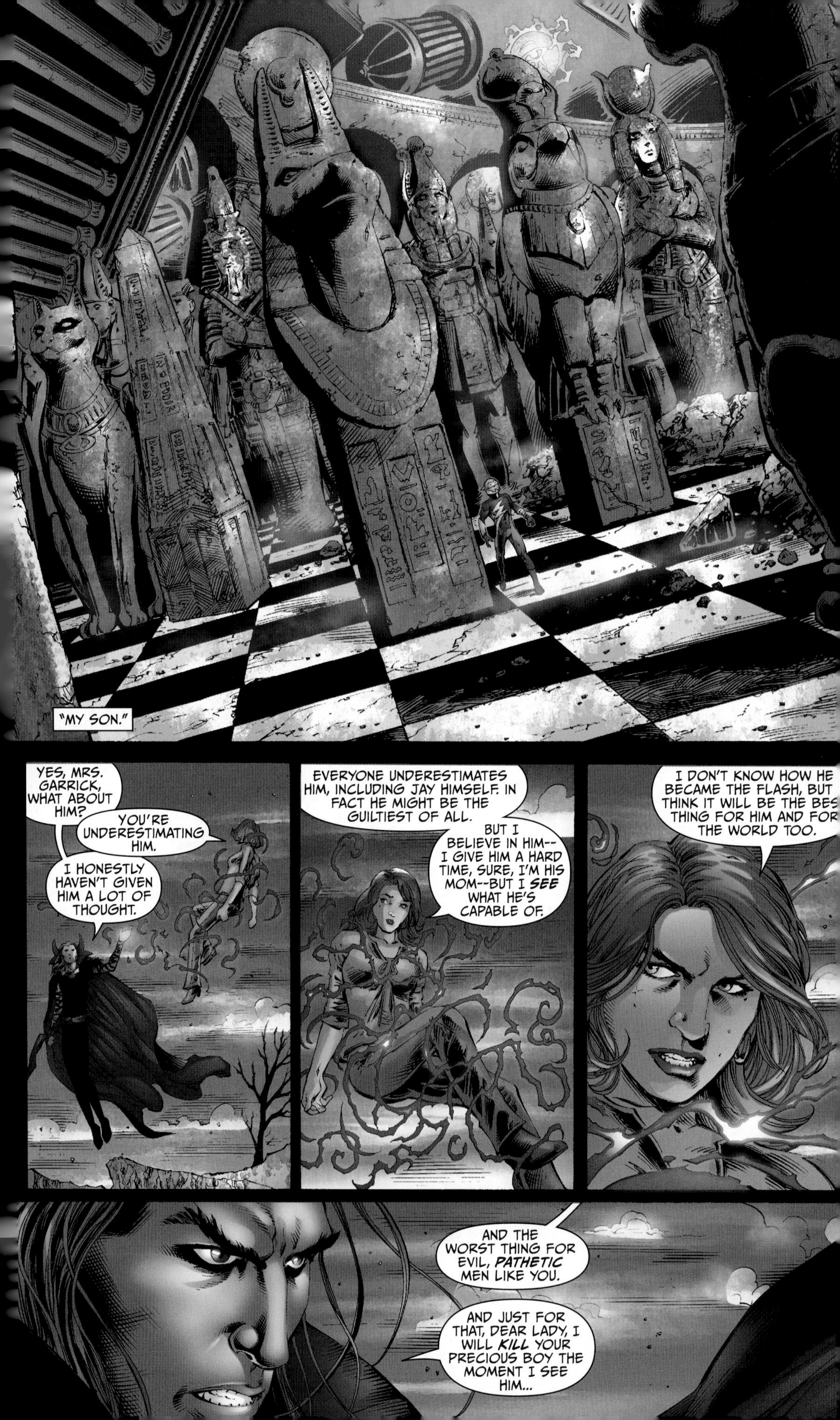
"MY SON."
YES, MRS. GARRICK, WHAT ABOUT HIM?
YOU'RE UNDERESTIMATING HIM.
I HONESTLY HAVEN'T GIVEN HIM A LOT OF THOUGHT.
EVERYONE UNDERESTIMATES HIM, INCLUDING JAY HIMSELF. IN FACT HE MIGHT BE THE GUILTIEST OF ALL.
BUT I BELIEVE IN HIM-- I GIVE HIM A HARD TIME, SURE, I'M HIS MOM--BUT I SEE WHAT HE'S CAPABLE OF.
I DON'T KNOW HOW HE BECAME THE FLASH, BUT THINK IT WILL BE THE BES THING FOR HIM AND FOR THE WORLD TOO.
AND THE WORST THING FOR EVIL, PATHETIC MEN LIKE YOU.
AND JUST FOR THAT, DEAR LADY, I WILL KILL YOUR PRECIOUS BOY THE MOMENT I SEE HIM...

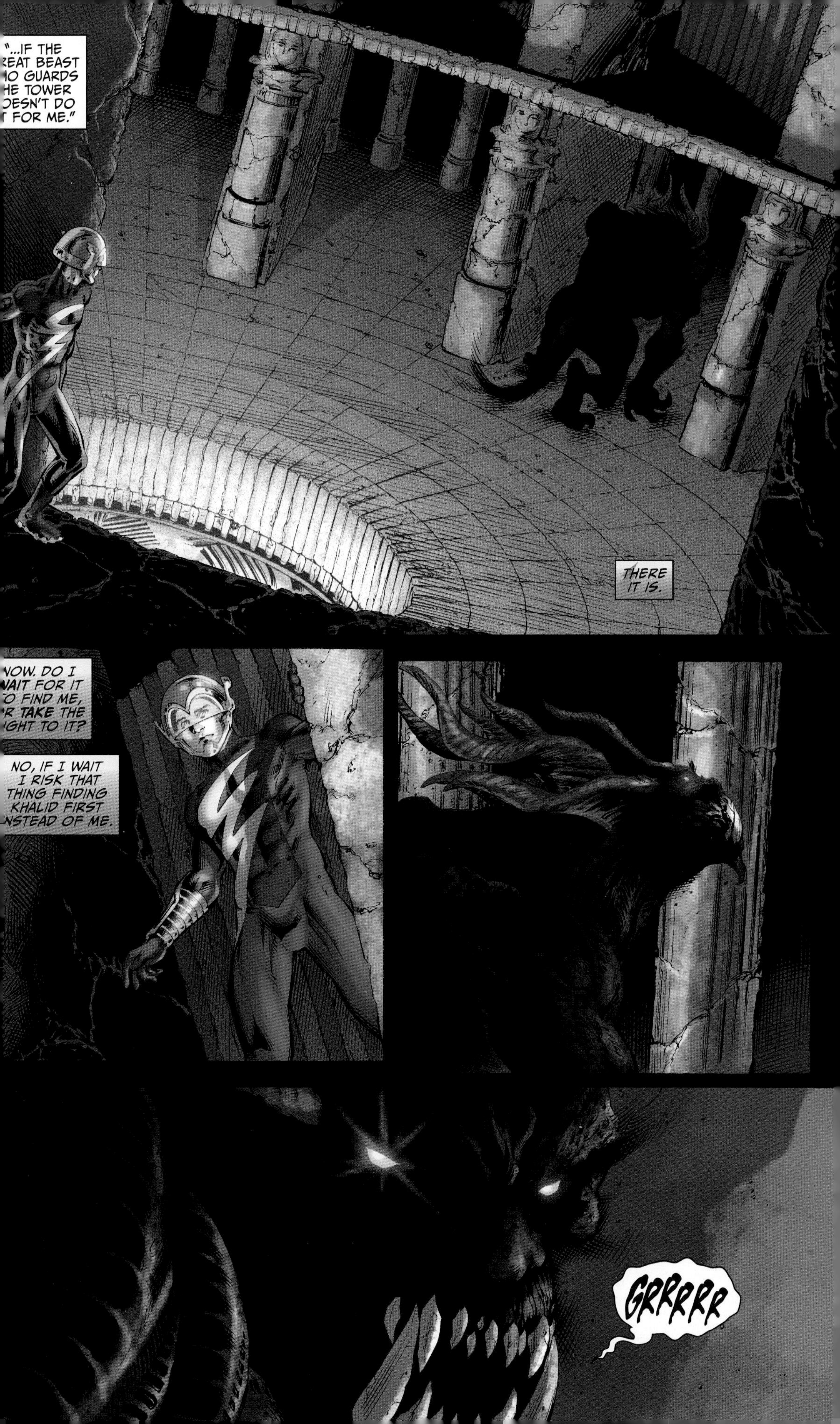
"...IF THE
EAT BEAST
O GUARDS
HE TOWER
OESN'T DO
FOR ME."
THERE IT IS.
NOW. DO I
AIT FOR IT
O FIND ME,
R TAKE THE
IGHT TO IT?
NO, IF I WAIT I RISK THAT THING FINDING KHALID FIRST
NSTEAD OF ME.
GRRRRR

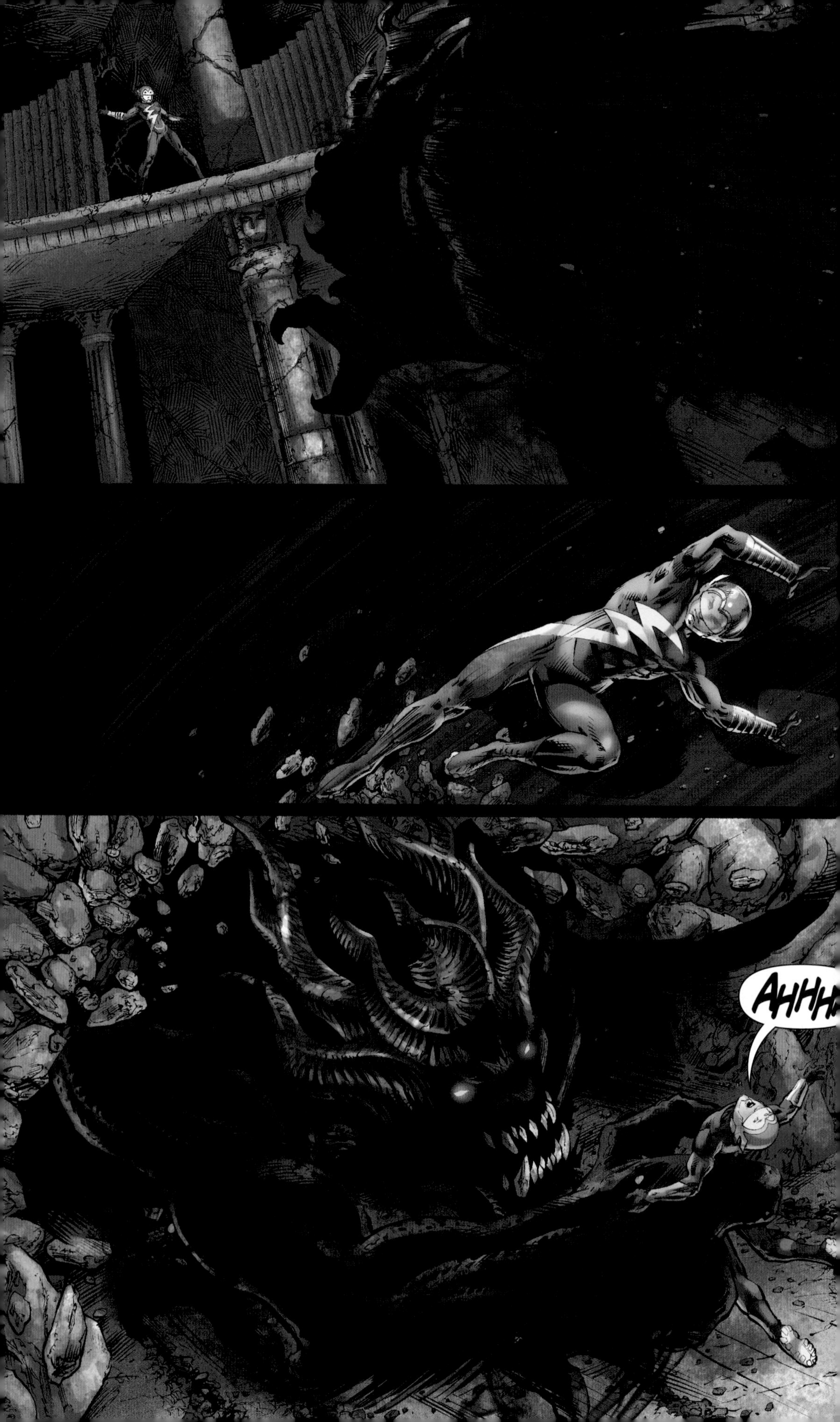
AHHH

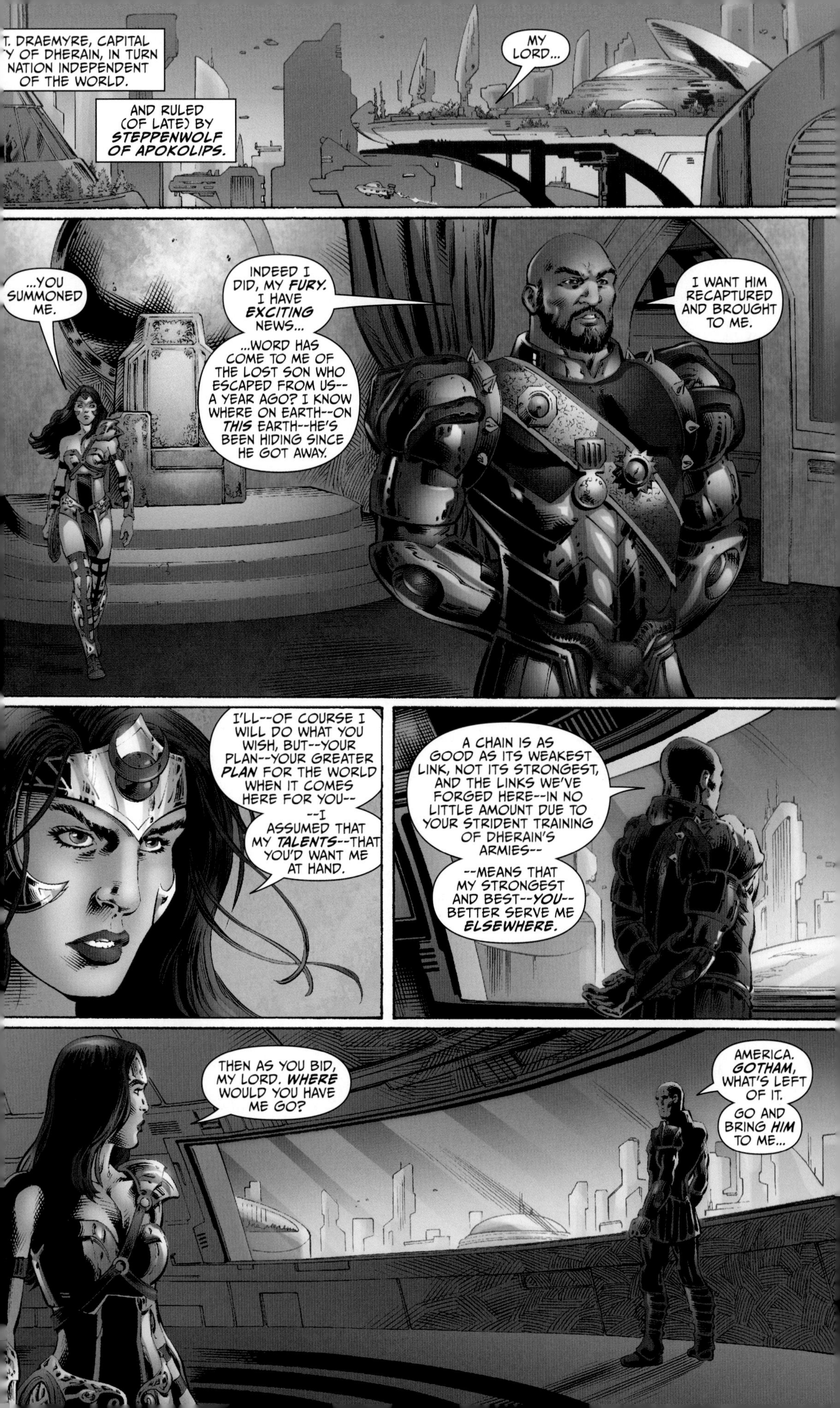
T. DRAEMYRE, CAPITAL Y OF DHERAIN, IN TURN NATION INDEPENDENT OF THE WORLD.
AND RULED (OF LATE) BY STEPPENWOLF OF APOKOLIPS.
MY LORD...
...YOU SUMMONED ME.
INDEED I DID, MY FURY. I HAVE EXCITING NEWS...
...WORD HAS COME TO ME OF THE LOST SON WHO ESCAPED FROM US--A YEAR AGO? I KNOW WHERE ON EARTH--ON THIS EARTH--HE'S BEEN HIDING SINCE HE GOT AWAY.
I WANT HIM RECAPTURED AND BROUGHT TO ME.
I'LL--OF COURSE I WILL DO WHAT YOU WISH, BUT--YOUR PLAN--YOUR GREATER PLAN FOR THE WORLD WHEN IT COMES HERE FOR YOU--
--I ASSUMED THAT MY TALENTS--THAT YOU'D WANT ME AT HAND.
A CHAIN IS AS GOOD AS ITS WEAKEST LINK, NOT ITS STRONGEST, AND THE LINKS WE'VE FORGED HERE--IN NO LITTLE AMOUNT DUE TO YOUR STRIDENT TRAINING OF DHERAIN'S ARMIES--
--MEANS THAT MY STRONGEST AND BEST--YOU--BETTER SERVE ME ELSEWHERE.
THEN AS YOU BID, MY LORD. WHERE WOULD YOU HAVE ME GO?
AMERICA. GOTHAM, WHAT'S LEFT OF IT.
GO AND BRING HIM TO ME...

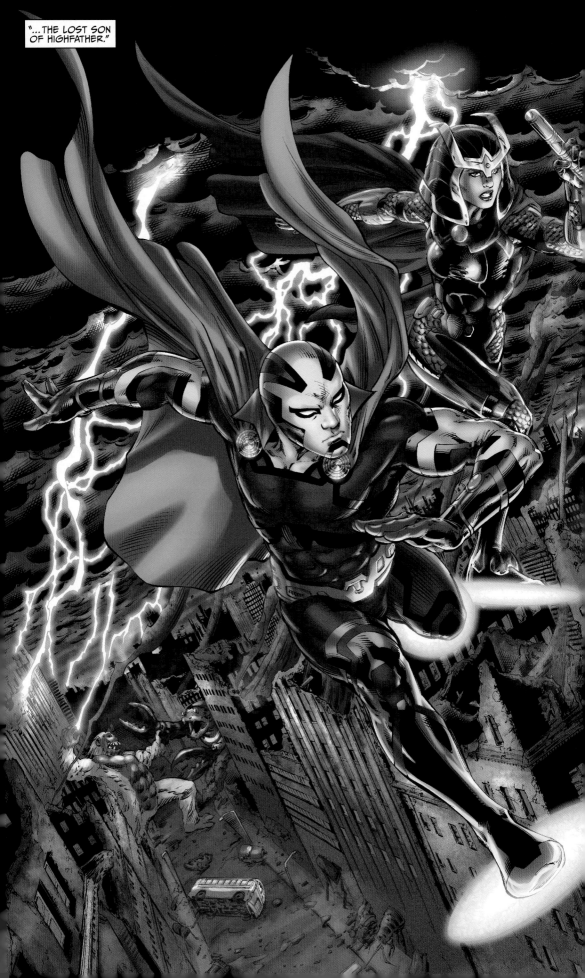

"...THE LOST SON OF HIGHFATHER."

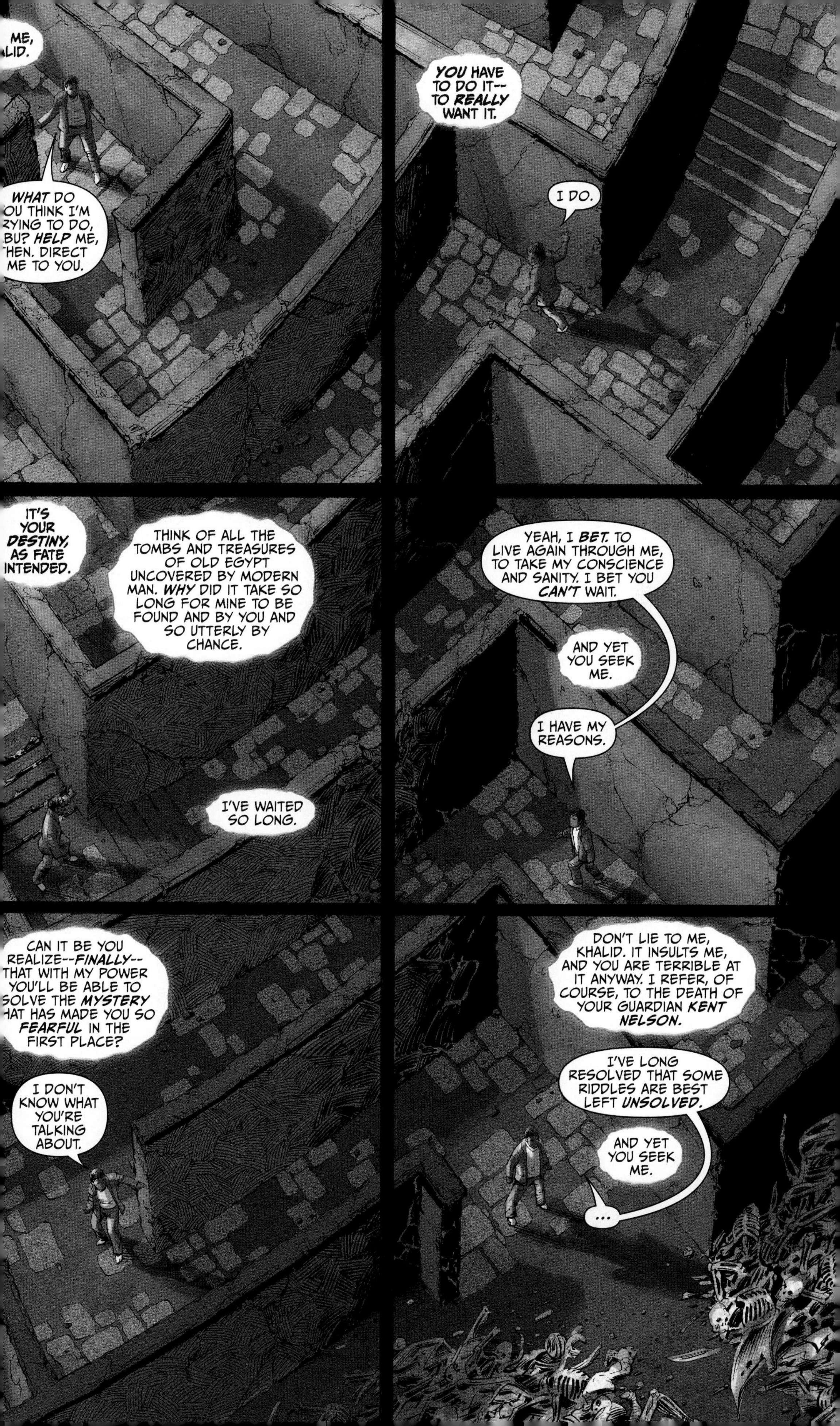

ME, LID.
WHAT DO OU THINK I'M ZYING TO DO, BU? HELP ME, HEN. DIRECT ME TO YOU.
YOU HAVE TO DO IT-- TO REALLY WANT IT.
I DO.
IT'S YOUR DESTINY, AS FATE INTENDED.
THINK OF ALL THE TOMBS AND TREASURES OF OLD EGYPT UNCOVERED BY MODERN MAN. WHY DID IT TAKE SO LONG FOR MINE TO BE FOUND AND BY YOU AND SO UTTERLY BY CHANCE.
I'VE WAITED SO LONG.
YEAH, I BET. TO LIVE AGAIN THROUGH ME, TO TAKE MY CONSCIENCE AND SANITY. I BET YOU CAN'T WAIT.
AND YET YOU SEEK ME.
I HAVE MY REASONS.
CAN IT BE YOU REALIZE--FINALLY-- THAT WITH MY POWER YOU'LL BE ABLE TO SOLVE THE MYSTERY HAT HAS MADE YOU SO FEARFUL IN THE FIRST PLACE?
I DON'T KNOW WHAT YOU'RE TALKING ABOUT.
DON'T LIE TO ME, KHALID. IT INSULTS ME, AND YOU ARE TERRIBLE AT IT ANYWAY. I REFER, OF COURSE, TO THE DEATH OF YOUR GUARDIAN KENT NELSON.
I'VE LONG RESOLVED THAT SOME RIDDLES ARE BEST LEFT UNSOLVED.
AND YET YOU SEEK ME.
...

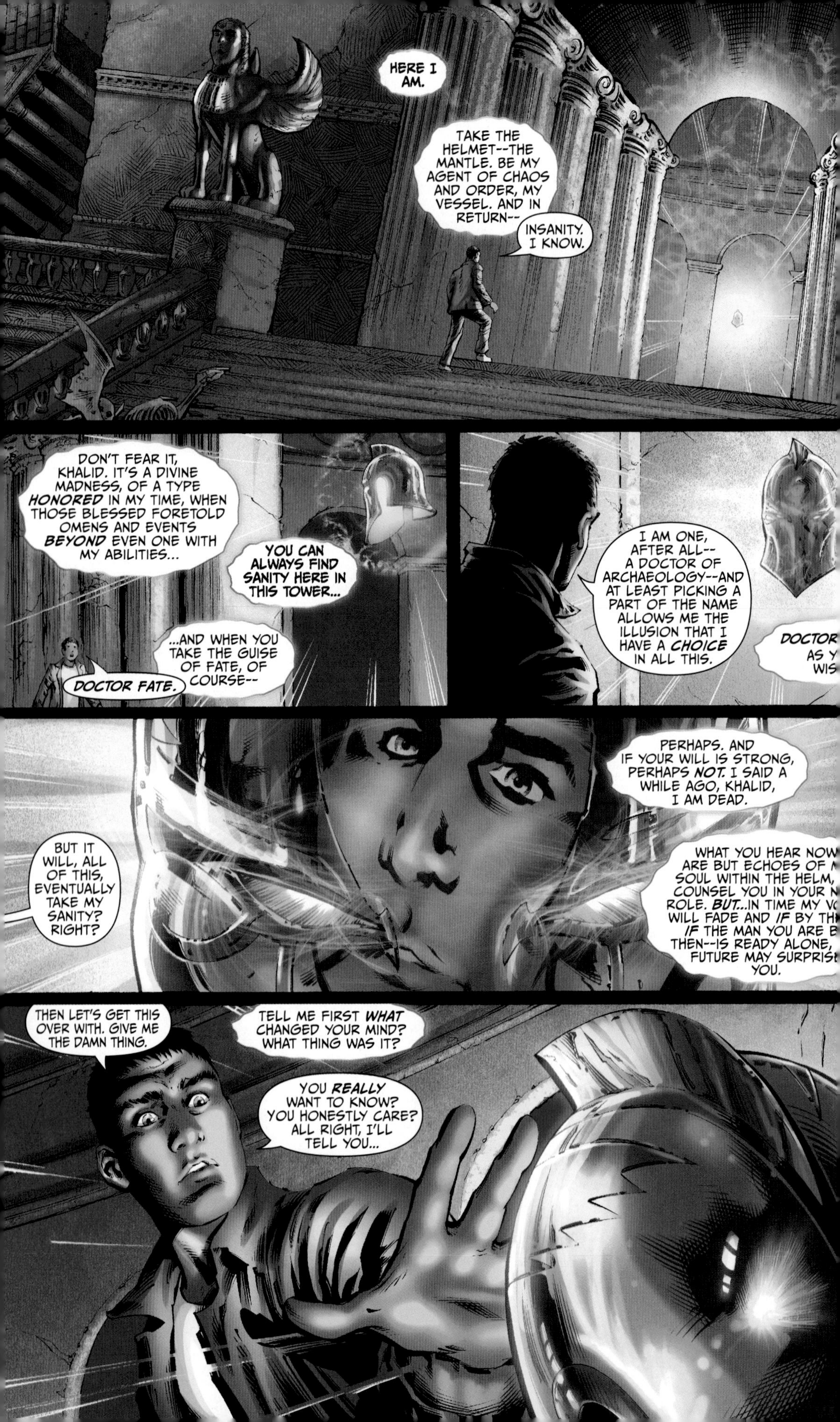
HERE I AM.
TAKE THE HELMET--THE MANTLE. BE MY AGENT OF CHAOS AND ORDER, MY VESSEL. AND IN RETURN--
INSANITY. I KNOW.
DON'T FEAR IT, KHALID. IT'S A DIVINE MADNESS, OF A TYPE HONORED IN MY TIME, WHEN THOSE BLESSED FORETOLD OMENS AND EVENTS BEYOND EVEN ONE WITH MY ABILITIES...
YOU CAN ALWAYS FIND SANITY HERE IN THIS TOWER...
...AND WHEN YOU TAKE THE GUISE OF FATE, OF COURSE--
DOCTOR FATE.
I AM ONE, AFTER ALL--A DOCTOR OF ARCHAEOLOGY--AND AT LEAST PICKING A PART OF THE NAME ALLOWS ME THE ILLUSION THAT I HAVE A CHOICE IN ALL THIS.
DOCTOR
AS Y
WIS
BUT IT WILL, ALL OF THIS, EVENTUALLY TAKE MY SANITY? RIGHT?
PERHAPS. AND IF YOUR WILL IS STRONG, PERHAPS NOT. I SAID A WHILE AGO, KHALID, I AM DEAD.
WHAT YOU HEAR NOW ARE BUT ECHOES OF SOUL WITHIN THE HELM, COUNSEL YOU IN YOUR ROLE. BUT...IN TIME MY V WILL FADE AND IF BY TH IF THE MAN YOU ARE THEN--IS READY ALONE, FUTURE MAY SURPRIS YOU.
THEN LET'S GET THIS OVER WITH. GIVE ME THE DAMN THING.
TELL ME FIRST WHAT CHANGED YOUR MIND? WHAT THING WAS IT?
YOU REALLY WANT TO KNOW? YOU HONESTLY CARE? ALL RIGHT, I'LL TELL YOU...

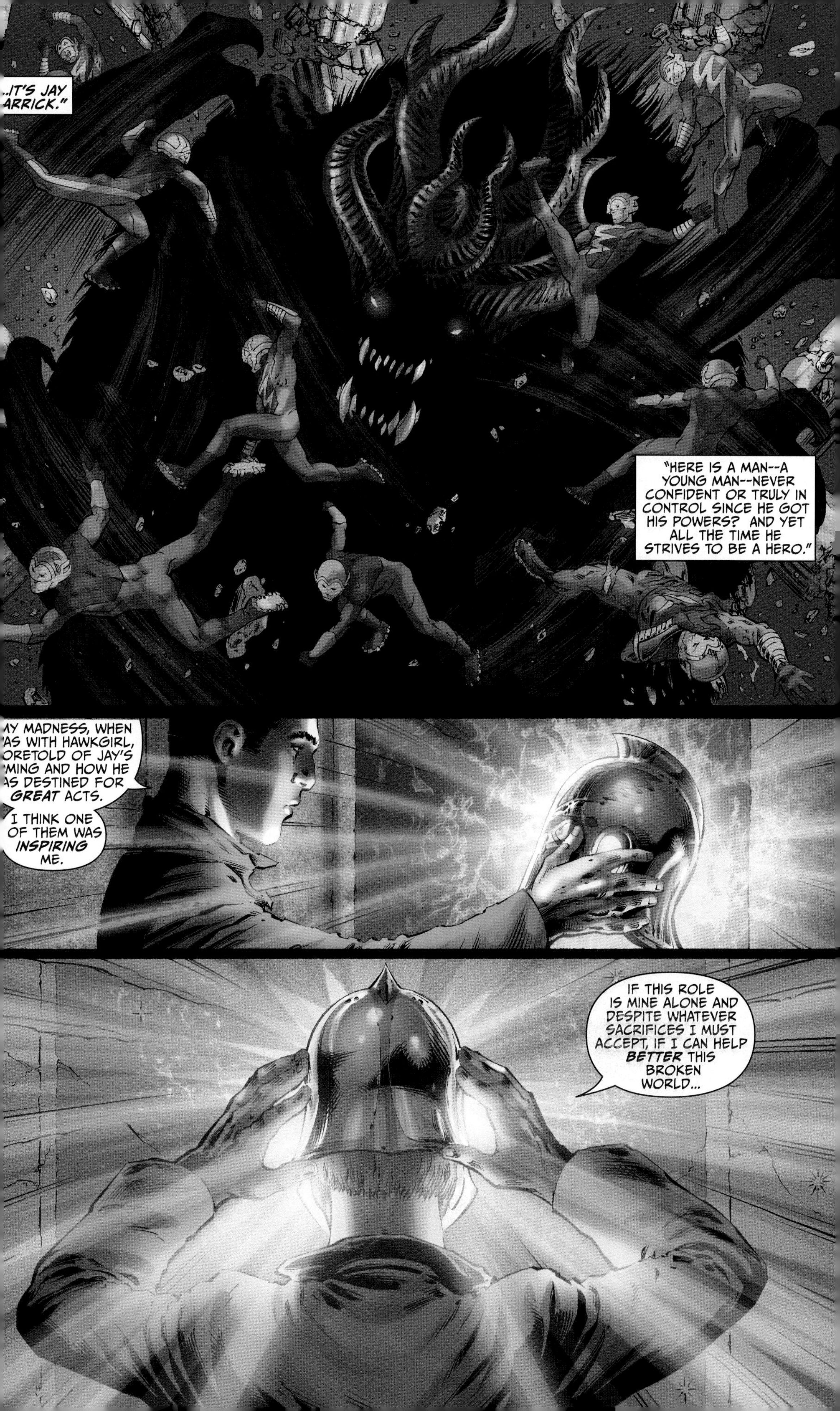
..IT'S JAY ARRICK."
"HERE IS A MAN--A YOUNG MAN--NEVER CONFIDENT OR TRULY IN CONTROL SINCE HE GOT HIS POWERS? AND YET ALL THE TIME HE STRIVES TO BE A HERO."
MY MADNESS, WHEN AS WITH HAWKGIRL, ORETOLD OF JAY'S MING AND HOW HE AS DESTINED FOR *GREAT* ACTS.
I THINK ONE OF THEM WAS *INSPIRING* ME.
IF THIS ROLE IS MINE ALONE AND DESPITE WHATEVER SACRIFICES I MUST ACCEPT, IF I CAN HELP *BETTER* THIS BROKEN WORLD...

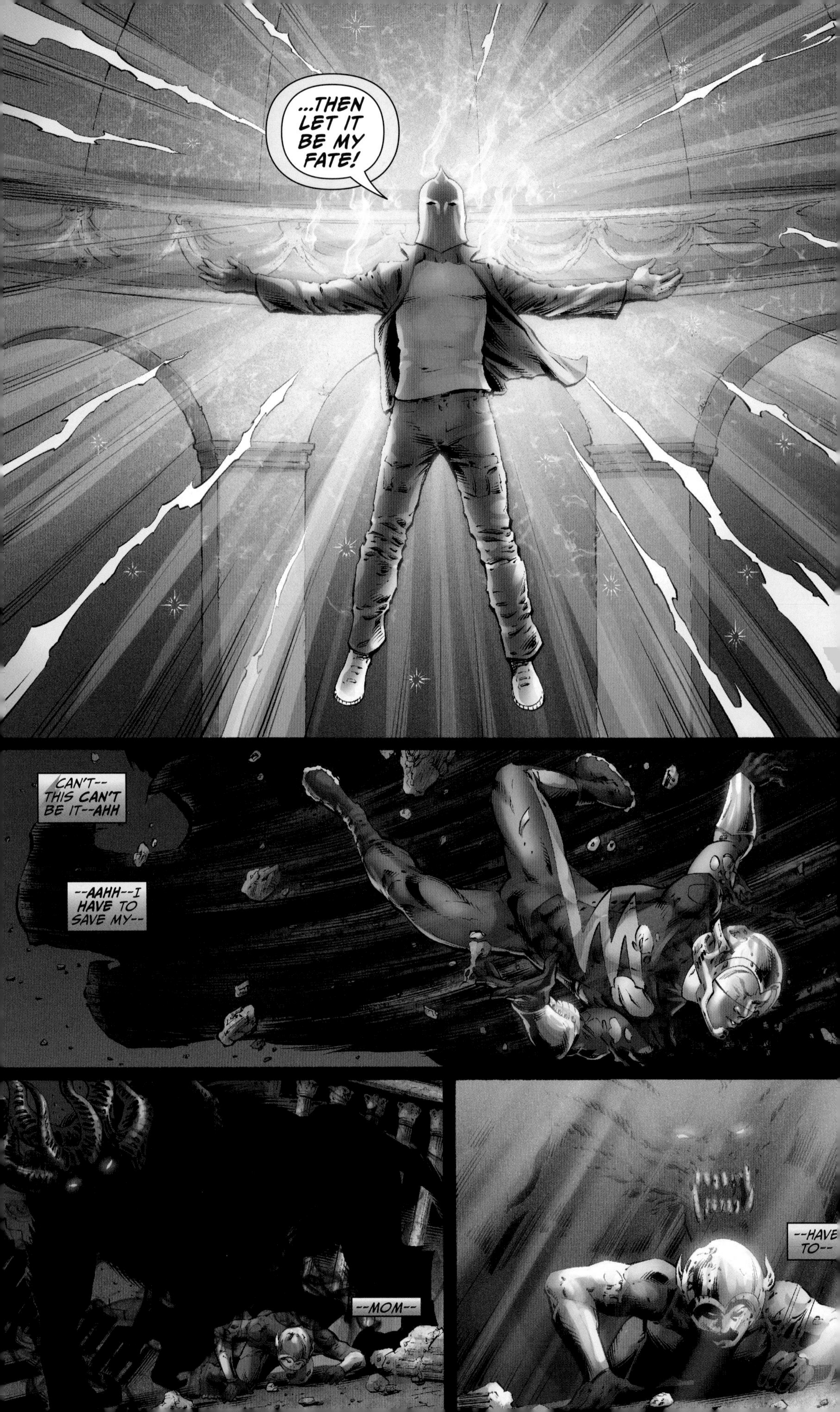
...THEN LET IT BE MY FATE!
CAN'T-- THIS CAN'T BE IT--AHH
--AAHH--I HAVE TO SAVE MY--
--MOM--
--HAVE TO--

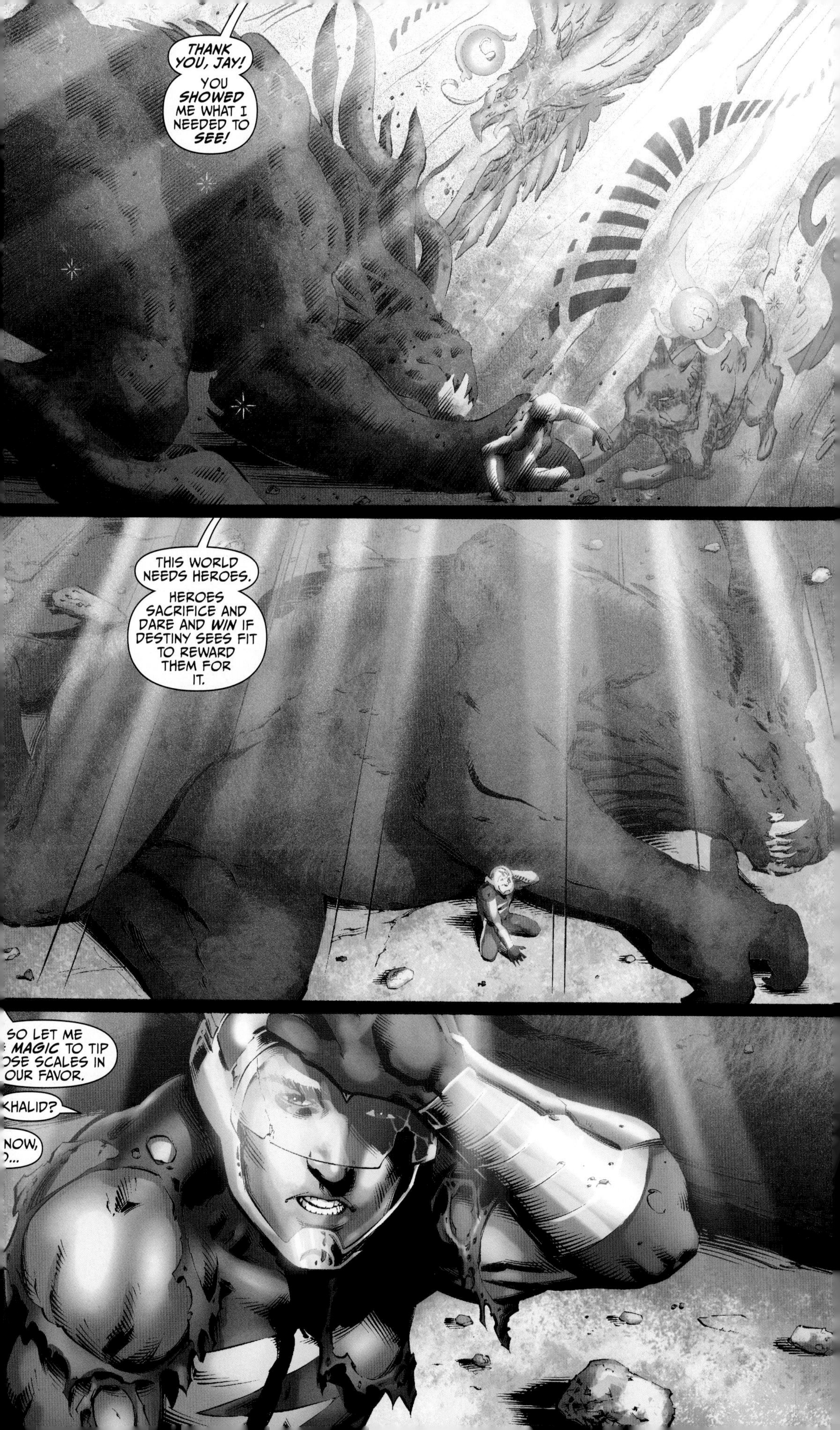
THANK YOU, JAY! YOU SHOWED ME WHAT I NEEDED TO SEE!
THIS WORLD NEEDS HEROES.
HEROES SACRIFICE AND DARE AND WIN IF DESTINY SEES FIT TO REWARD THEM FOR IT.
SO LET ME MAGIC TO TIP OSE SCALES IN OUR FAVOR.
KHALID?
NOW,

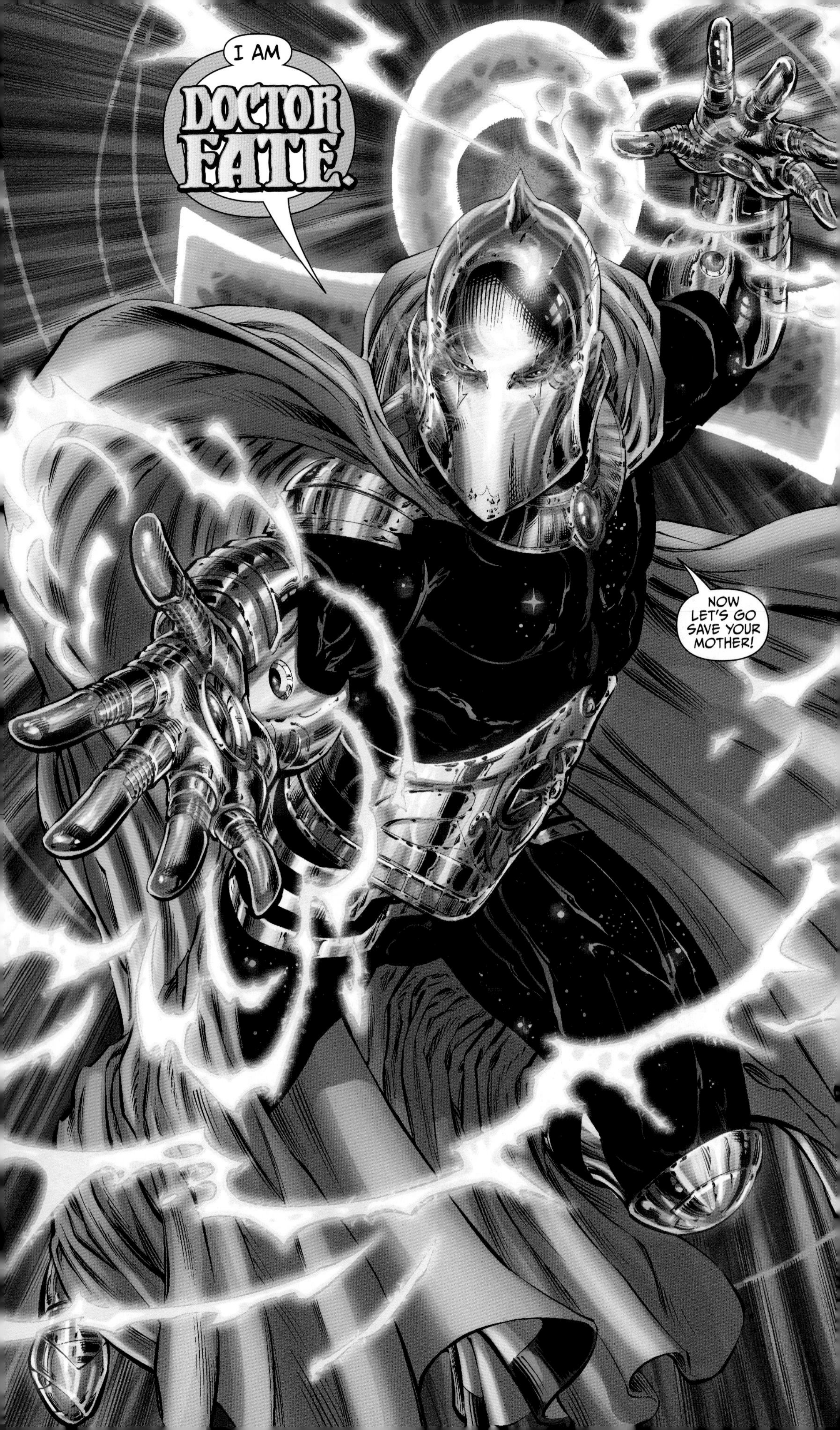
I AM
DOCTOR FATE.
NOW LET'S GO SAVE YOUR MOTHER!

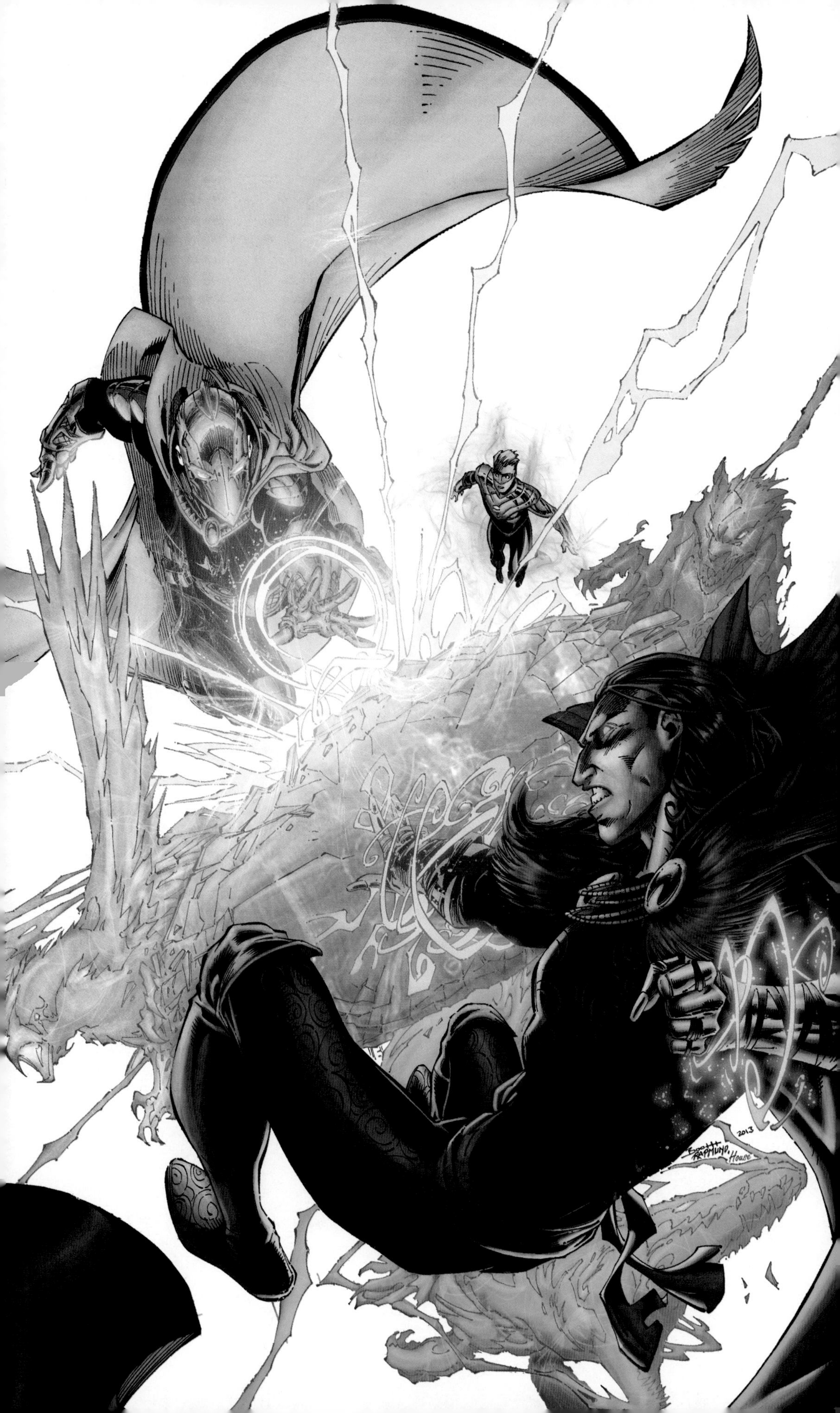
2013
RAPMUND, House

JAMES ROBINSON writer NICOLA SCOTT penciller TREVOR SCOTT inker cover by BRETT BOOTH, NORM RAPMUND & ANDREW DALHOUS

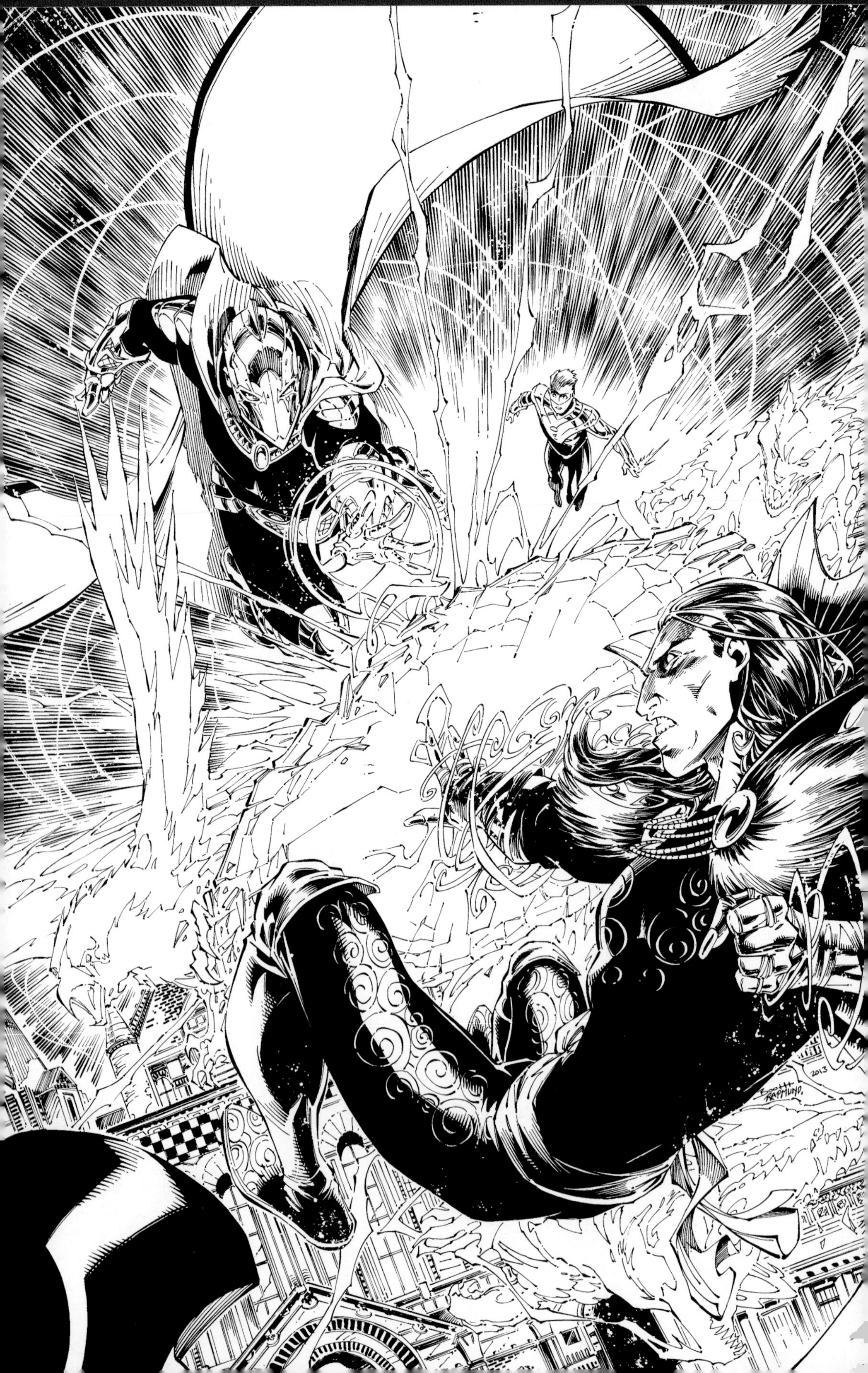

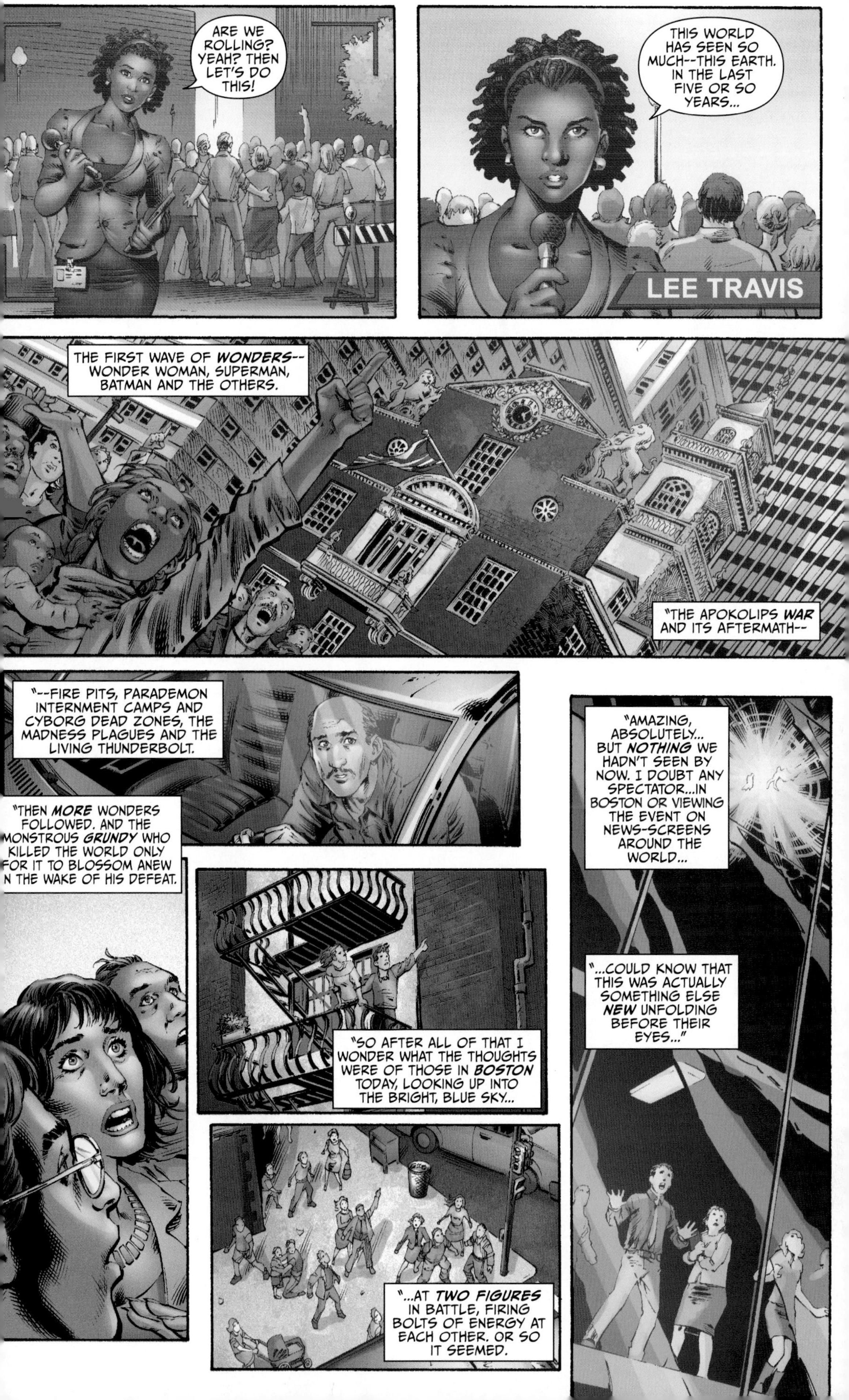
ARE WE ROLLING? YEAH? THEN LET'S DO THIS!
THIS WORLD HAS SEEN SO MUCH--THIS EARTH. IN THE LAST FIVE OR SO YEARS...
LEE TRAVIS
THE FIRST WAVE OF *WONDERS*-- WONDER WOMAN, SUPERMAN, BATMAN AND THE OTHERS.
"THE APOKOLIPS *WAR* AND ITS AFTERMATH--
"--FIRE PITS, PARADEMON INTERNMENT CAMPS AND CYBORG DEAD ZONES, THE MADNESS PLAGUES AND THE LIVING THUNDERBOLT.
"THEN *MORE* WONDERS FOLLOWED. AND THE MONSTROUS *GRUNDY* WHO KILLED THE WORLD ONLY FOR IT TO BLOSSOM ANEW N THE WAKE OF HIS DEFEAT.
"SO AFTER ALL OF THAT I WONDER WHAT THE THOUGHTS WERE OF THOSE IN *BOSTON* TODAY, LOOKING UP INTO THE BRIGHT, BLUE SKY...
"...AT *TWO FIGURES* IN BATTLE, FIRING BOLTS OF ENERGY AT EACH OTHER. OR SO IT SEEMED.
"AMAZING, ABSOLUTELY... BUT *NOTHING* WE HADN'T SEEN BY NOW. I DOUBT ANY SPECTATOR...IN BOSTON OR VIEWING THE EVENT ON NEWS-SCREENS AROUND THE WORLD...
"...COULD KNOW THAT THIS WAS ACTUALLY SOMETHING ELSE *NEW* UNFOLDING BEFORE THEIR EYES..."

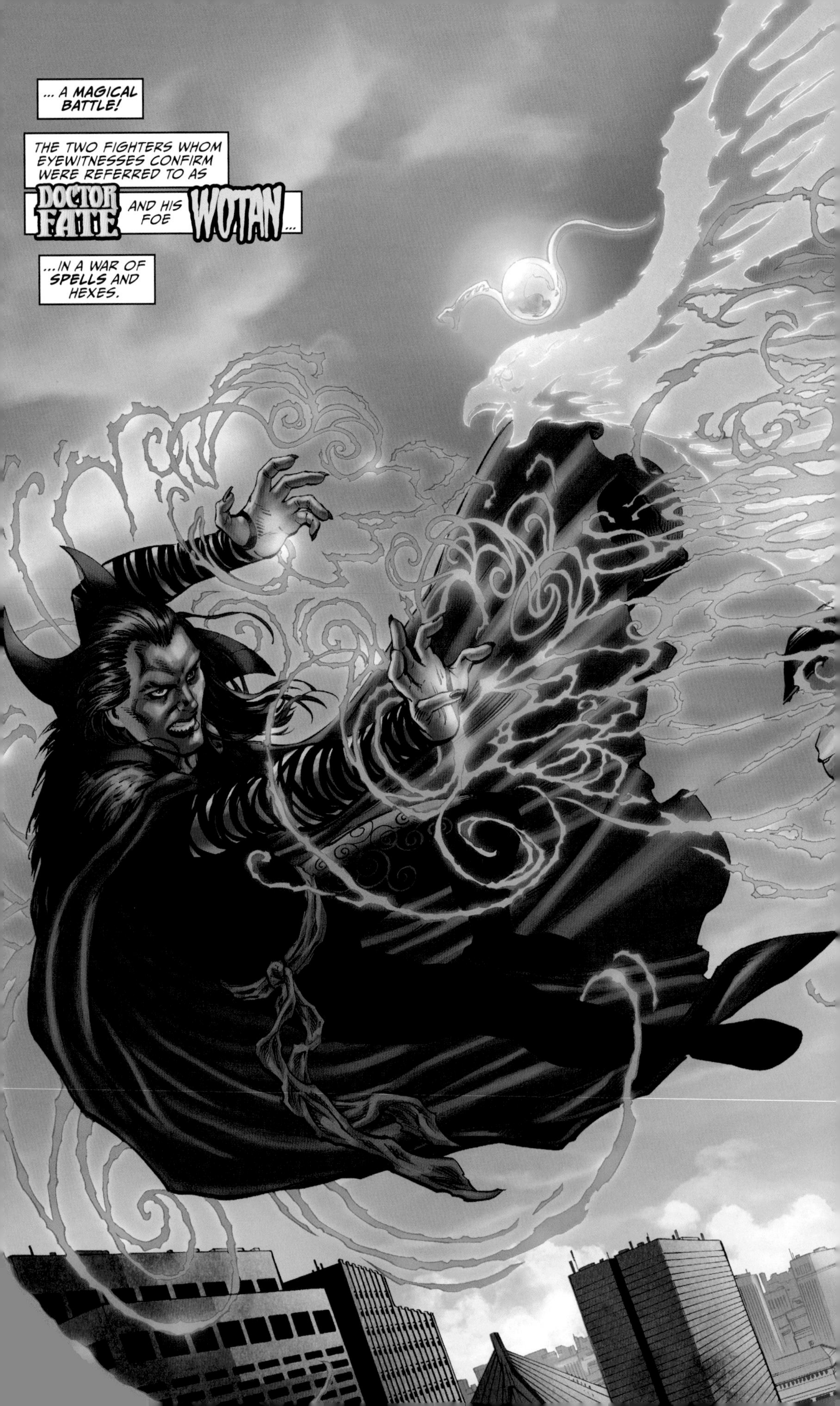
... A MAGICAL BATTLE!
THE TWO FIGHTERS WHOM EYEWITNESSES CONFIRM WERE REFERRED TO AS
DOCTOR FATE AND HIS FOE WOTAN...
...IN A WAR OF SPELLS AND HEXES.

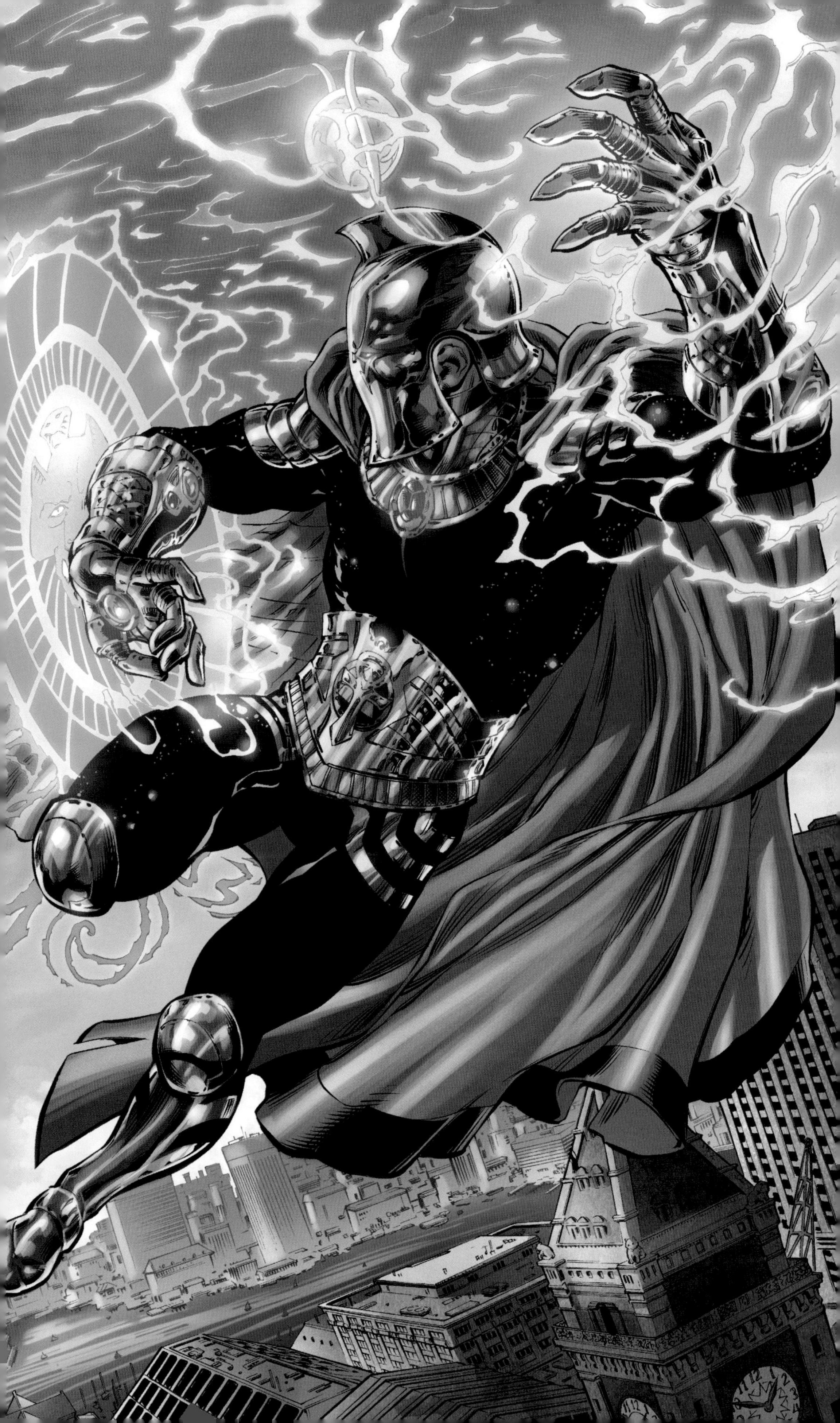

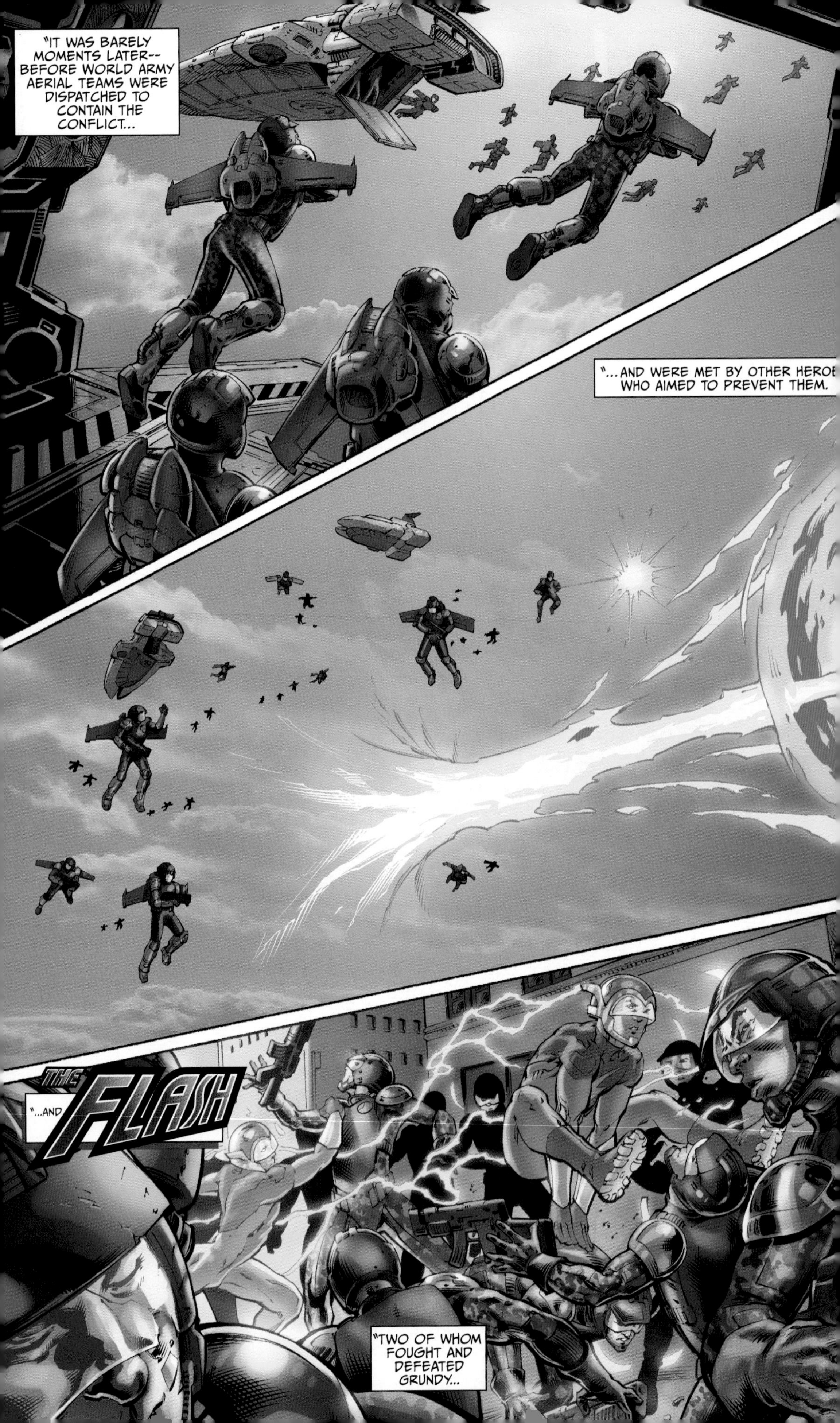
"IT WAS BARELY MOMENTS LATER-- BEFORE WORLD ARMY AERIAL TEAMS WERE DISPATCHED TO CONTAIN THE CONFLICT...
"...AND WERE MET BY OTHER HEROE WHO AIMED TO PREVENT THEM.
"...AND THE FLASH
"TWO OF WHOM FOUGHT AND DEFEATED GRUNDY...

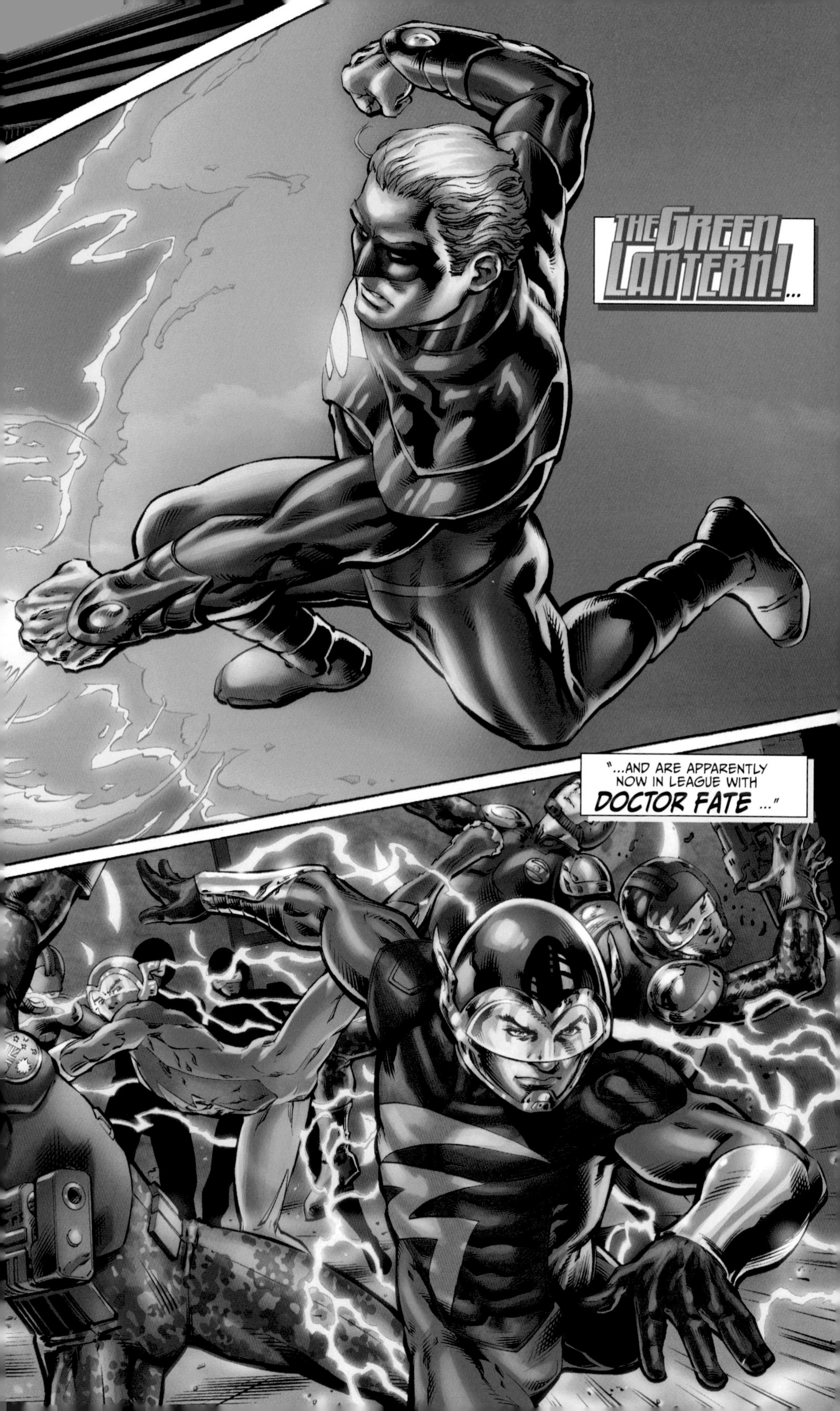

THE GREEN LANTERN!...
"...AND ARE APPARENTLY NOW IN LEAGUE WITH DOCTOR FATE ..."

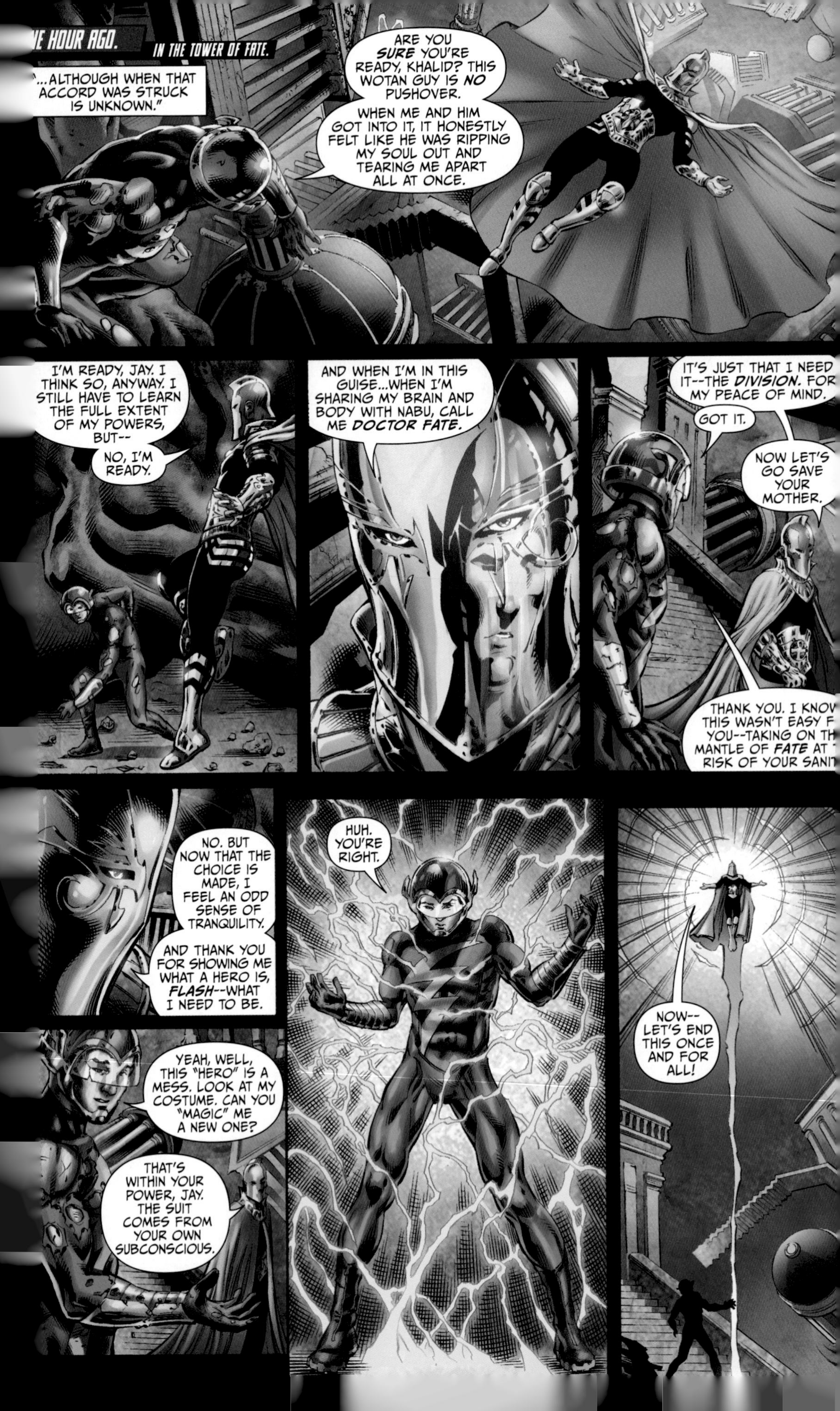

NE HOUR AGO.
IN THE TOWER OF FATE.
"...ALTHOUGH WHEN THAT ACCORD WAS STRUCK IS UNKNOWN."
ARE YOU SURE YOU'RE READY, KHALID? THIS WOTAN GUY IS NO PUSHOVER.
WHEN ME AND HIM GOT INTO IT, IT HONESTLY FELT LIKE HE WAS RIPPING MY SOUL OUT AND TEARING ME APART ALL AT ONCE.
I'M READY, JAY. I THINK SO, ANYWAY. I STILL HAVE TO LEARN THE FULL EXTENT OF MY POWERS, BUT--
NO, I'M READY.
AND WHEN I'M IN THIS GUISE...WHEN I'M SHARING MY BRAIN AND BODY WITH NABU, CALL ME DOCTOR FATE.
IT'S JUST THAT I NEED IT--THE DIVISION. FOR MY PEACE OF MIND.
GOT IT.
NOW LET'S GO SAVE YOUR MOTHER.
THANK YOU. I KNOW THIS WASN'T EASY F YOU--TAKING ON TH MANTLE OF FATE AT RISK OF YOUR SANI
NO. BUT NOW THAT THE CHOICE IS MADE, I FEEL AN ODD SENSE OF TRANQUILITY.
AND THANK YOU FOR SHOWING ME WHAT A HERO IS, FLASH--WHAT I NEED TO BE.
YEAH, WELL, THIS "HERO" IS A MESS. LOOK AT MY COSTUME. CAN YOU "MAGIC" ME A NEW ONE?
THAT'S WITHIN YOUR POWER, JAY. THE SUIT COMES FROM YOUR OWN SUBCONSCIOUS.
HUH. YOU'RE RIGHT.
NOW-- LET'S END THIS ONCE AND FOR ALL!

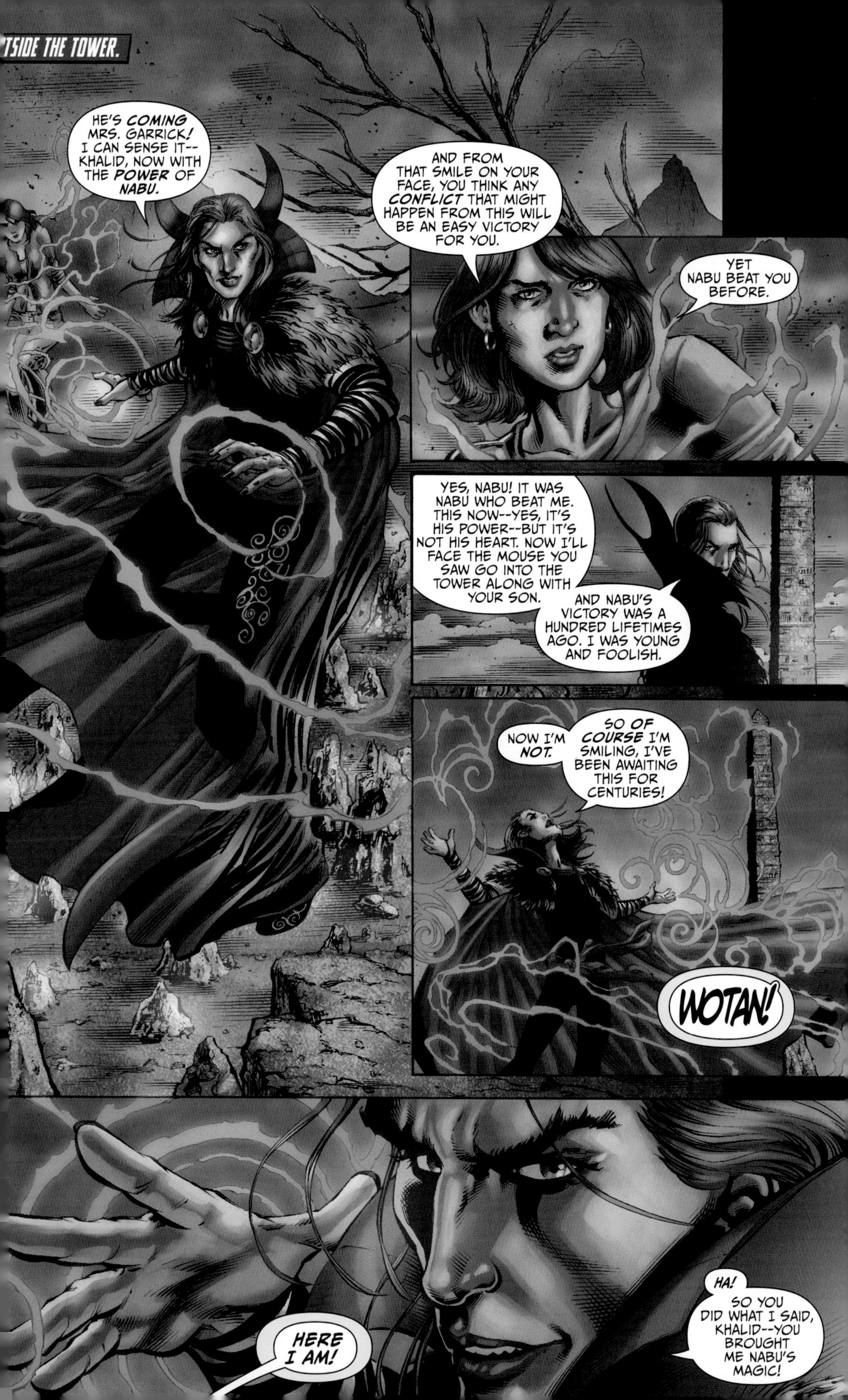
TSIDE THE TOWER.
HE'S COMING MRS. GARRICK! I CAN SENSE IT--KHALID, NOW WITH THE POWER OF NABU.
AND FROM THAT SMILE ON YOUR FACE, YOU THINK ANY CONFLICT THAT MIGHT HAPPEN FROM THIS WILL BE AN EASY VICTORY FOR YOU.
YET NABU BEAT YOU BEFORE.
YES, NABU! IT WAS NABU WHO BEAT ME. THIS NOW--YES, IT'S HIS POWER--BUT IT'S NOT HIS HEART. NOW I'LL FACE THE MOUSE YOU SAW GO INTO THE TOWER ALONG WITH YOUR SON.
AND NABU'S VICTORY WAS A HUNDRED LIFETIMES AGO. I WAS YOUNG AND FOOLISH.
NOW I'M NOT.
SO OF COURSE I'M SMILING, I'VE BEEN AWAITING THIS FOR CENTURIES!
WOTAN!
HERE I AM!
HA!
SO YOU DID WHAT I SAID, KHALID--YOU BROUGHT ME NABU'S MAGIC!

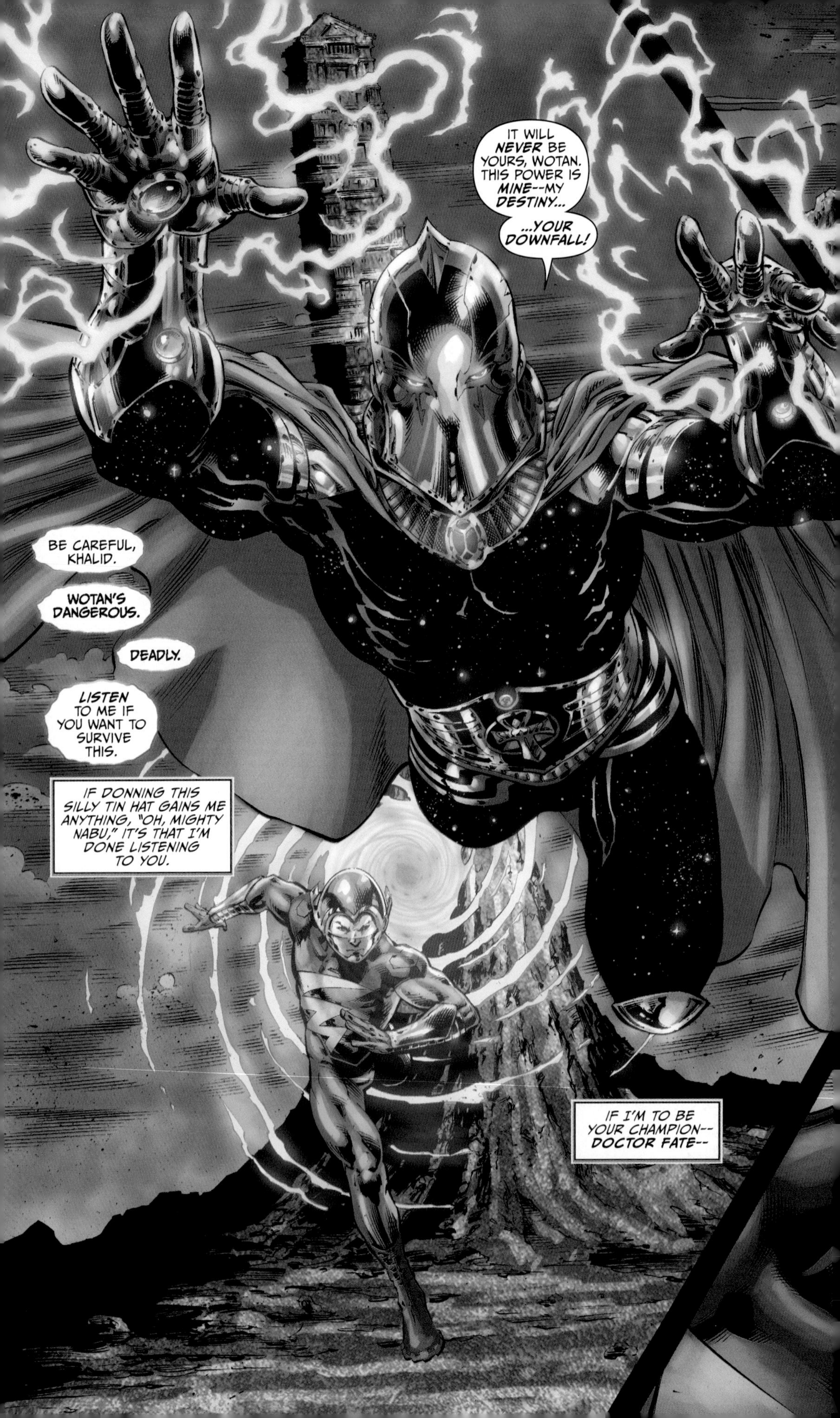
IT WILL NEVER BE YOURS, WOTAN. THIS POWER IS MINE--MY DESTINY...
...YOUR DOWNFALL!
BE CAREFUL, KHALID.
WOTAN'S DANGEROUS.
DEADLY.
LISTEN TO ME IF YOU WANT TO SURVIVE THIS.
IF DONNING THIS SILLY TIN HAT GAINS ME ANYTHING, "OH, MIGHTY NABU," IT'S THAT I'M DONE LISTENING TO YOU.
IF I'M TO BE YOUR CHAMPION--DOCTOR FATE--

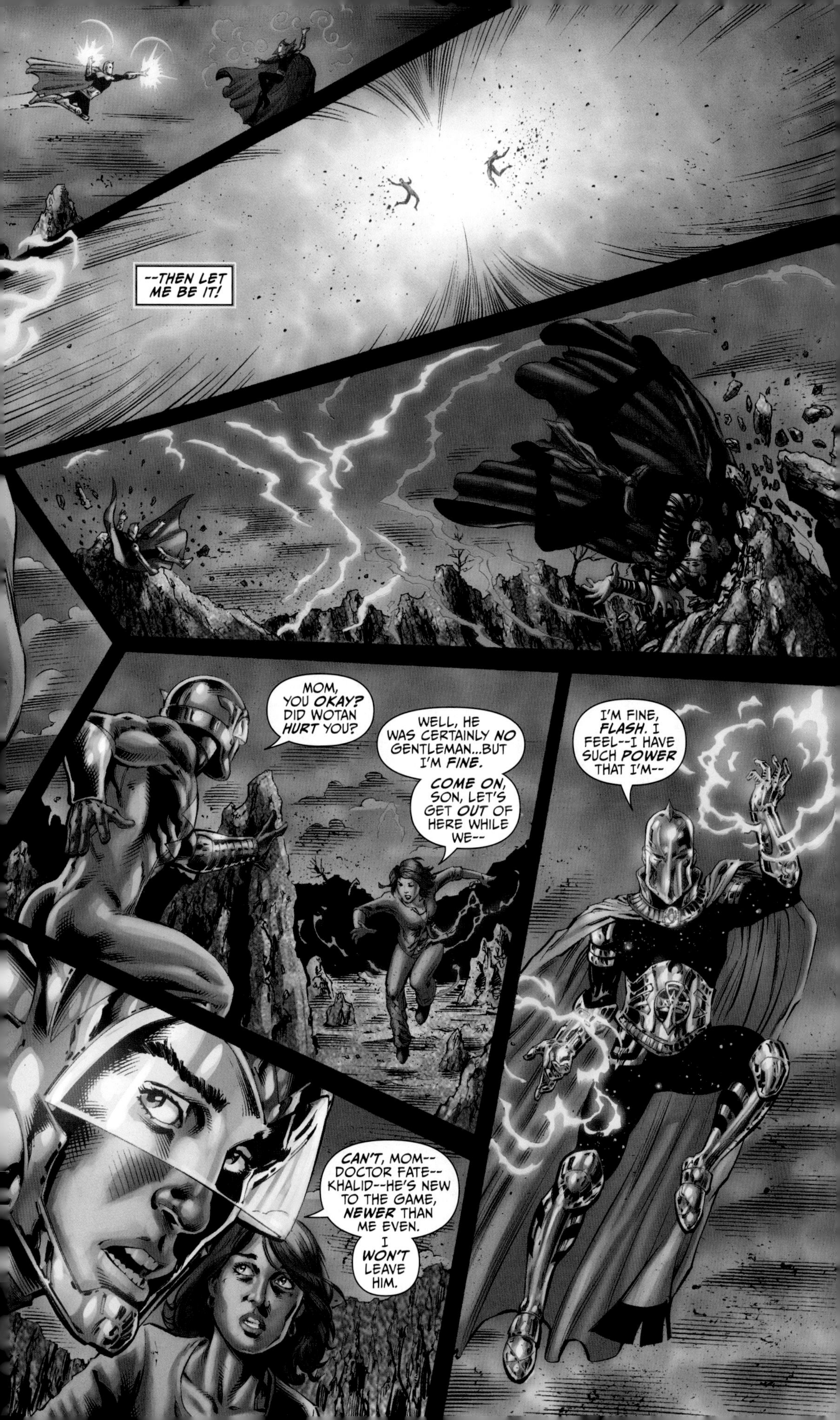
--THEN LET ME BE IT!
MOM, YOU *OKAY?* DID WOTAN *HURT* YOU?
WELL, HE WAS CERTAINLY *NO* GENTLEMAN...BUT I'M *FINE.*
COME ON, SON, LET'S GET *OUT* OF HERE WHILE WE--
CAN'T, MOM--DOCTOR FATE--KHALID--HE'S NEW TO THE GAME, *NEWER* THAN ME EVEN.
I *WON'T* LEAVE HIM.
I'M FINE, *FLASH.* I FEEL--I HAVE SUCH *POWER* THAT I'M--

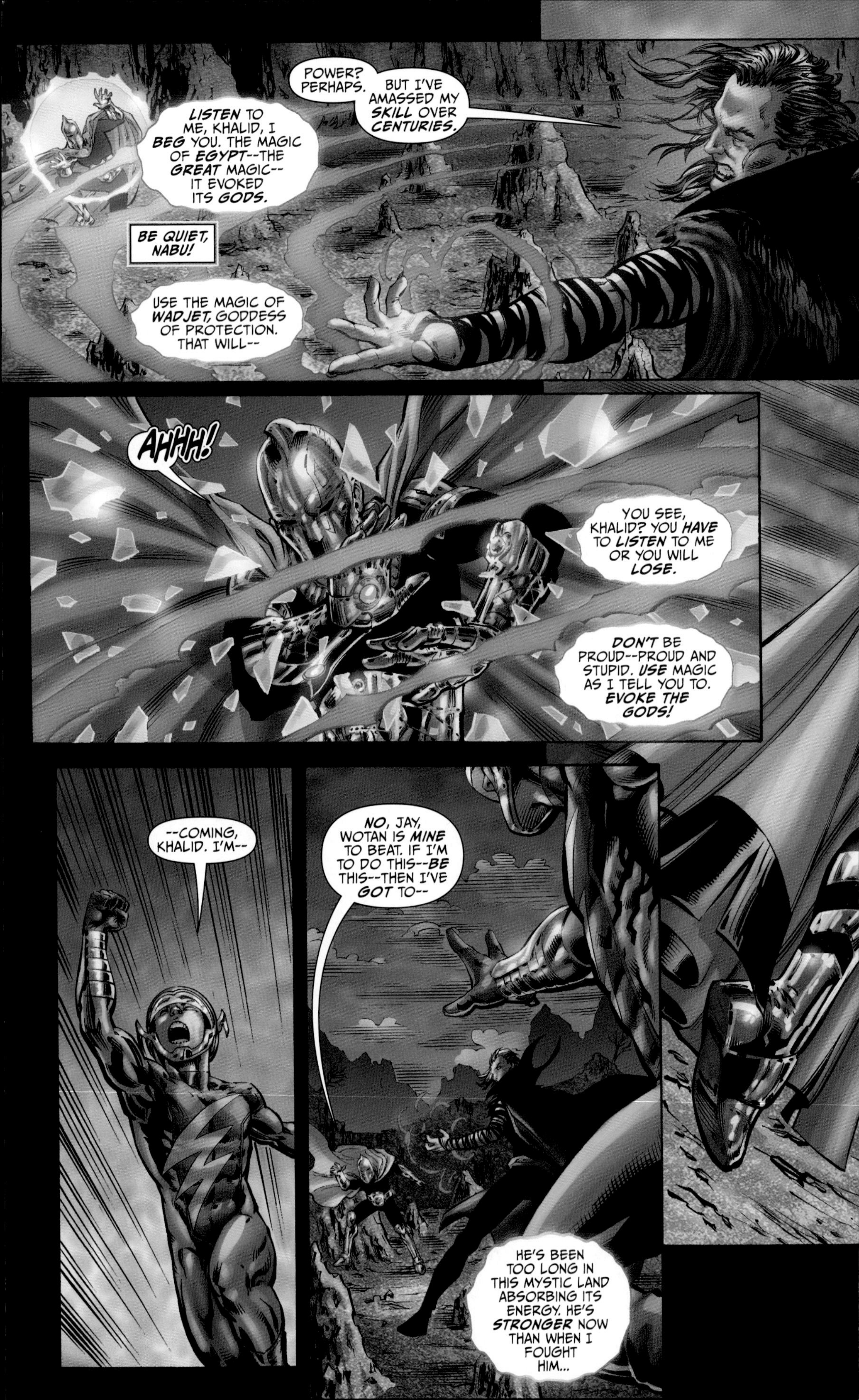
LISTEN TO ME, KHALID, I BEG YOU. THE MAGIC OF EGYPT--THE GREAT MAGIC--IT EVOKED ITS GODS.
POWER? PERHAPS.
BUT I'VE AMASSED MY SKILL OVER CENTURIES.
BE QUIET, NABU!
USE THE MAGIC OF WADJET, GODDESS OF PROTECTION. THAT WILL--
AHHH!
YOU SEE, KHALID? YOU HAVE TO LISTEN TO ME OR YOU WILL LOSE.
DON'T BE PROUD--PROUD AND STUPID. USE MAGIC AS I TELL YOU TO. EVOKE THE GODS!
--COMING, KHALID. I'M--
NO, JAY, WOTAN IS MINE TO BEAT. IF I'M TO DO THIS--BE THIS--THEN I'VE GOT TO--
HE'S BEEN TOO LONG IN THIS MYSTIC LAND ABSORBING ITS ENERGY. HE'S STRONGER NOW THAN WHEN I FOUGHT HIM...

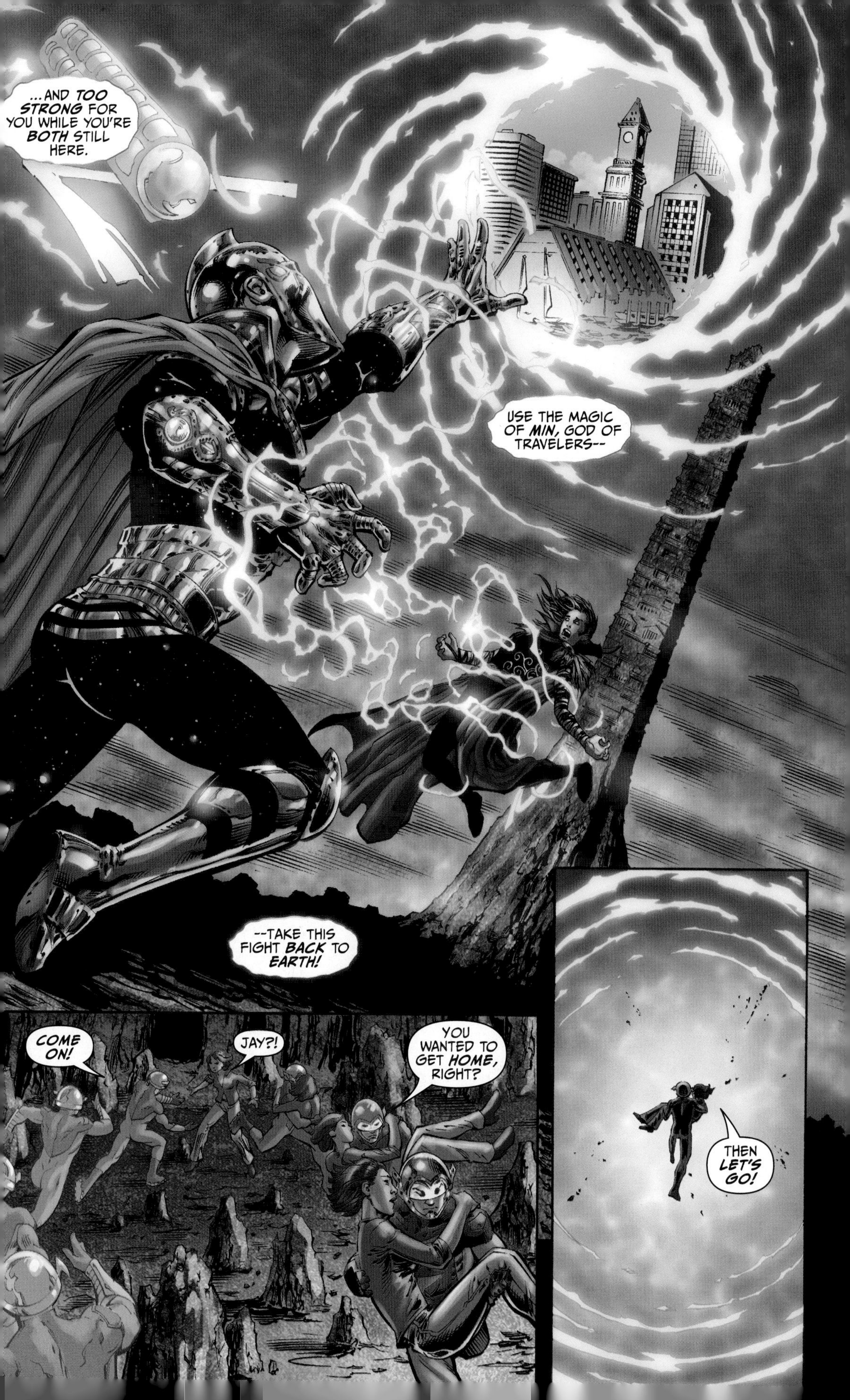
...AND TOO STRONG FOR YOU WHILE YOU'RE BOTH STILL HERE.
USE THE MAGIC OF MIN, GOD OF TRAVELERS--
--TAKE THIS FIGHT BACK TO EARTH!
COME ON!
JAY?!
YOU WANTED TO GET HOME, RIGHT?
THEN LET'S GO!

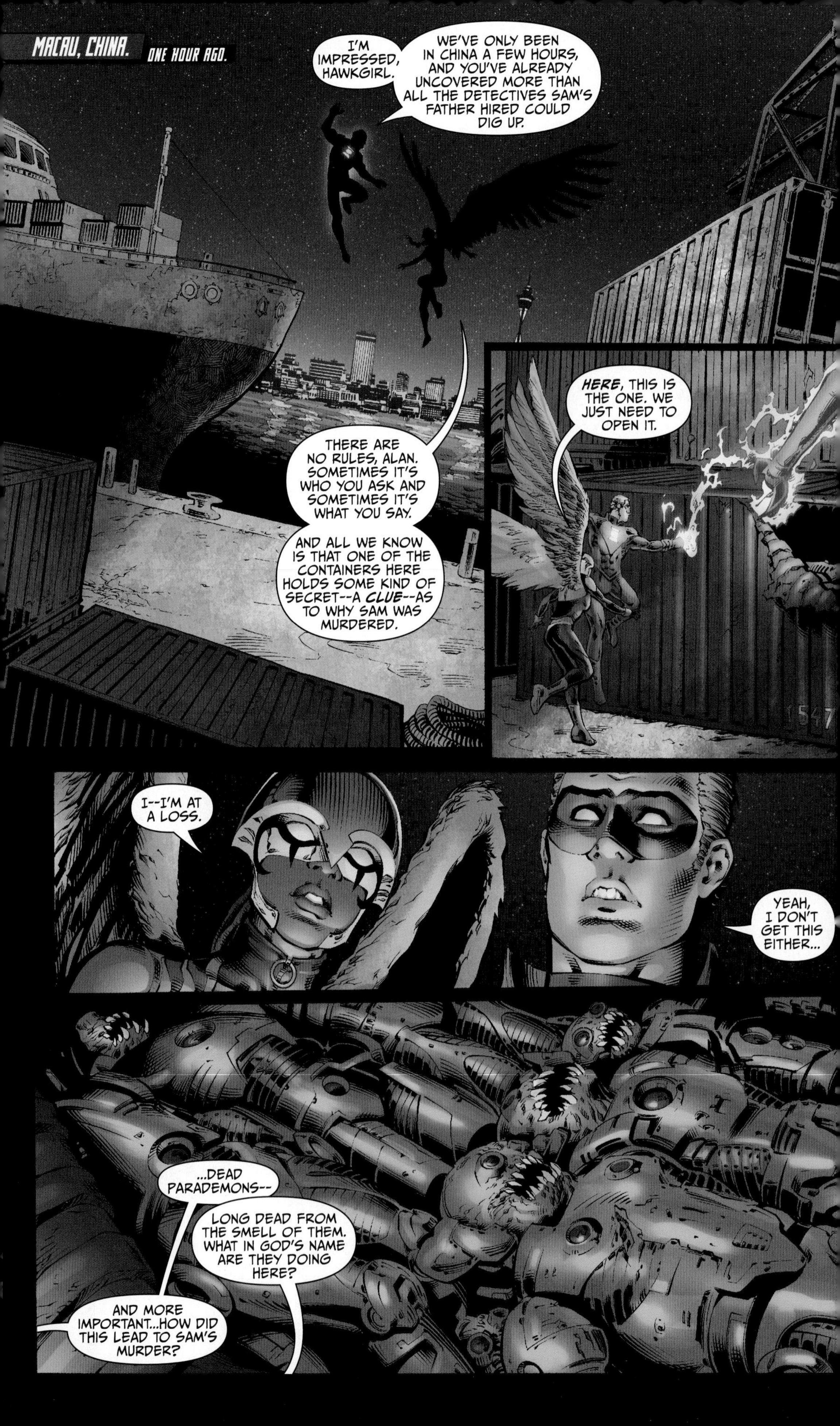
MACAU, CHINA.
ONE HOUR AGO.
I'M IMPRESSED, HAWKGIRL.
WE'VE ONLY BEEN IN CHINA A FEW HOURS, AND YOU'VE ALREADY UNCOVERED MORE THAN ALL THE DETECTIVES SAM'S FATHER HIRED COULD DIG UP.
THERE ARE NO RULES, ALAN. SOMETIMES IT'S WHO YOU ASK AND SOMETIMES IT'S WHAT YOU SAY.
AND ALL WE KNOW IS THAT ONE OF THE CONTAINERS HERE HOLDS SOME KIND OF SECRET--A CLUE--AS TO WHY SAM WAS MURDERED.
HERE, THIS IS THE ONE. WE JUST NEED TO OPEN IT.
I--I'M AT A LOSS.
YEAH, I DON'T GET THIS EITHER...
...DEAD PARADEMONS--
LONG DEAD FROM THE SMELL OF THEM. WHAT IN GOD'S NAME ARE THEY DOING HERE?
AND MORE IMPORTANT...HOW DID THIS LEAD TO SAM'S MURDER?

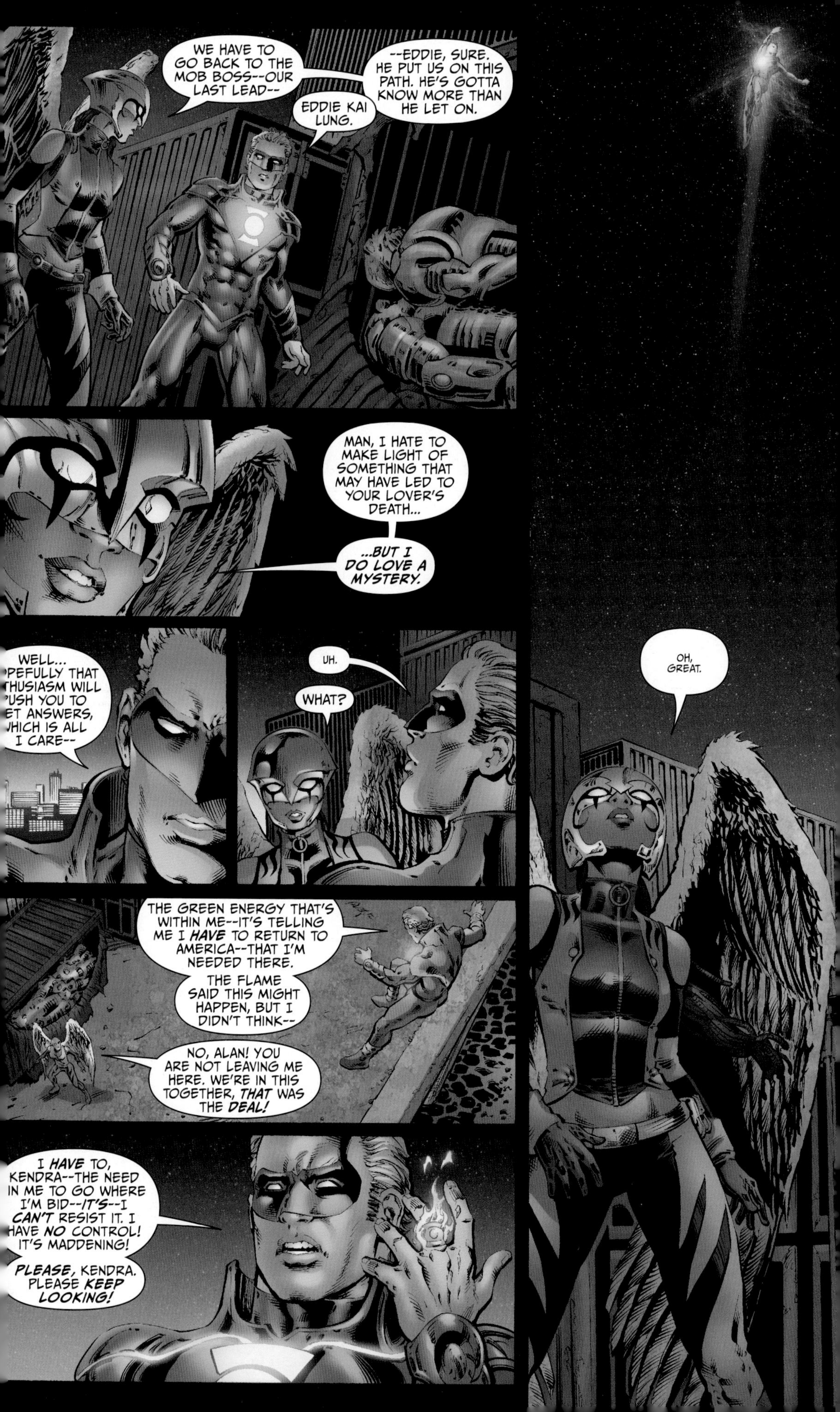
WE HAVE TO GO BACK TO THE MOB BOSS--OUR LAST LEAD--
EDDIE KAI LUNG.
--EDDIE, SURE. HE PUT US ON THIS PATH. HE'S GOTTA KNOW MORE THAN HE LET ON.
MAN, I HATE TO MAKE LIGHT OF SOMETHING THAT MAY HAVE LED TO YOUR LOVER'S DEATH...
...BUT I DO LOVE A MYSTERY.
WELL... PEFULLY THAT THUSIASM WILL USH YOU TO ET ANSWERS, HICH IS ALL I CARE--
UH.
WHAT?
OH, GREAT.
THE GREEN ENERGY THAT'S WITHIN ME--IT'S TELLING ME I HAVE TO RETURN TO AMERICA--THAT I'M NEEDED THERE.
THE FLAME SAID THIS MIGHT HAPPEN, BUT I DIDN'T THINK--
NO, ALAN! YOU ARE NOT LEAVING ME HERE. WE'RE IN THIS TOGETHER, THAT WAS THE DEAL!
I HAVE TO, KENDRA--THE NEED IN ME TO GO WHERE I'M BID--IT'S--I CAN'T RESIST IT. I HAVE NO CONTROL! IT'S MADDENING!
PLEASE, KENDRA. PLEASE KEEP LOOKING!

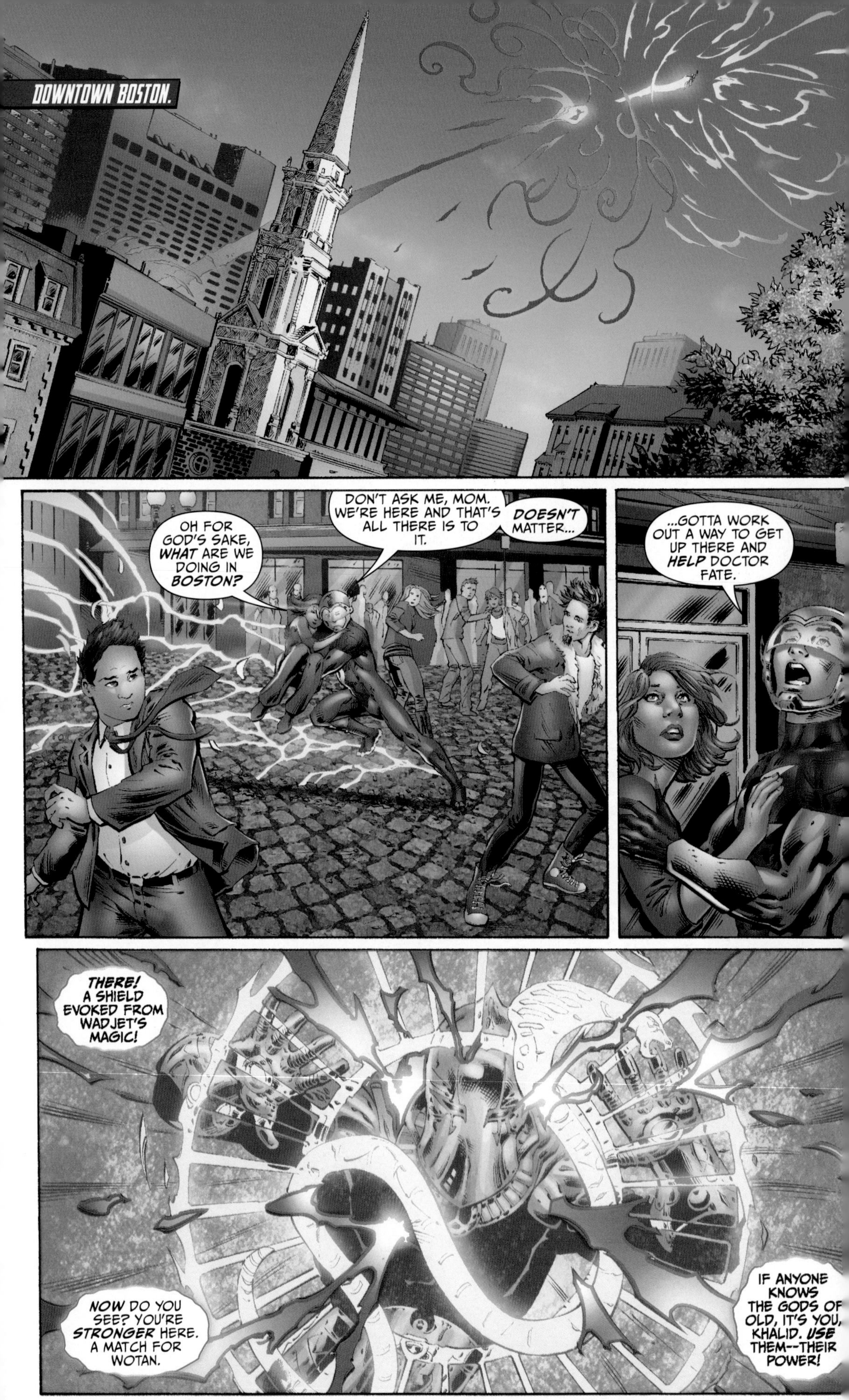
DOWNTOWN BOSTON.
OH FOR GOD'S SAKE, WHAT ARE WE DOING IN BOSTON?
DON'T ASK ME, MOM. WE'RE HERE AND THAT'S ALL THERE IS TO IT.
DOESN'T MATTER...
...GOTTA WORK OUT A WAY TO GET UP THERE AND HELP DOCTOR FATE.
THERE! A SHIELD EVOKED FROM WADJET'S MAGIC!
NOW DO YOU SEE? YOU'RE STRONGER HERE. A MATCH FOR WOTAN.
IF ANYONE KNOWS THE GODS OF OLD, IT'S YOU, KHALID. USE THEM--THEIR POWER!

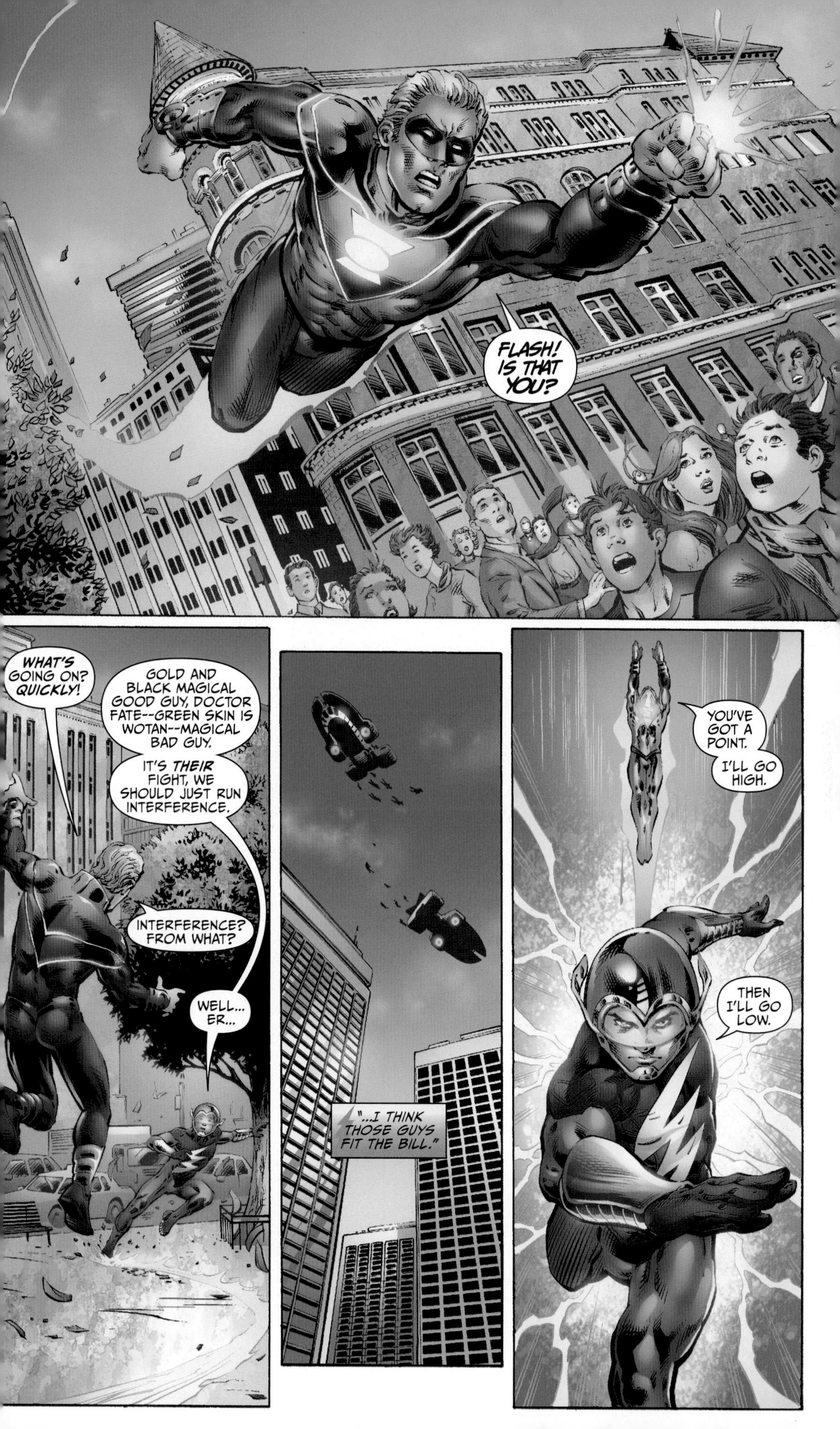
FLASH! IS THAT YOU?
WHAT'S GOING ON? QUICKLY!
GOLD AND BLACK MAGICAL GOOD GUY, DOCTOR FATE--GREEN SKIN IS WOTAN--MAGICAL BAD GUY.
IT'S THEIR FIGHT, WE SHOULD JUST RUN INTERFERENCE.
INTERFERENCE? FROM WHAT?
WELL... ER...
"...I THINK THOSE GUYS FIT THE BILL."
YOU'VE GOT A POINT.
I'LL GO HIGH.
THEN I'LL GO LOW.

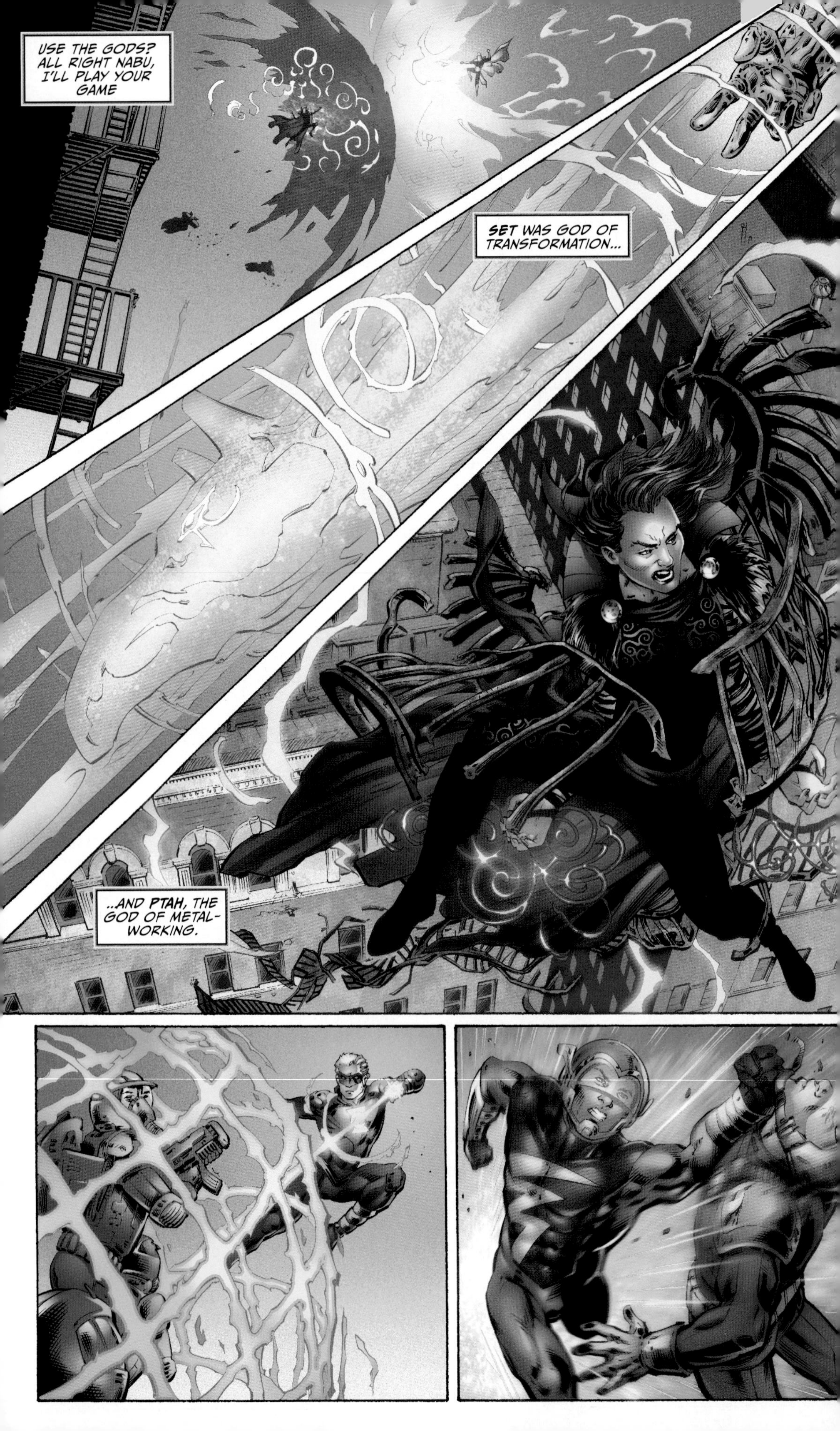
USE THE GODS? ALL RIGHT NABU, I'LL PLAY YOUR GAME
SET WAS GOD OF TRANSFORMATION...
...AND PTAH, THE GOD OF METAL-WORKING.

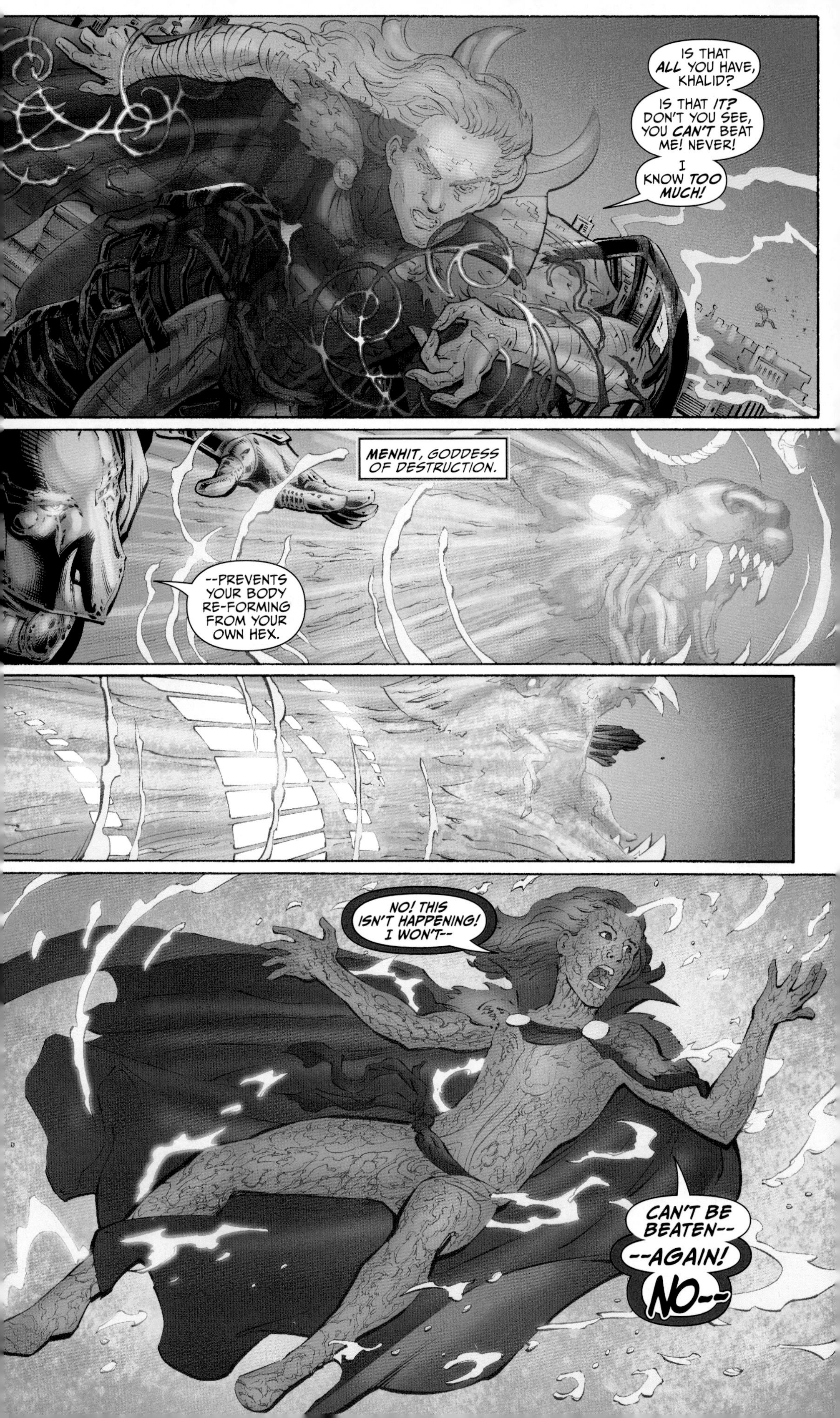
IS THAT ALL YOU HAVE, KHALID?
IS THAT IT? DON'T YOU SEE, YOU CAN'T BEAT ME! NEVER!
I KNOW TOO MUCH!
MENHIT, GODDESS OF DESTRUCTION.
--PREVENTS YOUR BODY RE-FORMING FROM YOUR OWN HEX.
NO! THIS ISN'T HAPPENING! I WON'T--
CAN'T BE BEATEN--
--AGAIN!
NO--

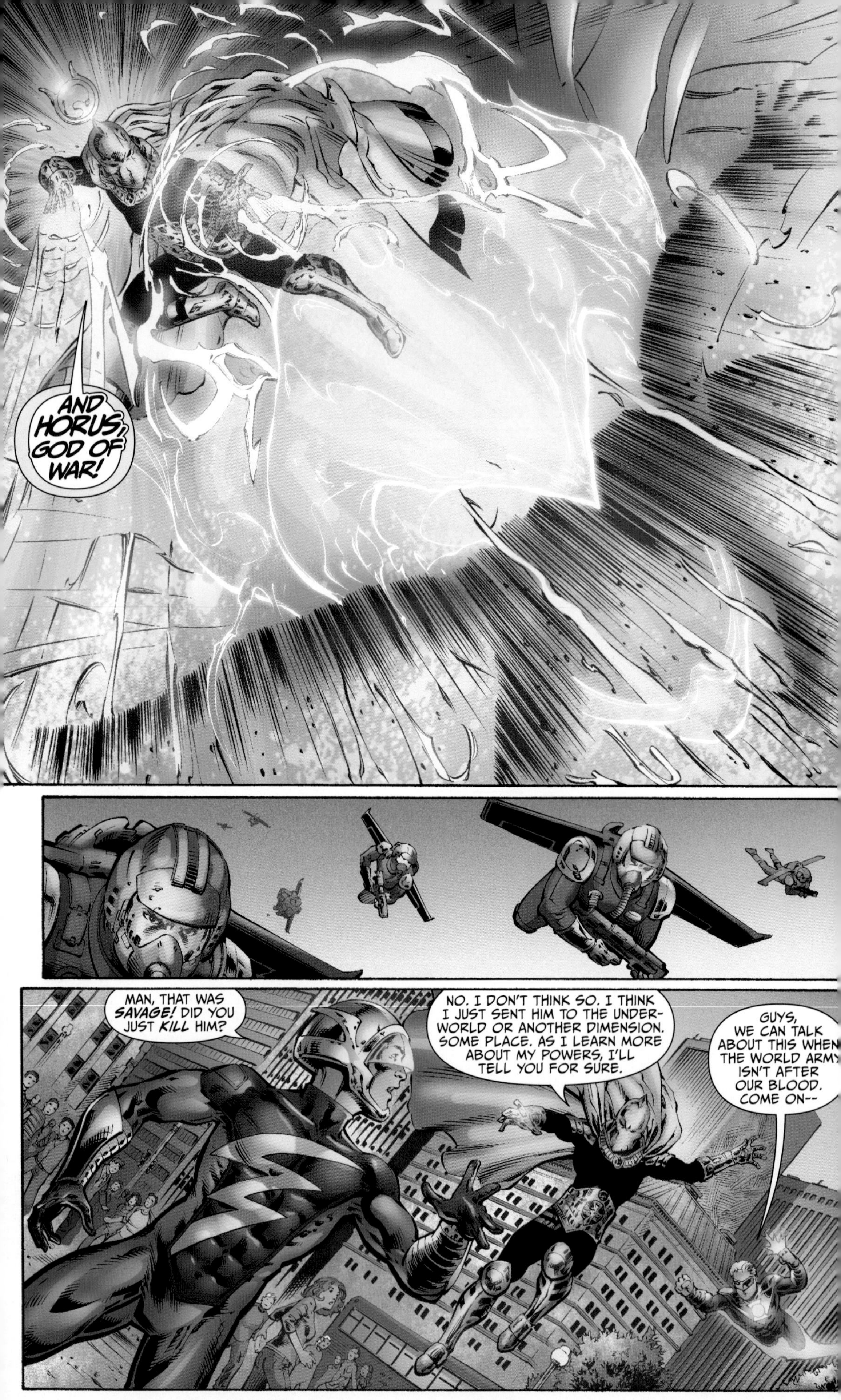
AND HORUS, GOD OF WAR!
MAN, THAT WAS SAVAGE! DID YOU JUST KILL HIM?
NO. I DON'T THINK SO. I THINK I JUST SENT HIM TO THE UNDERWORLD OR ANOTHER DIMENSION. SOME PLACE. AS I LEARN MORE ABOUT MY POWERS, I'LL TELL YOU FOR SURE.
GUYS, WE CAN TALK ABOUT THIS WHEN THE WORLD ARMY ISN'T AFTER OUR BLOOD. COME ON--

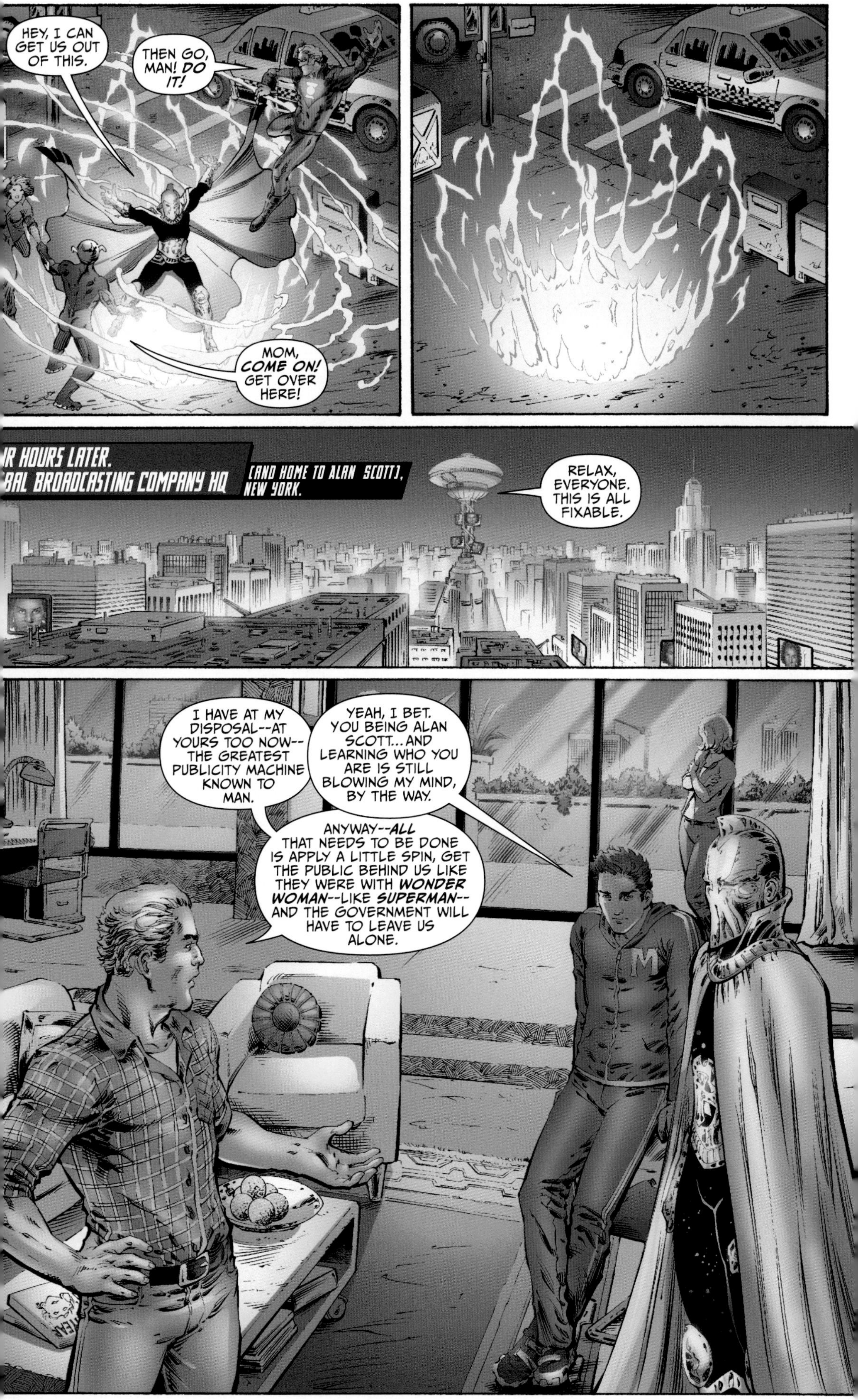
HEY, I CAN GET US OUT OF THIS.
THEN GO, MAN! DO IT!
MOM, COME ON! GET OVER HERE!
R HOURS LATER.
BAL BROADCASTING COMPANY HQ
[AND HOME TO ALAN SCOTT], NEW YORK.
RELAX, EVERYONE. THIS IS ALL FIXABLE.
I HAVE AT MY DISPOSAL--AT YOURS TOO NOW--THE GREATEST PUBLICITY MACHINE KNOWN TO MAN.
YEAH, I BET. YOU BEING ALAN SCOTT...AND LEARNING WHO YOU ARE IS STILL BLOWING MY MIND, BY THE WAY.
ANYWAY--ALL THAT NEEDS TO BE DONE IS APPLY A LITTLE SPIN, GET THE PUBLIC BEHIND US LIKE THEY WERE WITH WONDER WOMAN--LIKE SUPERMAN--AND THE GOVERNMENT WILL HAVE TO LEAVE US ALONE.

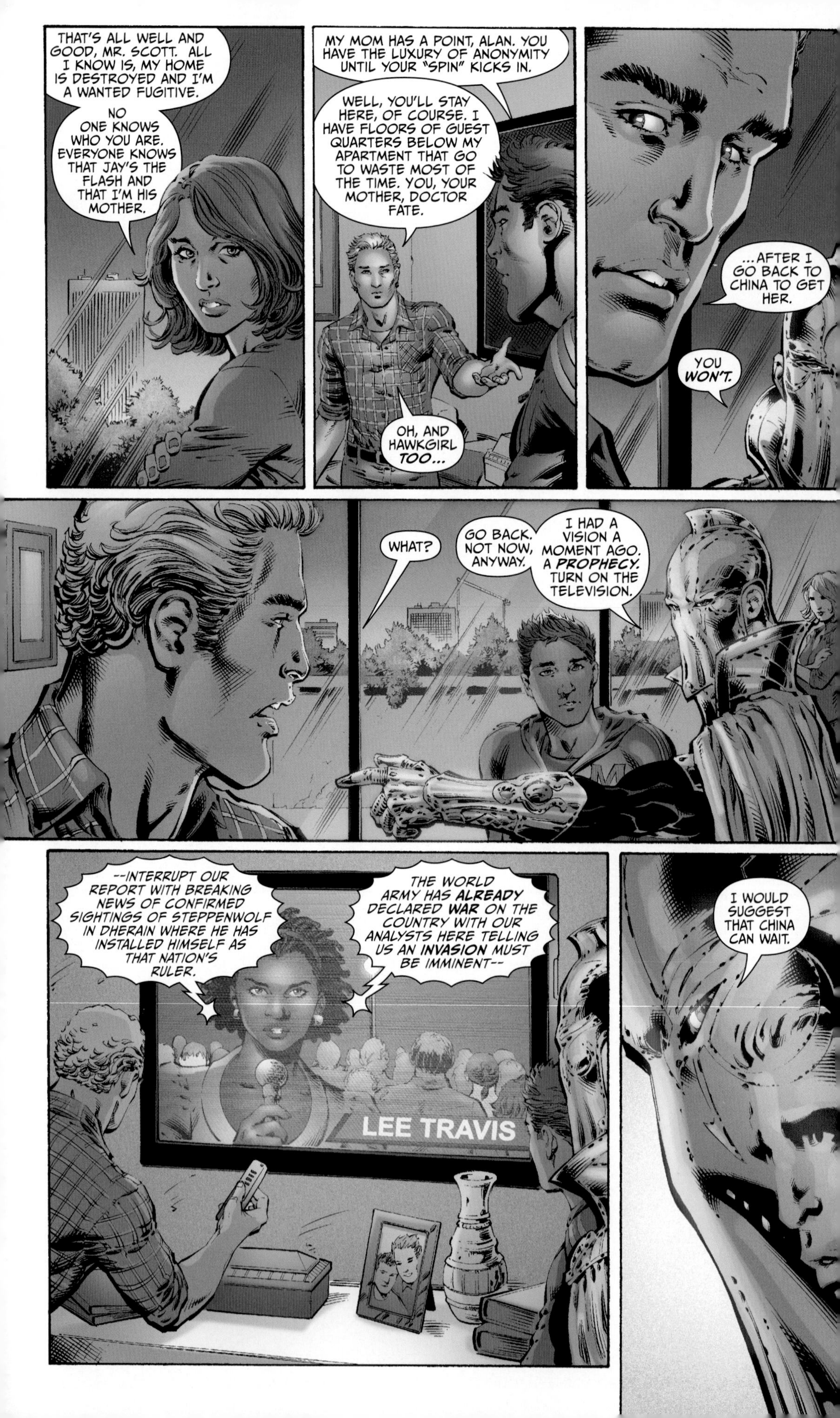
THAT'S ALL WELL AND GOOD, MR. SCOTT. ALL I KNOW IS, MY HOME IS DESTROYED AND I'M A WANTED FUGITIVE.
NO ONE KNOWS WHO YOU ARE. EVERYONE KNOWS THAT JAY'S THE FLASH AND THAT I'M HIS MOTHER.
MY MOM HAS A POINT, ALAN. YOU HAVE THE LUXURY OF ANONYMITY UNTIL YOUR "SPIN" KICKS IN.
WELL, YOU'LL STAY HERE, OF COURSE. I HAVE FLOORS OF GUEST QUARTERS BELOW MY APARTMENT THAT GO TO WASTE MOST OF THE TIME. YOU, YOUR MOTHER, DOCTOR FATE.
OH, AND HAWKGIRL TOO...
...AFTER I GO BACK TO CHINA TO GET HER.
YOU WON'T.
WHAT?
GO BACK. NOT NOW, ANYWAY.
I HAD A VISION A MOMENT AGO. A PROPHECY. TURN ON THE TELEVISION.
--INTERRUPT OUR REPORT WITH BREAKING NEWS OF CONFIRMED SIGHTINGS OF STEPPENWOLF IN DHERAIN WHERE HE HAS INSTALLED HIMSELF AS THAT NATION'S RULER.
THE WORLD ARMY HAS ALREADY DECLARED WAR ON THE COUNTRY WITH OUR ANALYSTS HERE TELLING US AN INVASION MUST BE IMMINENT--
LEE TRAVIS
I WOULD SUGGEST THAT CHINA CAN WAIT.

EARTH 2 #8 Variant cover by Nicola Scott, Trevor Scott & Gabe Eltaeb

EARTH 2 #11 Cover by Brett Booth, Norm Rapmund & Andrew Dalhouse

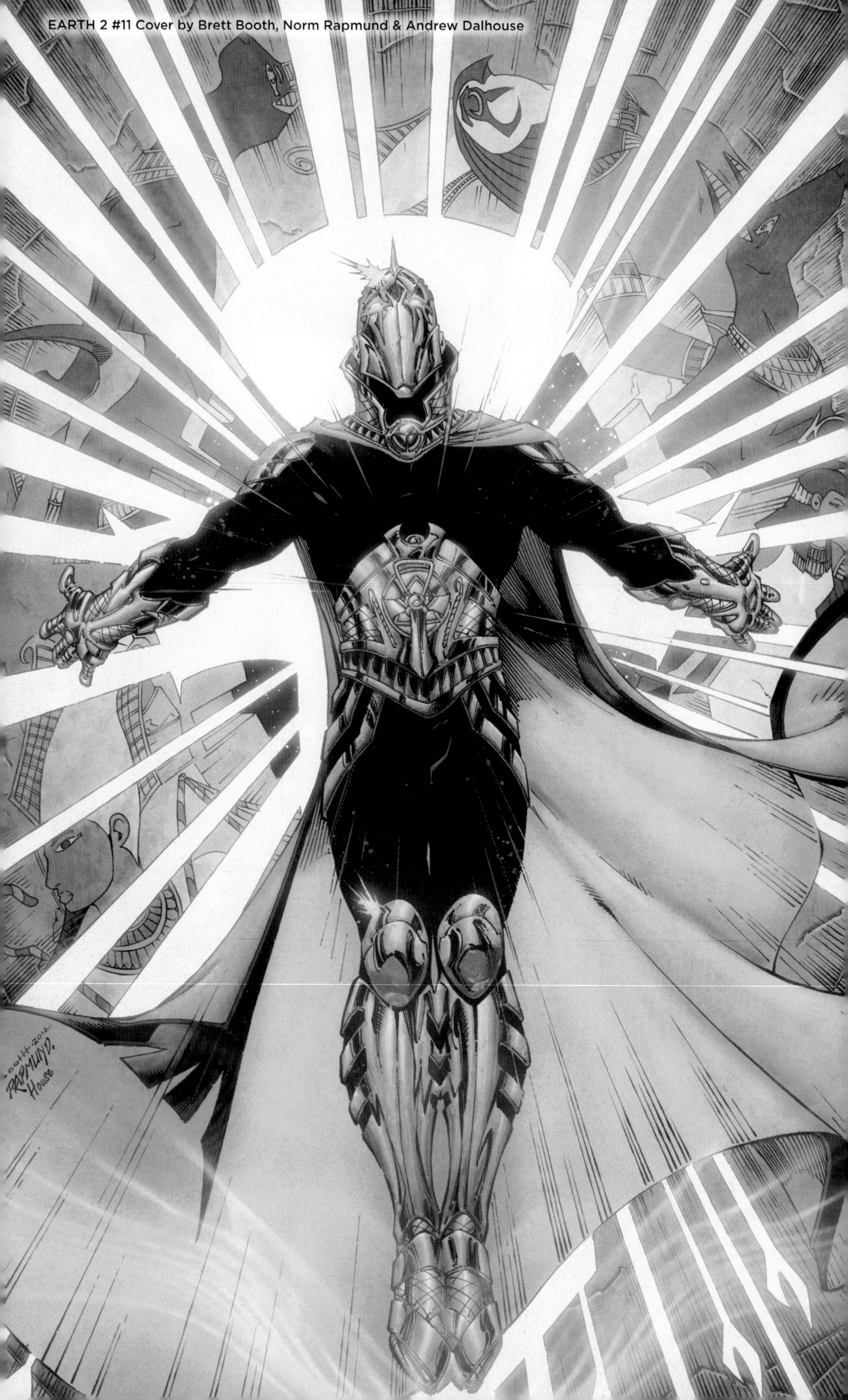

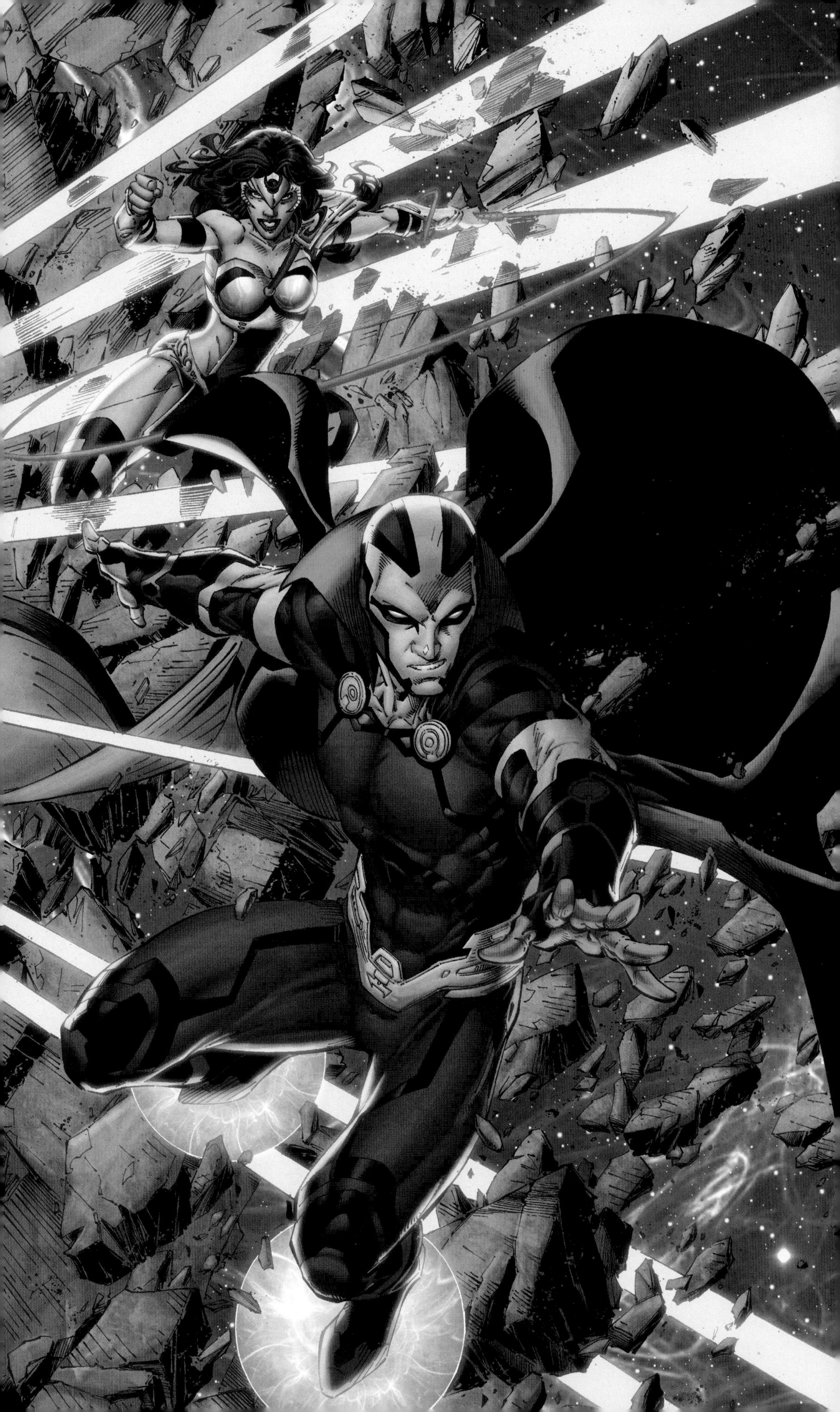

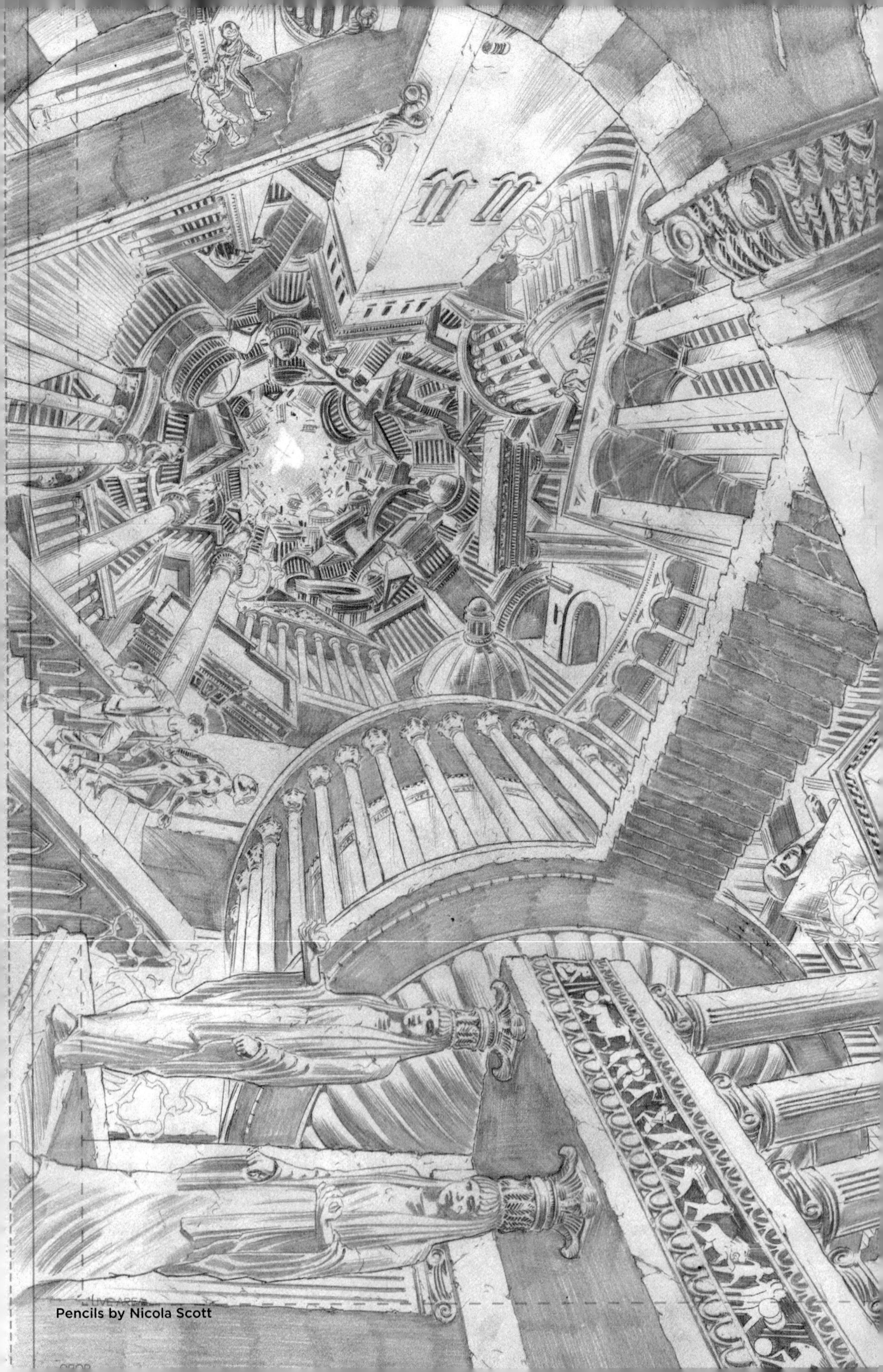

Pencils by Nicola Scott

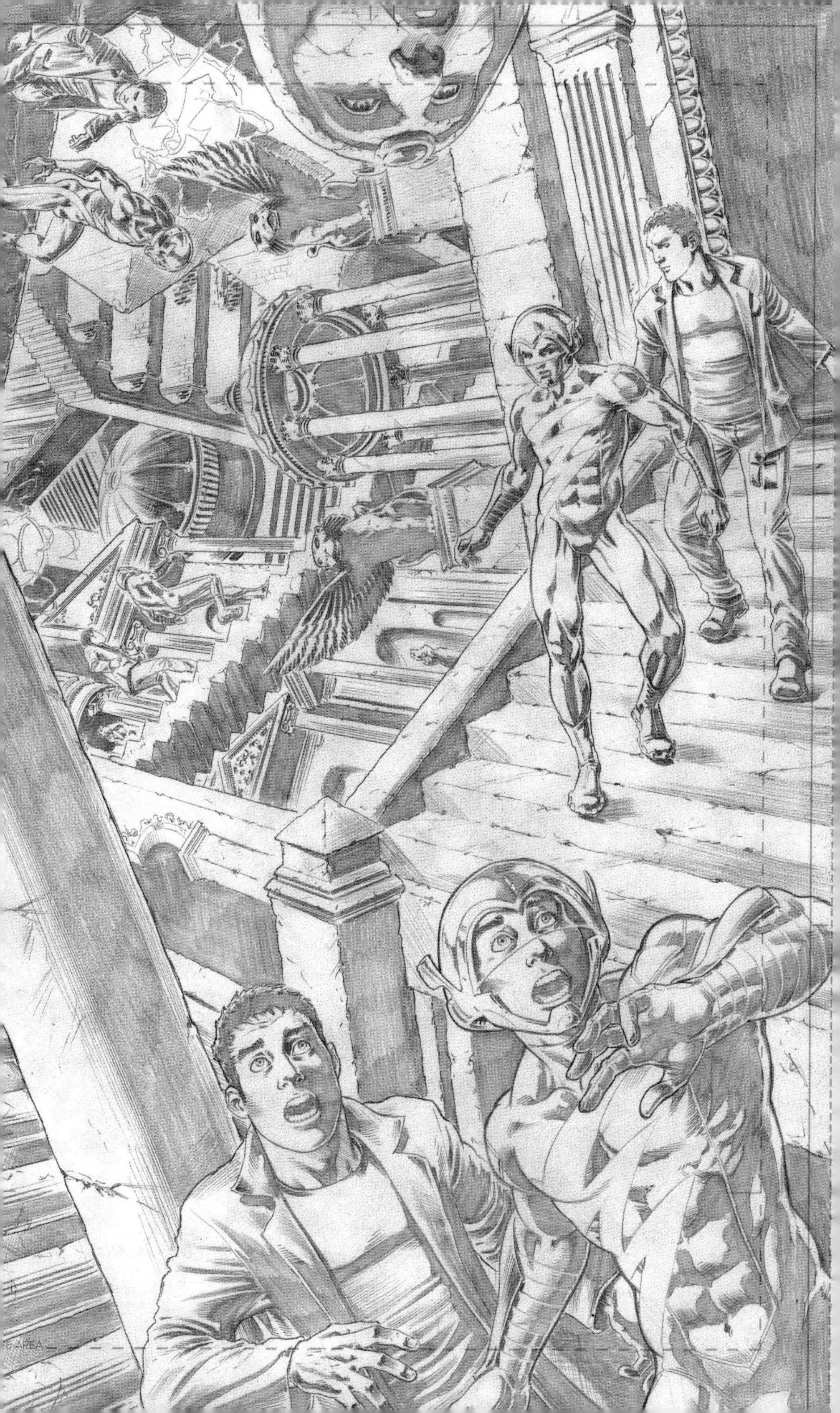

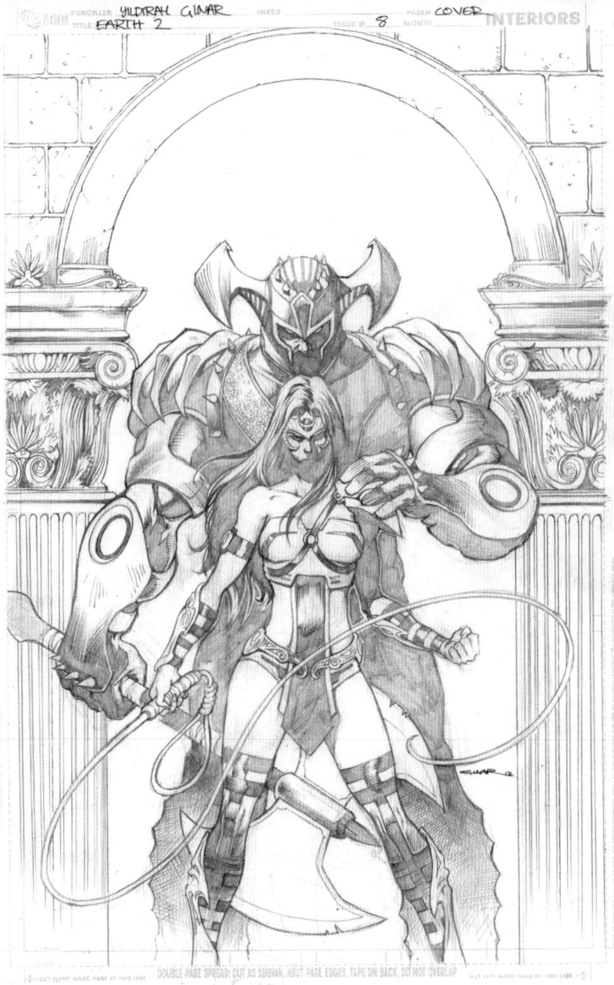
PENCILLER YILDIRAH CINAR
INKER
PAGE# COVER
INTERIORS
TITLE EARTH 2
ISSUE # 8
MONTH
DOUBLE PAGE SPREAD: CUT AS SHOWN, ABUT PAGE EDGES, TAPE ON BACK, DO NOT OVERLAP

EARTH 2 #8 cover pencils by Yildiray Cinar

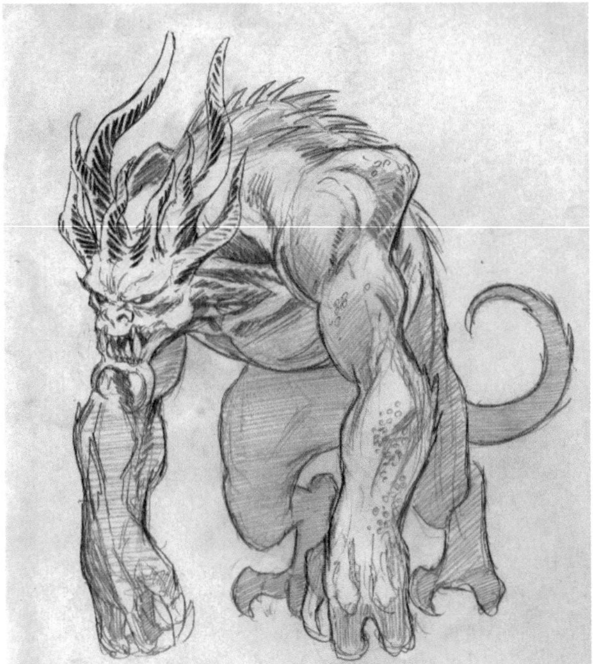

Sketch by Nicola Scott

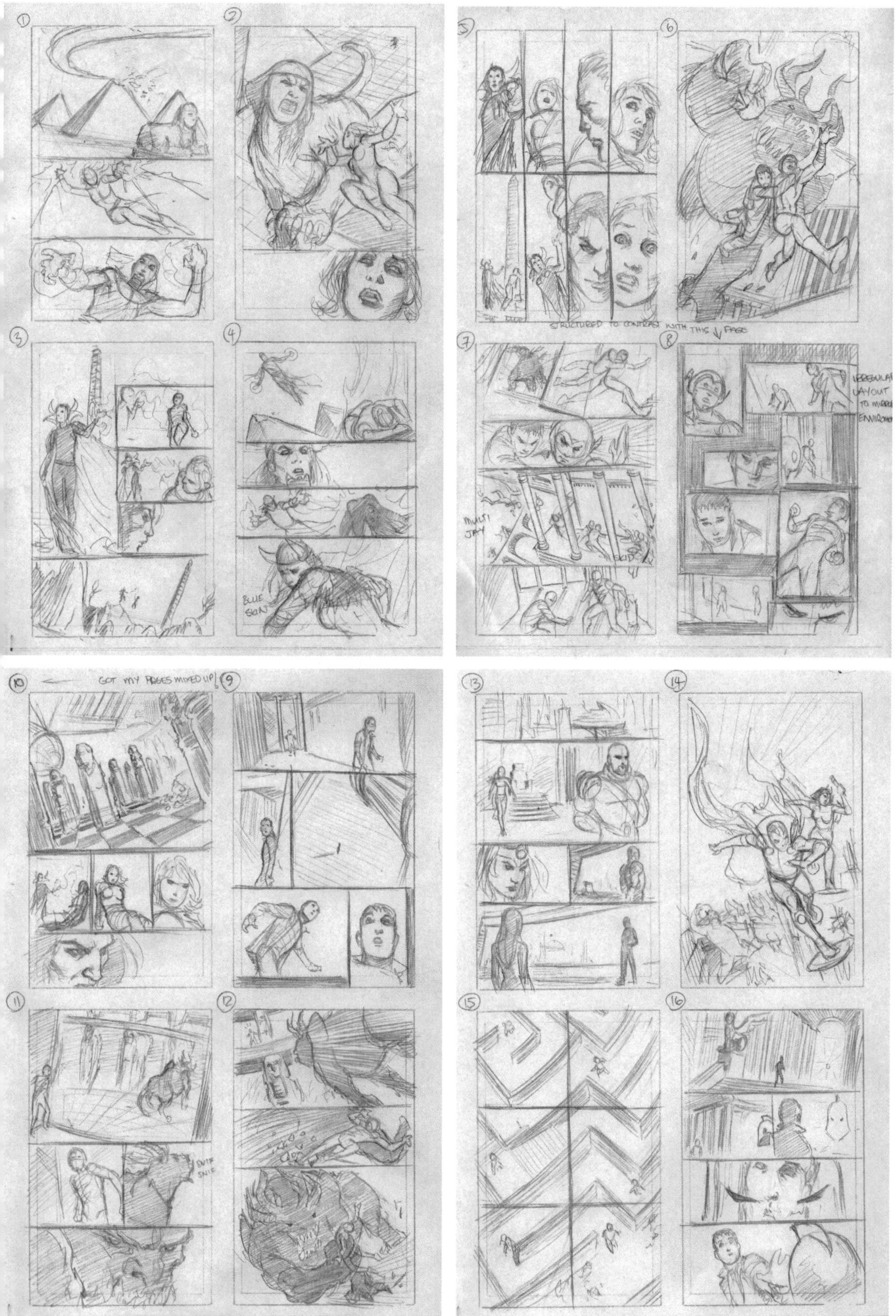
STRUCTURED TO CONTRAST WITH THIS PAGE
MULTI JAY
BLUE SKIN
GOT MY PAGES MIXED UP!
SNIF SNIF

EARTH 2 #11 layouts by Nicola Scott

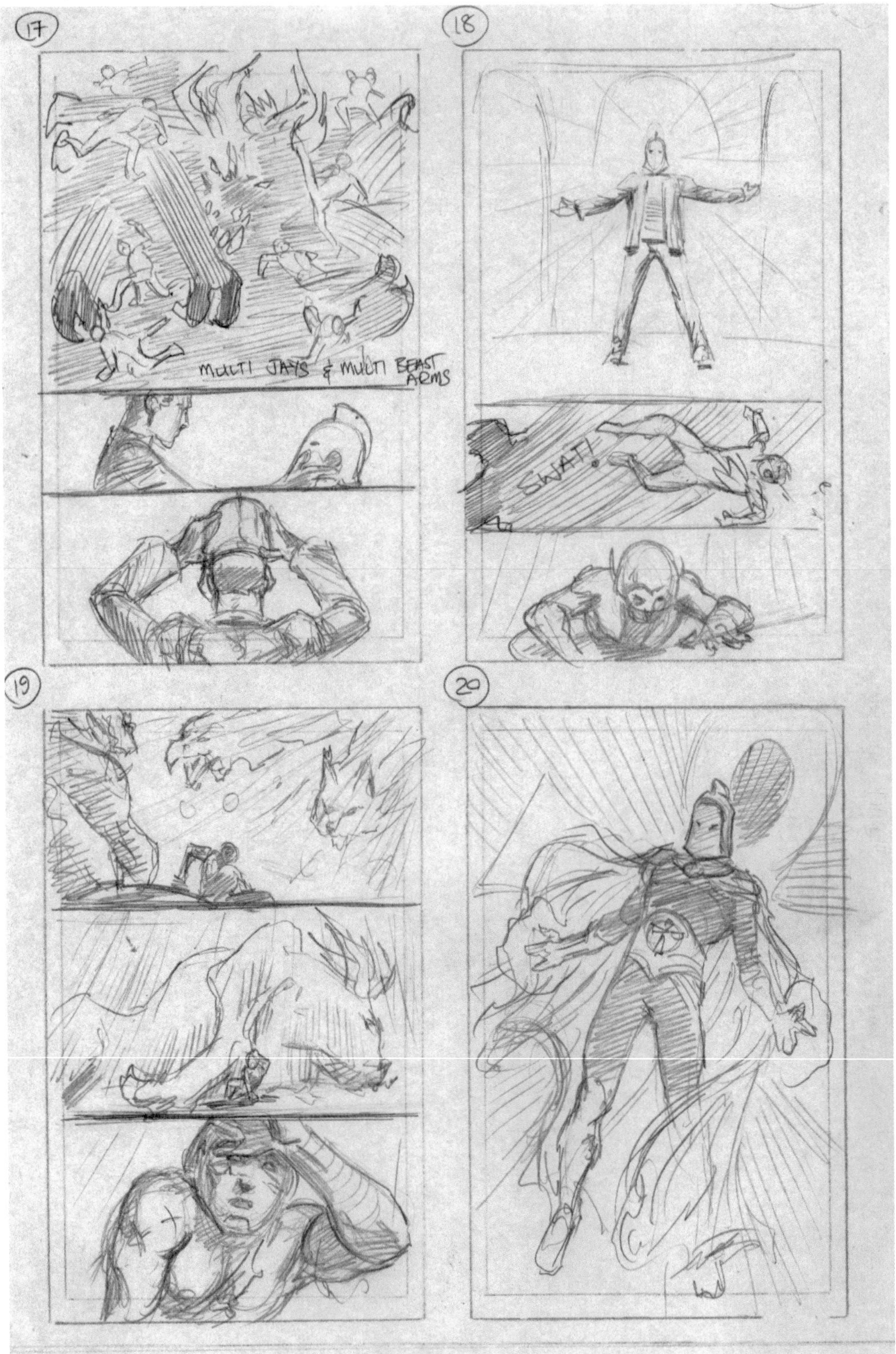
17
MULTI JAYS & MULTI BEAST ARMS
18
SWAT!
19
20